BROTHERLY TOMORROWS

BROTHERLY TOMORROWS

Movements for a

Cooperative Society

in America

1820–1920

Edward K. Spann

COLUMBIA UNIVERSITY PRESS

New York

COLUMBIA UNIVERSITY PRESS

NEW YORK   GUILDFORD, SURREY

COPYRIGHT © 1989 COLUMBIA UNIVERSITY PRESS

Library of Congress Cataloging-in-Publication Data
Spann, Edward K. 1931–
Brotherly tomorrows : movements for a cooperative society
in America, 1820–1920 / Edward K. Spann.
p.   cm.
Bibliography: p.
Includes index.
ISBN 0-231-06708-9
I. Collective settlements—United States—History
I. Title.
HX653.S62 1989
335'.973—dc19
88-17762
CIP

BOOK DESIGN BY JAYA DAYAL

PRINTED IN THE UNITED STATES OF AMERICA

*Casebound editions of Columbia University Press books
are Smyth-sewn and printed on permanent and
durable acid-free paper*

To
Laura,
Suzan,
and Jason,
the remaining three.

CONTENTS

v i i

Contents

viii

Contents

Contents

ACKNOWLEDGMENTS

I have benefited, in writing this book, from the work of others too numerous to mention, but I owe a particular debt to John L. Thomas and H. Roger Grant for their constructive criticism and to J. Robert Constantine for his generous support. Among those who have contributed to the preparation of the manuscript, Virginia Banfield, Janet Foster, Sharon Hinkle, and Susan Dehler have my special gratitude. Also, I wish to thank the staff of the Indiana State University Library for their ever-courteous assistance and the Indiana State University Research Committee for the research grants that have allowed me the time to complete this work.

INTRODUCTION

*B*rotherly *Tomorrows* examines a significant chapter in American social and cultural history. During the century after 1820 numerous groups of Americans attempted to transform what they saw as an excessively individualistic society into a cooperative one. Their efforts have often been labeled "utopian," but this term is a prejudicial one if we take Utopia in its usual meaning, a state of unrealizable perfection. The preferred term here is radical social idealism, since these American cooperationists did not seek perfection—which is the absence of life— but a new form of society which would nurture the better side of human nature.

Although this book gives some attention to various religious communities, it is not another study of sectarian societies set against "the world." Rather, it emphasizes essential secular efforts guided by secular ideologies and formed into organized movements for the transformation of the whole society. Many of these movements attempted to promote the formation of communities as the way to reorganize society, and others sought a social reorganization through national means. Whatever their specific design, they shared the common hope that cooperation could replace competition as the governing influence over human social behavior.

Generally, they were both reactions against the disintegrating effects of rapid social change and responses to the opportunities in a changing world to refashion the conditions of human life. *Brotherly Tomorrows* attempts to relate the various movements to this situation, most notably to modernization and to the westward movement. It also includes such influences as religion, particularly in its millenarian form, and class, especially the hopes and discontents of a broad middle class of intellectuals, professionals, small businessmen, and skilled workers. Beyond these general concerns, the essential aim of this book is to provide an understanding of the unique character of each of the cooperationist movements in connection with its special times.

The history of the cooperationist effort in America is a melancholy one. No movement was able to alter the course of society, although each had some effect on a significant minority. Briefly, in the early years of the twentieth century, Debsian socialism raised hopes for the triumph of the cooperative ideal, only to collapse under the impact of World War I and its aftermath. For those who judge the importance of a subject by its successes, this study of cooperative dreams and disappointing realities will have little significance. For those who have an interest in social philosophies and for those who appreciate the importance of social imagination in the conduct of human affairs, however, *Brotherly Tomorrows* may supply valuable insights into what is the most important subject of all, the striving of Modern Man to improve his social condition and to protect himself against his own growing powers over the world.

The collapse of socialism marks the end of a century-long effort to re-create society along cooperative lines. After 1920, Americans became even more individualistic and privatistic than ever before, encouraged by the hope that modern material abundance would make private utopias in individual households. The cooperative ideal was by no means lost, and was subsequently to reappear in various forms, most notably during the 1960s. This, however, constitutes a new and distinctive phase which demands a separate book. Perhaps, when such a book is written, it will explain why in our own times a second and seemingly more complete collapse of social idealism and of social imagination has taken place. *Brotherly Tomorrows* is intended to be a historian's work on history, an objective study of the human past, but it is also inspired by the hope that it can make at least a modest contribution toward reinvigorating the stagnated social imaginations of Americans so that they may better cope with the rapidly changing and troubling world that surrounds us all.

BROTHERLY TOMORROWS

The Challenge of the Century

In the 1820s, the United States saw the first of a succession of movements for a radical but peaceful transformation of society. Over the next hundred years, various "isms" from Owenism to Modern Socialism each offered the hope that through its special form of cooperative life it could bring the dreams of theologians and philosophers into earthly practice. Radical social idealism appeared in most of the modernizing societies of the North Atlantic World, but it developed a distinctive and especially hopeful direction in America.[1] The apparent newness and freedom from despotic institutions in the United States seemed to make it possible to begin the world all-over-again without the horrors of a radical social upheaval like the French Revolution.

It was no accident that the evolution of social idealism was spasmodic, a reflex to the periodic social and economic crises that afflicted the modernizing North Atlantic World. In the 1820s, the 1840s, the 1870s, and again in the 1890s, that world was shaken by increasingly severe "social earthquakes," each of which seemed both to demand and to make possible some radical social transformation. The dominant form of radical idealism was molded by the peculiar cultural as well as social conditions of its times. Although the differences among these movements were significant, they shared much in common: Each condemned the competitive side of society in the belief that competition was the source of a wasteful and brutal conflict that denied mankind the just and prosperous social life otherwise attainable on earth. Each believed that it was possible to create some rational basis for brotherly cooperation and so to unite the energies and talents of all for the good of all. Each was founded on the confidence that Man could free himself from the tyranny of the corrupted past if he would only commit himself to some new system of faith, which would serve as both a religion and science of brotherly cooperation.

The dream of a brotherly tomorrow had roots deep in the past, but the hope that it might actually be attained grew out of the interaction of two opposing faiths. One was the rationalism of the Enlightenment, the secular faith that through the exercise of human reason Man could eventually construct for himself a heaven on earth; that the truly good life and society was possible once humanity had cleansed itself of the errors that had corrupted the past. In most cases, rationalism inspired the confidence that "progress" would gradually bring humanity ever closer to the promised land, but it also encouraged the more radical in belief that the good life was attainable in a complete form in an immediate future. Likely, this would not have occurred if it had not been for the growing influence of the second faith, millenarianism, the belief that God, as part of his plan for Humankind, would Himself soon institute a heaven on earth to be enjoyed by those who had been his faithful followers.

By the end of the eighteenth century, the millennial idea had become of such popular interest that Samuel Hopkins, a noted Calvinist divine, published a full-length *Treatise on the Millennium* in 1793. On the basis of his interpretation of the Bible, Hopkins predicted that Christ-in-Spirit would eventually return to dominate the earth and establish a thousand-year kingdom, although this would occur only after a wrathful God had completed a great war against human wickedness that would "reduce and destroy mankind, so that comparatively few will be left." In the divinely governed new world to follow, all the faithful would be united by common faith and language into "one Family wisely seeking the good of each other in the exercise of the most sweet love and friendship."[2]

The joys of brotherhood would in this American heaven also involve substantial mundane rewards. New agricultural techniques would increase the productivity of the soil "sixty and perhaps an hundred fold," and new machines would enable men to level mountains and fill valleys so that "the crooked shall be made smooth, to render travelling more convenient and easy, and the earth more productive and fertile." These and various other improvements in productive techniques would make the planet a place of abundance for at least a thousand times its existing population. As all would be able to support themselves by two or three hours of labor, they would have ample time to invest not only in blissful worship but also in "reading and conversation, and in all those exercises which are necessary and proper, in order to improve their minds and make progress in knowledge."[3]

By Hopkins' biblical calculation, however, the millennium would not begin until sometime after the year 2000. The next half-century saw the appearance of various groups of deeply religious people who anticipated a coming-of-heaven-to-earth during their own lifetimes. Alienated from existing society and its orthodoxies, each of these religious sects formed its own cooperative society in order to prepare itself for the Millennium. That the United States became a special paradise for paradise seekers owes much to two such sects of millenarians, whose successes seemed to demonstrate that a truly brotherly world could be turned from fantasy into fact with the right leadership and principles.

In 1774, a small band of persecuted English Shakers landed in America under the lead of their prophetess, Ann Lee. They believed that the thousand years of heavenly order had already begun in 1770 with the spiritual return of Christ through his chosen medium, "Mother Ann," while she was imprisoned in a Manchester jail. The Shakers suffered a decade of often brutal persecution, which contributed to the early death of Mother Ann, but they succeeded in rooting their Millennial Church in American soil, thanks especially to the energy and organizing skill of some early American converts. It was Mother Ann's immediate successor, Joseph Meacham, who conceived and executed the idea of organizing the faithful into separate communities apart from "the world." In the decade after Mother Ann's death in 1784, they attracted enough new adherents to establish 11 distinct societies in eastern New York and in New England. Early in the nineteenth century, they extended their efforts westward, establishing eight more societies in Ohio, Kentucky, and Indiana. At their peak, in the three decades before the Civil War, these communities had some 6000 members, the majority of whom were women.[4]

The other sect, the Harmonists, migrated from Germany to the United States under the lead of their spiritual and temporal "Father," George Rapp. Rapp urged them to prepare a saintly society for the literal Second Coming of Christ, which he predicted would occur during their lifetimes. The Harmony Society, organized by the Germans soon after their arrival in 1804, never had more than 1000 members, but eventually it attracted much attention because of its remarkable success in establishing thriving towns. During their first decade, the Harmonists were able to wrestle a prosperous community out of the wilds of western Pennsylvania; in 1814, they sold this place and moved to the banks of the Wabash River in Indiana, where they created the even more successful town of Harmonie. This town soon acquired a unique distinction as the site for two very different efforts to establish ideal societies. In 1824, the Harmony Society sold its little heaven to the English rationalist, Robert Owen, and moved on to establish another successful town, Ekonomie, Pennsylvania, which it held until it died out in the early twentieth century.[5]

The two sects exemplified successful cooperation for generations of social idealists and students of cooperative societies. In her influential *Commitment and Community,* for instance, Rosabeth Moss Kantor depends heavily on them for her elaborate and possibly definitive sociological analysis of the necessary conditions for communal life. She rightly emphasizes their success in persuading individual members voluntarily to subordinate self-interest to group interest. It was this commitment, grounded in the belief that personal good could best be realized as part of a community, that led individuals to invest their energies and talents for collective benefit. In theory, such commitment could be a matter of rational self-interest, but, significantly, the communal successes of both sects derived from the millenarian faith of their members that, collectively, they directly served in a great divinely mandated enterprise which transcended all personal interests. Let ordinary mortals pursue their own selfish ends in a corrupted freedom, let the outside world shine with all its corrupting glamour, the inspired millenarians believed that they were joint heirs to a far greater world—the citizens of the Divine Kingdom soon to come or already come to earth.[6]

This sense of transcendent purpose was especially evident in their

4

approach to what they believed was the unsaintly mainspring of selfishness, human sexuality. Their solution, as severe as it was successful, was celibacy. The conviction of these millenarians that earthly reality would soon be replaced by heaven removed an essential justification of sex, the perpetuation of the species. Certainly, the continuation of heavenly life did not depend on the awkward couplings of men and women, because the source of all creation was, as both Harmonists and Shakers saw their God, a bisexual being embracing both Male and Female in one divine essence.[7]

Practically, celibacy helped both sects to achieve social goals of which most utopians could only dream. The demands of celibate life served to separate the true believers, ready to sacrifice their selves to the common good, from those who merely wanted an easy life. It also eliminated the exclusive relationships between men and women which had destroyed every paradise since the days of Adam and Eve. Devotion and loyalty did not focus on individual couples at the expense of the larger society, nor did individual family units demand the attentions of men and women at the expense of their commitments to the spiritual world and to their communities. The celibate life especially benefited women who were freed from childcare and the domestic responsibilities of the conventional family to participate in the essential business of their communities, often as the functional equals of men.[8]

Celibacy thus played a varied role as the linchpin of a tightly cohering communal family of relative equals. The Shaker authors of *The Summary View of the Millennial Church* expressed a view of shared by the Harmonists: "It is impossible for souls who really enjoy the unity of spirit to feel satisfaction with a separate enjoyment of which their brothers and sisters might, with equal propriety, partake with them. Their comfort, their peace, their happiness, their enjoyment of every kind, are greatly augmented by sharing them in union with their brothers and sisters." As members of what can best be called "total," communities, both Shakers and Harmonists lived, worked, ate, enjoyed, and suffered together, with few of the individual strivings, resentments, envies, and conflicts that tortured the world outside. In one of the several hymns which he wrote, Father Rapp described his society as one:

> Where all hate, strife, jealousy
> Cease their wicked stressing.

Harmonie means symphony—
Sphere of golden blessings.[9]

This strong sense of community owed much to celibacy, but it also resulted from a religious form of communism founded on the example of the first Christians. All things held in common for common need—the biblical ideal of property was taken up by the Harmonists and Shakers in their pursuit of sainthood, especially to prevent individual greed and ambition from weakening their spiritual commitment and social unity. It was in their communities that civilized humans came closest to realizing the essential ideal of pure communism: That each person give to the best of his ability and that each person receive on the basis of his needs. Communism worked because it was part of a larger order of sharing among people who believed they were God's faithful few united in one common interest in obedience to the Divine Will.[10]

This, as outsiders were quick to note, involved something more than a sharing of privations, since by the 1820s these religious communists had demonstrated a remarkable ability to transform the opportunities of America into prosperous communal economies. Beginning poor, the Harmonists and the Shakers had both been able to accumulate substantial communal property in the form of solidly built villages and thousands of acres of land. Although most of the Harmonists were employed in collective farming, they also constructed a variety of manufactories, equipped with the latest machinery run by water, steam, or animal power.[11] By the early 1820s, Harmonie had become the first industrial center in the still largely frontier state of Indiana. The Shakers achieved a simpler but also much admired worldly success by developing a more perfect practice of both agriculture and handicrafts than anyone else in America. Eventually, they established a profitable trade with the "world," benefiting, as in the case of the Shaker chair, from the reputation of their products for quality and durability. Most of the money earned in this trade was invested in land so that by the 1870s the 18 societies owned some 50,000 acres.[12]

By the late 1820s, both the Shaker and Harmonist communities had attracted the attentions of social thinkers in both Europe and America. This interest rarely involved much understanding of the profoundly religious character and rewards of these millenarian communities. For most observers, the distinctive doctrines of both sects were rather bizarre superstitions that had enslaved the ignorant to totalitarian leaders; one English visitor to Harmonie warned that George Rapp's society "presents the most extraordinary spectacle of a most complete despotism in the midst of a great republic."[13] Such critics, however, also noted that the millenarian communities had attained a high degree of order, harmony and material security—qualities that especially impressed Americans troubled by the increasingly unsettled and often slovenly character of their own society.[14]

Virtually all observers took special note of the material prosperity achieved by these religious communists, although it is noteworthy that the most enthusiastic assessments of this accomplishment came from Europeans who had not actually observed it. As early as 1817, Robert Owen (who was not to see a Shaker community until 1824) published in England an account of the Shakers to demonstrate, as he said later, "that even by a very inferior community life, wealth could be so easily created for all."[15] By the 1840s, this reputation had reached Germany, where it helped convince a young Frederick Engels of the virtues of communism. In 1845, Engels told Germans that the Shakers had achieved such abundance that there was no real need for them to work. "They are free, rich, and happy," he said of the members of the Society at Pleasant Hill, Kentucky. "They are happy and cheerful among themselves; there is no discord; on the contrary, friendship and love rule throughout their abode." That this was no temporary impression was indicated in the 1880s when Engels, in his last message to a dying Karl Marx, attempted to bolster the spirits of his friend with the exhortation "Remember the Shakers."[16]

By the early 1820s, the work of the German communists at Harmonie was also attracting much favorable attention. From Germany came praise of Harmonie as a model for social and economic policy: "A flower from Eden has made its appearance again." An English writer reported that among the Harmonists "perfect equality prevails, and there are no servants, but plenty of people to serve." Especially among Americans, the town won attention for its success in combining agriculture and manufacturing into one harmonious system, a matter of importance for those concerned with the disruptive effects of the new factory system on American society. Even Thomas Jefferson in 1822 rather left-handedly praised the Harmonist system for providing "as much happiness as Heaven has pleased to deal out to an imperfect humanity," although he said that communism would work only in small communities like Harmonie.[17]

Most of this attention came at a time when the North Atlantic World had been shaken into consciousness regarding the promise and perils of fundamental change by the French Revolution and by the early stages of the Industrial Revolution. For hopeful radicals, the sectarian communists seemed to have found a sure and peaceful way to utopia; the good societies of which a Plato and a Thomas More could only dream had been at least partly realized in communal form. The fact that the millenarians had succeeded by means of voluntary association offered the hope that they had not merely found the key to some private paradise for themselves but had actually forged the lever by which to overthrow a corrupted society. If all good men could be persuaded to withdraw from the corrupting institutions of existing society and to adopt the new ways, they could effect a peaceful revolution in human affairs that would redeem the world.

The success of the millenarian sects seemed to demonstrate that brotherly cooperation was a realistic alternative to the competitive individualism that had grown with the weakening of the bonds of traditional community. Was the key to this success to be found in their sectarian faith or in their cooperative formula? This question was to challenge generations of social idealists over the next century. "They show us a large society living in peace, plenty and worldly prosperity," wrote Thomas Low Nichols of the Shakers. "But how far are their religious system and ascetic life necessary for this success?"[18] If their narrow and seemingly irrational religious system were not necessary, then how much better could rational modern man work the communitarian formula for the benefit of all humankind. Was it possible to create some more rational form of cooperative community that did not demand the sacrifice of individual consciousness and freedom? Was it also possible to devise a rational system of faith, an Ideology, that could persuade rational men to commit themselves to cooperative society? For a small but growing number of Americans, this was the challenge of the century.

The dream of cooperative community appealed especially to those with sufficient social imagination and energy to be constructively dissatisfied with their societies. Many of them saw in the millenarian example hope that they could return to a more secure and more stable form of life than that which confronted them in a world shaken by commercial and

8

industrial change. Craftsmen, faced with competition from factory produced goods, could find a permanent place for their skills. The lost and
lonely could find the human intimacy and emotional security so absent
from an increasingly strange and impersonal world. For those concerned
with personal freedom and power, the community system offered an
escape from a world of increasingly remote force into a society over
which they could exercise meaningful control.[19]

The dream of cooperative community had a special attraction for a
small minority whose characters and experiences disposed them to dissent from social and religious orthodoxy. Often united by little more
than common hostility to prevailing beliefs and institutions, they constituted a "culture of dissent," a sort of rambling and often unkempt
ideological home for varied social idealisms over the next century. It was
a home without walls open to all regardless of class, sex, or nationality,
but most of its members were northern white males drawn from the
middling range of society. They were generally craftsmen, intellectuals,
professionals, and even businessmen whose natures and experiences
made them dissatisfied with existing social arrangements; they were
early advocates of what John L. Thomas has called the "Adversary
Tradition."[20] Convinced that existing society was fundamentally wrong,
they sought for new social formulas in the succession of "isms" which
swept through their world beginning with Owenism and concluding
with Modern Socialism.

The culture of dissent was to be the germinating ground for the
many and varied communitarian experiments that were launched in
search of the good society. In most cases, this search also included an
essentially religious quest for some seemingly rational system of belief to
replace a rejected Christian orthodoxy, a social religion of cooperative
brotherhood. Some dissenters were free-thinking rationalists like young
Frederick Evans, who dreamed of creating a community based on his
"materialistic" beliefs. In the late 1820s, after participating in one unsuccessful communitarian experiment, Evans resolved to found another
community "upon a proper basis, purely philosophical, and not allow in
it a single Christian." A stay in a Shaker community, however, convinced him that Shakerism was a satisfactory philosophical and social
alternative to established orthodoxies; eventually, Elder Frederick Evans
became the most prominent spokesman for the Shaker form of dis-
sents.[21]

Like Evans, most dissenters sought a way to combine modern rationalism with religious faith, generally in some millenarian form. Typical was the "New Jerusalem Church" founded in the eighteenth century by the Swedish scientist, technocrat, and religious mystic, Emmanual Swedenborg. Before his death in 1772, Swedenborg had convinced himself and a few others that he had been permitted to make repeated visits to the spiritual world where he had learned that the Lord was preparing to initiate His kingdom on earth.[22] Swedenborgianism appealed to several generations of Americans as a seemingly more rational and respectable equivalent of millenarianism, a system of belief which promised a world "wherein all things are become new." Although the actual membership in the New Church was limited to a few thousand before the Civil War, it had a wide-ranging influence within the culture of dissent. By the 1820s, Swedenborgianism had not only established itself in the major eastern cities but had also spread into southern Ohio and elsewhere in the Middle West thanks to the efforts of John Chapman, the legendary "Johnny Appleseed," who spent many years planting the seeds of the new faith along with his orchards.[23]

Swedenborgianism was perhaps the most formally religious of the various heterodox faiths that over the century attracted cultural dissenters. In varying degrees, every "ism" appealed to the hope for a rational alternative to existing religious life, one which would make all things new. The religions of dissent did not always inspire dreams of cooperative brotherhood, nor did they normally lead to communitarian activity. During the periodic crises that disrupted the progress of the century, however, they did play a critical role in raising efforts to realize the ideal of cooperative brotherhood in communitarian form. The first of such efforts began in the early 1820s after the Panic of 1819 had introduced Americans to their first national depression.

In 1821, a small group of New York professional men, mostly Quakers, formed a "Society for Promoting Communities," with the aim of convincing the "pious of all denominations of the propriety and duty of forming common[weal]ths on pure and just principles." They were moved by the sufferings of the poor in these depressed times to consider the cooperative community as a possible alternative to the heartless commercial and industrial society that they believed was growing up around them.[24] Convinced that the root of all evil was "the spirit of *self-ishness*," they attacked the prevailing emphasis on individual or "exclusive" rights as the source of social evils, and they called on every religious congregation to preach and especially to practice the principles of Christian brotherhood. This, they believed, could be done only if the pious were to separate from the corrupted world and form communities where they would be free to love one another. In this respect, they followed generations of pietists who attempted to preserve their purity by isolating themselves from "the world," but they went beyond the point where the pietists had stopped. They hoped that, by encouraging every religious denomination to form communities, they could initiate a whole new society dedicated to brotherly love.[25]

These New Yorkers attempted to demonstrate that the communal system could work on a national basis by resorting to the already familiar utopian tactic of citing the example of a distant—and largely unknown—place; in this case it was China, where the government acted "like the father of a family" who nurtured the interests of all his children. China had established a true community which had lasted for a thousand years. If under their heathen philosophy, the Chinese could maintain a society "so peaceful, agricultural, numerous, aged, and innocent," how much more could pious Christians accomplish in making brotherly love and cooperation the ruling force of society?[26]

The energy of the New York Society peaked in 1822 when its moderator, Dr. Cornelius Blatchly, published his *An Essay on Common Wealths* in the hope of mobilizing public support for a project to establish "communities of common stock" (i.e., common ownership) in a frontier area where large tracts of land could be purchased at small prices. For these communities, he advocated a system of religious communism on the grounds that only in a "community of wealth and interest . . . can *liberty* and *equality* exist in perfection." Private property, he believed, "generates that root of *all evil,* self-hood, or the *spirit* of selfishness, and *love* of money,' " from which had grown the oppressive rents, debts, banks, and monopolies that were beginning to trouble the lives of Americans. By creating "pure commonwealths" while land was still cheap and available, Americans could avoid the social miseries of Europe and

> Cause the forests of nature and the wilds of society to bloom as gardens; where women would no longer be considered inferior to men, and men would love them as equals; information and learning would abound; the youth would be nursed, and bred

with prudence, wisdom, and good associates; civil and religious liberty, justice, and mercy, would cause universal felicity, and God's will would be done on earth as it was in heaven.[27]

Blatchley anticipated at least two objections to this plan for piety and plenty. One was that the removal of the "salt of the earth" from society would serve only to make society even more despicable and corrupt; his answer came in the form of the familiar hope that one pure community would become "a city set on a hill," whose shining example would convert others to the cause. The extent to which it would become a shining example, however, depended on how well it refuted the second objection, that personal self-interest was the only dependable stimulus to labor and enterprise: Would not a community where all were supposed to work for the good of all be but a community of no work at all? Blatchley's response was that of a pious physician. He argued the religious communists had proven that social love was as natural a force on human behavior as self-love. "Ants, bees and beavers," he added, "live in communities, and manifest unceasing diligence, art and enterprise." Once freed from the selfish influence of private property, therefore, people would naturally labor artfully and diligently for the good of all.[28]

Blatchly and other communitarians thought they had found an ideal social model in Harmonie, whose principles seemed less eccentric and demanding than those of the Shakers. They generally believed, mistakenly, that the Harmonists had learned how to make communism work without the obnoxious practice of celibacy. Early in 1822, Edward P. Page, a member of the Society for Promoting Communities, wrote in a letter to Harmonie that if that community were democratic rather than autocratic in form, "I would go to the end of the earth and join a people so consistent as to encourage matrimony and the increase of home manufactured population." Several months later, Blatchly himself sent a copy of his *Essay on Common Wealths* to Frederick Rapp, the adopted son of the Harmonist leader, in the hope of learning the secret of the Harmonist success: "You have commenced a good work; you have set a good example; and stand like a city on a hill to enlighten others."[29]

A request for enlightenment also came from a Boston Swedenborgian, Samuel Worcester, whose interest in Harmonie had been awakened by Blatchly's work. Having discussed the communitarian idea with several other Bostonians, Worcester conceived the plan of establishing a colony of Swedenborgians somewhere in the West, but he was less sure than Blatchly that the example of ants and beavers proved that social love was natural to Man. There were many like himself, he wrote to Frederick Rapp, who thought that communism would "be useful and delightful" but who feared that the prohibition against private, individual property "would operate as an inherent and irresistible principle of disorder & decay." In particular, he asked Rapp, how had Harmonie resolved the basic problem of getting people to work energetically when all property and produce was commonly owned? What other than compulsion or self-interest could overcome inertia and indolence?[30]

The reply from Harmonie to these inquiries was not encouraging. Writing for his father as well as for himself, Frederick Rapp disabused Page of the notion that the Harmonists were any less sectarian than the Shakers: "There can be only one religious opinion here, for without being of the same mind, no union of the spirit and, consequently, no communal life would be possible." To Samuel Worcester the Rapps sent a more thoughtful reply out of respect for Swedenborg, a fellow mystic, but it was no less devastating to hopes for easy answers: Communism at Harmonie had escaped the disorder and indolence which concerned Worcester only because a deep and compelling spirit of Brotherly Love impelled "all sound Members in the body of the Community to care and provide for the good and welfare of their brethren without compulsion"; this spirit, in turn, depended on the willingness of all members both to sacrifice their self-interest to transcendent religious goals and to obey one man appointed to maintain those goals—without common goals and a common head there would be no real unity and no true commonwealth.[31]

As the creators of a successful community, the Rapps lent great authority to the view that communal heaven could be found only in a total community whose members subordinated their selves to the common good. If it were to avoid the use of brute force, a society of communists required a collective consciousness, a governing sense of having one's true being only in the collective self, part of one spirit, one body, one mind, and one transcending charismatic experience. For most of those who envied the harmony and prosperity of the millenarian sects, however, this was too heavy a price for earthly heaven. In his reply to Worcester, Frederick Rapp had offered to sell some of the Harmonist lands at "reasonable prices" for a Swedenborgian colony, but his emphasis on the necessity of total community was so discouraging that Worcester had not even bothered to respond. In New York, Blatchly's band of pious pioneers also found little encouragement in the Harmonist example and lost their momentum after 1822 as the nation began to recover from the depression.[32]

Blatchly himself sought comfort in a hope that became increasingly common to the generations of social visionaries to follow. He placed his faith in a great transformation in essential human spirit which he believed was taking place with the progress of society:

> For some centuries past, since printing and science have revived, the Spirit of God has been *consuming* that wicked man of sin; and we hope that the Lord will ere long destroy him by the brightness of his coming. We believe that the principalities, laws, customs, creeds, prejudices and doctrines of the world are about to terminate. We live in an age of revolutions and wonders. Monarchies, superstitions, ignorance and slavery, are affected with consumption. Republics, liberality, science, and liberty are diffusing innumerable blessings in America and Europe.[33]

Through the instruments of earthly progress, God was working a great millennial transformation in human outlook and behavior that would make for a heavenly commonwealth in the world once men accepted the responsibility of assisting this divine progress by founding communities.

Even without Blatchly's pious anticipations, the communitarian dream continued to attract cultural dissenters. Paul Brown, a freethinker and secular communist, claimed that he had begun to consider the idea of founding a community even before the formation of the New York Society, driven "to meditate on this subject by my suffering from the inadequacy of the existing institutions to extend justice to the poor, and the odious grinding influence of individual wealth and unequal usurped power which in several instances had bourne grievously afflictively upon me." Encouraged by Blatchly's work, he had began to contemplate "a new social order" in the belief that friendships and especially family relationships proved that human beings would naturally cooperate if they were placed in the right social circumstances. The times were ripe for a new social order, he wrote in 1825, for "multitudes, shaking off the shackles of a superstitious and contracted education, make no difficulty in admitting that investigation is no crime. The age of reason has dawned."[34]

Brown was anxious to proceed from social investigation to experimentation, but efforts to found commonwealths before 1825 were rare at best. The New York Society published a model constitution for a community with suggestions that "a premium should be paid for the best constitution for every religious persuasion," and Brown referred to a "colony" that was settled in Virginia, probably the work of the Society, but the results were negligible. Late in 1824 the shrunken membership of Blatchly's Society complained that they had encountered only discouragement from American leaders and neglect from the public. Their three-year campaign to promote the commonwealth cause had made barely a ripple outside the limited circle of dissent.[35]

In 1825, however, the communitarian ideal was suddenly brought to public attention by the advent of Robert Owen on the American scene. Even before that date, much of the limited interest in that ideal had been sustained by the apparent success of this English manufacturer and social idealist in making it work against the poisonous social conditions produced by the English Industrial Revolution. In his model company town at New Lanark, Scotland, Owen had created what he came to see as a successful community, which he publicized as such in his *A New View of Society* (1813) and in later writings.[36]

By the early 1820s, Owen's version of his accomplishments had reached the United States. Cornelius Blatchly published some extracts from *A New View* with his *Essay on Common Wealths* and presented New Lanark as proof "that communities of interests may be so managed, as to moralize even the *worst* of mankind, and to make them happy." What particularly impressed Blatchly—and other dissenters as well—was that Owen had worked this apparent communal magic without any recourse to sectarian religion: "His work is a great encouragement for irreligious people to engage heartily in establishing communities for their individual *health, benefit,* and happiness."[37] Viewed from afar, Owen seemed to embody their hopes for a new benevolent age of both faith and reason.

Ironically, Owen's own characteristically inflated confidence in himself as a maker of communities depended in part on his view, also from afar, of the Shaker and Harmonist communities in America. By 1816, he had discovered the Shakers, who he believed had attained wealth, health, and happiness "even by a very inferior communal life." If even these superstitious sectarians were able to demonstrate the value of the community system, Owen concluded, then his more advanced principles would make that system work even better for the benefit of all mankind. It was with this confidence that Owen attempted to initiate a correspondence with the Harmonists in 1820 in the hope of learning how they had been able to establish their successful "colonies." Typically, Owen introduced himself as the manager of "a colony here of about 2400 persons who I have already placed under new circumstances. . . . I am now in the midst of further development of the system I have in view."[38] Rapp did not respond to this effort to initiate a transatlantic partnership; probably his instinctive judgement of Owen's secular optimism was contempt.

Whatever the differences that separated these men in 1820, however, they were drawn together into a strange partnership only four years later, largely because they shared a millenarian restlessness over their respective "colonies." In the spring of 1824, Rapp, who only six months before had expressed pleasure in the continued upbuilding of Harmonie, suddenly began to prepare his followers for a new march to a new promised land. Why Father Rapp should have decided to abandon his town is unclear. Although he had become dissatisfied with both the climate and his neighbors in the Wabash region, he may have made his decision out of concern that his followers were growing soft in the comfortable world they had built. Whatever the reason, Rapp directed his saints to build a whole new town in western Pennsylvania, and in March 1824 he advertised that Harmonie was for sale at $150,000 to be paid in ten annual installments or $125,000 in five installments, the last without any interest.[39]

At that price, Harmonie—with its lands, improvements, houses, and mills—was a bargain; but even on such favorable terms the market for towns was an exceptionally limited one. Miraculously, however, Owen's restlessness in England made him as eager to buy as the Rapps were to sell. Within a year, he was to confront and for a time seemingly to overcome the challenge of the century in this new world on the Indiana frontier. Harmonie would become New Harmony, sectarian community would give way to rational community, and secular man would attempt to create a millennial kingdom for himself. The ultimate result would be both momentous and disastrous.

The Prophet of New Lanark

Robert Owen was one of the most notable personalities in the Anglo-American world during the first half of the nineteenth century. For not a few men and women, he was the heroic prophet who would lead humanity to paradise. For many more, he was a naïve visionary whose shallow optimism led to nowhere. Whatever, it was his destiny to begin a century's striving to establish a cooperative society on the basis of modern science and reason. As he neared the end of his long career in 1865, Owen wrote that "the mission of my life appears to be, to prepare the population of the world to understand the vast importance of the *second creation of humanity*."[1] For nearly half a century, he preached the same basic message, that humanity could create a millennial paradise for itself if only it would exchange its ignorant social ways for the God-given scientific truths which he had discovered and then had, so he believed, successfully demonstrated. Once the world learned to apply these truths, paradise would become real, and the troubles of life would prove to be only the nightmares of a restless sleep.

Robert Owen was born in 1771 to modest but respectable circumstances at Newtown, Wales. Much later, he described Newtown—the first of many "new" places with which he was to be associated—as "a neat, clean, beautifully situated country village" destined to develop into "a dirty but thriving manufacturing town." At the age of 10, he left this ordered little world to seek and soon to find his fortune. He was able to seize the new opportunities afforded by the Industrial Revolution to become an efficient factory manager and then, by 1800, a part-owner of the great textile mills at New Lanark, Scotland, with his father-in-law, David Dale.[2] By the age of 30, he had made himself a "prince of cotton spinners," but his success proved to be only the beginning of a career as a radical critic of capitalism and of industrial society. Eventually, this manufacturer, father of seven children and husband of an extraordinarily pious as well as patient wife, would declare war on his world and make himself a hero in the culture of dissent.

Owen began his mission by making New Lanark into a model industrial community, a "Happy Valley" set against the disorder and despair of the early Industrial Age. Here, he soon won public attention as a pioneer of welfare capitalism by providing pensions, cheap housing, and medical care for his workers while cutting their hours of labor some two hours below the existing norm. On the surface at least, New Lanark proved that it was possible to avoid the evils of industrialism while maintaining profits. Instead of higher wages, he provided a beneficial environment which kept his people dependent on him—a neat, orderly and enclosed organization where all inhabitants, as he said later, were "united and working together as one machine, proceeding day by day with the regularity of clockwork."[3] A more earthbound employer might well have been content simply to preside over this little society, but not Robert Owen.

Instead, he concluded that he had found the key to the great paradox of his industrializing world. On the one hand, the combination of applied science and technology seemed capable of eventually satisfying all human material needs; Owen estimated that twenty-five years of the Industrial Revolution had multiplied human productive power more than 15 times.[4] On the other hand, that increasing power for material plenty and for happiness was accompanied by the explosive growth of poverty, unemployment, human degradation, crime, and class hatred. How to deal with this paradox of poverty in the midst of potential plenty? A question which was to challenge social thinkers throughout the century posed no terror for Owen, because he believed that he had found the answer at New Lanark, and in 1813 he proceeded to tell the world about it in his tract *A New View of Society*.

In it, he boldly attacked the problem which seemed forever to deny hopes for a perfect world. Experience had taught that human nature was much too imperfect for mankind ever to achieve an ideal state. Owen chose to address this problem simply by rejecting the idea that such a human nature existed. Rather, Man's basic nature was neutral stuff, whose specific character was created by the social environment. All human evil and misery, therefore, originated from a defective society attributable to Man's ignorance and "fundamental errors of the imagination." Owen especially rejected the assumption that the individual was somehow responsible for his own character and conduct. On this assumption, society had created fundamentally vicious systems of rewards and especially punishments which, as he put it later, "deranged all the proceedings of society, made man irrational in his thoughts, feelings and actions, and, consequently, more inconsistent, and perhaps more miserable, than any other animal."[5]

The belief that society rather than human nature caused Man's misery and miserable conduct was common to advanced thinkers in Owen's times, but few pushed social determinism to the extreme position stated on the title page of his *New View*: "Any general character, from the best to the worst, from the most ignorant to the most enlightened, may be given to any *community, even to the world at large, by the application of the proper means.*" Owen was convinced that he had discovered a redeeming "science of the influence of circumstances" which would furnish all the means needed to establish social conditions that would make good and happy people.[6] He was confident that he had already successfully tested his science at New Lanark. Even more than most self-made men, he gave exaggerated importance to his own practical experience and little to the experience of the past as recorded in mere books. In defiance of theologies and philosophies, he had succeeded in redeeming the corrupted characters of his employees: "They were taught to be rational, and they acted rationally. . . . Those employed became industrious, temperate . . . faithful to the employers."[7]

He was especially proud of a device he conceived to train his workers to effective labor. Having rejected the idea of punishments and rewards, he invented a substitute for whippings and bonuses in the form of his "Silent Monitor," a wooden block with four differently colored faces that registered a superintendent's evaluations of worker performance: If the superintendent turned the black face forward, the judgement was bad; if the white face, the judgement was exceptionally good. Under this system, Owen said that he could tell at a glance how the workers in each department were performing. Not surprisingly, the preponderant color soon became brighter than somber black, leading him to conclude that "never before perhaps in the history of the human race had so simple a device created in so short a period so much order, virtue, goodness, and happiness out of so much ignorance, error, and misery."[8] How easy, then, to train the rest of the human race to live lives of virtue and happiness.

Even easier would it be to train children to become the good citizens of Owen's good society. At New Lanark, education became the keystone to both his social thought and social practice. Anxious to begin the process as early as possible, he admitted infants to his school as soon as they could walk. Convinced that books contained more error than truth, he banned them along with rewards and punishments from the early stages of education. Through the actual observation of tangible objects and the use of "sensible signs" like maps, the young were to be trained to become thoughtful, active students of reality capable of finding the same scientific truths which Owen had discovered. Only after they had learned how to distinguish truth from error would they move on to the use of books as a way of broadening their horizons. On graduation, they would be "rational beings, knowing themselves and society in principle and practice, far better than the best informed now know these subjects at their majority."[9]

That the school at New Lanark worked well in Owen's eyes is no surprise, particularly since the deck was stacked in his favor. As most of the children graduated at age 12 into his mills, he avoided the frustrating job of educating adolescents. Moreover, the closed context of New Lanark society made him the absolute, albeit benevolent, master not only of the children but also of his teachers whom he first trained himself and then supervised even more closely than his factory superintendents. Ignoring this fact, he concluded that he had invented the lever that could be used anywhere to move the world away from its stupendous ignorance to an intelligence and goodness yet unknown. When in 1816 he completed his educational scheme with the opening of his "Institution for the Formation of Character," he treated the event with usual hyperbole as a giant step toward the time when all people would be trained "in that knowledge which shall impel them not only to love but to be actively kind to each other in the whole of their conduct, without a single exception."[10] The "second creation of humanity" was within reach.

By 1816, Owen was beginning to reveal the millenarian tendencies that were to dominate most of his later life. In addressing the inhabitants of New Lanark on the opening of his Institution for the Formation of Character, he informed his listeners that he was about to divulge "the cause and cure" of wickedness and misery: The cause was the ignorance which Man had inherited from his forefathers. "When these great errors shall be removed, all our evil passions will be removed; no ground of anger or displeasure from one human being toward another will remain; the period of the supposed Millennium will commence, and universal love prevail." Convinced that he could lead a troubled world to this future and restless with the limited potential of New Lanark, he turned his attentions to promoting what in the *New View* he called "a national proceeding for rationally forming the character of that immense mass of population which is now allowed to fill the world with crimes."[11]

In 1816, he told his workers that he was preparing a scheme to establish new "communities," noting that he would begin elsewhere since New Lanark was still too much in the grip of "the old system" for him to begin operations there.[12] It soon became apparent that he intended to demonstrate that he could resolve all of the social problems associated with the Industrial Revolution. Although he first submitted his scheme in 1817 as a remedy for the mass poverty that had long haunted English society, it was evident that he believed that he could make an entirely new world of happiness and virtue for all, rich as well as poor, where all "the pretty jarring interests" of society would be united in cooperation and love.[13]

His idea involved a network of what he called "Agricultural and Manufacturing Villages of Unity and Mutual Cooperation." These largely autonomous cooperative villages, he said, would fuse the advantages of both rural and urban-industrial life, freeing humankind from both the debilitating atmosphere of industrial cities and the isolation that made rural people a generally ignorant peasantry. They would, by combining agriculture and industry into one communal whole, furnish each individual with a meaningful variety of employments which would enable him to develop fully as an individual, ending that dehumanizing specialization of work which often had turned a person into an "unhealthy pointer of a pin ... or clodhopper, senselessly gazing at the soil." In such communities of enlightened, broadly aware workers, Man could control the tremendous power of science and technology for his own good, turning the machine—the source of unemployment and misery—into a horn of plenty for all. Above all, cooperative life would assure an abundance of all things by eliminating the waste of isolated, individualistic living and by compounding the productiveness of human labor. Cooperative kitchens would, for instance, both eliminate the waste of food and free women from their domestic servitude to more rewarding labor in the community.[14]

Owen planned to house each village of 800 to 1200 people in one "large square, or rather parallelogram" of buildings containing communal kitchens and dining halls, public halls, private apartments, and a boarding school for all children more than three years old. This giant parallelogram and nearby industrial buildings would be situated on some 800 to 1500 acres, which by his optimistic assessment of agricultural productivity under his system would be sufficient to support the population in health and comfort. Here was "a machine" that would "simplify and facilitate, in a very remarkable degree, all the operations of human life."[15] Once the machine was in full operation, it would prove so simple to manage as "to render the business of governing a mere recreation"—a typically glib way for him to dismiss the complex and, for him, eventually fatal problem of political leadership and decision making.[16]

Owen's confidence in his cooperative villages grew even stronger when he learned of the Shaker and Harmonist societies in America. "It would be easy," he wrote, "to form other societies under all the regulations and principles of the Shakers which are really valuable—and rejecting of course, their idle peculiarities—foolish prejudices—and disgusting prohibitions." This reasoning led him into a formless communism based on the assumption that the ignorance of these sectarians had limited the potential of their system. Their "imperfect experiment," he said in 1825, "give sure proof of the gigantic superiority of union over division for the creation of wealth." What greater accomplishment, then, when this system was mated with enlightened mind in the form of his great parallelograms?[17]

Owen typically ignored the importance of the complex network of communal relationships that united groups like the millenarians. Whereas these sectarians had created total, all-embracing communities for themselves, he had designed something like a total institution resembling in important respects the "penitentiaries," "workhouses," and "asylums" that benevolently disposed contemporaries were beginning to erect for the lower classes. The parallelogram was essentially an instrument which, by bringing people together under the right management, would train them to live and work collectively. No dubious dependence on their willingness to make self-sacrifices was necessary, since they would automatically abandon their selfish and wasteful individualism when they experienced cooperative life "under the advantages that science and experience could give."[18]

As his vision expanded so did his conviction that he had found a rational and workable way to achieve the promised land during his own lifetime. "It is so easy," he wrote of his scheme, "that it may be put into practice with less ability and exertion than are necessary to establish a new manufacture in a new situation." His great machine seemed so obviously productive of good that Owen was confident it would be readily accepted by all unprejudiced men, rich and poor alike.[19] The general response to his scheme "to let prosperity loose on the country," however, was either indifference or ridicule. Probably most of his contemporaries agreed with Jeremy Bentham, a fellow reformer, who in the 1820s wrote that *"Robert Owen* begins in vapour and ends in smoke. He is a great braggadocio. His mind is a maze of confusion, and he avoids coming to particulars. He is always the same—says the same thing, over and over again."[20]

Like the prophet he had become, Owen met his critics with the stubborn conviction that he was right and his society wrong. If Englishmen failed to see the obvious virtues of his system, it was because there were radical defects in the English social order that kept them blind. One defect, Owen concluded, was the governing principle of industrial society, "immediate pecuniary gain," whose influence had warped all classes of society. Soon, he coupled his rejection of the profit motive with an even less forgivable sin, an increasingly shrill attack on orthodox religion. Like an earlier Deist and hero for radical dissenters, Thomas Paine, he openly charged that the religious dogma foisted on mankind by a "Satanic" and superstitious priesthood had blinded men to the clear light of reason and was ultimately responsible for the evils of the world.[21]

And so the prophet confronted a perverse world with his religion of reason, freedom, and cooperation in the conviction that his was the faith that God had really intended for mankind. He met resistance to his ideas with a secularized millenarianism:

> I must for a time offend all mankind and create in many feelings of disgust and horror at this apparent temerity of conduct, which, without a new understanding, a new heart and a new mind, they could never comprehend; but these in due time shall now [sic] be given to them. Ere long there shall be but one action, one language, and one people. Even now the time is near at hand—almost arrived—when swords shall be turned into ploughshares and spears into pruning-hooks—when every man shall sit under his own vine and his own fig-tree and none shall make him afraid.[22]

All that he seemingly needed was one village based on his principles, one demonstration to awaken a sleeping world to the harmony and happiness which lay within its grasp. Owen, however, could not raise the $500,000 he needed for his demonstration. Although in the early 1820s he had won some support from the English working classes, he had also cut most of his ties with the wealth and power of his society. Even his tie with New Lanark was at the snapping point, since his business partners in that enterprise turned against his "infidel" doctrines, going so far as to compel him to dismiss some of the teachers and to institute readings from the Bible in the New Lanark school.[23] How now to get to the promised land?

Fate answered in 1824 with the appearance in England of an agent appointed by the Harmony Society to sell Harmonie, a going village of unity and cooperation as Owen had long known, for the bargain price of $125,000. Owen's imagination leaped across the Atlantic to America, that new and open world where cooperative societies had been successfully established. By early December, he was in Ekonomie, Pennsylvania, the new town that the Harmonists were building, and there he first met George Rapp. The two prophets of paradise took to each other. According to Owen's son, William, Rapp expressed pleasure at meeting a fellow idealist and offered his help, even dreaming aloud of a frequent and profitable intercourse between the two societies should Owen buy Harmonie.[24] Another member of the Owen party, Donald Macdonald, was less sure that the Englishman and the German really understood one another, but hope and good cheer prevailed between the two men both at Ekonomie and then at Harmonie, where they celebrated the opening of the new year, 1825, by agreeing to terms for the sale of the village. In early May, the last Harmonists said a tearful goodbye to their old town, after an affecting sendoff by the new owner: "Mr. Owen caught the opportunity," said Macdonald, "to express aloud his great sense of their integrity, strict justice & kindness, and said that . . . he had never met with so honest and affectionate body of people. He was so much affected during his address that he could hardly speak."[25]

Owen, nonetheless, was happy to have undisputed possession of his town. New Harmony, with its preponderance of small houses, presented an appearance hardly pleasing to a man who dreamed of placing his people in a great, unified "parallelogram," but it was a solid town with the right mixture of manufacturing and agriculture. Besides, it included over 23,000 acres of land, plenty of space for the creation of true Owenite communities. The new owner soon located an ideal spot on which he planned to begin his first palatial parallelogram after a three-year apprenticeship to his system at New Harmony had prepared his followers to enter the promised land.[26]

As pleased as he was with his new possession, though, Owen spent little time there, preferring to concentrate on raising outside support for his plans. In fact, two days after he bought the place, he went off on an extended lecture tour that took him to Washington, D.C., where in February he was invited to speak in the chamber of the House of Representatives. There he told a distinguished audience, which included President James Monroe and President-elect John Quincy Adams, that the time had come for American leaders to choose between the continuation of poverty, ignorance, and social conflict and his New Society, where abundance would shower its blessings on all people. Cooperative society with its abundance would eliminate classes and class feelings, and it would make possible a complete system of education that would enable "the general intellect of society . . . to make greater advances in a year, than it has hitherto allowed to attain in a century." Universal wealth, intelligence, harmony, truth, and virtue—all were within easy reach. As impracticable as it might seem, said Owen, "the system which I am about to introduce into your states is fully competent to form them into countries of palaces, gardens, and pleasure grounds, and, in one generation, to make the inhabitants a race of very superior beings."[27]

As in England, Owen hoped to persuade the wealthy to help finance his plan. In his February speech, he suggested that all those who shared his principles and feelings form a great national corporation to build some of his parallelograms. In March, he returned to Washington to display a hastily constructed model of his "new combination of circumstances" designed for 5000 people, declaring that "like old machines, when a new one of very superior powers has been invented to supersede them, separate dwelling houses, villages, towns, and cities, must give place to other combinations."[28]

Owen's attempt to win the support of what he took to be the ruling establishment in America brought only silence or ridicule. During this period, most Americans were learning to channel their hopes and resentments into the new system of bipartisan democratic politics that appeared in the mid-1820s. In the future, the great majority of active citizens would look for the solution of their problems to the competition between political parties rather than to the theoretical benefits of cooperative society; the new politics had the practical virtues of neither threatening existing social arrangements nor obstructing private ambitions. The appearance of the partisan system, however, also evoked opposition to it as an oppressive influence. Many cultural dissenters in particular would agree with Tocqueville's warning that democracy threatened an intellectual despotism: "I know of no country in which there is so little independence of mind and real freedom of discussion as in America."[29] For them, Owen's naïve apolitical attitudes excited hopes for an escape into a new world of mental freedom.

Owen received considerable attention in the newspapers, which often reprinted his speeches with commentaries; one New York newspaper summarized his plan for cooperative villages and concluded that "if, the order of Heaven *can* be introduced on earth, such establishments must be the means of accomplishment."[30] Many of the people attracted to New Harmony probably had no higher motive than to benefit from the easy employment, good housing, and free education promised by this rich English paternalist; some of the first arrivals were nearby "backwoodsmen" who had envied and resented the prosperity enjoyed by Rapp's followers. More conspicuous if not more numerous, however, were various cultural dissenters, especially Rationalists and Swedenborgians, who came at their own expense from Cincinnati and other places in the Ohio Valley with the hope of finding the freedom and sense of community which they believed had been denied them by the oppressive orthodoxies of conventional society.[31]

From Zanesville, for instance, came William Pelham, a sometime publisher and newspaper editor, who soon was to help edit the *New Harmony Gazette*. Disgusted by what he saw as the grasping and limiting ways of society, he gloried in the "mental liberty" which he experienced in the new community: "I can speak my sentiments without fear of consequences." From Cincinnati came Josiah Warren, a many talented Rationalist, who became the director of the town band; Warren's eventual experience with Owen's scheme was to make him a pioneer in the development of a much different kind of radicalism, the philosophy and practice of modern Anarchism. From Philadelphia and Cincinnati came R. L. Jennings, an ex-Universalist preacher, who soon began to give secular sermons on Owen's system in the old Rappite Church; Jennings declared that if he were sent out as a missionary for Owenism he could soon win 30,000 converts to the cause.[32] Men like these gave New Harmony much of its character as a rallying ground for rationalism and cultural dissent in America.

By May 1825, enough people had gathered at New Harmony for Owen to form a "Preliminary Society" intended over the next three years to serve as a "halfway house" in which to train these recruits for full participation in his new world. Membership in the society was open to all men and women with the exception of "persons of color," who were admitted only as "helpers" or as apprentice missionaries for the Owenite cause among their own people. During this probationary period, he guaranteed each member a minimum subsistence allowance of $80 a year and established, as a concession to their yet-to-be remedied individualism, a system of limited rewards for work performance. One key article of the constitution of the Preliminary Society provided for the formation, during the third year, of a "Community of Equality and Independence"; the new community was to be located on part of the New Harmony property "purchased by its associated members" presumably from the wealth to be accumulated during the probationary period.[33] This provisions was soon to have fateful consequences.

The establishment of the Preliminary Society climaxed five months of giddy enthusiasm which had begun with the purchase of the Harmonist property. As his Washington speeches indicated, Owen's own enthusiasm was divided between New Harmony and the larger world. During this critical period, he had a choice between two roles: On the model of George Rapp, he could have chosen the role of "Father," the inspired and inspiring leader who directly involved himself in the affairs of his communal family; the successes of religious communities depended heavily on the animating presence of charismatic leaders. Owen, however, had largely abandoned this paternalistic role even before he had left New Lanark. Rather than attempting to make himself the leader of a communal sect, he preferred to pursue the role of "Prophet," the preacher of a new dispensation that would revolutionize the world. As founder of the system, he did appoint the committee which would govern the Preliminary Society during its first year, but otherwise he refused to recognize the need for his active presence at New Harmony. In June, after having appointed the committee and given his probationers a last lecture on his principles, he departed and did not return for more than seven months.[34]

These actions served to give Owen, unintentionally, another role— that of the "Good King," the leading influence in a larger world who could be expected to protect his local followers when they needed him. Unwittingly he had made himself the lead character in a local drama which in its secular way bore a curious resemblance to the scenario of the millenarians. After having raised expectations for heaven on earth, this good king had temporarily disappeared into another and larger world, leaving his disciples to develop his system in preparation for his second coming. During his absence, the work of the Preliminary Society was inspired with extravagent expectations regarding the new society which he would complete on his return. Having created this drama by his decision not to actively manage the Preliminary Society, it might then have been better if Owen had not returned for at least two years, leaving it to his devoted followers to form a real community of true believers. In January 1826, however, the good king reappeared to initiate his millennium. The consequences suggest that it might have been wiser for him never to have returned.

A New Harmony?

At Harmonie, George Rapp's German communists had developed a strong sense of communal unity based on their common cultural background and their shared devotion to a distinctive sectarian religion. The key to their success, though, was undoubtedly their personal and contractual ties with a strong, inspired leader. In exchange for Rapp's pledge to provide for their needs, they pledged to obey him in both secular and religious affairs. To have a successful community, said Frederick Rapp, "a man *is required as leader . . . to whom all the others must be obedient as well in spiritual as in natural regulations, and must submit themselves to his commands,* in order that *everything depends upon one will.*"[1] That system of government had yielded a high degree of brotherly cooperation. Over the next century, various religious cults were to achieve the same success through the same formula for total community. For most Americans, though, this "despotism" was neither acceptable nor necessary.

At New Harmony, Owen's largely American following attempted a radically different experiment in cooperative brotherhood, a democratic community embracing a diversity of people who had little common experience. They were the first of various voluntary communities founded on the hope that the "right" social mechanism would provide for communal cooperation without the sacrifice of individual freedom or even of individual interest. In this sense, New Harmony was the earliest of what Arthur Bestor has aptly called "Patent-Office Models of Society," inventions incorporating principles purportedly applicable to all men and all social situations.[2] For the constructively dissatisfied, there was nothing illogical about this hope. With the early triumphs of human reason, it did seem possible to construct a new and modern form of human community that could replace the varied but commonly flawed societies of the past.

If the Owenites had succeeded in transforming sectarian communalism into secular communism at New Harmony, they might have changed the history of the world. The experiment began with several notable strengths: an already formed and thriving town, a generally well-educated and enthusiastic population, a wealthy and prestigious leader, and the good wishes of many outsiders. In their belief that they were the pioneer creators of Owen's New World, the more ardent members had, in secular form, some of the same sense of transcendent purpose that had motivated the millenarians. Yet in less than three years after it began, Owen's great social machine destroyed itself, leaving behind a reputation that was long to cloud future hopes for cooperative communities.

Critical to this failure was Owen's blindness to his obligations as the exclusive inventor of the machine. Rosabeth Moss Kantor, an expert on the sociology of communal life, has noted the importance not only of a decisive, compelling charismatic leader but of some hierarcy of supporting secondary leaders to implement his will and to protect his inviolability as a source of the right and true.[3] Because of Owen's indifference to political considerations, he failed to provide the secular and democratic equivalent of these two essentials. Where Rapp's one directive will had prevailed, the new leader added to the problems of his experiment by his inconsistencies in dealing both with essential questions and with his most influential followers.

Few social experiments have gotten off to a faster start. In the month following the departure of the last Harmonists, the town managed to develop both a new character and the appearance of a rapidly maturing society. None of the newcomers seem to have appreciated the importance of the work of the Harmony Society in providing them with exemption from the crude frontier stage of development. Rather, they soon came to believe that the town was essentially their work under the inspiration of Owen. Thomas Pears, who had brought his family from Pittsburgh, wrote on June 2: "The schools are nearly organized, boarding houses established, smiths, carpenters, turners, etc. all employed, and agriculture going on almost as well as tho' we had been here a twelvemonth. And this has been accomplished by one man, who has drawn together people from all points of the compass, various in habits and disposition, to mix together like brethren and sisters."[4] Pears, who had arrived only a few days before, was destined to see little of that "one man," since Owen soon departed for the East and for England, leaving the new residents to begin the work of realizing his ideals during his absence.

In some significant ways, they succeeded. The New Harmony school, a centerpiece of the new society, was expanded until by the end of 1825 some 140 pupils were being boarded and educated at public expense: Under the system developed by Owen at New Lanark, they were to be taught to become "rational, just, charitable, and intelligent" beings who would be wisely aware "that they increase their own happiness in proportion as they increase the happiness of those around them." To educate the community and the world, a weekly newspaper, the *New Harmony Gazette,* began publication in October with the bold proclamation that "INDIVIDUALITY DETRACTS LARGELY FROM THE SUM OF HUMAN HAPPINESS." Even earlier, the great Harmonist church was converted into a town hall for meetings, lectures, and concerts. William Pelham was pleased to report that New Harmonians gathered at the former Rappite Inn "not to drink or carouse" or to talk of money "but for the purpose of rational conversation of a serious philosophical cast."[5]

The town soon established social routines in harmony with Owen's dream of a happy cooperative society: Parades and military drill on Monday nights; dancing on Tuesday; public meetings on Wednesday; concerts on Friday, and every evening, said Thomas Pears, "playing at ball, cricket, etc."—a community of good fellowship which seemed to demonstrate Owen's belief that his system could make any group of people into one happy family. By December, this happy community had grown to some 1000 people, leading the *Gazette* to boast that, so great were the advantages of life at New Harmony, the town could easily "have an increase of many times its present population," once sufficient housing was provided.[6]

The developing community did have some evident problems. "We ought to be in a new world," Pears wrote in September, "but most inhabitants have yet to put off the old man. . . . We have yet done with scandal, calumny, nor self-interest, nor the love of power and distinction." Whereas the old Harmonists had been disposed to talk little and to labor much, the New Harmonians showed the opposite tendency, their general record of productivity casting at least some doubt on Owen's earlier claim at New Lanark that "every individual may be trained to produce far more than he can consume." In part the disappointing level of production resulted from the absence of various necessary skills. Although in October one observer compiled an impressive list of available skills, he also noted a shortage of such needed workers as potters, saddlers, and especially operatives who knew how to run the Harmonist cotton and woolen mills, which were operating below capacity, in part because of unfamiliarity with the operation of their rather old-fashioned machinery. Industrially, the new society seems to have slipped back below the level of the Harmonists. Where Harmonie had developed a manufacturing sector oriented toward outside markets, New Harmony had more of the character of a frontier town whose isolation protected its craftsmen from outside competition.[7]

In general, though, these were the troubles of any new community, and ones balanced by some notable successes. If the mills ran at less than full capacity, other industries, like hat, shoe, soap-making, were thriving. Pelham reported in November that the brickyard south of town had made 240,000 bricks for the projected new village.[8] Moreover, the governing committee of the Preliminary Society was demonstrating at least some skill in the resolution of day-to-day problems. According to the *Gazette,* the superintendents of the various departments appointed to manage community affairs met every Saturday night with the committee to "consult upon anything that may be calculated to advance their common interest." Every Wednesday, the committee held a public meeting to report on its activities and to present to the inhabitants those matters which it believed should be settled by their majority vote.[9] In these and other ways, New Harmony seemed to be evolving into a real community, which was at least moderately successful in transforming Owen's abstract system into a practical human enterprise.

This communal effort was infused by what William Pelham called the "general sentiment" that, whatever the problems, "things will go better after the return of Mr. Owen." Owen was the "skillful pilot" who in the knowledge of the mysteries of his system would establish a sure course to the promised land. He was the good king who had declared his intention before he departed "to have every thing here of the best description in agriculture, manufactures, domestic arrangements, education, and whatever appertains to the improved state of society."[10] The dissatisfied explained their troubles in terms of Owen's absence: "The Master Spirit is not here," wrote Pears, "and I fear we shall advance but slowly until his return." The hopeful took comfort in the thought that the progress of the community without the presence of the Master Spirit was a guarantee of complete success on his return.[11]

It was natural, then, for at least some of the New Harmonians to believe that they had passed probation and were ready for the final stage of the new society. William Pelham looked forward to the time when the qualified would "enjoy an equal share with every other member of the immense benefit produced by mutual cooperation." The failures of the Preliminary Society, he said, could be attributed not only to Owen's absence but also to "the heterogeneous population hastily collected here," whereas the new community which Owen could establish "will consist of select characters actuated by feelings of common interest." This was a logical but, as it proved, fatally wrong reading of the function of the Preliminary Society; equally logical but also less than right was his conclusion that Owen as the sole proprietor of the New Harmony estate would find some way to place the property in the possession of the new community.[12] Whatever, Pelham could do no more than await the return of the good king to his domain. The anticipated advent came on January 12, 1826 amid rising hopes for the beginnings of the Owenite millennium.

During his seven months away, Owen experienced what his enchanted eyes saw as a confirmation of his earlier prediction that the United States "is ready to commence a new empire upon the principles of common property." Before sailing for England in July, he had lectured to several interested groups, and on his return to America in November he drew new audiences by displaying the most tangible result of his visit abroad, an elaborate, six-foot-square model of his great parallelogram. In New York, he unveiled the model and spoke for two hours to "a large respectable and literary company." He repeated his performance in Philadelphia; it was soon reported that some 900 Philadelphians were preparing to follow him to New Harmony.[13] Then, it was on to Washington, D.C., where he presented the model to President Adams with the enthusiastic prediction that the great parallelogram would, in Adams's words, "effect an entire change in the human character and in the proceedings of mankind."[14]

By the time he reached New Harmony in early January, the general enthusiasm was such as to give his return something of the character of a millenarian second coming. While his followers could now expect the Master Spirit to complete his arrangements, Owen himself found much encouragement in their accomplishments: "Upon examining the state of the new colony," he was later to write, "it appeared to me, that it had been managed in my absence much better . . . than any one who had a knowledge of human nature would have anticipated." His enthusiasm led him to conclude that the preliminary system in seven months had already prepared the New Harmonians for cooperative life. Less than two weeks after his arrival, he moved his timetable up by more than a year by deciding to begin a Community of Equality and Independence immediately, even though his first model village was still no more than a pile of bricks south of town.[15]

On January 26, 1826, after a series of lectures by Owen, the citizens of New Harmony elected a committee of seven to draft a new and "permanent" constitution. Following extensive discussion, it was approved in early February by a popular vote. "This is a delightful state of society," wrote William Pelham, "and such as I have long entertained in *idea,* but never expected to see realized."[16] Article I of the constitution boldly stated the dominant social ideal of "The New Harmony Community of Equality":

> All members of the community shall be considered as one family, and no one should be held in higher or lower estimate on account of occupation. There shall be similar food, clothing, and education, as near as can be furnished, for all according to their ages; and, as soon as practicable, all shall live in similar houses, and in all respects be accommodated alike. Every member shall render his or her best service for the good of the whole.

The government of the community was equally bold in its democratic character. All resident members of the community were to constitute an Assembly to make laws and appoint officers. The general business of the new society was organized into six departments, which in turn were

subdivided into occupational groups headed by "Intendents" to be selected by the members of their groups; the intendents in turn were to
select their departmental supervisors. Women members were given full
political rights, although most of their activity was limited to only one
department, that of "domestic economy."[17]

This experiment was an audacious one by any standard including
that which had prevailed at New Lanark. It abandoned the system of
rewards, punishments, and private property on which conventional society depended for work and order, replacing it with a vague new
system based on the belief that rational cooperative life would inspire
even more vigorous work and even greater harmony. It rejected the
ideological conformity of the millenarian sects in favor of a guarantee
that "every person shall enjoy the most perfect freedom on all subjects of
knowledge and opinion, especially on the subject of religion." Politically, it dispensed with rule by one strong leader in favor of a radical
new democratic system in which power would be exercised directly by
the community.

Even more audaciously, this radical new community was launched
without the selected membership which Pelham and others had expected from their reading of the Preliminary Society. The *Gazette* had
first described the projected change as involving the "organization of a
community from *amongst* the members of the Society" (emphasis added),
but the new constitution admitted any member of the Preliminary Society who simply signed it as a token of agreement with its principles.[18]
Since the first great parallelogram was yet to be built, the village of New
Harmony became the home of the new community rather than the
halfway house on the road to the model villages as Owen had first
intended.

The new "one family" was diverse in character and commitment, but
some kind of uniformity was assured by the refusal of a minority of New
Harmonians to join it. Having now been directly exposed to Owen's
thought and practice, they found much of it obnoxious, particularly his
open contempt for their religious pieties. Less than two weeks after the
approval of the constitution, some 100 inhabitants, mostly "backwoodsmen," seceded and established their own community of Macluria elsewhere on the New Harmony domain so that they might "hold their
prayer meetings undisputed." Another dissatisfied group also established a community, Feiba Peveli; the letters of this eccentric name

3 5

located the exact latitude and longitude of the new community according to a scheme of nomenclature devised by Stedman Whitwell, an English architect who had completed Owen's design for the great parallelogram.[19]

The departure of some 200 inhabitants did not disturb Owen, who agreed to sell them a total of 2700 acres of his domain on easy terms even though these tracts included some of his best agricultural land. Aside from relieving some of the overcrowding in the village, it satisfied his earlier expectation that the new "independent" societies to be formed out of the village would purchase their lands from him, an expectation that was becoming important in his thinking. By labeling the seceding societies Communities Two and Three, Owen was able to treat them as evidence of the spread of the new empire of peace and good will which he had predicted the year before.

Optimists also found hope in the proliferation elsewhere of Owenite communities, which had begun the previous year with the formation by Swedenborgians of the Yellow Springs Community in Ohio. By early 1826, that community was in trouble, but the year brought the formation of new societies in Indiana, Ohio, New York, and Pennsylvania. In May, a correspondent in the *Gazette* said that the Owenite empire had grown to at least ten communities, and he presented a long list of names for the hundreds which he predicted would follow.[20] In this "new social cooperative system," wrote one enthusiast, "all the federative societies would traffic and deal with each other in the spirit of equality, without the smallest fear of deception, over-reaching or cheating."[21] During these euphoric months of the new year, it looked as if New Harmony was becoming the capital of a rapidly expanding new world of unity and cooperation.

This period was marked by the arrival in early February 1826 of the much publicized "boatload of knowledge," a cadre of scientists and progressive educators from Philadelphia and elsewhere, who promised to make the village a center of advanced thought. Owen boasted that the boat, the *Philanthropist,* "contained more learning than ever was before contained in a boat," real, substantial learning and not the dead knowledge of the past. The most notable of this group was the geologist and educator William Maclure, who brought not only his talents but a considerable sum of money as well; eventually, he invested more than $80,000 in New Harmony.[22] The presence of this boatload of cosmopolitan talent, much of it from Europe, completed Owen's dream for a scientific and rational community. It was true that these newcomers and the estimated 50 tons of books and apparatus which followed them did not include the skilled craftsmen and new machinery which Owen previously had considered bringing to New Harmony, but such practical matters weighed little against the expectation that New Harmony would serve as a dynamic intellectual center for Owen's new rational world.[23]

The new infusion of talent and intellect at the least provided Owen with the ingredients needed to establish an improved version of his comprehensive institution for the Formation of Character. In the spring of 1826, the school established the previous year was expanded and reorganized by Maclure into a three-tiered system. At the base was an Infant School for children between 2 and 5 years of age headed by Mrs. Joseph Neef and Madam Marie Duclos Fretageot. Joseph Neef, an Alsatian immigrant to the United States, headed the Higher School where some 200 boys and girls between ages 5 and 12 were educated and boarded at public expense in a progressive environment removed from the influence of their parents.[24] Under the management of enlightened educators, they were to be schooled as one common family to a rational and scientific understanding of the world. Attached to the school was an industrial department intended to train them in the practical skills required by the community; each student was expected to learn at least one useful trade through actual practice. The top tier of the system was a School for Adults which provided evening classes and lectures in the sciences and other practical subjects for anyone above the age of 12.[25]

The establishment of this system deepened Owen's conviction that he had created the means to transform the New Harmonians into rational members of the Community of Equality. On the Fourth of July, he proclaimed a "Declaration of Mental Independence" from the tyranny of ignorance and superstition which had hitherto prevented mankind from achieving paradise: "Our principles will spread from community to community, from State to State, from continent to continent, until this system and these principles shall overshadow the whole world, shedding fragrance and abundance, intelligence and happiness upon all the sons of men." To mark the advent of the new age, the *Gazette* began to date its issue with the year 1, the first year of Mental Independence.[26]

By this time, however, reality was beginning to burst through the euphoria in the form of an accumulation of troubles which were to end the new age before the close of the year 2 M.I. In two Sunday lectures which followed his proclamation of Mental Revolution, Owen warned that "the Millennium" would not arrive until the community had achieved "a situation of pecuniary independence" and conquered its "feelings of anger and a want of charity."[27] Characteristically, he blamed these troubles on his followers, ignoring any thought of personal responsibility for the problems. At the least, however, he had upset the attainments of his followers as well as his own perhaps workable original plan by his precipitous decision to scrap the Preliminary Society.

The establishment of the Community of Equality had one immediate unfortunate effect. Unintentionally, it disrupted the communal arrangements developed during Owen's absence. The abrupt elimination of the established routines in favor of a radically new system created something like a leadership vacuum, and in less than a month the members found the system so unworkable that they persuaded the reluctant Master Spirit to take charge of their affairs for the next ten months.[28] For a time, Owen demonstrated some of the same managerial talents that had made him a success at New Lanark, enabling the *Gazette* to report in March that "the town now presents a scene of active and steady industry. . . . The society is gradually becoming reality . . . a Community of Equality." Owen also attempted to revive his original plan by appointing a "nucleus" of 24 persons to form a new community at New Harmony whose members it would select subject to his veto.[29] Neither Owen nor his nucleus, however, could resolve several basic problems which had been intensified by the creation of the Community of Equality.

One was the absence of a strong sense of unity and commonality among the membership, the result in part of the failure in January 1826 to begin the cooperative community with a selected membership. Owen was later to complain that the decision to admit all members of the Preliminary Society had retarded "the formation of one united Community . . . ; there were too many opposing habits and feelings to permit such a mass, without instruction in the system to act at once together." The decision was not his, but he did not intervene to prevent it.[30] Moreover, having disrupted the preliminary community by his haste in scrapping its institutions, he further weakened the sense of communal unity by thrusting the boatload of knowledge into the picture.

The arrival of these newcomers evoked a whirl of social as well as intellectual activity. Robert Dale Owen, one of the boatload, (and Owen's oldest son), later remembered "the absolute freedom of opinion in dress, and in social converse which I found there. The evening gatherings, too, delighted me; the weekly meetings for discussion of our principles . . . ; the weekly concert . . . the weekly ball, where I found crowds of young people, bright and genial." Whatever its intrinsic merits, however, this style of life deepened a basic rift in the community between those members who prided themselves on their refinements and those whom they saw as, to use the words of Mrs. Sarah Pears, "rough uncouth creatures." Out of the whirl of activity came a social faction, "the Literati," which soon showed a disturbing tendency to try to separate itself from the *hoi polloi.* Early in March 1826, the Literati (which included Robert Dale Owen and his brother, William) attempted to form a new community among themselves with the intention of taking over most of the valuable institutions of New Harmony.[31]

This attempted coup by the elite collapsed when Owen offered its members only a tract of wooded land to develop for themselves, but the social rift remained. One visitor to New Harmony, the Duke of Saxe-Weimar, wrote that Madame Fratageot had told him in German "that the highly vaunted equality was not altogether to her taste; that some of the society was too low," an attitude that she communicated to some of the young women in her charge. The Duke was hardly the most sympathetic judge of communal democracy, but he was probably right when he concluded that "in spite of the principle of equality which they recognize, it shocks the feelings of people of education to live on the same footing with every one indiscriminately."[32] Equality in the rough dampened enthusiasm for equality in theory and undermined commitments to the experiment. By further weakening the sense of community, this situation also complicated several practical economic problems.

One was the continued failure of the New Harmonians to produce more than they consumed, a problem compounded by the elimination of the practice in the Preliminary Society of giving extra credits to members proportionate to "the value of their services." One interested observer stated the problem in the *Gazette:* "What is to be the stimulus or encouragement to superior industry, activity, and utility in the community, where no merit is ascribed to anyone laboring better?" The only answer in the Constitution was a provision that "every member shall render his best services for the good of the whole."[33] In the logic of utopia, cooperation was intrinsically more productive than conflict, but logic did not provide a stimulus to work in the absence of rewards and punishments.

Owen had promised that he would make various new "arrangements" at New Harmony to increase productivity, especially by the introduction of new machinery and techniques, but his return brought no miraculous mechanisms. Instead he devised a technique, derived from his "Silent Monitor" at New Lanark, intended to shame New Harmonians into greater activity. Under the new constitution, superintendents of work were required to report their "opinion of the daily character of each person attached to their occupation." No provision was made for either rewards or punishments, but under Owen this scheme was applied in the form of weekly reports on everyone's work, the dominant measure being the number of hours spent by each worker on the job. Those who worked the fewest hours ran the risk of being signaled out for condemnation at public meetings.[34]

This system provided some basis for the management of labor, but it probably did as much to generate discord as to spur production. The emphasis on the number of hours of work rather than on actual productivity especially offended active and intelligent workers who believed that they contributed more in one hour than some others did in one day. Early in March, an increasingly discontented Sarah Pears complained:

> Instead of four or five hours of labor being sufficient for one's maintenance as people were led to imagine by Mr. Owen's representations; the bell is now rung at half past five to get up; at six to go to work, at seven for breakfast; at eight to work again . . . at six in the evening to return home. If those who are regularly employed are not punctual, they are liable to be reported at the nightly meetings of the intendents. If they are sick, they must have a certificate from the physicians. If this is not slavery, I know not what is.[35]

The work situation undoubtedly dissatisfied many of those had been drawn to New Harmony by hopes of greater freedom and leisure. As a woman, however, Mrs. Pears had some additional grievances against life at New Harmony. In describing the glories of his great parallelogram, Owen had promised that women would be freed from the domestic drudgery of individual households for more rewarding kinds of work.

In reality, wives and mothers like Mrs. Pears found a double burden, being expected to labor in the "domestic department" while also carrying on their traditional roles; after doing sewing, cooking, and cleaning for the community, they still had to take care of their individual households.[36] Owen, who had left his wife in England, seems to have been even less sensitive to this matter than to the other problems of communal life. When he finally was forced to notice the problem, he concluded that it had developed simply because women talked too much when they gathered for collective work: "now they can not talk and work too." Little wonder that Mrs. Pears should complain that "Mr. Owen in New Harmony is a very different personage from Mr. Owen in Pittsburgh, Washington, etc."[37]

Meanwhile, Thomas Pears and others were finding another worry and grievance in Owen's efforts to resolve probably the most troubling question raised by the hasty creation of the Community of Equality: Who actually owned the New Harmony property? Who could benefit from any increase in its value produced by the work of its inhabitants? Owen had, more or less, absorbed from the sectarians a vague commitment to the common ownership of property, but this capitalist turned communist had given virtually no thought to the matter. Although the constitution provided that "the real estate of the community should be held in perpetual trust forever for the use of the community," it did not alter the fact that Owen and not the community owned the New Harmony domain. If Owen had turned some of his real estate over to the community, he might have satisfied those who expected a real community of property, but this as a proprietor he refused to do.[38] Instead, he did nothing to resolve the question until he was forced to do so in defense of his own interests.

Soon after the Community of Equity was established, Owen began to recognize that New Harmony, rather than being the expected cornucopia of wealth for all, was becoming an increasingly expensive drain on his limited fortune, and at a time when he had hoped to find $40,000 to pay off his debt to George Rapp.[39] It was under these circumstances that he finally acted. In March 1826, he proposed that the community buy the village and its surrounding lands in 12 annual installments at 5 percent interest. Taken earlier, this step might have resolved the problem and limited the community to the truly committed. Having led his followers to expect an easy entry into paradise, however, Owen now raised much resentment and resistance, particularly when it was concluded that he would make a considerable profit from the deal. Thomas Pears wrote that the proposal produced an immediate collapse of energy and enthusiasm on the part of himself and others. Pears vowed that he would not make himself responsible for a share in the communal purchase, since he doubted the community could produce enough to pay off its mortgage to Owen.[40]

In April, Sarah Pears claimed that "I have no doubt that two-thirds of the Society would go if they had the means. Mr. Owen is growing very unpopular even with the great sticklers of the System." Within weeks, the Pears family was back in Pittsburgh, where Owen's enthusiasm had excited their dreams the year before. Thomas Pears apparently was the author of a poem that burlesqued Owen's fantasy for a great parallelogram at New Harmony:

> Yes, we shall see that glorious day,
> It's e'en beginning now;
> For we one tree have cut away
> Where Harmony shall grow
> And when we've got our palace built,
> No Harmonite shall sigh;
> Pain then shall cease and ev'ry tear
> Be wiped from Misery's eye.[41]

The great majority of New Harmonians continued to cling to their new society in the hope that things would soon go better, but most of the spirit that had given life to the community was fast fading away. After less than six months exposure to Owen and his policies, little remained of the animating faith in the benevolence and wisdom of the good king. This change was notably evident in the attitude of William Maclure, who had the cash as well as the talents which might have saved the experiment. Maclure and some of the other intellectuals drawn to New Harmony constituted a potential second tier of leadership which could have strengthened Owen's position, if the prophet had possessed the political wisdom to develop it. Earlier, the scientist had reassured Madame Fretageot that Owen's "immense mecanizm [sic] will require so broad and commodious a road that our childish plans will follow him without being obstructed by half the prejudice, superstition & bigotry we should have to fight unaided by him."[42] Soon after his arrival with the "boatload of knowledge," however, he became disenchanted with the workings of the "immense mecanizm" and began to take an independent interest in the governing policies of the community.

In mid-April 1826, Maclure proposed his own answer to the labor problem: "The thing most wanted is, to protect the industrious, honest members against the unpleasant, mortifying sensation of laboring for others that [sic] are either unable or unwilling to work their proportion necessary to keep up the expenditures of society, and pay their debts." His solution was to reorganize the community into various departments along occupational lines, assigning to each an equitable production quota, but otherwise permitting a department to regulate its own labor; each department would also purchase that part of Owen's property which it actually used. Decentralization of this sort, thought Maclure, would serve to reduce economic affairs to such scope as to directly engage the habits, knowledge, and loyalties of the members of each department.[43]

Owen rather reluctantly accepted the general idea, probably because it provided a way to sell part of his property. As was all too characteristic of his "arrangements," however, the actual rearrangement created essentially separate societies instead of interdependent departments. In late May, the one common family at New Harmony was divided up into an Agricultural and Pastoral Society, a Mechanical and Manufacturing Society, and an Educational Society, each of which contracted to buy its portion of the property. In theory, each society would perform the work which it did best, while continuing to share communal facilities and responsibilities under the general direction of a Board of Union. In fact, its chief effect was to produce a new set of conflicts that further complicated Owen's increasingly awkward relationship with both Maclure and the community.[44]

It did benefit Maclure and the Literati by giving them control over the New Harmony schools and an extensive property, but the new situation soon turned sour when the farmers' and mechanics' societies refused to pay tuition for the schooling of their children.[45] Owen himself further compounded tensions when at the end of August he attempted to set up a rival educational enterprise. After noting a "disturbing want of cordiality among you," he persuaded the entire community to meet in the village hall three evenings a week for a program of "community education." This new system, he promised, would bring parents and children together, enabling the older members both to benefit from the supposedly superior knowledge of the young and to test the effectiveness of the Education Society in educating their children. If anything, this scheme seems to have intensified tensions within the community, and in a few weeks Owen abandoned it.[46]

By September, Maclure had concluded that the Master Spirit was spoiling his own experiment by his presence. In his view, Owen's dominating enthusiasm and wealth had discouraged the members from taking an active and responsible role in the community; as a result, "all their instruction has been to consume not to produce." Convinced that New Harmony was headed toward a "vortex of ruin and destruction," Maclure eventually took advantage of Owen's money problems to "collect" the Education Society for himself in exchange for paying the $40,000 which Owen still owed the Harmonists.[47] Others were forming the same opinion of Owen. In August 1826, a group of New Harmonians united to condemn his policies:

> We have witnessed only a rapid succession of new undigested projects, some of wh. are actually at variance wi. ye. vital principles of ye. Community System as promulaged in yr. publications. . . . We see around us only confusion, inequality, apathy or jealousy, ill will, & conflict of opposite feelings instead of order, regularity, equality, voluntary industry, & a mutual spirit of accommodation.[48]

These critics were particularly upset by Owen's apparent preoccupation with the sale of his property. Among them was Paul Brown, one of those Americans who like Cornelius Blatchly had formed their ideal of "common wealths" before Owen had appeared on the scene. When Brown was finally able to get to New Harmony, he said later, he was shocked by the contrast between his expectations and the "mercantile" feelings raised by the effort of "the lord proprietor . . . to get an assemblage of people that were willing to sign a contract to pay for the estate."[49] This view was shared by Joseph Neef, the head of the Higher School (and a future father-in-law of two of Owen's sons). Neef had grown disillusioned with the lord proprietor when in the spring Owen had rejected a proposal that he turn 2500 acres of his domain over to the community.[50]

Throughout this period, Owen betrayed a characteristic obtuseness regarding the character and requirements of community. He might still have been able to save the one common family if, like George Rapp, he had made himself a full member of it; but this was not the manner he had learned at New Lanark. Instead of the good father, he acted more like a lord proprietor who made remote judgments regarding his tenants. When he was asked whether he would turn the domain over to those who pledged to go the whole way with him, he replied that he believed the people were not yet ready for a community of common property: "I shall be ready to form a community whenever you shall be prepared for it." Having convinced himself that he had created the circumstances which should have made the population ready for paradise, he complained that his plan had been stymied by stubborn defects in the character of that population.[51]

In less then nine months after his return, Owen had broken the mainspring of his own communal enterprise by his bumbling leadership. His lack of even ordinary political sense left him isolated from his own community. The true extent of the damage was concealed for a time by the apparent stability of population at New Harmony. Most people were not yet ready to abandon whatever personal stake they had in the community; those who did leave were replaced by newcomers who, whatever their faith in Owen's system, saw something to be gained from it. In October, the *Gazette* celebrated its second anniversary with the declaration that "a mutual confidence has been established" between Owen and the people, but even its determined optimism could not obscure signs of communal decay, notably in the form of vandalism, theft, and drunkiness; Owen, a temperance man, had tried to exclude the devil of intemperance by closing the old Rappite distillery.[52] The Master Spirit attempted to save the situation by making another government headed by himself and four associates, but his new "energetic government" did nothing to reverse the downward spiral.[53]

This accelerating demoralization was reflected in the disenchantment of William Pelham, a faithful member of the Preliminary Society and one of the first editors of the *Gazette*. Early in 1826, he had been swept up in the millennial enthusiasm of Owen's second coming, calling him "an extraordinary man—a wonderful man" who had constructed a social machine which soon would "go like clock work." By August, however, he was willing to join in the complaint over Owen's mismanagement of the machine and by the end of the year his dreams of paradise had given way to despair: "Our Rope factory burned down," he wrote in January 1827. "Our Society is still tearing down the log buildings for firewood, and the women sometimes cannot agree among themselves who is the cook." By this time, Pelham was looking forward to leaving New Harmony for another projected community experiment in the spring.[54]

Owen himself completed the collapse when early in 1827 he ordered all those who were not productively employed at New Harmony either to leave his domain or to join one of the "societies of common property, equality, and kindness" which were to be formed on his lands outside the village. This fifth reorganization in a year evoked more forced optimism from the *Gazette:* "New Harmony, therefore, is not now a community; but, as was originally intended, a central village out of, and around which, communities have been formed, and more continue to form themselves."[55] Although Owen pretended otherwise, it was soon evident that the new communities were but the fragments from an exploded experiment. In June, he left for England and when he returned one last time in 1828 he discovered that the ten colonies had been dissolved away by what he called the spirit of "individual gain." He was able to retrieve most of his domain, which he then deeded over to his sons, but the three years of the experiment had left him much poorer if not wiser, costing him about $100,000 of the estimated $250,000 he had made during his days of profitable capitalism.[56]

New Harmony probably would have eventually disappointed the extravagant hopes associated with it, but why did the experiment fail so fast and so completely? The best answer involves the familiar "ifs" and "mights" of utopian history: If Owen had adhered to his original plan— if he had stayed with his developing community from the beginning—if he had turned part of his domain over to the community—if he had recognized the need for a secondary tier of supporting leaders—if he had supplied the community with new machinery—if he had avoided disrupting changes, then New Harmony might have evolved into a successful community of benevolent rationalists.

It would be as easy for men to become angels, however, as for him to have behaved differently than he did. Although he thought otherwise, he was also a creature of circumstance. His nature and experience made him what he was: an English businessman and prophetic visionary whose Mount Sinai was a company town. Having formed his science and system from his apparent successes with a dependent British factory population, it was his destiny, thanks to George Rapp, to attempt to realize his millennium in the American West among a heterogenous population of rationalists, Swedenborgians, and other cultural dissenters attracted by his promise of liberation from the restraints of conventional society. Although Owen was wise enough to recognize some need to adjust his system to the new circumstances, his blindness to his own limitations made it impossible for him to adjust himself to the community he was trying to create. It was probably inevitable, then, that his good intentions should eventuate in complaints that he was a greedy landlord who was attempting to establish what Neef called "a kind of feudal barony."[57]

Robert Owen virtually ignored New Harmony after his last departure in 1828 except to complain that it had actually been conducted by other people who did not understand his principles; but he did turn to the United States one more time in an effort to realize his vision. In 1844, he turned up in Washington, D.C., where, complained John Quincy Adams, he "mesmerized me . . . with his lunacies about a new organization of society," the starting point to be a new community with $3 million to be raised by Congress. The failure of Congress even to consider his proposal did not dampen his hopes.[58] In 1845, he convened at New York a "World's Convention" of radical reformers with the intention of affecting "in peace the greatest revolution ever yet made in human society." A small convention was actually held but without notable effect, and in 1847 he left the United States never to return.[59]

After New Harmony, Owen continued to attract some attention, particularly as a prophet of unlimited material abundance. In the early 1840s, he predicted that "machines and chemistry" rightly managed would enable "the few to oversupply the wants and wishes of all consumers," making things so plentiful that all could provide for their basic needs without cost or restraint and eliminating forever the material scarcity which had degraded both individuals and society. In this material paradise, everyone would be equal in that each person would have sure access to everything which he really needed. Rational men, therefore, would have no reason for envy, resentment, or competition over wealth. By making all things as freely available as air or water, the new system would release humankind from its foolish preoccupation with material wealth so that it might develop its full moral and intellectual potential. Out of the material plenty made possible by modern productive power, then, would emerge the Millennium which Owen called "the New Moral World."[60]

Although his dream was founded on technology and science, Owen was no mere technophile. The only machine that evoked his enthusiasm was his own great parallelogram, a social machine involving his "superior" social arrangements. He believed that, without a fundamental reorganization of society, Man would forever squander modern plenty. Although wealth could be expected to increase even in a defective society, it would be largely wasted under circumstances that drove men into disruptive rivalries and destructive wars. Individualism, private property, and competition served merely to produce a corrupted society dominated by "priests," "warriors," and other parasites whose interest it was to waste rather than to produce wealth. Only in a cooperative community rightly constituted would the "illimitable" power which God had intended for human benefit be realized.[61]

As a prophet, Owen encouraged an interest among radical social idealists in the invention of some kind of social organization whose "superior" arrangements would yield the Millennium. As the attempted creator of a social machine at New Harmony, however, his influence was more negative than positive. A few Americans continued to be attracted to his form of nonsectarian communism; feeble movements in that direction were to appear and disappear during most of the century. For most American idealists, though, the example of New Harmony served merely to prove that communism was workable only in its original sectarian form. Owen himself was chiefly remembered as the foreigner who had not only proven that point but also offended the cherished values of the nation by his attacks on individualism, private property, and the conventional family. The next notable efforts to invent ideal social organizations would give special respect to all three of these values, in the process creating distinctively American forms of cooperative brotherhood.

Whatever the long-term influence of New Harmony on the cooperative dream, the next decade after the debacle on the Wabash saw the near disappearance of communitarianism in nonsectarian form. In 1834, George Henry Evans (the brother of the Shaker convert Frederick Evans) and Lewis Masquerier considered establishing an Owenite community in northern Illinois; but eventually both men rejected Owen's communism in favor of a long-term effort to reform the national land laws so as to assure a "homestead" to every individual. Josiah Warren, a member of the New Harmony community, did establish a short-lived community, Equity, in Ohio, but this was founded on principles diametrically opposed to those of Owen. Warren's experience at New Harmony led him to develop an American version of anarchism which was to have some influence throughout the century.[62]

In part, the decline of communitarianism resulted from the collapse of New Harmony, but it also resulted from a change of circumstances. It was at least a minor part of Owen's misfortune that he began his experiment at a time when America had recovered from the worst effects of the Panic of 1819 and had begun a decade of rapid development. During these generally prosperous years, most people were too busy pursuing the individual opportunities of an expanding economy to even notice prophecies of collective plenty in any form. Both their hopes and resentments found release in the expanding system of popular politics, whose disputes involved the management of existing society rather than basic social and economic arrangements.

In 1837, however, a new financial panic initiated a sequence of economic collapses which by the early 1840s produced the deepest and longest depression which the nation had yet experienced. In this gloom there appeared a new light kindled by a new generation of radical social idealists. Although that light would also eventually fade, it marked a far more influential phase of communitarianism, one which had significant implications for the society and culture of the modernizing nation.

Individuality and Brook Farm

The early 1840s brought an efflorescence of radical social idealism which made the decade of Owenism a mere prelude in the search for cooperative brotherhood. Essentially, the culture of dissent achieved a critical mass sufficient to give it self-sustaining life over the next eighty years. During the 1840s the literature of radicalism reached major proportions, particularly in the form of a radical press that included such influential newspapers as Horace Greeley's New York *Tribune* and William Lloyd Garrison's *Liberator* as well as more limited journals devoted to a single cause like the *Harbinger* (Fourierism), the *Practical Christian* (Christian Socialism), and the *Oneida Circular* (Christian Communism). Social idealism had found a powerful albeit uneven voice that was to affect the social thought and behavior of the next generation. The two decades after 1840 brought hundreds of plans for the attainment of some form of heaven on earth and at least fifty actual communitarian experiments dedicated to the ideal of cooperative brotherhood.[1]

This was the special work of a small but brilliant group of young social thinkers born during the first two decades of the century.[2] Men like Horace Greeley, Albert Brisbane, and George Ripley all came of age during the great period of modernization in the North Atlantic world that followed the Napoleonic Wars; most reached maturity in the years between 1824 and 1836, the first of several periods of extraordinary progress and prosperity which during the next century were to raise hopes that a truly good society could be created on earth. That nearly all of them were born in New England, the most rapidly modernizing section of the country during this period, had a double significance, for it exposed them not only to progress but also to radical religion.

By the 1820s, New England had entered an extraordinary phase of religious ferment highlighted by the kind of millennialist expectations expressed by Samuel Hopkins at the end of the previous century. Although the young idealists often had very different views of the millennium, they did agree that the first step toward it was to break with a corrupted society and a corrupted Christianity, to "come-out" from existing churches and other institutions in order to create new forms of devotion and social life.

The members of this group were by training and disposition preachers in religious or secular form—ministers, educators, and journalists who challenged existing orthodoxies and the orthodox by preaching a new dispensation attuned to their progressive age. Without exception, they were devoutly anti-political, convinced that the sleazy world of competitive partisan politics was the road to hell and that existing government was the most corrupt institution of all. Some were founders of new religions like Perfectionism and Trancendentalism while others preached more secular "isms" such as Fourierism, Communism, and Anarchism. Whatever the form of their faith, they were driven by a combination of personal ambition and personal commitment to strenuous efforts to make that faith the basis for a new and better society.

Most of them attained a mature voice at a time when the world seemed to need a new dispensation. After 1837, the progressive years gave way to a disturbing new period of deepening poverty, unemployment, and desperation. In late 1843, a convention of social idealists in Boston listed the social evils that challenged the hopes for progress:

> The inefficiency of all modes of Public Charity to relieve or prevent *Pauperism* . . . , the injustice of our common system of *Wages;* the unequal distribution of means and opportunities for *Culture, Refinement, Recreation and Social Pleasures;* the imper-

fect character and degree of *Popular Education,* both for children and adults; the unnatural subservience of *Woman;* the distinctions of *Caste* based upon outward and artificial circumstances; the universal war of *Competition;* and finally the tendency of our Industrial, Commercial, and Financial Transactions to the establishment of a MONEYED FEUDALISM.[3]

This crisis of the corrupted world seemed to provide the opportunity as well as the need to reorganize social life on the basis of some form of brotherly cooperation where a harmony of interests would assure all a share of the benefits of progress. Having rejected politics, government, and the other institutions of society, the radical reformers adopted communitarianism as their instrument of change with the hope that by forming one successful cooperative community they could begin the conversion of the troubled world.

The new communitarianism first erupted in New England in 1840. "We are all a little wild here with numberless projects of social reform," said Ralph Waldo Emerson. "Not a reading man but has a draft of a new community in his waistcoat pocket."[4] By 1842, three of these projects had been realized in notable form. One was Brook Farm, the special concern of Transcendentalists. Another was the Northampton Association of Education and Industry, founded in western Massachusetts by a group headed by George Benson, William Lloyd Garrison's brother-in-law; this community reached a peak population of 180 before it encountered financial problems and collapsed in 1846, leaving behind what eventually became the village of Florence. A smaller but more successful community was established by Adin Ballou and his sect of Practical Christian Socialists. This "Fraternal Communion," which based its social life on the principles of the Sermon on the Mount, survived for over a decade, only to expire in the mid-1850s after having established the successful manufacturing town of Hopedale.[5]

These cooperative experiments, along with others to follow, were significantly different in their respective social principles, but they did share a common distaste for communism. In part, this resulted from memories of Owen's disastrous experiment at New Harmony, which had only proven that common ownership of property could not be divorced from religious sectarianism. Beyond considerations of property, however, there was a deeper concern over human personality that led to a rejection of communism in religious as well as secular form. The focus of this concern was "Individuality," an idea which neither Owen nor the Shakers could appreciate. In place of the naïve Owenite view that human social nature was uniform stuff that could be uniformly transformed by a social machine, the new generation believed that no cooperative community could succeed which did not allow for a diversity of unique individual personalities; the problem was to create a system of cooperation which would eliminate the competitive selfishness of existing society while providing for the full development of each distinctive individual self.

In New England, the idea had a varied influence. The Christian Socialist, Adin Ballou, said that "perfect *individuality* is a fundamental idea of the true man" and vowed that his ideal Christian community would provide for "unabridged individuality of mind, conscience, duty, and responsibility"—a promise that to a great extent he was able to keep.[6] William Ellery Channing, the great Unitarian thinker, declared that "Individuality, or moral self-sufficiency," was a necessary basis for the truly good life. The idea had special importance for the small but influential band of Transcendentalists, who had rejected traditional religion and churches in favor of the view that every individual had within himself a spark of divinity which gave him a distinctive potential for personal goodness and happiness.[7]

This ideal became important at a time when changes in American life were weakening social institutions in favor of individualism, a social fact noted and first named in 1840 by Alexis de Tocqueville in the second volume of *Democracy in America*. Emerson, ever sensitive to social tendencies, said that "this is the Age of Severance, of Dissociation, of Freedom, of Analysis, of Detachment. It is the age of the first person singular. The man steadily sunders himself more from his holdings. Every man for himself."[8] The dissolution of social constraints and conventions had its strong positive side in that it freed every person to develop his own inherent potential for goodness and happiness. On the other hand, the breakdown of protective social ties also threatened to set individuals adrift to be controlled and manipulated by the anonymous forces of their new society, a particularly ominous tendency during the crisis years after 1837. The problem of making a society for individuality would evoke many attempted answers over the next century.

Emerson tried to solve the problem by teaching every individual to have faith in the potential and power of his own self-sufficient self, in the belief that "as we come to our stature we shall inherit not only forms & churches & communities but earth & heaven."[9] What Emerson preached his friend Henry Thoreau put into practice at Walden Pond. From mid-1845 to the late summer of 1847, Thoreau lived there in solitude in order "to transact some private business with the fewest obstacles." His private business was with his own life, to measure in himself the full capacities of an individual man. In society, he believed, the clutter of things to which men had become attached distracted them from developing more than a small part of their total selves and had dulled their sense of what was possible. To demonstrate that anyone could escape from such dullness, Thoreau devoted himself to living a life of "simplicity, simplicity, simplicity." By meeting his needs with no more than six weeks of work a year, he believed that he had found a sure way to break from society's limiting influences in order to sound the full depths of his self.[10]

Thoreau abandoned his community-of-one in 1847, eventually to advertise it in one of the great books of the century. The stone which he cast into Walden Pond was to create more than a few ripples around the world. Yet there was a significant weakness in his private paradise which had already led to some of his Yankee compatriots to reject it. Lacking any great need for society, Thoreau had found it easy to declare his independence of it, but this also meant that he gave virtually no attention to developing a social context for his ideal; for him, the ideal society was one where everyone would live on his own square mile of land, a fruitless fantasy even on the frontier. Thoreau might pretend that society was little more than a phantom, but for nearly everyone else it was a reality from which there was no desirable escape.[11]

For at least some well-educated, advantaged New Englanders the problem was not that society refused to leave them alone but that it left them with nothing worthy to do. In 1844, when Emerson attempted to explain the character of New England reformers, he noted that the last quarter of a century had seen "a gradual withdrawal of tender consciences from the social organizations."[12] Educated to pursue a life of high idealism, they encountered what they felt was a world dominated by sleazy politics, dead religions, sterile professions, and dollar-dominated businesses. It was a world which promised them material comforts but seemed to deny them access to life itself, insulating them from the challenge of real life at the expense of the full development of their individual selves. Their discomfort and resentment was intensified by the feeling that this shallow existence was lived also at the cost of those who were closest to life, farmers and workers, classes enslaved by their poverty to oppressively hard physical toil.[13]

How to restore a lost wholeness to individual life and to the life of society? The answer demanded some meaningful labor that would enable each person to combine the physical and intellectual sides of his self. "Am I not defrauded of my best culture," said Emerson, "in the loss of those gymnastics which manual labor and the emergencies of poverty constitute?" Theodore Parker, concerned over the opening gap between wealth and poverty in New England's industrializing society, declared that "things will never come to their proper level so long as thought with the Head, and Work with the hands are considered incompatible."[14] For Parker and others, it was important that labor be made attractive and available so as to allow individuals to exercise their full physical as well as mental potential. It was equally important that the life of the mind which they enjoyed also be made available to the less advantaged so that they too could develop the full potentials of their selves. These were the aims of Brook Farm, the special creation of one New Englander who had a particularly serious interest in combining muscle and mind in the pursuit of individuality.

George Ripley (1802–1880) followed a familiar New England road to radicalism. After his graduation from Harvard in 1826, he broke with the orthodox Congregationalism of his Puritan forebearers to become a Unitarian minister. Eventually, he became restless with Unitarianism and in 1836 helped to organize the Transcendental Club, which marked the appearance of Transcendentalism as an organized movement.[15] Along the way, Ripley developed a strong belief in the perfectability of individual man: Every person, as God's creature, "constantly communes with an ideal perfectness." In this divine nature, Man had the potential to achieve a perfect character and to make a heaven of his society; inspire the human soul "with filial love of God, and you make a paradise at once." For Ripley, however, the religion and society of Boston seemed dead to filial love, and their influence seemed only to deflate the soul.[16]

Ripley's uneasiness with the life around him grew into outright antagonism after 1837. In Boston, the increasing numbers of desperately poor people highlighted the advantaged position of his own class, deepening his resentment against the essential spiritual failure of society. "I cannot witness the glaring inequalities of condition, the hollow pretensions of pride," he told his Purchase Street parishioners in 1840, "the burning zeal with which they run the race of selfish competition, with no thought for the elevation of their brethren, without the sad conviction that the spirit of Christ has well-nigh disappeared from our churches, and that the fearful doom [of divine punishment] awaits us."[17]

Some of Ripley's contemporaries shared his anguish and frustration. "When I see how false our life is," wrote Emerson in 1840, "how oppressive our politics, that there is no form of redeeming man appearing in the whole population, & myself & my friends so inactive . . . heroism seems our dream & our insight a delusion. I am daily getting ashamed of my life."[18] Others, too, grew restless, ashamed of words and thoughts that had no effect, a generation of idealists awaiting a heroic example. In New England, it was Ripley who supplied the example. Convinced of the spiritual hollowness of churches, he resigned his ministry early in 1841 with the announcement that he was "a peace man, a temperance man, an abolitionist, a transcendentalist, a friend of radical reform in our social institutions." By then he had already formed a plan to begin the work of spiritually regenerating society, a plan inspired by the model of the Primitive Church, "a band of brothers emancipated by submission to Christ from all external authority."[19] It was the same model that the millenarian communists had followed, but Ripley's version developed along different lines under the influence of his Yankee concern with individuality. The result was Brook Farm.

He worked out the essential character of his Christian community in the summer and fall of 1840. Convinced that the gap between intellectual and manual labor was at the root of the social crisis, he planned to establish a voluntary cooperative life that would furnish each person with some suitable combination of intellectual and physical activity. In association, mind-workers and hand-workers could unite as a brotherly community of common work, eliminating the class gap which had meant the loss of a physical vitality for the one and the loss of mental and moral development for the other. In a community where all work suited the need of the individual, everyone would labor willingly for the common good, aware that in cooperation rather than in competition he could best realize the full potential of his self.[20]

Ripley intended to begin this community on a farm sufficient, "under skillful husbandry," to support a population large enough to provide the practical skills needed for self-subsistence. To this he planned to connect "a school or college, in which the most complete instruction shall be given from the first rudiments to the highest culture." Aside from providing a place for intellectuals to work, the college would furnish the opportunity for every member to develop his special skills and talents. Once in operation, said Ripley, "our farm would be a place for improving the race of men that lived on it; thought would preside over the operations of labor, and labor would contribute to the expansion of thought; we should have industry without drudgery, and true equality without its vulgarity."[21]

Ripley's utopia was also noteworthy for what it omitted. It did not promise a life of leisure to those who joined it; rather, it offered a full-time life of labor to satisfy the needs of active, creative, purposeful men. It did not provide for a select membership; to the contrary, it required a heterogeneous population that included Ripley and, as he put it, a "good washerwoman." It did not demand adherence to a common standard or body of doctrine like the millenarians; it was open to all people of good will whatever their religious views. It did not require celibacy or the abolition of marriage; it was open to families and single people alike without reference to sexual behavior. Above all, it did not, like Owen's scheme, involve some elaborate "system": As much a practical man as theoretrician, Ripley developed his plan in general terms, expecting the community itself to evolve forms and practices suited to the needs of its members.[22]

He planned to initiate this venture as a small and simple experiment without publicity and fanfare, but he did hope to win the tangible support of fellow Transcendentalists. "I can imagine no plan which is suited to carry into effect so many divine ideas as this," he wrote to Emerson. "If wisely executed, it will be a light over this country and this age." The time seemed ripe for such an enterprise, and he was willing to sacrifice his own private interests in the belief that such a boon might never appear again.[23] He hoped to win Emerson's support, but Emerson refused to involve himself in the experiment, chiefly on the grounds that he was not made for a society "which is not either very large or very small & select." He put his reasons more bluntly to his brother: "Can I not get the same advantages at home without pulling down my house?"[24]

Ripley was not to be deterred from what was becoming his mission. With the sympathetic support of his wife, Sophia, he was able to move his family along with several other people into the house on the farm in the early spring of 1841 and to begin operations on a small scale. Among the early members was young Nathaniel Hawthorne, who chose Brook Farm as an escape from the routine job he had had in the Salem Custom House. Hawthorne, however, soon began to lose his enthusiasm for manual labor when physical fatigue prevented him from pursuing his writing career. Where Ripley hoped to find "the divinity of labor," Hawthorne after a long stint of shoveling manure concluded that "A man's soul may be buried and perish under a dung-heap . . . as well as under a pile of money." Less than seven months after his arrival, he left, although he waited a year longer before he formally resigned his membership.[25]

On the other hand, Ripley himself found immense satisfaction in his release from the increasingly arid theological controversies of Boston. For him, the general work of a farmer provided a much welcomed balance to his other role as an intellectual and teacher. Others, too, found a satisfying balance of jobs in their cooperative life. George P. Bradford, who joined the farm in the late spring, remembered the first months as a time of exhilaration and joy: "Besides the agricultural knowledge and experience so interesting to many of us, there was a feeling of healthy reality in knowing and coming into close contact with some of the coarser forms of labor and drudgery." Bradford was one of the men who volunteered to hang out the wash to dry on the communal wash days in order to ease the domestic burdens of women. Young Charles A. Dana, who came to the Farm in September to recover from eyestrain, also found satisfaction in becoming part of a mixed population of "literary people," workers, farm-hands, and others who lived and labored together in democratic equality. Having broken off his education at Harvard, Dana soon became a leading member of the Farm and stayed with it until its end five years later.[26]

By August, the Farm had succeeded in developing a flexible labor system suited to its intentions. Work was organized into various departments, whose directors were responsible for determining what had to be done, leaving it to the members to volunteer for a particular kind of work on the basis of skill, interest, and good will. Everyone was obligated to provide the same number of hours a week (60 in the summer and 48 in the winter), but were free to choose the work they liked.[27] Forty years later, Emerson wrote of the Brook Farmers that "one man ploughed all day and one looked out of the window all day, and perhaps drew his picture, and both received at night the same wage," but this misrepresented a pattern of productive work which enabled Ripley to claim in December that the Farm had realized "ten per cent gain on the value of the estate"; by one estimate, the efforts of the members tripled the value of their property within three years.[28]

In September 1841, they decided to raise needed capital by forming themselves into a joint-stock company, the Brook Farm Institute of Agriculture and Education. From the beginning, they had determined to found their cooperative community on a noncommunistic form of collective property ownership. In line with their individuality, they had pooled only so much of their personal property as they desired, keeping most of their property in their own hands. Now, in order to buy the farm property and to expand their educational as well as agricultural operations, they issued $500 shares in the Institute. Each share was to yield a guaranteed 5 percent interest per year and no more—a provision that reflected both their confidence that cooperative work would yield an annual "overplus of money" and their resolve to keep the profit motive from perverting their paradise. As residents, shareholders were not exempt from the obligation to pay for their weekly board with either six days labor or $4 in cash. Ten people agreed to subscribe for the first $12,000 in shares, Ripley and his family taking a full third of the total.[29]

The original $12,000 was earmarked chiefly for the purchase of the Farm property which had been lent to Ripley by its owner. Unfortunately, only about a third of the subscription was actually paid in cash, forcing Ripley to take out a $6000 mortgage on the property. He hoped to finance the much-needed expansion of facilities in the community by selling shares to outsiders. In December, he asked Emerson to buy one or more shares, noting that in return for a secure if not lucrative return the purchaser would provide much needed aid "in this time of our infant struggle and hope." The Sage of Concord seems to have ignored the invitation, although he already had investments in the stock of banks and insurance companies. Other reformers were no readier to provide hard support for the experiment, forcing the Farm to take out a second mortgage to finance its expansion.[30]

If words had been dollars, Ripley's financial problems would have been resolved, since the Farm did receive generally favorable notice. William Ellery Channing gave it his blessings, although he worried over the possible loss of "individuality, animation, force, and enlargement of mind" in such associations.[31] His protegée, Elizabeth Peabody, contributed a long and laudatory article on the Farm in the *Dial*. After praising it as an effort to realize "Christ's idea of Society," Peabody gave some special attention to what she took to be the effort to combine education and culture with an agricultural way of life: "If it succeeds in uniting successful labor with improvement in mind and manners, it will teach a noble lesson to the agricultural population, and do something to check that rush from the country to the city, which is now stimulated by ambition, and by something better, even a desire for learning." She was careful, however, to distance herself from the project and to spend nearly a third of her article in giving critical advice to its members on the management of their affairs.[32]

More perceptive and less adulterated praise in 1842 came from Ripley's friend and fellow reformer, Orestes Brownson, in an article for the *Democratic Review*. After having himself formed a plan for the organization of what he called "corporations," Brownson had already begun to question whether communitarianism could succeed unless it involved a Shaker-like theocracy that would repress individuality; eventually, he was to reject the communitarian approach in favor of the Roman Catholic Church as the only way for the redemption of Man.[33] In 1842, however, he praised the Farm for its success in reconciling human social needs with the needs of individuality. These who like Emerson preached individual self-reliance overlooked the fact that "man is not sufficient for himself," while those who like Owen favored a system of communism had neglected the importance of giving every individual a personal and private place in society. "Individual property is recognized and secured," wrote Brownson from his observations of life at the Farm, but individualism had been socialized by the practice of "eating at a common table and laboring in common and sharing in common the advantages of individual excellence there may be in the community." This success had been achieved because Ripley had evolved his plan out of "the simple wants of his soul as a man and as a Christian" rather than basing it on some theoretical scheme that had little relationship to his own personal needs and experience.[34]

Brownson saw the Farm as a model which other Americans could follow in their own ways. A great advantage of Ripley's approach was that it demanded no radical break from the relationships of existing society. Rather than threatening conventional family life, it extended family feelings and relations to include the community; the nuclear family so increasingly common to modern society was preserved and strengthened by placing it within an extended social family based on common interests and experience. Other Brook Farms could be established by groups of families willing to pool enough of their resources to provide the $15,000 to $20,000 needed to initiate communities. Brownson passed on a bit of advice from Ripley that each such community have "one main object to which it directs its energies. We are a company of teachers. . . . Others may have companies of manufacturers or of agriculture." Another visitor said that the Brook Farm plan could be adapted to cities where a group of like-minded persons could form a community to live "in some large hotel, or block of houses, agreeably suited." That idea was to have a long history.[35]

This public notice brought little money, but it provided at least modest encouragement to continue the experiment. Undoubtedly, it contributed to the popularity of the Brook Farm school which under Ripley's management provided a progressive education designed to meet the individual needs of students and to make schooling an integral part of community life. The greatest strength of the school lay in its six-year college preparatory course which required at least one hour a day of work in the community as well as study with Ripley, Mrs. Ripley, and four young male scholars. If this regimen was often not an easy one, students found much release and satisfaction in their free access to the life of the community. "The young people," wrote Emerson, "agree that they have had more rapid experiences than elsewhere befell them."[36] Although much of the experience was in the form of dances, dancing classes, songfests and picnics with the residents, it also included their work for the community. Beyond that, the older students enjoyed a ready access to some of the finest minds in New England. Besides Ripley, there was Charles A. Dana, destined to be the powerful editor-owner of the New York *Sun,* and John S. Dwight, later the most influential American music critic of his times; both men were an integral part of the community.[37]

The school was, in significant respects, a measure of the life of the community. George William Curtis, a student there, remembered that in agriculture "there were never such witty potato patches and such sparkling cornfields before or since."[38] If perhaps there was more mind than muscle in the labor, most of the work was actually done. By 1842, the Farm had grown to some 60 members who with varying degrees of enthusiasm contributed their skills to the community. "The association of labor makes distribution [of the work] according to taste and ability easy," said one visitor, "and this takes the sting out of fatigue. . . . Bodily labor does not fatigue as much when the mind is active and elevated." Although the Brook Farmers discovered that their soil was too meager to support an easy agriculture, they were able with the liberal use of fertilizers to increase not only its value but its productivity; "we got more money from an acre of ground in five days," recalled one member, "than any of our neighbors did in six." They were able to sell milk, vegetables, and hay to the outside world, benefiting like the Shakers and Harmonists from the high reputation of their products.[39]

Despite its problems, Brook Farm seemed to be evolving itself into a heaven on the stony earth of Massachusetts. Ripley had responded to some local curiosity about the goals of his community by saying that he hoped to establish "a model of life which shall combine the enchantment of poetry with the facts of daily experience," and in some ways he succeeded. Many would later remember their lives there as an idyllic existence. John Codman, who arrived in the spring of 1843 as a student, recalled that he found true happiness in the activity of the Farm: "Oh, the independence of it! To be able to do everything, and with love of it, knowing no high or low of work—all its honor and no shame." One member remembered that the Brook Farmers enjoyed virtually every minute of every day.[40] The idyllic character of the Farm also attracted many outside visitors who found at least momentary contentment there. Even Emerson, who was becoming increasingly critical of its collectivism, could note in his journal in 1843, that he had a cheerful time on a visit: "Fine weather, cheerful uplands, and every person you meet is a character and in free costume." During these early years, Brook Farm entered the New England memory as a special time of enchantment.[41]

Ripley himself, however, was less than satisfied with the situation. He had intended to establish a new and better form of society, not simply to create an idyll for students and visitors, and in a significant practical way the Farm was less than a success. Expansion of its facilities especially to accommodate the school was expensive—too much so for the limited earning power of its largely agricultural operations. The income from the school and from board paid by some of the visitors helped to balance the books, but that was hardly an adequate basis for a viable society. Moreover, the members seemed to lose some of their zeal as they settled into their new routines; enjoyable work did not necessarily mean productive labor, nor did communal picnics necessarily make for a deep commitment to brotherhood. Like his Puritan ancestors, Ripley believed that the good society depended "on the power of self-sacrifice in man, not on appeal to his selfish nature," and like them he found that this was a power difficult to sustain.[42]

Confronted by the devolution of his serious-minded social experiment into a combined boarding school and summer camp, Ripley grew increasingly exasperated with the financial constraints that prevented him from completing his plan for a cooperative community embracing all classes of society. Having mortgaged the Farm to the limit, he could not find the money needed to provide facilities for craftsmen and industrial workers. The inadequacies of existing housing and work facilities were beginning to wear down the spirits even of committed members. Forgoing his true interests, Ripley finally forced himself to try to raise the needed money in New York, but he failed; in September 1843, he complained that "with property amounting to $30,000 the want of $2,000 or $3,000 fetters us and may kill us." In a capitalistic world, even Christian brotherhood seemed to depend on the dollar. By autumn, however, a new inspiration was beginning to revive his hopes, leading him in October to begin to recruit industrial workers for the Farm and to plan a new workshop building to accommodate them.[43]

In 1843, New England was beginning to encounter Fourierism, the complex system of the French social visionary Charles Fourier. Although Fourier had died in 1837, his ideas had been taken up by a handful of young disciples who began to catch the attention of social idealists throughout the North Atlantic world. In January 1842, the editor of the *Democratic Review* introduced a four-part series on the new gospel written by Fourier's American disciple, Albert Brisbane, with the observation that the times demanded some notice of a growing movement which might contain "the germ of a new civilization destined to overspread the earth."[44] Emerson, with his usual sensitivity to trans-Atlantic trends, soon observed in the *Dial* that there was a notable increase in Fourierist activity and enthusiasm, especially in England where Fourierists had established a journal *The Phalanx*.[45]

Emerson refused to be moved by the new enthusiasm. Although he did publish one of Brisbane's articles in the *Dial,* he rejected Fourierism as another social system which like Owenism seemed to include every-thing except "the faculty of life, which spawns and scorns system and system-makers." Elsewhere, he warned against any form of association-ism: "The union is only perfect when all the uniters are isolated. It is the union of friends who live in different streets or towns. Each man, if he attempts to join himself to others, is on all sides cramped and dimin-ished of his proportion." His growing hostility to what he saw as a trend may have added to his willingness to support Thoreau's experiment in individuality at Walden.[46]

Emerson, however, had lost any claim to Brook Farm's attention by his indifference to its needs. By late 1843, Ripley and his associates had determined to reorganize their society along Fourierist lines. Probably they were influenced by Horace Greeley, whose New York *Tribune* was taken on a regular basis at the Farm. Having made his newspaper a conduit for Fourierism, Greeley had the previous year urged Dana to consider the new system as a solution to what he saw as a primary flaw in Ripley's plan: That plan would succeed if all were equally willing to work, but suppose a few members decided "to enjoy and not to earn," he asked. "Will not their example weigh heavily on the spirits and influence the conduct of all?" Faced with a growing mortgage and dwindling energies, Ripley was attracted to Fourierism in part by its promise of a more productive system of labor. Moreover, he hoped to win substantial financial support to expand the operations of the Farm from what seemed to be a burgeoning national movement.[47]

Emerson's criticisms were perhaps best answered in 1845 by John S. Dwight, who presented a radically different idea of individuality. True individuality, he said, could never be attained through Emersonian individualism. To the contrary, the full nature of every man could be realized only as a member of a community organized along Fourierist lines: "Only in the Combined Order, only when the solidarity of man-kind shall be realized, can healthy individuality find place." An even more radical rejection of individualism came from Dana, who after months of hesitation had arrived at the conviction that Fourier was "the profoundest thinker of these modern times." He wrote to his friend Isaac Hecker that he found in the new movement something "worth a life-labor to reach, namely, forgetfulness of self—not the forgetfulness of contemplation and introspection, but true, natural action."[48]

Ripley also found in Fourierism a new life and faith as well as a program for action. Although his dream of brotherly cooperation remained the same, his new enthusiasm betrayed a hostility to the gentle Transcendentalism with which the Farm had previously been associated: "We shall suffer no attachment to literature, no taste for abstract discussion, no love of purely intellectual theories, to reduce us from our devotion to the cause of the oppressed, the down trodden, the insulted and injured masses of our fellow men."[49]

The changeover was formalized in January 1844, when the community incorporated itself under the name of "the Brook-Farm Association for Industry and Agriculture." In explanation of the change, Ripley and associates said that the community had previously been largely "a private experiment" but that now they believed it important to publicly avow their new principles, in part to promote public understanding of Fourierism and in part to attract the capital needed to transform the Farm into "a perfect Phalanx" along Fourierist lines. After noting that their property was worth nearly $30,000, they promised that purchasers of its stock (at $100 a share) could hardly lose their investment "in an Association whose means are devoted mainly to productive industry," a practical note mixed in typical Fourierist fashion with promises of the paradise soon to be attained on earth.[50]

Ripley's efforts to bridge the gap between mind and muscle in the interests of individuality for everyone had entered into a dramatic new phase that took Brook Farm out of its tight little orbit around Boston. By publicly avowing their new faith, Ripley and his associates had cut their connections with Concord: John Codman, who had entered the school during the changeover, later said that they were "practically deserted by Emerson and his coterie." For Ripley's old friends, the new faith was too mechanical, too materialistic, and "too French." Orestes Brownson called Fourierism "nothing but material pantheism, a polite name for atheism," while Hawthorne "was thoroughly disgusted" with the preoccupation with food, luxuries, and sex which he found in some of the Frenchman's works.[51]

For a time, however, Ripley could afford to dispense with the meager support of his Transcendentalist friends. In 1844 and 1845, Brook Farm went through a remarkable period of energetic reorganization and renewal that brought an expansion of its population and industrial operations. Idyll became industry as Ripley acquired some of the skills and capital needed to complete his plans, and with promises of more to come. By the fall of 1844, the Farm had erected its workshop-building to provide employment for workers, and it had started to build a large "unitary dwelling" to meet its housing needs. The next year it was able to get a formal charter of incorporation from the state legislature under the name of the "Brook Farm Phalanx," with authority to hold up to $100,000 in real estate, a strikingly large sum for an experiment that had begun with only a few thousand dollars four years earlier.[52]

Events would soon indicate that Ripley had staked the future of Brook Farm on a movement destined to explode and that the conversion was a leap in the dark toward disaster. For one glorious period, however, the Farm was able to lift itself out of its insular life and into the excitements of a wider and wilder world of dreams and desires. The next two years were to be perhaps the richest and most exciting years in the entire history of the search for a brotherly tomorrow.

Fourierism

The conversion of Brook Farm to Fourierism in 1844 was a signal victory for a rapidly developing movement to revolutionize the world and to restore humankind to the Garden of Eden. This new species of secular millenarianism drew its inspiration from a prophet who had conceived a social vision far richer and more respectful of human individuality than Robert Owen's New Moral World. In Fourierism, Americans found a new prophetic inspiration, and one which was not embarrassed by the presence of the prophet himself. While Owen had helped sink New Harmony by his involvements in its affairs, Charles Fourier conveniently died before his movement took form, bequeathing to his disciples a mass of writings for them to interpret and to exploit. Owen tried to dismiss his French rival as being "No more than a clerk in a merchant's counting-house . . . without experience of the world or knowledge of mankind," but no one could deny that Fourier was one of the most richly imaginative social thinkers in all history.[1]

Fourier's life was a triumph of imagination over external circumstances. Born at Besançon in southeastern France in 1772, he was only a year younger than Owen, but both his life and his thought were essentially different. The son of an affluent woolen-draper, he had lost his wealth and nearly his life during the tumultuous days of the French Revolution. Later, he settled into a series of dull commercial jobs first as a traveling agent and then as a correspondence clerk in Paris with the American firm of Curtis and Lamb of New York. A bachelor and a loner who hated children and spiders and loved cats and flowers, he spent most of his later life uneventfully in rented Paris rooms, there to die in 1837 virtually unnoticed by the world.[2]

Fourier's inner world, however, was as magnificantly exciting as his external life was dull. By 1800, he had begun to conceive a social vision which he believed would radically redirect human history. "I alone," he wrote in 1808, "have confounded twenty centuries of political imbecility, and it is to me alone that the present and future generations will be indebted for their boundless happiness." He had, he thought, discovered the secrets of nature which would enable him to restore human life to the form that God, the creator, had intended.[3] He would, if given the chance, unleash a power far stronger and more benevolent than that of Owen's New Lanark, the power not of mechanical force but of life itself.

The essence of Fourier's system was his doctrine of Passional Attraction. Conservatives might view human emotions as essentially evil and Owen might see them as neutral stuff shaped by environmental influence, but for Fourier the passions were dynamic forces implanted by God within His creatures to guide them to a perfect life. How could it be otherwise if God, the creator, were all-wise and benevolent? Without exception, every natural human emotion, taste, prediliction and inclination was part of the divine plan for a just, happy, and harmonious society. Man's desire for pleasure, his cupidity, his love of intrigue, his passion for variety and the rest of the 12 basic passions, and their 405 subdivisions which Fourier identified would, under the right conditions, realize the heaven that God had intended for man on earth.[4]

Unfortunately, civilized man had thwarted God's intentions by devising false moral codes and faulty social organizations based on the foolish assumption that the passions were evil: "Morality teaches man to be at war with himself, to resist his passions, to repress them, to believe that God was incapable of organizing our souls, our passions wisely." In the idiocy of their conventional wisdom, said this lifelong bachelor, parents insisted on compelling their children to eat bread when they wanted sweets, thus opposing the divine intention that mankind grow sugar rather than wheat, a cereal which Fourier condemned as being both obnoxious and labor-consuming.[5]

Such eccentricities aside, the doctrine of Passional Attraction was a serious effort to explore the psychological and social implications of an assumption that was to have an immense influence in the nineteenth and twentieth centuries: that evil and misery in the world originated from the repression of natural human emotions. By devising a false society at war with his natural tendencies, Man had alienated himself from his own true nature and from his fellow beings. In what was tantamount to a radical revision of Christian traditions, Fourier attacked the whole of civilization as a violation of the divine plan for a perfected humanity in a perfect world. Where God had intended brotherly love and cooperation, man had invented war; where God had intended joy, man had invented misery; where God had intended the ecstasy of work, man had invented drudgery; where God had intended a plenty of all things, man had invented poverty; where God had intended a garden of delights, man had invented hell. As long as a false organization of life continued to pervert Man's god-given nature, every effort to improve the human condition would simply produce a new kind of misery. Industrialism, "the latest of our scientific chimeras," said Fourier, was in existing civilization bringing a new "mercantile feudalism" that was reducing the majority to industrial slavery with the certainty that "poverty should be the offspring of abundance."[6]

Well-intended men like Owen had attempted to resolve this paradox by creating radically different social organizations based on the principle of cooperative action, but Fourier believed that only he had discovered the way to make such organizations work. In contrast to Owen's casual and almost simple-minded principles, the Frenchman developed an elaborate and fussily detailed system of social psychology designed to accommodate human diversity. While Owen assumed that all humans were fundamentally alike, Fourier believed that God had intentionally created not one but varied human types, each a special combination of the passions. Only when society was reorganized to accommodate the individual needs and powers of every human type would the passions do what God had designed them to do. Although there were unnumbered possible combinations, Fourier built his system around some 810 basic human types. He envisioned a world in which all mankind would be grouped into communities or "phalanxes" of some 1600 to 1800 people each, a number small enough to assure close, communal relationships among the members and large enough to provide for a complex mixture of human types, male and female.[7]

The phalanx would especially accommodate those passions which the Divine Planner had intended to inspire men to work cooperatively and creatively for the good of all creation. All work would be free and self-fulfilling, involving only what a person desired to do. In order to assure that necessity would not limit freedom, each phalanx was to guarantee every member a generous subsistence regardless of what he did. To provide a job suited to every distinctive taste and talent, work was to be subdivided into many specialized tasks. As Fourier believed every person naturally desired variety in his work and life (if God had intended otherwise, "he would have given us a taste for monotony"), each task would involve no more than one to two hours of labor so that during a week an individual could work at some 30 different jobs suited to his particular passional makeup. The population constituting the phalanx would group itself and regroup itself again and again into temporary bands of individuals with a shared taste for a particular task; during one day, an individual might work variously with those who shared his preferences for, say, chicken raising, orchardry, rose growing, and shoe-making. Under such circumstances, every person could satisfy his particular range of passions through work, and so work would become a pleasurable way through which he could realize his individuality.[8]

In his planning, Fourier did not neglect the desire for gain and the competitive drive that existed in varying degrees in every person. He condemned the nebulous communism and naïve equality that Owen had adopted at New Harmony as the "poison" of association, since it subverted some of the most powerful human impulses for work. Although the property of the Phalanx was collectively owned, the wealth it produced was to be distributed, beyond guaranteed subsistence, on the basis of the money, talent, and effort that each person invested in the community; those who performed such repugnant forms of work as the cleaning of sewers were to receive extra compensation. From this system would come a dynamic world of collective capitalism where everyone would be able profitably to exercise his special talents whether he were by nature a laborer, farmer, technician, investor, artist, or aristocrat. In such a community, the wealthy and the talented would be justly rewarded without feelings of guilt over their advantages or without the resentments of others. There could be no French Revolution in the harmonious world of the phalanx, because the natures of all would be fulfilled by an abundance of satisfactions available to all.[9]

Once a phalanx was properly organized, it would naturally become a community of work and pleasure, a dynamic organization of groups driven to frenzies of effort by uninhibited passion. The collective power and talents God had implanted in humans for their prosperity and happiness would be realized as each person fulfilled his individuality; the immense power of life itself would be awakened as every individual, impatient of sleep, gave his energies to an extended day of effort—on occasion doing what Fourier himself sometimes did, work for 24 or more hours straight. While Owen and other utopians dreamed of six- and even four-hour work days, this enemy of drudgery outlined a typical work day that began at 3:30 in the morning and included more than 14 hours of labor. In such a community, self-indulgence would inspire unprecedented feats of achievement: "Behold at dawn thirty industrial groups issue in state from the palace of the Phalanx and spread themselves over the fields and workshops, waving their banners with cries of triumph and impatience. . . . Such will be the athletes who will take the place of our mercenary and languid workman, and who will succeed in making ambrosia and nectar grow upon a soil which yields only briers and tares to the feeble hands of the civilized."[10]

Fourier envisioned great industrial armies, formed from thousands of phalanxes and embracing millions of men, whose collective diligence would furnish a power beyond human dreams, able to dig great canals through the Isthmus of Panama and through continents and able to remake the earth into a paradise for Man. Such armies would repair the damage done to nature by civilization, replanting forests and improving crop land; they would turn the sterile deserts into fertile fields and even convert the frozen polar regions to Man's use, modifying the climate so that the earth would be able to support the some three million phalanxes which eventually would cover the globe. The collective power of impassioned individuals would make a new Eden of pleasure and profusion where all desires would be met and all talents realized, where, along with billions of happy people, there would be "thirty-seven million poets the equal of Homer, thirty-seven million mathematicians the equal of Newton"—although presumably only one Fourier.[11]

Fourier shared with Owen the utopian penchant for embodying his dream in grandiose buildings, but, in contrast to the palacial coldness of the Englishman's parallelogram, his "Phalanstery" resembled a great resort hotel seething with life and passion. It would be a self-contained unit of society embracing interrelated apartments, recreational facilities, banquet halls, ballrooms, meeting halls, and workshops in one extended building set amid the fields, orchards, fish ponds, and chicken-runs required to produce food of every variety. Fourier planned the Phalanstery so as to facilitate a communal interaction among its members. All parts of the building were interconnected by interior streets or "galleries of association," some 18 to 24 feet wide and three stories high, where the ever busy throngs could meet on their way to work or pleasure, protected from rain or cold. Outside, a network of interrelated paths connected fields and orchards, binding them together while enabling work groups to shift quickly from one task to another, providing a living landscape of human activity where all groups were "in activity, shaded by colored awnings, working in scattered companies, marching to the sound of instruments and singing in chorus as they change the location of their work."[12]

By combining cooperative effort with individual development, Fourier expected to realize the full productive power of the human race, producing such a profusion of wealth that even the dullest and least productive member of the Phalanx would be able to meet his material needs; all would in some degree be possessors of the communal wealth. Material possession, however, was simply the foundation for the real life of the Phalanstery, for this community of work was even more a community of satisfied and gratified passions, a highly erotic world where even the strangest and rarest of desires would be free to play—a Garden of Eden of perpetual delight. Fourier was in advance of the awakening modern consciousness regarding sexuality. Certainly, he needed no Sigmund Freud to teach him that the repression of sexual energies warped the human personality, nor did he have to learn from a popular song that it was love that made the world go round.

In his "New Amorous World" (the title of one of his unpublished notebooks), there would be no repression to poison the wellsprings of love but complete freedom for sexuality to develop in all its forms. "Love in the Phalanstery," he wrote, "is no longer, as it is with us, a recreation which detracts from work; on the contrary it is the soul and the vehicle, the mainspring of all work and of the whole of universal attraction." In this world, women as well as men would be freed from moral repression and from family responsibilities to form a richly varied web of passional relations among themselves involving all. The imagination of this lonely bachelor conceived of a society where all forms of heterosexual and homosexual love would be admitted to a refined and elaborately contrived system of love—even his own rare and secret "sapphianism" (love of lesbians), which he estimated governed only 33 of every million people.[13]

In the Phalanstery, every individual would be bound by passional attraction to a living community infused with something like a subtle and perpetual orgasm. In the extravagance of his fantasy, Fourier found an idea of community which had a checkered history in utopia, that of a communal composite of individuals so complete that it constituted a "PASSIONAL OR COLLECTIVE MAN," each phalanx a superorganism enlivened by all the passional drives and the talents that God had given the human race. The fulfillment of individuality, therefore, would also lead to the organic unity of the human race itself and ultimately with the universe; so would be restored the seamless web of life which God had planned and which civilization had torn asunder.[14]

Humanity, thus, could regenerate itself and reclaim the harmony, unity, happiness, and divinity which God had intended for it, *if* only the world would give Fourier a chance to actualize his system. Perhaps his ultimate fantasy was that he would attract unlimited support if he were only understood. In particular, he expected men of wealth to pour their money into his phalanxes as profitable investments. He published four books on his system, but no rich man knocked at his door; and he was largely ignored except by a small group of young disciples who were too poor to establish his model society. While Owen even in failure enjoyed the limelight, Fourier found only neglect until his death. His doctrines were not unimportant ingredients in the ferment that eventually produced the great modern movements of European radicalism, but it was on the other side of the Atlantic, in a world he never saw, that his influence was most tangible, thanks to the movement initiated after his death in the United States by Albert Brisbane.[15]

Brisbane was well prepared both by his circumstances and his disposition for Fourier's message. Born in 1809 at Batavia, New York, into a wealthy landowning family, he was given a materially easy life which left him hungry for something worthy to do. As a young upper-class American sent to Europe to complete his education, one day he was in Paris eating ice cream when came the thought that was to determine his future role in life: That the farmers who rented and worked his father's

Genesee lands had paid for his indulgences. Had he done anything for them? He had not. That these American farmers might not have required his help perhaps crossed his mind, but he soon convinced himself that they did need him and in a way suited to his own interests and temperament.[16]

He was able to find a foundation for this conviction in the thought that the common American belief in a special destiny for the United States was an illusion. To the contrary, both Europe and America, belonged to the same "gigantic, restless, modern world! seething, striving, battling, incoherent, producing on the surface wealth and show and privileges, while at the bottom reigns poverty, drunkenness, degradation, vice, crime, almshouses, work-houses, and all the complex antagonisms of cliques and parties and sects." Whether cloaked in velvet or buckskin, the existing institutions of this trans-Atlantic world were fundamentally vicious, constituting a "social hell" that demanded redemption, a challenge worthy of the talents of a bright, imaginative, and uncomfortably idle young man.[17]

Brisbane had found his mission, but he did not find his message until 1832 when in Berlin he read Fourier's *L'Association Domestique-Agricole*. The book evoked in him a "tumult of emotion" as a whole new realm of human possibilities opened to his imagination. Here was a dream society without guilt or fear, free of both the idle rich and the degraded poor, where the upper classes were "the true leaders of the world, instead of its oppressors." And where a sensitive, well-educated man like himself could find a meaningful role: "I saw a healthy, rich humanity organizing everywhere its universities—its sources of mental development. In my enthusiasm, I saw a million universities scattered over the globe, and the means of solving the great problem of human destiny." Having experienced, as he remembered it, "the first gleam of intellectual satisfaction" in his life, Brisbane hurried back to Paris, where he soon persuaded Fourier to give him 12 lessons at five francs a lesson.[18]

Brisbane's exposure to Fourierism left him with a deep conviction that Fourier was "a mighty Genius who had penetrated the secret of the plan of God, and revealed the glorious Destiny reserved to Man on Earth." The young American was drawn into the richly colored paradise detailed by his mentor, into "a mighty epic . . . of a World redeemed and regenerated," but for him the Frenchman was much more than another Dante or Milton. Like other men of his times, Brisbane felt the need for a science of human society, a "Sociology," as immutably true and as effectual as physical science but more life-oriented than the dry mechanics of Newtonian physics. Fourier, rather than being simply a painter of pretty utopian pictures, was "the great Pioneer in Social Science" who by discovering the underlying laws of life had given mankind the knowledge it needed to control its social destiny.[19]

The new science was ideally suited to Brisbane's temperament and personal needs. It offered him a mission in life free from the limiting burdens of leadership since it provided him with an active role as the promoter of a new social system whose scientific character would make it so automatic as to operate without his personal direction. In that system he thought he had found "a mechanism suited and adapted to human nature, so that human nature can follow its laws and attractions and go rightly, and be its own guide." Neither the science nor the system, however, would resemble the spiritless sciences and mechanisms of civilization. Like the New England Transcendentalists, he believed that essential truths could be found through the intuitive powers of the mind and soul. As a science, Fourierism appealed to him because it was derived not from the observation of a limiting material reality but from a combination of logic and intuition which had pierced "the veil that covers the mysteries of the universe" and had revealed the cosmic design of the Creator.[20]

In Fourier's science, then, Brisbane believed that he had also found a social religion that would free him from the need to choose between two unpalatable alternatives. One was the irrational enthusiasm of the revival religion which had enflamed the common folk in the area around Batavia; the other was what he later called "the cold atheism of my father," a lifeless rationalism that left no room for his spiritual yearnings. In Fourierism, he believed he had found a way to reconcile religion and science, putting an end to the age-old conflict between faith and reason which had prevented Man from discovering the cosmic laws which God had intended to guarantee a heaven on earth.[21] Here was a cause worthy of his talents and yearnings, and one which, with the death of Fourier in 1837, he could make essentially his own.

Brisbane returned to the United States determined to spread the new gospel. His first efforts had little effect, but the publication of his first book, *The Social Destiny of Man* (a translation and condensation of

Fourier's works) in 1840 did win some favorable notice. The *Boston Quarterly Review,* for instance, declared its "entire sympathy with the fundamental principles of the work, especially since in demanding associated labor, it by no means sacrifices individual property." During this depression year, at least some Americans must have taken special note of the contention boldly stated in the book's subtitle, "Our Evils are Social not Political; Political Evils are the results of the False Organization of Society," perhaps the first American proclamation of the new doctrine of "Socialism" then being evolved from the hopes and fears of the North Atlantic world.[22] Moreover, he was able to attract the support of at least two of the ablest publicists of their day. One was Horace Greeley, the young editor of the *New York Tribune,* who allowed Brisbane to advocate the new gospel on the front page of his newspaper. The other was an even younger journalist, Park Godwin, the assistant editor of the New York *Evening Post* and the editor of the short-lived radical journal, the *Pathfinder.*[23]

These three men shared a common concern over the growth of an increasingly ugly competition among individuals and interests in the new urban-industrial society which had appeared along the Northeastern seaboard. Under "our anarchical commercial and financial system," warned Brisbane, this competition was "contaminating all the practical affairs of life with fraud, injustice and double dealing" and degrading the "higher faculties of the mind" required for cultural and scientific advance to the level of "the mere ability of money-making." The combined power of money and of machinery in the hands of the few, moreover, was reducing the wages and increasing the toil of the working classes, spreading a degrading poverty which threatened an eventual social upheaval at the expense of everyone including the rich themselves.[24]

The young Fourierists saw little hope of returning to the traditional, more stable rural America, because rural society was itself crumbling before the anarchical force of the new age. Although most Americans were as yet at least one step removed from the perils of industrialism, they were abandoning rural areas for the uncertain life of the rapidly expanding cities. This flood of people served to intensify the degrading competition for jobs and wealth in urban-industrial society. Why had people rejected the independence of rural life in favor of this anarchy? Greeley, himself an expatriate from the countryside, believed that the essential cause was the inability and unwillingness of individualistic farmers to collectively organize their economic and social resources; as a result, rural areas were poor, powerless, culturally backward, and socially unsatisfying.[25]

Most American were content to seek solutions to such matters in politics, but the Fourierists held that these problems were "organic" to society and would only grow worse without radical surgery. In this general sense, they were "socialists": men who believed that cooperation must replace competition as the governing principle of modern society if man was to avoid disaster and to reap the true benefits of modern progress. "The emancipation of the human intellect from its ancient fetters," said Godwin, "at first so productive of scientific and social advancement has in the end conducted us to a state of wild disorder and individualism. . . . There is a complete want of unity in our aims as well as opinions." The rapid growth of poverty in the age of potential abundance convinced him that the modern world confronted a fundamental social problem which had to be solved if mankind "wishes to prevent the commotion with which all civilized society is menaced—a question which in Europe and perhaps ere long in this country will leave the studies of philosophers . . . to take up arms in the streets"; this was four years before the Revolution of 1848 in Europe and the publication of the *Communist Manifesto*.[26]

For the young disciples, Fourier was "a magnificent genius" who had both accurately diagnosed the problem and provided a practical remedy. The doctrine of passional attraction seemed to furnish the basis for a true science of human behavior which Godwin predicted would show mankind how "the discordant interests of individuals can be harmonized at the same time that their rights are secured." Passional attraction had led the Master into some weird and morally outrageous fantasies, but his disciples were confident that the doctrine could be stripped of such extravagances and made a sure scientific formula by which individual energies and talents could be so coordinated as to make a social harmony beneficial to all. In this society, material prosperity would satisfy human wants without the crass materialism which was subverting both morality and "the high faculties of mind," and the opportunity to achieve one's distinctive individuality would be available to everyone—rich and poor, men and women, workers and businessmen and intellectuals.[27]

If there was much vagueness in Fourier's social science, his phalanxes seemed to provide practical solutions to various problems. They could, for instance, remedy the essential defects of rural life by organizing the inhabitants of the countryside into compact societies possessing all the advantages of cities with none of their defects; in general, they could affect a fusion of rural and urban benefits into a new social form suited to the tastes and interests of all. Even more concretely, they could eliminate the great waste of land, labor, fuel, and other resources associated with single-family living: The "unitary" kitchen and laundry of just one phalanx would replace 300 kitchens and laundries, thus avoiding waste and also freeing women for more productive and rewarding roles.[28] The prospect of a world reorganized into phalanxes excited Brisbane's imagination:

> A traveller on the Globe in future ages of Social Harmony will see, at every few miles distance, sumptuous palaces of various architectural styles rising before him, surrounded by magnificent parks and gardens, by orchards, vineyards, fields, and woodlands, interspersed with fountains, works of art, and monuments of every kind varying the landscape, and enhancing the effect of natural society.[29]

Having brought this vision down from its Parisian mountaintop, Brisbane made a strenuous effort to persuade the people to accept it. In the dark years of the early 1840s, he and his fellow disciples attempted to create a mass movement, a unique one which did not depend on a charismatic leader like Robert Owen, nor even on any particular devotion to Fourier himself. As they presented it, their cause was "Associationism" rather than Fourierism, and their system the invention not of an imaginative Frenchman but of God himself. They emphasized the practical benefits of the phalanx rather than the perilous beauties of passional attraction, and they promised that their new system could be established "without disturbing a single vested right."[30] After much effort, they aroused more criticism and ridicule than enthusiasm, but they did succeed in launching an indigenous movement that would affect thousands of Americans over the next four decades.

The Movement

The 1840s was a decade of extraordinary social ferment throughout the North Atlantic world. In Europe, that ferment boiled up into the Revolution of 1848 and eventually into the birth of modern socialism. In the United States, social radicalism took a less earthshaking course that involved a distinctively American quest for cooperative brotherhood. In the mid-1840s, the Christian Socialist William H. Fish said that by the beginning of the decade, "the old order of society had come to be felt by many of the most progressive class of minds to be selfish and burdensome." After noting that these social concerns had attracted the interest of some of the best minds in both Europe and America, Fish declared:

> The experiment will be *thoroughly tried*. Too many men of ability and influence have enlisted in it to give up in despair. . . . And if one plan fail they will try another and another and another still, till they find the right one. For somewhere there must be a better system of business and living than the one that now prevails—one more equalizing. If not, we had better give up in despair of the long-talked of, and hoped for, Millennium.[1]

Indeed, the apparent collapse of the social order did inspire hopes that gloomy times could be made to yield the kingdom of heaven on earth. The search for the Millennium took a much varied though generally communitarian form. Fish himself helped his colleague, Adin Ballou, establish a sectarian community of Practical Christian Socialists at Hopedale while another Yankee millenarian, John Humphrey Noyes, created his own form of community based on biblical communism first at Putney, Vermont, and then at Oneida, New York. Unlike earlier sectarians, these men aspired to convert the nation to their millennial ways with the typical American confidence that what they practiced could be practiced by all.[2]

National attention, however, was caught by a more secular and universalist drive for cooperative brotherhood. Ignoring sectarian warnings that only strong and governing religious commitments would make real brotherhood possible, the majority of radical idealists placed their hopes in the perfection of some social design which they believed would finally bring society into conformity with Man's true nature. Although Owenism experienced a modest renewal in the early 1840s, the radical scene was dominated by Fourierism, which temporarily took on the character of a national movement, complete with a press and a network of societies —a potential rival of political parties. This resulted from the proselytizing work of a small group of writers and intellectuals headed initially by Brisbane, Godwin, and Greeley. By the mid-1840s, their efforts were augmented by the writings and organizational work of several other idealists, most notably William H. Channing, the nephew of William Ellery Channing, and three members of the Brook Farm community, George Ripley, Charles A. Dana, and John S. Dwight.

In this age of individuality, it was not surprising that there would be differences among these seven men, and that in 1843 four of them should each have his own periodical: Greeley, his *Tribune;* Brisbane, his *Phalanx;* Godwin, his *Pathfinder;* and Channing, his *Present.*[3] In essential ways, however, they shared an intensely personal interest in the transformation of their society; they were one of several groups of young men who in Europe and Ameri made themselves notable for their intent to make a radical break with the crumbling world of their fathers. These Fourierists shared a strong distaste for the opportunities afforded them by society, particularly for the traditional professions of the ministry and the law. Godwin tried both careers and found them wanting, while Ripley, Dwight, and Channing were ministers who had rejected their churches. Greeley, the only one of them without a substantial education, had escaped from the limiting life of the countryside to seek a career in New York City. Although his wealth exempted him from the need for a profession, Brisbane had been privately educated for an intellectual life which had little place in democratic America. Eventually, nearly all of them found a satisfying career in journalism or literature, but even for Greeley this was an as yet dim and distant future.[4]

Whatever the prospects, the dissatisfaction with society involved far more than a simple concern with making a living. The young Fourierists were part of a culture fascinated with romantic heroes and with the idea of inspiring, redeeming genius. To replace what they saw as the raw materialism and groveling politics of their times, they dreamed of a new age of heroic achievement where the poet, artist, and intellectual would have a prominent place. Others would try to realize this dream in literature and art, but these Yankees, bearing the consciences of their Puritan forefathers, sought their heroic achievement in the redemption of society. Although they had abandoned established churches, they wanted a religion which would fuse their intellectual, social, and spiritual aspirations into one faith governed by what William Henry Channing called "a desire to glorify God in a PERFECTED SOCIAL LIFE."[5]

Moreover, they wanted a social faith in harmony with their scientific age. The times demanded, said Brisbane, a reconciliation of Religion and Science, something which could not be done "until the dogmas of Religion are taught with scientific purity." Since physical science seemed able to discover the laws governing God's physical creation without threatening religion, the Fourierists believed some science of society could accomplish the same regarding mankind. Brisbane dreamed of finding "the Science most important to Man—namely SOCIOLOGY or the SCIENCE OF SOCIETY," one which he said in 1842 would reveal "the true and natural System of Society."[6] Godwin also believed that, with the triumphs of the physical sciences, the time had come for a Social Science which would reveal the laws that God, the "great Engineer of the Universe," had intended to govern the development of mankind.[7]

Fourierism seemed to meet this need for a mission and for a science. In contrast to the arid and simplistic rationalism of Owen's science of circumstances, Fourier's all-embracing vision apparently had been able to capture the rich complexities of God's universe. For intellectuals, he was the mighty genius who had created a complex system of social science that would make for a lifetime of profitable study. For would-be redeemers of society, he had provided a rational diagnosis of and practical remedy for social evil. For religious dissenters, he had discovered the faith which God had intended for humankind. In 1845, the disciples proclaimed their mission: "Against a false and rotten system we have sworn a holy and undying hostility. Nor are we alone in the conflict. On all sides brave and true souls come up to mingle in the struggle. Panoplied in reason, armed with science, consecrated to the love of God and Man, they press to the redemption of the holy city of Jerusalem."[8]

The early 1840s were exciting times. Brisbane later remembered that "a great vision floated before my mind," one which inspired him to a great ambition to serve mankind. During these days of the apparent collapse of the old order, it seemed possible to seize the moment for the new cause. "All men are dissatisfied with the present," declared Godwin in 1843. "Society is vibrating with new and strange *isms.*" For him, at least, a new stage of history was about to begin. Anticipating the *Communist Manifesto* by four years, he predicted that "civilization," the fifth stage of human history, during which Man had completed "his social infancy," was breaking down under its anarchical tendencies. Out of the collapse of the older order, he predicted, would rise a new and more glorious phase of human history, the period of "Guaranteeism," in which it would be possible to combine the separate interests of all the classes into one cooperative social unity beneficial to all.[9] The logic of history, then, supported the Fourierist effort to realize their secular Millennium.

Generally, the dissatisfaction with society took a strong anti-government form especially in New England and its colonized zones in the West; this rebellion against politics was especially encouraged by the radical religious press, notably by William Lloyd Garrison's *The Liberator.*[10] Although the rebellion drew most of its energy from radical religion, the Fourierists believed that they could use it to raise national aspirations in general above the level of politics. In his *Democracy, Constructive and Pacific* (1844), Godwin argued that a "destructive and revolutionary democracy" had established the principle of individual freedom, only to leave the individual helpless before the anarchical forces of the new industrialism. Because destructive democracy dominated politics, neither of the existing political parties could solve this problem: The policies of the Whig party would only "consecrate" the tyranny of industrial capitalism, while those of the more individualistic Democrats would only strengthen the "element of disorder." What was needed, then, was an entirely new movement dedicated to organic social change and to a social form of democracy.[11]

To rally the people to their cause, the Fourierists adopted the techniques of political democracy. Recognizing the power of a partisan press, they attempted to establish their own journals. The *Tribune,* the *Pathfinder,* and the *Present* each contributed to the movement, but the Fourierist propaganda effort first came to a focus in 1843 with the founding in New York of the monthly *Phalanx: A Journal of Social Science* under the motto "Our Evils are Social, Not Political, and a Social Reform Only Can Eradicate Them." Edited by Brisbane and Osborne Macdaniel, it listed among its expected contributors Greeley, Channing, Godwin, and two New York Swedenborgian ministers, Benjamin F. Barrett and Solyman Brown; also included in this list was Mary S. Gove, probably the most active female radical of her day and the later wife of Thomas Low Nichols.

The *Phalanx* survived on a shoestring basis until 1845 when it was replaced by the *Harbinger,* a weekly initially published at Brook Farm and edited by George Ripley and his associates. Charles A. Dana said that the new journal was intended to provide "a central school speaking authoratively upon the doctrinal questions." Over the next four years, the *Harbinger* greatly enriched the discussion of what it called "the cause of radical organic social reform," publishing a wide range of articles on social and cultural matters by the leading lights of the movements.[12]

In addition to these efforts, Brisbane between 1840 and 1843 published two books plus various articles in such periodicals as the *Democratic Review* and the *Dial,* while Godwin added two short books, both published in 1844. Although the total audience for all of these publications probably was no more than a few thousand readers, the effort was assisted by occasional notices in various other sources with wider audiences. In 1844, the *Christian Examiner,* the influential Unitarian quarterly, devoted most of its July issue to a series of articles on Fourierism, and the Swedenborgian *New Jerusalem Magazine* published at least two articles on the subject. Even *Hunt's Merchants Magazine* gave some favorable publicity by publishing a review of Godwin's *A Popular View of the Doctrines of Charles Fourier* in which the reviewer predicted that Fourierism "must in its full realization embrace all reforms and produce a harmony and order in the moral and social world."[13]

This success owed much to efforts to Americanize Fourier's doctrines. Although the disciples acknowledged their debt to his inspiring genius, they allowed themselves the freedom to ignore his eccentricities. Unencumbered by the presence of the Master himself, they were able to present their cause as "Associationism," a practical philosophy in harmony with the American tradition of voluntary association adapted to American conditions and needs; its joint-stock principle of property ownership was suited to a nation that was coming to depend on the business corporation. In their version, passional attraction was stripped of its erotic overtones and became "attractive industry," a force for economic and social harmony. They were particular anxious to convince the American public that their movement, far from being a threat to religion, would bring the practical realization of true Christianity. Greeley said that Association was "the application of Christianity to the Social Relations of mankind," while William H. Channing declared that "Jesus was the Father of Association." Even though the Phalanx could hardly be identified with the Primitive Church, it was possible for John S. Dwight of Brook Farm to describe it as "the Body of Christianity," where brotherly cooperation would provide the basis for the full realization of the Christian spirit.[14]

The Associationists hoped to create a popular movement based on a coalition of classes. In part, they appealed for support to people very much like themselves. In Association, said Brisbane, "men of talent and genius" would find the opportunity to develop their full potential with the assurance that their talents would receive the recognition and material rewards denied by existing society; after all, Fourier had provided for rewards to Talent as well as to Labor and Capital. Moreover, such men would be able to meet their special spiritual needs. "The organization of attractive industry," said John S. Dwight, "will be reconciliation of spirit and matter, of religion and the world." Brisbane promised the full development of the "intellectual riches of the soul," while Godwin spoke grandiloquently of enabling each man to "attain his true destiny" as a moral being.[15] In the new society, men of talent and sensibility would be able to enjoy all the benefits of cooperative brotherhood in association with those whom Brisbane pleased to call "the Mass" without the least sacrifice of their individuality or their dreams.

More broadly, the Associationists spoke to those Americans who were disturbed by the disrupting effects of Jacksonian democracy, industrialism, and the prolonged depression which had followed the Panic of 1837. Dispensing with Fourier's embarrassing emphasis on emotional repression as the source of human ills, they provided explanations for contemporary problems in contemporary terms. All organic social evil, they claimed, arose out of modern man's irrational preference for a haphazard system of competitive individualism over the orderly system of cooperation which God had intended to govern the Earth.

Under the competitive system, Godwin warned, social conflict was spreading into every aspect of life, producing a "commercial feudalism" where the rich and powerful few had come to dominate the many. Even in America, "Capitalism is swallowing labor—and the masses are yearly becoming more and more enslaved to its despotism." Although he attacked the anarchy and despotism of competitive capitalism, Godwin did not attack the capitalists themselves, since like other Associationists he believed that the root of the problem lay not in class malevolence but in the absence of a cooperative social order: "The misery of modern industrialism was that it set out without plan and without organization." The answer, then, was not to overthrow capitalism but to give it the right organization under the ruling spirit of Associationism. Unless competition were replaced by cooperation, neither religion nor politics nor anything else would prevent the descent of society into the hell of commercial anarchy and despotism.[16]

The new Associationist order, since it was founded on divine science, would benefit all and hurt none—a point given special emphasis by Brisbane in his textbook for the movement, *Association; or Concise Exposition of the Practical Part of Fourier's Social Science* (1843) based on the articles which he had written the previous year. Here, as elsewhere, Brisbane was careful to distance Fourier from Owen, whose attacks on the sacred institutions of society had given the cooperative ideal a bad name: Unlike Owen's crude radicalism, Associationism would not endanger either the family or religion, nor would it threaten the profit-motive and private wealth; instead, the new system would elevate and sanctify them. Rather than destroying the class system, Association would perfect it by creating a unity of classes: "The favored classes will, as soon as Association is established, make it their pride and ambition to provide for the gradual Elevation of their favored fellow-men, but they will not be called upon to sacrifice their feelings and comfort in promiscuous association."[17]

Brisbane and his allies depicted a collective society that would meet the needs of every group. To small employers and businessmen fearful of being crushed under what Godwin called "the colossal wheels of large properties and enterprises," they offered a secure place in their own colossal enterprise.[18] To skilled workers confronted by the factories of the new industrial age, they offered a vision of "Beautiful Halls of Industry," where workers would control the tempo and condition of their work. To those trapped in drudging and dreary rural life, they offered the hope of attractive labor and a richly varied society on collective farms.[19] For everyone, they pictured a richly satisfying life in the collective splendor of the great "Edifice of Association," in which all members would reside, each family in its own private apartment suited to its tastes and its wealth, a world of privacy in balance with the world of cooperative effort.[20]

The Associationists offered material profits as well as a pleasurable life to every class. Although they condemned what they saw as the anarchical capitalism of their times, they tried to harness the pervasive capitalistic ethos in America to their cause by presenting Associationism as a superior form of capitalism suited to progressive times. Unlike the communism of Owen, the new system would maintain the energy and creativity of self-interest. Unlike the existing civilization, it would incorporate all interests into a well-ordered economy by giving everyone a chance to be a capitalist, even the humble being able to acquire by their labor one or more shares in the joint-stock property of their Association. Each share entitled its owner to a portion of the immense wealth to be produced by the hyperactive phalanx, a full-quarter of the product being set aside for the shareholders. Although all would have a chance to become capitalists, the chief beneficiaries would be wealthy investors who would profit from an association even if they did not live or work there; they could buy or sell their shares in much the same way as they did with their stock in a business corporation.[21]

This appeal to capitalism was at least partly motivated by the need for a substantial capital investment even to begin the work of transmuting dreams into gold. Owenism might attempt to demonstrate its magic in a small Indiana town, and Brook Farm could begin with a few people; but a phalanx required a more definite size and context. It was only in a large and well-organized group, said Brisbane, "that all varieties of talents and capacities, as well as the proper capital, skill and knowledge can be combined." Without the proper combination, the incomplete phalanx, like some incomplete chemical formula, would not fizz or bubble and passional attraction would not work its magic. Although he was willing to allow associations with as few as 400 persons, he insisted that any association begin with a minimum of $400,000 in capital and 1000 acres of land.[22]

Even at $1000 a head, that was a cheap price to pay for admission into paradise. A properly funded and constructed "Edifice of Association" would furnish "a beautiful spectacle of architectural unity, in comparison with which our present little and isolated constructions would appear most insignificant and discordant." Set among lavishly cultivated fields and gardens, the full-fledged phalanx would so satisfy every need and taste as to persuade Americans to give up their solitary homes for the grand communal life. Once the proper number of people were assembled, then even one Association would demonstrate the power of attractive industry to produce nearly unlimited wealth. Other associations would soon be organized, multiplying at an accelerating rate until, like some benign organism, the new paradise had spread over the entire nation and over the Globe: "The work of a universal social reform, which now appears gigantic and impracticable, will in reality be simple and easy."[23] If only a few hundred people could be convinced to back his dream with hard cash, Brisbane could validate his social science and begin to transform the world.

In New York, the money capital of America, his enthusiasm caught the attention of some influential Americans, although not always to his benefit. After encountering Brisbane at a social gathering in 1842, Emerson wrote home: "He wishes me 'with all my party,' to come in directly and join him. What palaces! What concerts! What pictures, lectures, poetry and flowers"; the Sage of Concord commented in his private journal that a big city, with all its diverse entertainments, was phalanx enough for him.[24] Brisbane, though, did succeed in winning the support of various people, including some Swedenborgians and other cultural dissenters. With the special assistance of Greeley's daily and weekly *Tribune,* he was able to broaden the field of Fourierist propaganda. By July 1842, the *Tribune* could announce the formation of the Fourier Association of New York and the opening of a large lecture hall in the city where for 6 cents a week people could learn the basics of Associationism.[25]

The ambition of the New York Fourier Association was to form a network of societies throughout the country to act under its direction in support of one demonstration project. Nine months later, it launched a formal campaign to raise $400,000 for its projected North American Phalanx to be located near New York or Philadelphia: "The Philanthropist will find in it the highest end to which he can direct his benevolence—the Capitalist will find in it the amplest and most unequivocal guarantee of safety and profit for the investment of money."[26] There was no great rush of capitalists to the Fourierist gold fields, but the movement did spread to other parts of the country. In September 1843, a Western Fourier Convention was held at Pittsburgh, with Greeley's encouragement; and soon after Brisbane brought the gospel to central and western New York state, where his lectures attracted large audiences in the major towns. The movement also found support in New England despite the sneers of Emerson and the opposition of many reformers. By December, Brisbane was able to boast that "the name FOURIER is now heard from the Atlantic to the Mississippi," and to ask: "What will the next ten years bring forth?"[27]

Over the next few months, the movement received the support of social reform conventions in Boston, Cincinnati, Rochester, and several other places. By April 1844, it had attracted enough recruits in the Northeast for the New Yorkers to host a general convention of delegates from various associations in Maine, Massachusetts, New York, Pennsylvania, and Virginia (Wheeling). After choosing George Ripley as its president, the convention approved a declaration that "this is a religious meeting" and then detailed the many social, cultural, and economic benefits that would automatically flow from a properly organized and funded phalanx. As the last day of the meeting was Fourier's birthday, the delegates gathered at the Apollo Saloon to celebrate his cause with "soul-stirring speeches" and many toasts that reached a grand climax with a toast to friendship given as the assembled group held hands around the table, "producing an electric thrill of emotion through every nerve."[28]

Brisbane and his associates had reason to be satisfied with the results of their proselytizing work. By 1844, however, a weakness had developed in the movement which assured its failure. The original aim of Brisbane's campaign had been to create a network of coordinated societies to raise support for one demonstration phalanx, but the proliferation of societies soon gave the movement a direction of its own. Having been convinced that paradise and profits were within reach, many of the new converts rushed out to establish phalanxes on their own, dispersing the meager capital available even for one demonstration. The New York convention tried to restrain this tendency by urging Associationists to concentrate on a few demonstrations, an effort reinforced by a warning from the *Phalanx:* "There have been several excellent experiments started in different parts of the country, the failure of which . . . would bring grievous disparagement upon the cause."[29] Such cautions, however, had little effect on the new enthusiasm.

In one sense, the propaganda campaign had succeeded too well. Although it failed to attract the big money of capitalists, it did tap into a broad vein of expectation and frustration in American society. The collapse of the economic boom in 1837 had made many Americans deeply dissatisfied with their lot in life. A few were essentially speculators whose dreams of quick wealth were dampened by stagnating business and depressed property values. Others were skilled workers, dissatisfied by the uncertainties of urban employments, and small farmers frustrated by the meager social as well as economic benefits of their isolated farms. These workers and farmers supplied much of the capital for the various Fourierist enterprises that sprung up after 1843, investing their tools and lands as well as some cash to boost the dreams of abundance, security, and satisfaction into actuality.[30]

Generally, these people were also dissatisfied with the social and cultural orthodoxies of conventional society; for them, Association offered an immediate escape from both economic depression and social and cultural oppression. Brisbane, with his private dream of bringing society into harmony with the Cosmos, might urge patience on the grounds that his scheme was "founded upon precise mathematical calculations, and incapable of application to the arbitrary caprice or fancy of individuals."[31] For many, however, Associationism was an immediate prescription for their troubles; in it, they saw the opportunity to make their own independent worlds suited to their individual "caprice or fancy" which they could control in their own interests. Having promised salvation for individuality in the cooperative paradise, Associationism drew to it some of the very anarchical individualism which it was designed to eliminate.

Brisbane's plea for careful preparation was ignored in the rush of enthusiasts to seize the benefits of this new venture. That rush began in March 1843 when some of his New York colleagues formed the Sylvania Association and, eager to "profit by the vast Economies" of Fourier's system, committed their meager resources to an ill-chosen site in the hills of northeastern Pennsylvania some five miles by rocky road from the Delaware and Hudson Canal. Sylvania collapsed in less than two years with the loss of most of the $14,000 actually invested in it.[32] This failure, however, was not quick enough to caution the thousands of people who in the years between 1843 and 1846 founded some 30 more associations throughout the northern United States. Among these phalanxes were the Clarkston (upstate New York), the Leraysville (Pennsylvania), the Trumbull (Ohio), the Alphedelphia (Michigan), the LaGrange (Indiana), the Integral (Illinois), and the Wisconsin.[33]

Most of the associations, with a characteristic American confidence that land was wealth, invested all-too-much of their limited capitals in large tracts of cheap and isolated lands in disregard of Brisbane's rule that they locate close to major urban centers. John Humphrey Noyes, an intelligent student of Fourierism and other forms of Socialism, said that this "lust for land leads off into the wilderness, 'out west,' or into by-places, far from railroads and markets; whereas Socialism, if it is really ahead of civilization, ought to be near the centers of business." Where they should have striven for some sophisticated economic basis, the pretended phalanxes often committed their partly urban populations to the primitive economy of frontier agriculture. At Sylvania, for instance, 75 largely citified adults (apparently, none of whom were farmers) found that they had to wrestle a living from 2394 acres of "barren wilderness," an unintended retreat to a frontier stage of life.[34]

Confronted by a situation which he could not control, Brisbane dressed it in a chilly optimism: "These trials are upon so small a scale, and are commenced with such limited means, that they exhibit but few features of the system. They are, however, very important commencements, and are small beginnings of a reform in some of the most important arrangements of the present social order."[35] Multiple small beginnings might look good to a determined optimist, but for a system dependent on a big beginning they boded ill for the future.

The General Convention in 1844 attempted to make the best of this situation by urging the existing phalanxes to form a cooperative union for mutual support, and in May 1844 six newly established associations in western and northern New York (inspired by Brisbane's lecture tour a few months earlier) did form a "Confederacy," the American Industrial Union, in the hope of creating an independent Fourierist world. The confederacy had strong possibilities, comprising some 4000 apparent supporters, 5000 acres of land, and over $100,000 in capital commitments.[36] The capital, however, existed largely on paper or in land, while the people were ill-prepared for the hard work of founding new communities. Failing to achieve the expected "vast economies" of the Fourierist system, the six associations soon vanished and with them went the enthusiasm for Association. A second Fourierist lecture tour of the area encountered meager audiences.[37] Elsewhere, other feeble fragments of the dream, lacking even the promise of joint support, also soon collapsed. A few, however, showed greater promise.

The Wisconsin Phalanx survived for six years, long enough for it to suffer from the hopeful cupidity raised by Fourierism. Conceived during the fruitful winter of 1843–44 by the Southport (Kenosha) Fourier Club, this phalanx took vigorous root in the virgin soil of Ripon township. It was one of the most businesslike of the phalanxes, founded by a struggling frontier middle class that expected practical social and economic benefits. One proponent of the idea told the Southport Club that it could be viewed as "a common business partnership" which would enable its members "to produce all that is required for the support, comfort and convenience of the human family . . . with less toil than is now required for the laborer while association affords facilities for education, moral and intellectual culture."[38] The idea must have looked good for those who felt trapped in a socially and economically stagnant frontier area by the depression which had followed the collapse of the western land boom.

Much of the character and attitude of these associationist pioneers was reflected in the life of one of their leaders, Warren Chase. Born in New Hampshire in 1813, Chase's early life made him a natural dissenter from conventional society, the "Lone One" as he called himself in his first autobiography. At age 10, he was orphaned and set adrift in a hard world with the conviction that it was God who had killed his mother, a conviction which left him with a permanent distaste for Christianity. He tried to find a new faith first in rationalism and then in the fashionable new "sciences" of phrenology and mesmerism, but these provided little solace in what proved to be a life of much hardship and little success. By stages, he drifted westward to Wisconsin where in 1843 he took stock of his life and discovered that after 30 years he had a "sickly wife, the mother of three children," one of whom was sick and soon to die, plus "a little cabin for the family, and one larger for the cow."[39] In this bleak year of general depression, he had little to look forward to, but before it closed he was to discover the works of Fourier, and his life was to change dramatically for the better.

Fourierism offered him an escape from loneliness, drudgery, and privation. "Its vast economies, its equitable distributions, its harmony of groups and series, its attractive industry, its advantages for schools, meetings, parties, and social festivities, all seemed to make its theory invulnerable to attack." Convinced that Association was salvation for himself and his family, he sold his little property to help fund the new phalanx and then, as its business agent, made a successful effort to get it legally chartered as a joint-stock company by the Wisconsin territorial legislature.[40] These contributions and Chase's innate business sense helped get the new enterprise off to a successful start.

By 1848, the Phalanx had achieved a modest prosperity. "It had," recalled Chase, "a good and successful system of rewards for labor; by which they were not troubled by the drones." Hard work and cooperation had brought into being a hastily constructed little village called Ceresco which included some workshops, a gristmill, a schoolhouse, and a large unitary dwelling for some of the members as well as various temporary shacks for the rest; they added over 300 acres to their domain and expanded their farming operations.[41] By frontier standards, the 150 members achieved a rather successful social life. Chase said later that "they danced without rum, or vulgarism and profanity. They had meetings without prayers and babies without doctors." Although they made some provision for religious services, they were generally free-thinkers like Chase, "a great reading community" who provided themselves with a reading room and no church.[42]

What successes they achieved, however, were at the expense of their enthusiasm for Association, which suffered from an attack of rising expectations. It was not long before some began to complain that they were not receiving rewards for their skills commensurate with outside wages and to grumble that they were the victims of "the extravagant form of usury" resulting from the allocation of one-quarter of the product of their labor to capital, much of it to nonresident stockholders.[43] Others were disappointed in the extravagant expectations raised by Fourierism for a pleasurable social life suited to their individual needs. Having constructed a crude and uncomfortable unitary dwelling for some of themselves, the members disagreed over the merits of building a great phalanstery to house them all, and there was resistance to the practice of dining together at a "unitary table," a dispute which Chase believed was a major factor in the social failure of the experiment.[44]

This weak sense of community combined with the modest economic success of the Phalanx made it vulnerable to the temptation to make individual profit. This was virtually assured by the fact that many of the newer members were recent settlers in the area who had been attracted less by the theoretical delights of Fourierism than by the actual advantages of an organized social life. It was not surprising, therefore, that some members and stockholders became interested, as one said later, in accumulating property for themselves "by any and every means called fair in competitive society."

In 1849, Chase and other dedicated Associationists tried to save their experiment by issuing a call for $20,000 to buy out dissident stockholders, but the call was unanswered. Therefore they decided as their last collective act to dissolve the Phalanx and to divide its wealth, which had grown considerably due primarily to a tenfold increase in the value of its lands. Even Chase, who had hoped to find "a new heaven and new earth," agreed that termination was necessary and took on the responsibility of "paying every debt on the stock and three dividends" before he closed accounts in 1852. What had been a phalanx was absorbed into the thriving new town of Ripon, a typical booster enterprise founded in 1849 on nearby land which the Association had been unable to buy from its owner.[45]

The end came more quickly and less voluntarily for the Brook Farm Phalanx, even though it was the most protected from the booster spirit. When Ripley's little but prestigeous community reorganized itself in early 1844 as the "Association for Industry and Education," it added much hope to the Fourierist cause. While Brisbane and the other disciples paid little attention to the Wisconsin Phalanx, they exulted over the Farm's decision "to institute an attractive, efficient, and productive system of industry."[46] The new phalanx, the most idealistic of them all, quickly became the intellectual center of the Fourierist empire. It provided a new home for the *Phalanx,* the monthly journal of the movement, which in 1845 was converted into a weekly under the name *The Harbinger,* a substantial part of which was written by Ripley, Dana, and Dwight.[47]

Benefiting from its closeness to Boston, the Farm seemed to grow stronger under Fourierism. Enthusiasm for the cause gave the revitalized community new energies and ambitions, leading it to announce that it anticipated "great results from applying the principles of universal order to industry." By the end of 1844, it had completed a large workshop building for varied kinds of skilled work to lessen its dependence on agriculture and education.[48] The women as well as men were inspired to industrial activity. The eighteen-year-old daughter of John S. Dwight, Marianne, joined with other women to form a "fancy group" to produce caps, capes, and other articles for the Boston market; they hoped that the arrangements would free them from their domestic burdens and open a new field in which women could attain economic independence: "By and by, when funds accumulate (!) we may start other branches of business, so that all our proceeds may be applied to the elevation of women forever."[49]

Much of the new energy and enthusiasm soon came to a focus on the construction of a "Phalanstery or Unitary dwelling" to house the phalanx. From the beginning, the Farm had not been able to provide satisfactory housing for its members, particularly those with families. By converting itself into a phalanx, it transformed this annoyance into the basic problem of providing an adequate container for its unitary social life. Encouraged by Brisbane, who brought vague promises of financial support and, said Marianne Dwight, some pictures of "a Phalanstery and its domain in full harmony," the members began to construct a wooden building 175 feet long and three stories high containing a hundred rooms and a dining hall for three hundred people—this at a time when the whole community had only ninety inhabitants. In their enthusiasm, they dreamed of an even grander building, which they would erect when the Phalanx achieved its full power.[50]

During their first year under the new regime, the Brook Farmers believed that they had much reason for gratitude to Fourier, the prophet who had opened the way to paradise. On April 7, 1845, they met to celebrate the seventy-third anniversary of his birth. In a room enlivened

by plants and flowers from their new greenhouse, they gathered together, reported the *Phalanx,* in "perfect social equality of all present,
alike of the server and the served," to pay tribute to the great genius
who had "comprehended and revealed the sublimest truths of nature."
Speeches were given by Ripley (whom Marianne described as being
never "so happy or so great"), Brisbane, Dana, and others. Enthusiastically, one young member said that earlier as a college student he had
despised "Ambition," but now under Fourier's influence "I confess, by
Heaven, I am ambitious. I will be omniarch of the globe." It was indeed
a springtime of hope and joy.[51]

A year later, however, there was neither hope nor joy. In the fall of
1845, there began a sequence of disasters that destroyed the experiment.
The first blow was an outbreak of varioloid (a mild variant of smallpox)
that virtually paralyzed the community and disrupted its school. Although no one died from the disease, the epidemic had severe financial
costs at a time when the Farm had exhausted the money needed to
complete its building program. Work on the Phalanstery had to be
suspended, leading Marianne Dwight to mourn that "we must have
$10,000 at least before spring, or we may as well die."[52] Fourier's
heaven, the members were beginning to discover, had an expensive
price which they had to strain every resource to meet. Then came the
final blow, when on one disastrous night in March 1846 their still
unrealized dreams of paradise went up in the smoke of a spectacular fire
that completely destroyed the building. Having failed to insure the
Phalanstery, they were left only with ashes and a debt they could not
pay.[53]

Their pleas for money to rebuild brought no response from the
national movement. Having overextended both their ambitions and their
resources, they believed that they had no choice but to liquidate their
experiment. In August 1847, a meeting of stockholders and creditors of
the Farm voted to sell it, and in 1848 Ripley arranged its sale to the
Town of Roxbury for use as an almshouse—an ironic end for an experiment which four years before he had announced was not intended to be
"an almshouse, an asylum for those who have become maimed . . . in the
contests of civilization." Brook Farm was terminated with honor; after it
had settled its affairs, said Dana, "we owed nobody a dollar." It was
long remembered as a community of special grace and joy.[54]

The experience might have survived as something more than a pleasant memory if its leaders had had a greater will to overcome their adversities. Despite its disasters, the Farm had a potential for survival, but it was one which Ripley did not try to exploit. The founder and mainstay demonstrated a notable lack of interest in saving his creation even when the majority of the members seemed ready to fight to preserve their way of life. With the establishment of the *Harbinger,* he had given much of his attention to the national movement, writing a large share of the articles in the new journal as well as serving as its editor.[55] After the fire, he apparently convinced himself that his cooperative society was too small and poorly endowed to make an adequate industrial association along Fourierist lines. Unwilling to go back to his original experiment, he was ready to sacrifice the Farm in order to go forward into the new Associationist future: "We have never professed to be able to represent the idea of Association with the scanty resources at our command; nor would the discontinuance of our establishment . . . in the slightest degree weaken our faith in the associative system." In July, Marianne Dwight rather bitterly classified Ripley along with Dana as "promulgators," who were more interested in promoting the movement than they were with life on the Farm.[56]

In fact, Ripley and other leaders had moved away from their preoccupation with phalanxes. Less than three months after the fire at the Farm, they launched the American Union of Associationists, whose primary goal was to "indoctrinate the whole People of the United States with the Principles of Associative Unity." The new organization proclaimed Association "the only peaceful mode of removing a principle of evil," that principle being competitive individualism which served only to strengthen the "power of Combined Capital" over nearly every aspect of modern life. It asked a question which was to be raised by social radicals during every industrial crisis over the next century:

> How is it that amidst innumeral and incessant improvements in agriculture, inventions in mechanics . . . intensely stimulated powers of production, accumulating national wealth, and such overflowing abundance that markets sufficient to absorb the surplus are in vain sought—poverty, destitution, crime, popular degeneracy are yet increasing in appalling ratio?

Progress *and* poverty—the problem had to be resolved if ever America was to avoid either a "destructive radicalism" or a brutal and brutalizing servitude to the wealthy few. Only the peaceful revolution offered by Associationism could avoid impending disaster: In "the Principles of Joint-Stock Property and Cooperative Industry we hold out to the capitalist and laborer—in contrast with the infernal horror of industrial Feudalism—the Eden-like peace and prosperity of Universal Unity."[57]

The American Union established a discrete distance from Fourier by announcing that its cause was "independent of every merely *individual* influence." Similarly, it said nothing about phalanxes beyond a vague reference to cooperative "townships." On the other hand, it attempted to identify the movement even more closely with religion, a step especially favored by William Henry Channing. Channing hoped to make the Union a missionary organization to promote what he called "a living church in a Combined Order of Society" based on his own version of Christianity. In this, he was supported by John S. Dwight, who proclaimed a new "Church of Humanity" founded on Associationism: "What a faith is ours. We reject the doctrine of the inherent depravity and disharmony of the human passions as impious atheism, not only libelling but denying the good God." As part of this effort, the Associationists in Boston began to hold regular Sunday meetings with Channing as the preacher.[58]

Nationally, the Union attempted to launch an ambitious program to maintain twelve full-time lecturers whose mission was to propagate what Godwin called "the eternal principles of Social Harmony." It was supported by various "affiliated unions" in Philadelphia, Providence, Wheeling, Cincinnati, and several smaller places mostly in New England. At the first annual meeting of the Union in 1847, it declared that its "Central Policy" was "to organize into one living active body, a series of Affiliated Unions of Associationists scattered over the whole country, and to organize them in such a way as will best promote a thorough scientific training and moral development of the members of this confederacy." In time, the members of these local unions would be prepared to establish a new round of model associations.[59]

This resort to apostolic tactics included some attempt to organize the working classes. In 1847, as the new editor of the *Harbinger,* Godwin warned workers that they needed Association to protect themselves against enslavement to capital, and he warned everyone of the menace of "mechanical improvements" under the conditions of anarchical competition: Under these conditions, machines "come into competition with laboring people, and throw them out of work, and although they greatly cheapen products, of what use are such products if laborers have not the wherewithal to purchase them?"[60]

Despite Dana's confidence that workers "can hardly help looking to us for advisors," however, labor demonstrated little faith in would-be leaders from the advantaged classes, particularly in men who tried to discourage the attempts of workingmen to protect themselves through strikes and through agitation for a ten-hour workday. Henry Kriege, a German immigrant and a former member of Marx's Communist League, probably spoke for many ordinary workers when he said that "Fourier found his support among the well-to-do, the so-called people of culture," and warned that Association was a scheme for the control of labor in the interests of capital. By 1848, the *Harbinger* had little to say about the efforts to organize the workingman.[61]

Undoubtedly, the Associationists wanted especially to win over the well-to-do and respectable. During the depressed and depressing early 1840s, they had captured considerable attention by their promises of profits and culture, and by their warnings that industrial capitalism threatened what Godwin called the "reduction of the middling classes." Later, however, the phalanxes failed to demonstrate their promised magic—a failure highlighted by the return of national prosperity. Moreover, many middle class Americans had become at least vaguely aware of Fourier's ideas regarding sex, leading them to suspect that Fourierism was a threat to morality and to the family. Although the Associationists attempted to allay these concerns, they sometimes added to them. Godwin, for instance, did say that the passional system would include men of "the most feminine tastes" and women with "tastes decidedly masculine," and Dwight did concede that in Association "the relationship of the sexes will be very different from what they are now."[62] Passion but no profit—whatever the truth of this reputation, it further weakened the already limited appeal of the movement for the middle class.

The movement also suffered from a significant shift in public concern during the decade. In the early 1840s, Associationism had provided at least some kind of answer to the apparently deepening economic and social problems of a period of depression. Social radicalism, however, had its greatest appeal in the same reform and dissenting circles that were also concerned with another evil—slavery. Almost from the beginning, Associationists had been forced to argue that they were attacking a deeper and broader form of slavery than that involving black people alone. In 1845, Greeley declared that he was less troubled by slavery in the South than he was by slavery in New York City.[63] Such arguments had little effect. By the mid 1840's the growing concern over the spread of slavery induced by the annexation of Texas and the Mexican War shifted attention away from the organic social evil of competitive capitalism to the organic moral evil of the "Slave Power," a shift highlighted by the organization of the Free Soil party in 1848.

By 1850, it was evident that Associationism was a lost cause. The American Union of Associationists was hurried into oblivion by its failure to raise money to support its lecture program, although at its last annual meeting in 1848 it attempted to carry on by appointing John Allen, president of the Lowell affiliate, as its "traveling agent." The movement also found it difficult to maintain the *Harbinger*. After the demise of Brook Farm, the journal had been moved to New York City, taking a reluctant Ripley with it. Godwin, who earlier had served as chairman of the Central Executive Committee of the movement, soon became its new editor. Neither the change of place nor of editorship, however, enabled it to become self-supporting.[64]

For a time, Godwin and other Associationists found some hope in the prospect of a fruitful connection with European Fourierism, particularly when the Revolution of 1848 in France seemed to give the French Fourierists, in the words of the American Union, "the balance of power between the conservatives . . . and the Radicals seeking a leveling Communism." Brisbane, who in 1844 had been appointed to represent America to "our Fellow Associationists in Europe," was in Paris in 1848 and threw himself into the fray. The prospects for a Fourierist coup, however, quickly evaporated, and with them the last hope for the American cause. Although in early 1849 Godwin declared that the previous year had begun "the grand developments which are destined to take place in the nineteenth century," it was only to embellish his notice that the *Harbinger* was suspending publication.[65]

Channing temporarily revived the periodical under the title *The Spirit of the Age,* with the promise that the times were bringing "an era of reconciliation, when order and freedom shall be harmonized by unity of interest, and universal goodwill shall be proved and perfected in universal justice." Despite Channing's hopes to unite reformers and "Socialists" of varying schools behind him, his journal soon expired and with it went what little remained of the movement.[66] For many years, however, fragments of Associationism continued to survive; a movement which had touched the lives and thoughts of thousands was bound to have some long-term influence. In 1871, Channing said that Brook Farm was "only a small specimen twig" of a greater cause and predicted that the world would eventually apply the Associationist method to many aspects of public and private life.[67] In the early 1850s, the vigor of one "specimen twig" in particular served to sustain such hopes. This was the North American Phalanx in New Jersey which had survived the collapse of the phalansterian boom to become the most vital and authentic of all the Associationist experiments. It also was to fail, but not before it had made an independent and significant chapter in the search for a cooperative society.

VII

The Phalanx in Dream
and Reality

Associationism, like most radical movements, contained fundamental ambiguities, most of which developed out of essential differences between its leadership and its following over the embodiment of its social ideals, the phalanx. Although they sincerely avowed a concern for individuality, the disciples were the first of several generations of American intellectuals who sought their heaven in the harmony and efficiency of a well-ordered cooperative system embracing all elements of society, justifying Emerson's contention that the phalanx "was the perfection of arrangement and contrivance."[1] On the other hand, Associationism excited the activity of those who believed that it offered them a good organization suited to their own interests. They were the citizens of a world where business corporations, benevolent societies, and hotels had taught them to see the voluntary association as a way to both profit and satisfaction. The result was a spate of what Brisbane called "primitive Experiments" founded on "a low practical ideal" that debased Fourier's dream.[2]

Brisbane most fully described this dream in his *Treatise on the Functions of the Human Passions,* an exploration of Fourierist theory written after the collapse of the movement. Probably because he no longer felt any obligation to reduce theory to acceptable terms, he insisted on the need for a full-fledged "Integral Phalanx" of approximately 1800 people. Only this number could assure the complete range of passions which Fourier had predicted would, with proper organization, naturally form "the complete Passional Man," a superorganism with divine attributes.[3] And it was only in the rightly organized Phalanstery that the Passional Man could be brought to life: "The Palace of the Association should be an Architectural Organism perfectly adapted . . . to the nature and requirements of the Collective Soul that is to inhabit it."[4] Above all, it was only in the Integral Phalanx that the individual could fully realize his self, could experience the full vitality of his diverse passions and the inifinite heights of satisfaction which God had intended for all.

Brisbane's fantasy of the Integral Phalanx served his later insistance that Fourierism had not failed but had never really been tried. Especially in his early career, however, he himself had given much emphasis to the "low practical" ideas which might attract popular support. On the one hand, his phalanx was a corporate form seemingly large enough to turn modern science, machinery, and organization to practical advantage. "We must give to labor," Brisbane wrote in 1846, "a *good Organization;* we must dignify it and make it attractive; we must apply to it all the resources of science and invention, so as to increase production greatly —four, six, eight fold. By this means we can secure abundance to all."[5] On the other hand, the phalanx was scaled to the world which most Americans tended to idealize, the world of small local communities and small enterprise, of petty craftsmen and yeoman farmers, that for decades before 1840 had begun to suffer from the competition of factory production and western agriculture.

This scale governed Brisbane's ideal of good labor organization. The functional organs of the phalanx were its Groups and Series of Groups, each of which performed a particular task. One Series, for instance, specialized in the manufacture of hats, another in the raising of pears (a favorite of Fourier). In turn, each Series was subdivided into three or more Groups which minutely specialized in producing one kind of hat or one variety of pear. This minute division of labor would enable every individual to apply one of his talents and to satisfy one of his interests in useful production. Were a member to prove incompetent to a particular task which he had chosen, he would be directed out of the Group by its "Secretary" to a more congenial job. As a further safeguard, all who applied to a particular Series were obliged to begin as apprentices until they had learned the required skills.[6]

Even in a limited Association of 400 people, there would be at least 50 Series and 150 Groups. Of the Series, approximately 8 would be devoted to livestock raising, 22 to agriculture, 10 to manufacturing and mechanics, 6 to household labor, and 4 to the arts, science, and education; the preponderance of agricultural over industrial pursuits was a fair reflection of a time when agriculture was still believed to be the social and economic basis of life. In this economy, where every job would be matched to a specialized talent and interest, all work would be performed skillfully and enthusiastically. There would be no need for coercion or bosses or factory walls.[7] Women would benefit from this system as much as men; the unitary household would free women to participate in the joyous working world without the loss of the benefits of family life.[8]

Associated industry would also satisfy the social needs of all, since most work was performed by groups of like-minded individuals. Each group was a guild, a small community of friendly workers bound together in cooperation by common instincts and motivated by a common pride in the work. "Friendship-Paternity-Love," promised Brisbane, would prevail in Association. "By means of the organization of the Groups and Series, both sexes and all ages can take part together in most of its occupations; parents and children, friends and lovers will be united in the same Groups, so that these three beautiful sentiments will be gratified jointly with the prosecution of useful pursuits."[9]

In this, Brisbane evoked one of the most powerful and persistent of human impulses, the desire for stable family and fraternal ties. It was a time when the movement of Americans to the frontier and the cities in search of opportunity had raised much sentimental regret over the loss of old associations with families and friends; the resulting sense of individual loneliness and insecurity was compounded by the primtive state of communications in an age which was only beginning to use the railroad and the telegraph. By providing a full range of opportunities within a well-organized community, the phalanx would prevent the separation of husbands from wives, children from parents, and friends from friends; the stable family and community associations of traditional life would be anchored against the temptations as well as the dangers of modern life.[10]

This ordered and intimate social life would control one temptation that seemed to be tearing American society apart, the urge to find fulfillment through the maximization of monetary profits. Greed or, as Fourier preferred to call it, "cupidity" was a natural human passion, but under the anarchical conditions of present society it had become the greatest threat to the social and moral order. In Association, the passion for profit would be gratified in such a way as to make it work also in favor of a stable community order and to the benefit of everyone. If in one respect attractive industry would satisfy every psychic and physical need, it also would provide material rewards calibrated to the real contribution made by each individual to the common good.[11]

Every year, approximately one-quarter of the surplus product of the phalanx would be apportioned to capital, to which Brisbane gave preference as "the first source of wealth," since it provided the materials and tools of production. The rest was to be distributed to labor and skill on the basis of a complex formula designed to assure a just return to all members. In this capitalistic paradise, all pay was in the form of a "division of profits" rather than of wages, a system which would make everyone a capitalist in one degree or another, thereby eliminating the widening gap between capital and labor that had begun to trouble the industrial world.[12]

Each Series under this system was to receive a share of the profits based on its classification as a Necessary, Useful, or Attractive occupation. If its work was particularly repugnant or required special skills needed for the health and harmony of the Association, it could expect the highest return: Physicians and garbage collectors thus could expect premium pay. Conversely, those engaged in especially desirable kinds of work like pear raising would get the highest psychic rewards but the lowest return. If a series attracted too many or too few volunteers for the work to be done, its rank and pay could be lowered or raised until the situation was equalized. Since each member would receive dividends from the various Series to which he had belonged in the year, the total would be an exact reward for his contributions beyond the individual satisfactions he earned from his work.[13]

Ideally, the Association was a self-adjusting social organization. General matters of internal governance would be handled by an annually elected Council of Industry whose chief responsibilities were to determine land usages and to equip the phalanx with the best machinery and scientific techniques, but its role would be advisory.[14] In this world without politics and politicians, the effective decisions would be made by the work groups themselves in the same way that the guilds had done in the past. In the broadest sense, the Association would embody in a miniaturized way the whole range of modern opportunities without sacrificing the intimacy and accessibility of local communities.

At a time when social change was becoming increasingly uncontrollable, the phalanx would have the size, mass, and completeness needed to make an autonomous little world which its inhabitants could control for themselves. Autonomy, however, would not mean a retreat to the backward conditions associated with isolated rural life, since the phalanstery could reach across space and time to avail itself of all the benefits of human progress. Besides a library, newspaper, and other cultural media, Brisbane equipped each phalanx with a "telegraph and signal tower" to communicate with other phalanxes and to facilitate necessary social, cultural, and economic exchanges.[15]

In an age of great but uneven progress in the material conditions of family life, the Unitary Household of the Phalanx promised to provide everyone with the advantages of modern domestic facilities and to effect economies of money and energies by replacing the hundreds of kitchens, heating apparatuses, and living spaces of "isolated households" with a more compact and efficient organization.[16] Unitary kitchens equipped with the latest and best equipment and managed by the most enthusiastic and skilled cooks would produce better meals at less cost than the solitary housewife laboring in the solitary household. Central heating would replace dirty and inefficient stoves and fireplaces. In general, the phalanx would provide all the advantages of urban life without the troubling uncertainties of the city. By pooling their wealth and talents in a cooperative system, all Americans could acquire the benefits of gaslighting, indoor plumbing, and the other amenities then enjoyed by a minority of city-dwellers. They could escape from smoky lamps and smelly outhouses into a lavish new world where from their private apartments in the Edifice of Association they would have ready access to all that they might need. Set amid artistically cultivated gardens and beautifully cultivated fields, this "town or city under one roof" would truly be the palace or mansion for the people.[17]

Association also promised to resolve some of the most intimate and often anguishing problems of middle-class Americans. It offered a way by which parents could ease the burdens of child care and yet also assure that children would remain part of the parents' world. Collective life could provide nurseries for infants, and it could provide a complete system of education—formal and informal—within the household, so that children would be kept out of the hands of alien schools and educators. In its most complete form, it could furnish the next generation with the needed skills and jobs in its own economy which would keep them at home.[18] At a time of growing concern over both the preparation of children for life and the weakening of traditional family ties, these were important advantages.

Even more significant were the promised benefits to women. For them, the Unitary Household offered freedom both from child care and, even more, from domestic drudgery. The combination of household machinery, and coordinated labor made possible by the collective life would release women from pan-and-broom servitude to more rewarding kinds of activity. In the complete Unitary Household, they would still be responsible for domestic work, but their labor would be socialized and transformed into a wage-earning activity like other forms of work. The phalanx, said Brisbane, would emancipate women "from pecuniary dependence on man, from domestic servitude, and from a low sphere of actions," thereby ending the age-old battles of the sexes and establishing harmony at the root of society.[19]

This miniaturized world would guarantee everyone "admission to the public tables; the possession of a good apartment; changes of comfortable and genteel clothing; the privileges of using the libraries, reading rooms, baths, etc., and the right of attending concerts, festivities, the amusements of the Association, and social unions and public assemblies." While assuring a rich social life, it also would meet the need for privacy by providing families with a choice of individual apartments suited to their tastes and incomes. Under the security of these social guarantees, every person would be freed from the disturbing anxieties and selfish yearnings of conventional life to enjoy the life which God had intended for Man. Brisbane agreed with conservatives that this guaranteed security would lead to indolence so long as labor was made repugnant, but he emphasized that this would not occur in a society based on attractive industry.[20]

Little wonder, then, that he and other Associationists should believe that the Phalanx would excite the world's attention. It retained the freedom and energy of capitalism without its anarchical and brutal character. It offered the advantages of the welfare state without its inertias and restrictions. It reconciled individualism with social order and personal ambition with unity of direction. It combined a due respect for class differences with a commitment to human brotherhood. It was a well-oiled social mechanism which drew its energies from individual self-activity and the individual's search for self-fulfillment.[21]

In theory, this mechanism would not work without the prescribed minimum of 400 members and $400,000 in capital. In practice, its promised glories inspired the rash of poorly funded experiments which began with the Sylvania Association. The disciples themselves contributed to these brash beginnings by their own ambiguities regarding the size and nature of the phalanx. Officially, they declared that the phalanx had to be a completed social mechanism in order to perform its magic. "The garden of Eden was prepared before Adam was placed in it," wrote George Ripley; "and the manufacturer knows that the manufactory must be built and the machinery in order, before the operatives are introduced." On the other hand, Ripley's own Brook Farm had evolved from small beginnings out of the activity of its members. Moreover, Godwin told Americans "to adopt what *details* they please" from the Associationist scheme, while Horace Greeley described an Association as a substitute for "the smallest Social Organism above the Family" and advised his readers that it could begin with "two or three hundred" members. Even Brisbane said that "small Associations of about two hundred persons . . . can be established which will offer great advantages, as regarding economy, profit, material comfort and judicious application of labor and capital," much less than what he expected from the complete phalanx but enough to satisfy most interested Americans.[22]

These ambiguities were to afflict the North American Phalanx, the most successful and durable of the Associationist experiments. In March 1843, soon after the formation of the Sylvania Association in New York City, some upstate Fourierists formed what they called the Albany Branch of the North American Phalanx. Brisbane vacillated in his response to this project. He urged caution and briefly refused to grant the name "North American" to it; apparently, he also refused to become its head, although he had already been elected president of the model phalanx. When he finally ceded the name, however, he helped the Albany Branch find a site for its experiment near Red Bank, New Jersey. Although they were able to raise only $7000 in cash and the less than enthusiastic endorsement of the New Yorkers, the Albanians determined to push ahead and bought a rundown New Jersey farm of some 670 acres on a mortgage held by friends of the experiment.[23]

The North American Phalanx had one of the least imposing beginnings of any of the associations founded in the years between 1843 and 1845, but it had at least two long-term strengths. One was its location within 40 miles of the resources and markets of New York City, a fulfillment of Brisbane's requirement that no experiment be begun away from a major urban center. Over the first years, the North Americans were able partly to reinvigorate the soil of their wornout farm and to make it the basis for market gardening and orchardry. In New York, they found a profitable market, eventually served by two steamboats which they partly owned, for their fruits, vegetables, flour, and other products. By 1852, the total value of their production had risen to $60,000 (four times what it had been in 1846), much of it derived from their extensive milling operations. Although rarely numbering much more than one hundred members, including children, and starting with capital no more than one-fiftieth of what Brisbane believed necessary, they were able to create a viable communal economy through their collective labor.[24]

The second and more crucial advantage enjoyed by this phalanx was the character of its membership. Unlike Brook Farm, its leaders had little prestige, but they were men with some money and much practical sense. Most of the early founders and members were small business and professional men and skilled workers drawn from Albany and its surrounding towns. As members of the urban middle class, they had a variety of skills and a varied knowledge useful to the community. Although few had experience with farming, at least some brought an awareness of scientific agriculture that helped them adapt their farming operations to urban conditions. One useful skill, also evident at the Wisconsin Phalanx, was a familiarity with accounting procedures, much needed in this esentially capitalistic utopia to provide some objective understanding of its economic situation. Charles Sears, the most prominent North American, said in 1851 that most communal experiments "failed because the accounts were not clearly and faithfully kept," a conclusion that could be applied to Brook Farm, where bookkeeping seemed less a skill than an exercise in wishful-thinking.[25]

While the North American and Wisconsin phalanxes resembled each other in their business success, they differed notably in their commitments to Fourierism. The North Americans were able to combine a practical business sense with a strong devotion to the Fourierist ideal. In their general policies, they were ready to sacrifice the chance of rapid growth in order to maintain the integrity of their experiment. They were selective in admitting new members, generally requiring some proof of good character, a useful skill, and a commitment to associationism from applicants; of 59 people who applied for admission between 1847 and 1850, they admitted only 18, and this was after they had decided to expand on a controlled basis.[26] As a result of this policy, and the loss of some of their early members, they grew slowly from approximately 90 residents in 1844 to a population of no more than 150; but in the process they were able to develop a cohesive community which defied the warnings of the Shakers (whom they had consulted at the beginning) that no communal society could survive without the elimination of conventional families.[27]

Part of this cohesion stemmed from the resolution of a fundamental issue of governance. According to Charles Sears, the long-term Secretary and later historian of the North American Phalanx, its first year ended in conflict over its basic organization. Its first president, Allen Worden of Albany, favored a system of management from the top, much like that of a modern business corporation. Although this scheme was favored by some of the nonresident stockholders, the majority of members rejected it, because it "would be merely to repeat the institutions of civilization; that Association would be devoid of corporate life, would be dependent on individuals, and quite artificial."

Instead, they committed themselves to a system intended to give every individual a role in decision-making and to enable him to be "his own employer, doing that which he is best qualified by endowment to do, receiving for his labor precisely his share of the product, as nearly as can be determined." The early years also saw much internal controversy, but, rather than attempting to suppress dissent, the majority chose "free criticism and personal liberty," a policy which enabled the members to resolve most of their difficulties. These decisions did not create perfect harmony, but they did begin an important experiment in industrial democracy along Fourierist lines based on the aim of giving every member total "enfranchisement" in the whole affairs of life, economic and social as well as political.[28]

For more than a decade, they successfully practiced their Fourierist version of democracy. Although their limited numbers prevented them from attaining the radical specialization of labor envisioned by Brisbane, they did create an appropriate organization of work, dividing the whole population—men, women, and children—into seven semi-autonomous work groups responsible, respectively, for agriculture, livestock, manufacturing, the mechanic arts, education, domestic service, and entertainment and culture. Each year, the leaders of the community met to work out a general economic plan for the community and to set the goals of the various work groups; after these goals were posted, members signed themselves into those groups which had their interest, the whole operation being balanced out either by persuading members to volunteer for labor-deficient groups or by hiring outside labor. The members of each work group selected their own leaders, who met every evening to plan the next day's work.[29]

The Phalanx evolved its own version of the Fourierist wage system. With a one dollar per ten-hour workday as the standard, wages were determined for each group by the degree of necessity, usefulness, and agreeableness of its work; the actual pay of each worker in the group was then determined by his hours of work, his skill, and his contribution to capital. Wages under their system ranged in the early 1850s from sixty cents to $1.13 per day, while the average cost of food, lodging, and laundry was $2.00 per *week*. It was a matter of considerable pride to the community that the system covered all groups, including those responsible for domestic service and entertainment, a conscious policy which in particular rewarded women for their contributions to the communal welfare.[30]

The Phalanx also tried to provide its members with some freedom of choice as consumers. All wages were paid in money, eventually in scrip issued by the community, which could be used to pay room rent and to buy food and other necessities generally at cost. This system enabled the community to resolve at least one of those seemingly petty disputes that contributed to the downfall of communal experiments like the Wisconsin Phalanx. In this case, it was a dispute raised by the demands of a vegetarian minority of North Americans that the community exclude "animal-food" from its dining hall. Given the quasi-religious character of vegetarianism, this was an explosive issue particularly in a close community but it was defused when the members adopted "restaurant" dining with a menu from which each person could choose foods suited to his tastes, beliefs, and purse.[31]

The Phalanx was less successful in defusing another issue raised by the complaints of some of its members that their skills were not adequately rewarded by outside standards. Very early, its leaders discovered that they had not escaped the problem of most communal societies in attracting and holding skilled workers; this was an important factor in the failures of New Harmony and of the Wisconsin Phalanx. In 1853, the community explained its relative slowness to develop a manufacturing capability by noting that in its early years "we invested over $5,000 in buildings and machinery for mechanical purposes, and when they were ready for occupation, the men for whom they were mainly built, left us." Even their maximum wage of $1.13 per day was little more than half that paid to housepainters in nearby New York City. Eventually, the North Americans did develop some complementary industry, especially flour-milling, but their failure to meet outside wage-levels for skilled labor retarded their economic development.[32]

Community leaders like Charles Sears admitted that the Phalanx did not pay wages equal to those outside, but they also pointed out that living costs in their community were lower because of its internal economies and its ability to buy at wholesale prices which cooperation made possible.[33] They also pointed out that beyond wages workers received benefits not available outside. In their terms, the Phalanx was a "guaranty" society which guaranteed to all members the necessities of civilized life. It gave them sure employment at a just wage and supported them when they were incapacitated by sickness or old age. It provided aequate housing and a good environment for families and a good education for children. Its physical conditions were such as to lead Sears later to boast that during its 12 years only nine of some 120 to 150 members had died: "It is the lowest death rate I have ever seen recorded."[34] The Phalanx had at least in a rough form achieved the social welfare system toward which the modern world had then only begun to imagine, and had done so while respecting human individuality and personal freedom.[35]

The benefits of cooperative life provided the leaders with a justification for their refusal to meet outside wage levels, but this was not the most basic factor in their response to what they called the "class issue." To yield to the "class" system, they believed, was to give up the heart of the experiment. They had set out to create a new social order which would combine "attractive social relations, a true religious unity, a practical Christianity, and the means of unlimited growth" for the benefit of all members. Higher wages for skilled workers might promote more rapid economic growth, but wages determined by market demand rather than by the Fourierist formula would threaten the mutualistic basis of the Phalanx. Short-term gains would be at the expense of opening the way for the very "Industrial Feudalism" which Associationism was intended to replace, a feudalism, which in the anarchic society of competitive enterprises sacrificed the interests of the weak to the ambitions of the strong.[36]

The community gave some special attention to protecting the interests of women. Cooperative living and work combined with labor-saving devices (the Phalanx used the power from a small steam engine for washing, churning, and other chores) reduced domestic drudgery and, said a visitor in 1852, enabled one woman to do the work of ten women in single households. Beyond that, women were paid more equally for their work than outside, the result of a conscious effort to protect them from the wage exploitation especially common in the New York garment industry. In the 1850s, a young New England woman by the name of Mary S. Paul, who earlier had worked in the textile mills of Lowell and Manchester, explained why she was planning to join the community: "A woman gets much better pay than elsewhere. . . . There is more equality in such things according to the work not sex. You know that men often get more than double the pay for doing the same work that women do." She seems not to have been disappointed with life at the Phalanx.[37]

This commitment to equal pay for work judged equal by Fourierist standards involved something more than money. In wage equality the Associationists saw the key solution to the problem of sexual relations which was becoming increasingly troublesome in the world. To charges that Fourierism threatened conventional marital relations, they replied in 1852 that they were creating the conditions for greater harmony and unity between the sexes by endowing women with the "social position and pecuniary independence" which would give them an equal voice in determining the character of their relationships with men. The new relations would be more secure than existing ones because they would be founded on joint satisfaction and mutual consent. Although it is not possible to calculate the satisfaction of women at the North American Phalanx, it is noteworthy that, when in 1852 male members voted 50 to 4 in favor of a statement defending their system, the 11 women who voted were unanimous in supporting it.[38]

Much of this devotion to a mutuality of interest was inspired by Charles Sears, the long-term Secretary and "leading mind" of the Phalanx. Little is known of Sears, who seems to have been too busy with the practical affairs of life to leave much of a written record. A. J. Macdonald, the first student of American utopianism and a frequent visitor to the Phalanx, said simply that he was "rather tall, of a nervous temperament, the sensitive predominating, and was easy and affable." Although he was overshadowed by the disciples, he may have been the most devoted Fourierist of them all. As the leading spokesman for the Phalanx, Sears maintained that it was far more than an economic entity. "It was, in fact," he wrote in 1879, "a complete commonwealth, embracing all the interests of the state, differing only in magnitude. Indeed, it might be deemed a model state in miniature." It was a miniature commonwealth characterized by an organic unity of all interests including its weaker members, women as well as men and children as well as adults.[39]

This ideal also governed Sears' views of education. In 1852, he spoke of a "natural method" of learning which involved the young not only as pupils in school but also as wage earners in the community of work: "Commencing with the nursery, we make, through the living corporation, through adequately endowed institutions that fail not, provision for the entire life of the child, from the cradle upward; initiating him step by step, not into nominal, ostensible education apart from life, but in the real business of life, the actual production and distribution of wealth, the science of accounts and the administration of their affairs." Although this system seemingly resembles Owen's educational ideal, it differed in that it made education the province of the whole community not simply of the school, of parents as well as educators.[40] It promised not to divide children from their parents, as Owen's scheme seemingly had threatened at New Harmony, but to permanently incorporate them into the world of their fathers, a not unimportant consideration at a time when young men and women had begun to desert their parental homesteads in droves for the greater opportunities of the frontier and the city.

Neither Sears nor the other leaders believed that their "complete commonwealth" was a total success. By their own accounts, it fell far short of realizing the enormous productivity promised by the Fourierist system, and it was unable to maintain anything better than an ordinary one-room rural school house. The leaders, however, believed that they were making steady progress without the sacrifice of their basic ideals. In the early 1850s, the Phalanx was able to make some profits and to increase its wage levels. Also, it was able to expand both its productive base and its living quarters to accommodate an enlarged population. According to A. J. Macdonald, Sears in 1853 "was of the opinion that in five years they would be able to show something tangible to the world." The year before, young Frederick Law Olmsted said that a visit to the Phalanx had convinced him that "the advantages of cooperation are manifestly great, the saving of labor immense, the cheapening of food, rent, etc. enough to make starvation into abundance."[41]

Certainly, the North American Phalanx was worthy of public attention. As a developing effort to create a guarantee society in the mutual interest of all its members, it was becoming a significant social laboratory which had great potential importance for the larger society. It was perhaps the most important social experiment, the most productive of social good, ever initiated in the United States, one deserving of support from all those who dreamed the cooperative dream. And yet in less than three years after Sears had made his prediction, this one surviving star in the Fourierist firmament had been extinguished and with little protest or regret even among its supposed friends.

There were several immediate causes of this failure, but the basic cause lay in the ambiguous relationship which had developed between the Phalanx and the leaders of the Fourierist movement outside. That relationship was much like the one which had existed between early Brook Farm and its "friends" in New England. When it suited their interests, Fourierists like Brisbane treated the community as a nice place to spend a summer weekend and as an object of occasional pride. Horace Greeley reportedly said that he would rather be president of the North American Phalanx than President of the United States—a remark he may have remembered in 1872 when he was humiliatingly defeated for the presidency by Ulysses S. Grant. Greeley and a few other New Yorkers had bought much of the Phalanx stock and so had contributed to its capital, but this was hardly an act of charity, since they received a 5 percent dividend on their holdings. During its first four years, the Phalanx paid out over $4,000 in dividends.[42]

With the exception of Greeley, however, Fourierist leaders did not take the Phalanx seriously. Although the North Americans named the highest rise on their farm "Brisbane Hill," they seem to have received even less support from the chief disciple than he gave to Brook Farm; he was later to say that they were destined to fail, because their experiment was "without ideality." Generally, they received little tangible aid. At least until the demise of Brook Farm, they were left alone to work out the problems of creating a community. This had its positive side, since their efforts helped develop a sense of unity and identity which contributed to their success; relative neglect means relative freedom from outside meddling in their affairs. However, they were frustrated in their plans for expansion and threatened with stagnation in somewhat the same way that Ripley had been at Brook Farm in 1843.[43] Like Ripley, they came to the conclusion that they would have to appeal to the national movement for money if their social experiment were to continue.

In 1847, they stated their case in the *Harbinger* to "the Friends of Social Re-organization." They said that even with their limited numbers and resources they had satisfied themselves of "the possibility of Harmony in Association." They were sensitive about their disappointing size and made some effort to justify their experiment on its own terms: "Our views are that true Divine growth of the Social as of the individual man is the Progressive Development of a Germ: and while we would not in the slightest degree oppose a scientific organization upon a large scale, it is our preference to pursue a more progressive mode, to make a more immediately practical and controllable attempt." In order to advance that progress, they asked their "friends" for $10,000 to build a phalanstery for at least 300 people and for $15,000 to expand their economy. Even though they numbered only 65 residents and 30 nonresident stockholders, they assured their friends that $25,000 invested in an expanded phalanx would be a safe investment, since the estimated value of their assets was almost three times their debts.[44]

Their appeal initially had little effect. In 1847, the disciples were attempting to rebound from the failure of Brook Farm and other disasters by reinvigorating their national campaign. At the annual meeting of the American Union in May, Edward Giles, a New York Fourierist, did propose that the Union support at least one of the surviving phalanxes (the North American, the Trumbull, or the Wisconsin), but this evoked an "animated discussion" and the subject was referred to a committee which reported a recommendation that the subject be deferred until the next annual meeting.

Eventually, however, Greeley and some other New York Fourierists began to recognize that the North American was the last if not the best hope of the course. In early 1848, they formed the Phalansterian Realization Fund Society to raise up to $35,000 in loans for its support. Typically, the first aim of the New Yorkers was to provide money for the construction of a grand phalanstery suited to their idea of phalanx life, but the more practical sense of the North Americans prevailed. Eventually, they received $5900 in loans, $2000 for a phalanstery, and the rest for more productive improvements. With the help of the New Yorkers, they were also able to legally reorganize themselves in 1852 as a corporation, a step which they hoped would enable them to raise capital for further expansion. By the fall of 1852, they had increased their capital stock from $18,000 (in 1844) to approximately $60,000.[45]

The first result of these developments was a quickening of activity. In 1851, the North Americans completed their new 85-room Edifice, which was described by one observer as appearing to be "but a wing of a more extensive design, intended to be carried out at some future time." Whatever its place in the future, the new building with its steam heat and gas lighting provided comfortable accommodations, suited to varied tastes and incomes, both for themselves and for the new members whom they now planned to receive. It contained a large public hall which could accommodate 200 people at dinner; the new space and facilities enabled them to establish their "restaurant" mode of communal dining and to lessen the burdens of women. In appropriate phalansterian style, a covered walkway connected it with some of the other buildings in which some of the members continued to live and work. While the phalanstery contained ample social space for communal life, it also met at least some of the need for privacy by providing individual rooms and family apartments; members could also build their own homes on the "Cottage Plain" away from the new complex.[46]

With the new money, the North Americans were also eventually able to construct new mill facilities and to expand their milling operations; it was apparently at this time that they began to market what has been called the first boxed cereal in America. By 1853, they could claim that since their early years they had quadrupled their annual production and increased their net earnings nearly six times.[47]

Progress, however, also meant perilous new entanglements with the outside world. Expansion brought new members who, whatever their devotion to the ideal, did not have the sense of community which had developed among the pioneers. At least three had come from failed phalanxes elsewhere and two from other cooperative experiments, each bringing with them their own ideas regarding cooperation. John Gray, for instance, had spent five years with the Shakers; he enjoyed the greater freedom of phalanx life but complained of the relatively low wages for his skills as a cloth-dyer. Gray soon tried the "old" conventional society outside, found it not to his liking, and returned to the North American with greater appreciation of its life but probably with little better understanding of its ideals.[48]

Progress also made the community more vulnerable to outside stresses. Much of the new activity was a reflection of the larger prosperity that had begun in the United States with the California gold rush. Inevitably, the economic expansion of the Phalanx involved it in a world of rising material expectations. According to Joshua K. Ingalls, a critic of Fourierism, these expectations affected some of the stockholders in the Phalanx. On the basis of some comments which he had heard made by one of them in 1853, Ingalls later charged that they desired the stock in the North American "boomed by declaring large dividends," a concession to capitalism which he believed had assured the failure of the experiment.[49]

A more immediate problem grew out of the fact that its expanded operations increased its dependence on skilled labor. After several years of relative calm regarding the "class issue," leaders again were confronted with wage complaints from skilled workers, and again they refused to recognize this class interest. Tensions increased further when the Phalanx had to decide on a site for its new mill. Initially, the majority decided to locate the mill away from the phalanstery at nearby Red Bank in order to reduce the costs of transportation in their milling operations, but this decision was reversed by Charles Sears, who had been away when it was made, on the grounds that it would separate the mill from the community.[50] Sears' apparently dictatorial use of his authority and his preference for communal unity over economic advantage intensified resentments at a time when the community had also to confront another problem from outside, an increasing disposition of its "friends" to meddle in its affairs.

The Phalanx's particular problem was one of its oldest benefactors and largest nonresident stockholder, Marcus Spring. A wealthy New York merchant, Spring had increased his holdings in its stock to $6000 by the early 1850s and was also the leading figure in the Phalansterian Realization Fund. Although he built a summer house on the property, Spring kept himself separate from the community and its ideals. He seems to have been relatively satisfied with its economic progress, but he grew dissatisfied with what he and some other friends saw as its cultural and spiritual failures. By the late 1840s, Spring had fallen under the influence of William Henry Channing who was attempting to harness what remained of the national movement to his hopes for a new church of unity. Concluding that the North American had sacrificed spirituality to materialism, both men intended to introduce religion into what seemed to be an agnostic community; they would give a soul to the material body which the community had built and so would animate that body to new powers.[51]

Sears and other members, however, resisted these well-intended concerns on the grounds that whatever the benefits of formal religion to other communities it would be a poison to theirs; many of them were free-thinkers, Swedenborgians, Universalists, and other cultural dissenters at war with the world's orthodoxies. Some had convinced themselves that life at the Phalanx was a form of practical Christianity that orthodox religion had neglected to practice, a point made by a former clergyman: "Here is the true church of Christ's gospel, and in this way it must be that the Kingdom must come." Having founded their community on a public neutrality regarding what they viewed as private beliefs, they warned that to introduce "sectarianism" of any sort would serve only to admit the world's troubling ways into their experiment.[52]

The religious question, however, was internalized when in 1849 the community accepted Spring's brother-in-law, George Arnold, as a member. Arnold was a Unitarian minister, but he came highly recommended for his agricultural skills and in 1850 was elected president of the Phalanx. Arnold probably was responsible for the appearance of religious missionaries at the North American whose efforts to make converts angered Sears and other free-thinkers; this resistance in turn angered Spring, and in 1852 he persuaded Arnold and some 30 other members to join a new community which he had decided to form at Perth Amboy, New Jersey.[53]

Spring's new Raritan Bay Union got off to a fast start in part because it was able to sop up most of what little money there was for social experimentation. It succeeded in raising $40,000, a sum which the North Americans had never been able to get, most of which was used to build a grand edifice 250 feet long. The Union committed itself to achieving the "higher" forms of industry, education, and social life that critics found absent in the North American. It did succeed in attracting people of education and culture, including the painters George Inness and William Page and the abolitionist-educator, Theodore Weld, who opened a private school in one wing of the building.[54] As a social experiment, however, the Raritan Bay Union was a dead end. Lacking both the unity and the ideological commitments of the North Americans, it failed to develop as a community, and by 1855 Spring had begun to lay out its property for suburban real-estate development with the help of Henry Thoreau as a surveyor.[55]

Spring's benevolent meddling cost the North American about one-quarter of its membership and the loss of possible new capital. Moreover, it further embarrassed the relationship between the North Americans and their few remaining friends. The common impression seems to have been that the Phalanx had achieved economic success at the expense of the higher ideals of Fourierism. One visitor declared that "the labor of the members is well remunerated and both sexes stood upon a footing of perfect equality," only to conclude with a denunciation of the North Americans for the inadequacy of their library and for allowing cigar smoking even among boys. In 1853, a correspondent for the *New York Tribune* rendered the judgment that the Phalanx had sold its soul for the "mere gratification of the animal appetites," and concluded that it was a total failure: "There must be intellectual and spiritual life and progress; no matter can move itself."[56]

The North Americans rallied to defend themselves. When Greeley, one of the largest stockholders, began to question their achievements, they issued a long public statement in which they detailed their accomplishment and called for added support as well. What they needed, they said, was neither good advice nor critical judgment but $65,000, part of which they earmarked for educational purposes.[57] In the course of their defense, they issued a final challenge to their friends:

When we first took interest in the Social Movement, we supposed that there was an organization of wise, experienced men, who had the command of means, and were devoted to the idea of

Social Reform, and who were ready and willing to work for an idea, as men usually work for their private interests; and in this particular we have been more greatly disappointed then in any other, respecting the movement. Concerning measures, we have not greatly misjudged, but men have failed us constantly.[58]

They did not evoke the support which they wanted, but they were able to complete their new mill, using hired immigrant labor when necessary, and to attract new members. One of the newcomers was the New England factory woman, Mary S. Paul, who joined the Phalanx in 1854 in the hope of finding fair treatment for her sex. She was not disappointed. During her first year there, she enjoyed its general conditions of life as well as the freedom to choose the kind of work which best suited her: "Life here has many attractions which no other life can have, and imperfect as it is I have already seen enough to convince me that Association is the true life." Yet, in writing this opinion to her father, she also warned that in less than a year the experiment would be terminated and she and other members thrust back into the world.[59]

What indeed had looked like a self-generated communal reinvigoration in 1854 became a mortal illness a year later as a result of a series of events which the North American could not control. The cruelest blow came in September 1854 when their large new mill burned to the ground, and with it went some $3000 in grain which they had purchased on credit from neighboring farmers, adding a new debt to that acquired for the construction of the mill. In itself, the fire was less devastating than the one at Brook Farm eight years before, since the North Americans had a more viable economy and also had taken the trouble to insure their property. The winter of 1854–55, however, brought a short but deep depression that virtually paralyzed the economy of New York City and its surrounding areas. The results were the bankruptcy of the company that had insured the mill and also pressures from some of the stockholders to liquidate the experiment.[60]

During that winter, Sears and other leaders made a desperate effort to find the money they needed, even offering to sell the still undeveloped half of their farm to the Shakers, but the Shakers, normally habitual land-buyers, refused. Although Greeley reputedly was ready to lend them what they needed, the leaders finally concluded that they had reached the end. By their accounting, to survive meant accumulating a total debt of $42,000, which at prevailing interest rates would be met only by diverting most of their income to creditors. Moreover, they could not agree on where to rebuild their new mill, raising once again an issue that involved the essential character of the experiment. They might still have gone on if they had confidence in their friends, but for years they had struggled against adversity with little financial and even moral support from the national movement. They had given their all to maintain the integrity of the experiment, and now they had little energy or will left to cope with their greatest crisis. To make matters even worse, they had to compete for attention with a new project headed by Brisbane and by Victor Considerant, the leader of French Fourierism, to establish a cooperative colony in Texas.[61]

In 1855, therefore, the community and its creditors agreed to liquidate the Phalanx, and to sell off its lands in parcels ranging from 150-acre farms to 5-acre plots. By 1856, the property had been sold at auction for about $80,000, enough to pay all debts and to return to stockholders, by Sears' calculation, 57 percent of their investment.[62] Most of the members either dispersed into the general population or went to Considerant's Reunion Colony in Texas, but at least a few bought portions of the property and remained on the old domain. The buildings and part of the land were acquired by the Bucklin family, members of the Phalanx, who for many years operated a canning business there; the cannery continued to give life to the old domain, which was described twenty years after the dissolution as consisting of "still well-cultivated fields and thrifty gardens."[63]

In the 1870s, the Bucklins put a new roof on the Phalanstery, whose rooms they rented to various tenants; it was in this rambling building that Alexander Woollcott, the author and humorist, was born in 1887. Over the years, the area changed and decayed. By 1938 all that remained was a small hamlet called "Phalanx" and the rotting old building. Eventually, a few persons awoke to the historical significance of this last remaining artifact of the Fourierist movement, and in the early 1970s an effort was made to raise money for its restoration. Before anything could be accomplished, however, the building was burned to the ground, the victim of apparent arson.[64] And so in New Jersey the last ember of a once glowing dream flared up and went out. Aside from the North American Phalanx, though, there was at least one more chapter in the history of American Fourierism, a chapter which was to cover most of the last half of the nineteenth century.

VIII

A Twilight Long Gleaming

Even after the death of the North American Phalanx in the mid-1850s, traces of Fourierism lingered on for many years. In the spring of 1855, as she prepared to leave the North American, Mary Paul wrote to her father in New England: "I know many will exalt in the downfall of this place, but each are shortsighted. Charles Fourier's doctrines, although they contain many absurd ideas, have enough of truth in them to keep them alive until the world shall be ready for them." The year-and-a-half experience of this bright ex-factory girl at the Phalanx was enlightening and deeply satisfying, one which she was not likely to forget; but it was also one which she would not repeat. By 1856, she had returned to New England, eventually to marry, to become a mother, and to experience all the joys and pains of single-family, nonunitary living.[1] As Mrs. Mary P. Gould, she disappeared from the record without divulging her secret dreams and hopes.

Undoubtedly, many of the others who participated in the thirty-odd phalanxes established after 1842 carried a fragment of the Fourierist dream with them when they dispersed into the general population, but for most of them, like Mary Paul, it was the dream of an irretrievable past. There were, though, some exceptions like the Longley brothers of

Cincinnati. That city had been a stronghold of social and of cultural dissent since the days of Owenism. In 1844 a group of Cincinnatians had established the Clermont Phalanx on a "splendid domain" along the Ohio River 30 miles above the city.[2] The Clermont disbanded two years later with the loss of much enthusiasm for Association, but the cause was carried on by Elias Longley, the recording secretary of the Cincinnati auxiliary of the American Union and, later, the editor of *Type of the Times*, a journal devoted to social reform. In the mid-1850s, he was joined by his younger brother, Alcander Longley, who had been a member of the North American Phalanx. In late 1857, Alcander began the publication of the monthly *Phalansterian Record* from his brother's printing office with the aim of revitalizing Fourierism.[3]

Longley's objective was to establish a "Fourier Phalansterian School," which he described as an "Integral School of Science and Art," where some 500 people would gather to learn the theory and practice of Fourierism. This was to be the germ from which he expected a successful phalanx to grow — if only he could persuade enough people to initiate it. Early in 1858, he announced that he had purchased "the nucleus of a domain" in the form of a 220-acre farm in southern Indiana. By the summer, however, he was forced to drop the project "for want of means" and both the School and the *Phalansterian Record* soon vanished. Alcander Longley, though, had merely begun what was to be a half-century of effort to create a cooperative community in some form, ultimately to set something like a world's record for the number (at least six) of attempted communities.[4]

Such efforts to revive the phalanx movement provide only a crude measure of the continued influence of Fourierism into the 1850s and later. In radical circles, it survived as a social science and possible basis for organic social reform. At least for a short time in 1858, it was given a new voice in Longley's paper and also in *The Movement*, a weekly started in New York City by John Allen; Allen, a former Universalist preacher, had served as the last lecturer of the American Union. *The Movement* was founded with the hope "that a great socialistic revolution is brewing, and soon to be developed," but its own future apparently was very short, since less than six months later Allen died in Iowa at the age of 42.[5] A more enduring support for Fourierist science came from the first disciple, Albert Brisbane. Although Brisbane had partly withdrawn from the propaganda campaign in the 1840s, he remained active enough in the next decade not only to lend his support to a new Fourierist project in Texas but also to be arrested by the New York police in 1855, when they raided a meeting of social radicals he was attending. Over the next thirty years, he continued to argue in various writings and speeches the superiority of Fourierist science over what he viewed as the superficialities of "modern scientific speculation."[6]

The broad influence of Fourierism on American thought and imagination during these decades was hardly pervasive, but it did have some significant effect particularly within the culture of dissent. Whatever its limitations, the Associationist campaign in the 1840s had touched the dreams and ambitions of many people. Probably more than a few Americans agreed with Thomas Low Nichols when he said that, while the phalansterian system was not made for this world, "no one can read Fourier without being fascinated with its beauty, splendor and apparent practicality."[7] Although it failed even to dent the obdurate orthodoxies of its times, Fourierism did make itself the key impulse for the notable broadening and deepening of the dissenting culture which occurred in the middle of the nineteenth century; in this way, it at least indirectly influenced the rich variety of radicalisms spawned by that culture during the second half of the century.

It was, for instance, a factor in the explosion of heterodox religious sentiment which took place after 1830. In itself, it appealed to those who, like the disciples, hungered for some faith to replace what they saw as the spiritually and intellectually arid religion of their times. Many of its advocates also discovered a natural affinity between it and Swedenborgianism, the most intellectually respectable of the heterodox faiths that were appearing around them. Emmanual Swedenborg, the eighteenth century scientist and mystic, became the favorite theologian and philosopher of the *Harbinger,* in part because he depicted a heaven organized on principles much like those of Fourier. It was apparently the example of the Swedenborgian New Church that inspired the effort of men like Channing and Dwight to make Fourierism the basis for a "Church of Humanity."[8]

In spreading Swedenborg's spiritualistic ideas, Fourierism contributed to the explosive growth of Modern Spiritualism, which by the 1850s affected the thought and imagination of millions of Americans; Warren Chase, a leader of the Wisconsin Phalanx, later became one of the most influential exponents of the Spiritualist theology.[9] Out of this general spiritualistic ferment, in turn, would develop such cult communities as Thomas Lake Harris' Brocton Community, which had at least vague Fourierist overtones; as a young New York minister, Harris had been a delegate in 1847 to the convention of the American Union of Associationists.[10]

Fourierism also contributed to the stew of heterodox ideas regarding sexual relations which had begun to boil by the 1850s. Although the disciples downplayed Fourier's "French" sexual ideas, their emphasis on passional attraction and on greater freedom for women did challenge sexual conventions. Moreover, what they were unwilling to do, their enemies accomplished by attacking Fourier's doctrines as a threat to marital and family relationships. In 1846, for instance, the New York *Courier and Enquirer* maneuvered Greeley's *Tribune* into a debate over Fourier's sexual ideas which called public attention to them. Many people recoiled in horror at Fourier's "immorality," but others—especially cultural dissenters—were encouraged to challenge sexual conventions. The mating of Fourier's theory of passional attraction and Spiritualism was the chief source of the doctrine of "free love" that became conspicuous in the culture of dissent by the early 1850s.[11]

The British positivist Henry Edgar, who had spent five months at the North American Phalanx, said in 1854 that Fourierism had spread more widely in the United States than elsewhere and that the number of those affected by "the passional theory is very great. The principal elements of it have been promulgated in various forms throughout certain classes. Popular acceptance it has certainly not met—it could never meet. But the anti-domestic notions involved cropped out in all directions and in various forms."[12] One influence for these notions was Brisbane, who was alleged to be the "chief" of a secret Free Love League in New York. Whatever the truth of this allegation, Brisbane did end his *Treatise on the Human Passions* with a lengthy chapter on "amatory relations" where he described a future phalansterian world which provided for "the full, free, natural, and harmonious development of Love in all its shades or varieties" and guaranteed to women the "liberties of self-possession" they needed to achieve conjugal equality with men.[13] Much of this kind of sexual radicalism was later suppressed by a conservative backlash, but some of it survived to influence the twentieth century.

Associationism also introduced into American culture Fourier's fantasies of peacetime armies that would perform heroic acts of constructive work. In his *A Popular View of the Doctrine of Charles Fourier,* Godwin described great "Industrial Armies," formed from the eager workers of many phalanxes, which "will render Humanity more and more the Master of the Globe," able to reclaim deserts, swamps, and polar icefields for human use and eventually to control the earth's climate: "The union of bodies, taken from different countries, and each executing its tasks according to the methods of its own engineers, will excite a powerful emulation. They will engage in veritable industrial battles, and their triumphs, celebrated with pomp, will resound over the whole earth. The labors of industrial armies will be accompanyed by greater glory than ever attended the labor of warriors." In 1848, under the heading "Industrial Armies," Godwin gave his editorial praise in the *Harbinger* to the plan of Louis Blanc in France to organize the unemployed into a great working army intended to produce rather than to destroy.[14]

Brisbane also envisioned Industrial Armies which would conquer nature in the accomplishment of the Fourierist millennium. It was apparently this vision which inspired a scheme (published in 1858) for the organization somewhere in the West of a "Levianthan Farm" whose 200,000 acres were to be tilled by "two rivalized establishments, with military organization of labor, gigantic machinery to plow, plant, reap and render harvests." This scheme, devised in response to the unemployment caused by the Panic of 1857, was to provide the world with a model "Industrial Commonwealth" based on associationist principles.[15] The influence of such visions was not great, but they helped prepare the way for Edward Bellamy and others who popularized the idea of industrial armies in the last decades of the century.

On a more practical plane, the Fourierists also helped teach Americans the virtues and techniques of cooperative organization. Godwin and Greeley, for instance, urged workers to form cooperative building associations to enable them to buy their own homes, thus helping to introduce a form of association which eventually would evolve into savings and loan associations. In 1846 and later, the *Harbinger* suggested that the affiliated societies of the American Union advance the cause of guaranteeism by forming cooperative stores to reduce the price of necessities and also other kinds of cooperative ventures to provide themselves with "guarantees of aid in sickness, of intellectual and educational privileges, in reading-rooms, classes, etc."[16] The failure of the affiliated societies prevented a test of this idea, but in 1858, a Fourierist proposed that workers form "industrial clubs or fractional Phalanxes" to furnish themselves with jobs under their control. In helping to introduce the idea of producer-consumer cooperatives, the Associationists made at least a modest contribution to a tradition which over the next half century emphasized various forms of worker cooperatives over wages-and-hours oriented unionism.[17]

Fourierism had a more evident influence on one form of cooperation that caught the special attention of young professional men and women, the Unitary Household, a scaled down version of the Phalanstery. In 1846, John S. Dwight proposed that the affiliated societies each form "an Associative club-house" in which their members could evolve cooperative living arrangements that would assure them of some of the economies of the Phalanstery.[18] A decade later, the idea became reality in New York City when Stephen Pearl Andrews and Edward F. Underhill founded their Unitary Home. This was a nonprofit cooperative residential hotel designed to provide the benefits of, in the words of Underhill, its manager, "the wholesale purchase for cash; the cooperation of numbers, the use of machinery, and the guarantee of mutual security between cooperator and manager." Residents paid rents based on the size and location of their particular rooms plus a portion of the costs entailed by a common parlor, dining room, nursery, and other communal facilities.[19]

The Unitary Home was so successful that by 1858 it had grown to include a block of four row houses and about 100 residents, many of them young professionals who were attempting to establish themselves in the city. One member was the later poet and literary scholar, Edmund Clarence Stedman, who spent over a year there with his wife. He recalled that it was possible to eat "a banquet of five courses" in the communal dining hall for 30 cents and to live in some style in expensive New York for $5.00 a week, enjoying both privacy and an active social life including twice-a-week "refined dance-receptions" in their exclusive little world. Occasionally during the summer, the inhabitants visited the property of the recently defunct North American Phalanx, where they ate in its dining-hall and enjoyed the landscaped grounds of this "modern Eden." Forty years later, Stedman was to remember its "economy of cooperation" as one aspect of Fourierism at least that had use for the twentieth century.[20]

He left this collective household in 1859, however, and a year later the experiment was terminated. Underhill explained that he lacked the money required to expand it to a size large enough to "admit of its properly remunerating him for his time," but it also seems to have suffered from public suspicions that it was a den of free-lovers and other sinners. In 1860, the New York *Times* published a charge that residents of the House had abandoned it when "the leading spirits of the enterprise were detected in evil practices" ranging from "unblushing adultery" to the seduction of children.[21]

Whatever the truth of this accusation, the idea of the Unitary Household survived. In the mid-1870s, for instance, Joel A. Ellis and some 30 others formed a "family" in a cooperative home at Springfield, Vermont. Ellis dreamed of even larger homes where "from three to five hundred persons live together in comfort and plenty, and where they are furnished with constant and profitable employment." He argued that the evident economies and efficiencies of "large Unitary Homes" made them practical business propositions sure to generate ample profits from the $50,000 which he estimated could build a Unitary Home for 100 people. With the advantages of collective housekeeping, cooperative labor, and the use of machinery, the Home would reduce the costs of living almost by half. With typical booster optimism, Ellis predicted that one fully funded effort would start a rush to build cooperative homes that would "soon absorb all the working people and capital in the country," eventually sixty billion dollars in capital and over a hundred million people.[22]

If Ellis's Unitary Home displayed the booster side of Fourierism, another Unitary scheme reflected the Fourierist concern with liberating women and with liberalizing relations between the sexes. In 1868, Melusina Fay Peirce, the wife of the philosopher and scientist Charles S. Peirce, observed that modern women like herself had come to loath the burdens of housekeeping "more and more every day." Melusina Peirce's remedy was to take these responsibilities out of the individual household and to turn them into a business in the form of a "Cooperative Housekeeping Society" run by women. Essentially, the society was like the Fourierist domestic series extracted from its phalansterian setting. The individual household would be preserved, and collective housekeeping would be incorporated as a distinct institution which would self domestic services to the separate households. Peirce dreamed of a well-organized association whose cooperative kitchen department would supply meals to member households, whose clothing department would supply the clothes, and whose laundry department would take care of the laundry—all "for cash on delivery." In this way, women could create profitable vocations for themselves in harmony with their own talents and also eliminate the hated kitchen from their private homes and lives.[23]

Peirce predicted that the Society, benefiting from the economies of cooperative work, would soon take over most of the retail clothing trade and would also expand into new areas, developing charitable and health departments and providing places for women lawyers, doctors, and journalists to practice their skills. Independence and wealth would soon enable women to develop their talents in the arts and literature, thereby making a new "feminine civilization" parallel to that of men. By separating "the hitherto jumbled interests and responsibilities of the two sexes," cooperative housekeeping would eventuate in "a splendid society, presided over by ladies famous for their beauty, their wit, or their tact, where every graceful element of human achievement may have free play, and every kindly impulse of human feeling full encouragement." Society and sexual relations thus could be revolutionized, if women would only begin the work by forming their first cooperative association to take advantage of big-house efficiencies.[24]

In 1869, Peirce began a housekeeping society which rented a house, elected officers, and began a laundry business, but it did not get enough partronage from member households to make it profitable, and less than two years later the house was closed. For Peirce, the experiment failed because men had discourged their wives from participating, another abuse of that "HUSBAND-POWER which is very apt to shut down like an invisible bell-glass over every woman as soon as she is married." Defeated but undaunted, she continued at least sporadically to pursue her dream; as late as 1918, she advocated the idea of "national housekeeping" as a solution to women's frustrations.[25]

All of these unitary schemes were at best only the bits and pieces of a broken dream. The hopes for a regenerated world of integral phalanxes had died with the national movement. By the early 1850s, most of the disciples had abandoned what was evidently a failed crusade and had focused their talents and energies on more rewarding pursuits. "As to those who constituted the *avant guard* in propagandism thirty years ago," said Brisbane in 1877, "they naturally fell away when the direct practical object they had in view was demonstrated to be impossible."[26] Dana, Dwight, Ripley, and Godwin along with Greeley became successful journalists while Channing became a distinguished cleric, eventually being chosen chaplain of the United States House of Representatives.

Only Brisbane himself, abetted by his wealth, spent his life on the cause, but he, too, showed some signs of weariness. In the mid-1850s, he supported the efforts of Victor Considerant, the French Fourierist, to establish a "Europeo-American" colony in Dallas County, Texas, even though this Reunion Colony was no model phalanx, being intended simply "to bring together the social elements most favorable to associate life under conditions of perfect freedom and leave them to assume their *natural forms.*" The scheme, originally conceived by Considerant as refuge from the tyranny of Louis Napoleon, excited some hopes among American social radicals for a new movement toward a cooperative order. In 1855, a "Texas Emigration Union" was formed, and it was rumored that the North American Phalanx was to be made "a branch of the Texas movement."[27] Despite predictions that thousands of Europeans and Americans would soon gather in North Texas, however, the Reunion Colony failed; its most notable effect was to assure the termination of the North American Phalanx.

These twin failures provided a formal end for a movement which had already died. After 1856, what was left of it was drawn into the conflict over slavery. Greeley, Ripley, Godwin, and Dana all supported the Republican party and, then, the Union cause in the Civil War. As journalists, Godwin and Greeley helped transform the war to restore national unity into a war to free the slaves, while Dana became a major influence for the organization of the Union military machine, first as a special military commissioner and then as a member of the War Department.[28] For more than a decade, the attack on "the Slave Power" overshadowed organic social reform.

After the War, however, Fourierism experienced a modest revival, in part because of the publicity given it by its most persistent critic, John Humphrey Noyes. Noyes belonged to the same generation of social radicals as the disciples. In the 1840s, while they were attempting to convert the nation, he was forming his small sect of Perfectionists into a successful community. Under a system of religious communism, his Oneida Community had, by the 1860s, achieved a level of material prosperity and social which approximated the Fourierist dream. On the basis of this success, he ridiculed Brisbane's claim that Fourierism was a science. Any true science, said Noyes, had to stand on empirical and experimental grounds, and plainly Brisbane's theories had come "from the closet and not from the world of facts." Whatever the value of Fourierist intentions, "we do not expect to get a *working* theory of social reorganization from men who do their thinking without experiment."[29] In contrast, successful religious communities like Oneida had passed the test of experience and had demonstrated that religious devotion was an essential ingredient of any practical social science.

Noyes, however, also was drawn to Fourierism as the dominant secular form of cooperative society. In 1853, he declared that religious faith was a far greater force for cooperative union than the passional attraction of Fourierism, but he added that "we expect . . . to learn many things about externals from Fourier." During the troubled decade that followed the Civil War, he conceived the idea of forming a coalition of Fourierists and other radical idealists under his influence and in 1870 began to implement the idea by publishing his *History of American Socialism.*

This book, which has enduring historical value, was in itself a reflection of the connections among forms of radical idealism. As Noyes took care to note, part of it derived from materials collected before the Civil War by A. J. Macdonald for a book on American communitarianism. Macdonald, who migrated from Scotland in 1842, was an Owenite by enthusiasm, but his enthusiasm had dimmed over the years. He died in 1854, before he could complete his book—one of the many victims of a cholera epidemic. Eventually, his materials fell into the possession of Noyes, who used them in a way suited to his objectives.[30] Noyes omitted the material relating to "colonies of foreigners" such as the Harmonists and added much new material, particularly regarding the phalanxes, with the aim of making his book a history of the American "national experience." His general objective was to demonstrate that socialism, the ideal of cooperative society, was in its varied forms thoroughly American in its origins and relationships.[31]

Six years after the publication of his *History of American Socialisms,* he extended this strategy by transforming his house organ, the *Oneida Circular,* into a new weekly, the *American Socialist,* which he intended to make into a great national newspaper dedicated to all forms of cooperative society. Over the next three years, he and his associate editor, William Alfred Hines, attempted to make the new journal "the largest and best Socialistic paper in the world" dedicated to publicizing every kind of American cooperative endeavor in order to encourage what he took to be a renewed interest in socialism: "The final practico-Socialistic organization of society, it seems to us, is to come, like a great railroad system, out of *American* thinking carried on in connection with a vast system of American experiments."[32] He had little doubt that this socialistic railroad would eventually take Americans to Oneida communism.

This strategy, instead, proved to be a disaster for Noyes and his form of American communism. The time and attention dedicated to the new cause was at the expense of his role as the leader of the Oneida Community, a critical factor in the startling collapse of that thriving community in 1879. His work, however, was a boon for radical social idealism in general and for Fourierism in particular. More than half of his *History* was devoted to the Fourierist movement and to the various phalanxes. In the *American Socialist,* he published extensive selections from the writings of "the Old Guard of Socialists," especially the Fourierists, and allowed Brisbane to air some of his current thinking.[33] Although this publicity was less than that generated by the propaganda campaign of the 1840s, it did help revive some interest in Fourierist theory and practice among the sympathetic.

Nothing like a new national movement developed, but it is worth noting that in April 1879 some 60 people gathered in Boston to celebrate Fourier's 107th birthday with a toast: "An organized, redeemed and harmonious Society will yet do honor to the great discoverer of the fundamental laws of a *True* Social Order." As late as 1895, Dana in a long lecture on Brook Farm at the University of Michigan, could sympathetically summarize Fourier's doctrines and then say that future generations might have "reason to thank the infinite Father for conferring upon His children the manifold blessings of industrial attraction and passional harmony."[34] And the Fourierist revival was not confined to words, since it was accompanied by a modest new round of actual effort in part inspired by Horace Greeley.

Greeley never had much enthusiasm for, or understanding of, Fourierist theory, but he did have a deep interest in Association as an instrument of social reform.[35] In his *Recollections of a Busy Life* (1868), he condemned the social anarchy of individualism and expressed the hope that Association would eventually prevail: "Our dwellings, our fields, our farms, our industries, all tend to belittle us; the edifice which will yet lodge commodiously and agreeably two thousand persons, giving each requisite privacy and independence, though as yet unconducted, is not a chimera; no more is the prosecution of agricultural and other labor by large bands, rendered picturesque by uniforms, and inspired by music . . . ; it shall yet be proved that the combined efforts of many workers make labor efficient and enobling, all things tend unconsciously toward grand, comprehensive, pervading reforms."[36] Greeley himself avoided anything like a grand association, with or without uniforms and music, but he did commit himself to one of the more successful experiments in cooperation during the century.

The prime mover in this project was another veteran of the phalanx period, Nathan C. Meeker, who had been a leading member of the Trumbull Phalanx established in eastern Ohio by a group from Pittsburgh. With some 250 members, the Trumbull Phalanx was perhaps the largest of the phalanxes and one of the more successful; it survived for four years and might have survived longer, according to Meeker and other members, if the area had not been a prolific breeder of "fever and ague."[37] This experience left Meeker with little faith in the guaranty side of phalansterian life, since an unusually high proportion of sickly, disabled, and indolent members had been a heavy weight on the fledgling experiment; he was later to say that, because people were "given to laziness and cheating," no form of socialism would work without a strong despotic leader and a dominant religious idea to compel its members to work for the common good. On the other hand, he retained a strong enthusiasm for cooperation as a way by which people like himself could satisfy their needs and ambitions. In 1866, he said regarding the North American Phalanx that "to this day do members, and particularly women look back to that period as the happiest in their lives."[38] It was a beautiful dream that had failed, but he hoped to repeat it in a more modest and enduring form.

Eventually, Meeker became the agricultural editor for the *Tribune,* and in the late 1860s he persuaded Greeley to back a scheme to establish a cooperative colony in the wide open spaces of northern Colorado. Twenty years before, Greeley himself had proposed that an association be formed in the East for the purpose of creating a civilized settlement on the frontier. In 1858, a New Englander used the idea to promote a

scheme for his "Exodus Colony" to be established in Iowa. Industrialization and the hordes of European immigrants in the East, he said, had
made it "the 'manifest destiny' of our eastern people" to settle in the
West, but there would be great inconvenience and possible dangers in
individual settlement. It was far better to form associations to colonize
the frontier: "The great idea of this movement is to transplant New
England institutions with the emigrant, so that we may have the advantages of the East, combined with those of the West."[39] After the Civil
War, this new version of an old Puritan idea inspired a wide variety of
colonizing efforts, beginning with Meeker's Colorado plan.

His basic idea was to form a land-purchase cooperative through
which easterners could amass sufficient capital to buy and to irrigate the
cheap but dry land of the West; the land was then to be apportioned
among the members of the cooperative as individual holdings. Although
individualism was the dominant note, this proposed "Union Colony"
had elements of Fourierism. It was conceived to be a compact agricultural community centered around a town, where all could benefit from
the advantages of cooperative life. The old dream of work by Series and
group was left in the past, but Meeker hoped that this community
would provide its members with the benefits of cooperative buying and
selling as well as of some collective management of its resources.[40]

A key feature of the plan provided that the money received from the
sale of the town lots be used to pay for such public improvements as a
town hall, schoolhouse, and library. In this way, the increased value of
town lands created by the development of the surrounding agriculture
would be used "for the benefit of the whole people" rather than filling
the pockets of a few land speculators. Under this scheme, cooperation
would bring rapid economic development along with a "refined society
and the advantages of an old country." To further assure a refined
society, all title-deeds to the land contained a prohibition on the manufacture or sale of intoxicating liquor, an exclusion common among the
phalanx populations of the past. In general, the scheme was intended to
provide its members with the advantages of associative life compatible
with individual initiative and ambition.[41]

Meeker's plan reawakened in Greeley an old interest in creating
cooperative communities to relieve American cities of their surplus populations. He began to dream of a whole network of colonies to develop
the waste lands of the West and to provide opportunities for the jobless

and the underemployed. At one meeting in New York City, he advocated the founding of a thousand colonies where the jobless and low-wage workers could make their own lives: "I dislike to see men in advanced life working for salaries in places where perhaps they are ordered about by boys. I would like to see them working for themselves." He had long believed that many of these men had been driven to settle in the cities by the economic, social, and cultural disadvantages of isolated rural life, and in the 1840s had supported the phalanx movement chiefly because it promised to establish the benefits of urban life in a rural setting. A thousand colonies formed on the Union Colony plan would, he hoped, achieve this end, reversing the mass migration to the urban centers which had long depopulated rural areas and overcrowded the cities.[42]

No thousand colonies were ever established, and the plan proved to be the last hurrah for the old Associationist. Greeley became increasingly involved in politics, venturing into his disastrous and humiliating campaign for the presidency in 1872. His defeat at the hands of Grant and the near simultaneous death of his wife broke his spirit and in late November he died insane, convinced that he had "done wrong to millions while intending only good to hundreds."[43] It was a sad ending for a man who had had the courage to dream publicly of a better society, but the facts of his life indicate that he had no reason to fear the meeting with his God. Among the many monuments to his good will was the Union Colony, in which he had invested some of his money as well as his public support.

The Union Colony Association was formed in 1869 with 442 members, mostly eastern farmers, artisans, and small businessmen (one exception was the noted showman P. T. Barnum). This new rally of the old Fourierist classes brought tangible results in the formation of the town of Greeley, Colorado, and the agricultural development of thousands of acres of Colorado plains near the confluence of the Cache de Poudre and South Platte rivers. Seven years after it was initiated, the colony was commended for realizing "the splendid hopes and theories of certain prominent thinkers. Briefly, here in the Great American Desert the principles of cooperation have been applied to agriculture." Through Association, the frontier wilderness was conquered by the civilized East. Although its idealism was soon overwhelmed by its individualism, Greeley developed by 1900 into a prosperous town of 3000 people with a strong sense of community centered on its tree-lined streets, its public park, its temperance character, and its schools; it boasted of having the highest per-capita high-school enrollment in the nation. This "Garden City of the West" became a model for later colonies which helped populate the drylands of the West.[44]

Most of the investors in the Union Colony prospered, but one who did not was its creator, Nathan Meeker. By his account, he refused to speculate in Greeley land, denying himself the easiest benefits from the success of his ideas. Burdened by debt, he was forced to take on a new role as government agent to the Ute indians. The ever hopeful idealist attempted to convert this tribe to cooperative agriculture, pressuring them so insistently that in 1879 he was finally killed by "the enraged Utes."[45] And so his cooperative adventure, which had begun with Fourierist fantasies in Ohio, came to a grisly end on the plains of northern Colorado.

Another oldline Fourierist had a more peaceful if not more successful life. He was Charles Sears, the former Secretary of the North American Phalanx and perhaps the most dedicated of all American Fourierists. At the North American, he had fought to maintain the guaranty side of phalanx life, to make it a "complete commonwealth" which would provide for the needs of all of its members, and he believed that he had succeeded. In 1879, he defended it against charges that it had proven only that Fourierism was doomed to fail:

> It had abolished lawsuits within the society; it furnished no criminals nor paupers to tax the public; it had no children growing up without literary education, or ignorant of the ways and means of life; and the death-rate, taken for a period of thirteen years, was less than that of the Shakers.
>
> As an experiment in compact, closely graded Industrial and Social organization, extended to agricultural and domestic labor as well as to manufactures, education and amusements, it was successful.
>
> As an experiment in new societary relations, including the intimate association of families, and the making equal to both sexes alike all the industrial, social and political franchises, it was successful.[46]

The termination of the Phalanx in 1856 was a great disappointment to Sears, but after the Civil War he reappeared as an advocate of Fourierism, encouraged by the hope that "another tidal wave of socialistic discussion and effort at organization has fairly set in." The earlier experiments had failed, he said, because they had been premature as a response to the problems of industrial society, but by the 1870s the results of industrial anarchy could no longer be ignored. He warned that the frontier, the traditional escape, would soon be used up and Americans would have to confront the accumulating problems of their chaotic society: "Our unsystematic husbandry and trades are draining the country of its sources," and the unemployment created by the Panic of 1873 had produced a disturbing new victim of industrial anarchy, the jobless, rootless, and wandering "tramp," a figure who was to haunt the American social imagination for the next two decades.[47]

Sears believed that the key to this problem was the American farmer, whose individualism and unsystematic husbandry had left him helpless before the business corporations and combinations that were rising out of the economic chaos. Businessmen had demonstrated the advantages of association for themselves; now it was time for farmers and for workers and other Americans to organize themselves along Associationist lines.[48] Although the North American Phalanx was an irredeemable part of the New Jersey past, Sears believed he had found a new Fourierist model in the form of a new community established by an ally in the phalansterian campaign, Ernst Valeton de Boissiere.

De Boissiere, a French Fourierist, had apparently been an early investor in the North American Phalanx. In 1851, he had fled to the United States to escape from the dictatorship of Louis Napoleon and eventually formed a friendship with Sears. In 1868, De Boissiere, Sears, Brisbane, and E. P. Grant (a founder of the shortlived Ohio Phalanx established in southern Ohio in 1844) began a campaign to revive Fourierism. They were able to raise enough money to enable de Boissiere in 1869 to buy 3500 acres of prairie land near Princeton, Kansas. In that year, he said that he hoped to attain "the happy state" once enjoyed by the North American Phalanx. Although Brisbane soon backed out of the scheme, de Boissiere was able to gather a small community originally called the Kansas Cooperative Farm but better known as Silkville for its avowed intention to raise silk. By the mid-1870s, he was able to lay the basis for silk culture and to build a 60-room stone phalanstery to house the 40 or 50 people who had gathered there.[49]

Silkville was founded on a modified Fourierism. In an advertising circular issued in 1874, de Boissiere described its basic ideals: "A leading feature of the enterprise is to establish the 'Common Household' of Fourier—that is, a single large residence for all the associates. Its principal aim is to organize labor, the source of all wealth, in such a manner as to make it both *efficient* and *attractive*. Guarantees of education and subsistence . . . to be provided as soon as the organization shall be sufficiently advanced to render them practicable."[50] This was a Fourierism chastened by sad experience—absent were the extravagant dreams regarding passional industry and serial labor, but it did offer the hope that the members would eventually be free to "distribute themselves into organizations for industrial operations, and select or invent their own kinds and mode of cultivation and other practical processes."[51]

Silkville remained small, its population never exceeding 50 people, in part because it required a $100 deposit and the payment of two months rent for membership so that the experiment would not be "embarrassed by admitting the totally destitute." It did, however, achieve a modest prosperity, especially after Sears joined it in 1875. Under Sears' management, it developed a small silk culture and a modestly successful agriculture. Silkville survived for two decades, but in the mid-1880s Sears died and de Boissiere returned to France; the Frenchman's death in 1894 formally terminated what remained of his experiment. The property became the DeBoissiere Odd Fellows' Orphans' Home and Industrial School.[52]

By the mid-1890s, only two of the original disciples remained alive. Greeley had died in 1872, and eight years later Ripley followed, to be honored by Charles A. Dana as the harbinger of a time to come when the earth would be converted into "an abode of peace and beauty, excelling the mythical Eden of old." Dana himself lived until 1897 surviving another old Brook Farm colleague, John S. Dwight, by four years. The last survivor, Park Godwin, died in 1904 long after he had retired from active social reform.

In 1895, at the beginning of a great new ferment that would give life to Modern Socialism in America, Dana made a point of distinguishing Fourierism from the proletarianism of Marx and Engels: "Its adherents were all people who had gathered in the fruit of the highest education, the highest refinement that was known to American society in those times." It had not accomplished much, he admitted, but "what it did accomplish was a good deal for those who were concerned in it." It certainly was good to Dana, the once dissatisfied college student, who by way of Brook Farm and the *Harbinger* was able to find a career in journalism and a powerful voice as the editor of the New York *Sun.* Greeley, Ripley, Dwight, and Godwin had also benefited as journalists and critics from their connections with the Associationist campaign.[53]

Albert Brisbane remained true to his faith until the end. For over a half a century, the chief disciple had hovered over the movement which he had initiated, keeping himself deliberately remote from the actual practice of the phalansterian way. Occasionally, he settled to earth; he once joined his new converts at Brook Farm and awed them, said Marianne Dwight, by talking of "our meeting 35000 years hence under Saturn's ring; and we agreed to do so!" As a matter of both policy and personality, though, he refused to commit himself to any of the "incomplete" experiments which he had helped inspire. "His mind seemed to roam the universe," said his second wife, Redelia, while the man "stood in the midst of his epoch almost an impassive observer."[54]

The little triumphs and greater failures of the phalanxes barely affected a man who viewed them as premature and imperfect. In the midst of their failures, his Social Science remained as true as before. "No practical trial of it," he later wrote, "has been made which in the remotest degree either proves or disproves the truth of its principles." Throughout, he retained his faith that Fourierism was the true science, because it had been deduced from the eternal principles of God's Cosmic Order and not from the imperfect observations of Man's imperfect society. The various systems of society that had prevailed in the past, he believed, "have all been founded by instinct, or, to use a higher term, by the intuition of leading minds." Although Fourier's system had its imperfections, the Frenchman in his intuitive grasp of the Cosmic Order had laid the basis for that science by which Man could establish a heaven on earth.[55]

Brisbane participated in the Fourierist revival of the 1870s. In 1876, he published two books relating to Fourierism as part of a projected *Sociological Series* and contributed various articles on Fourierism to Noyes' *American Socialist.* Except for a brief interest in the Silkville experiment, however, he remained aloof from the actual cause. He "retired into his own mind," said Redelia Brisbane, in order to concentrate on "scientific research" into the mysteries of the Fourierist universe. Although he preferred theory to practice, he also took some interest in technology, designing a new kind of steamship and an oven for baking without "yeast and other artificial means of raising bread and pastry." It was while working on this oven in the cold and rain of the winter of 1889–90 that Brisbane contracted the influenza which broke his health. He died on May Day in 1890, a not inappropriate day for a man who hoped to elevate human labor to a new level of dignity and joy. Long before, he had written of himself:

My spirit goes out unto the Future
With a redeemed and regenerated race!
My joy and my ambition are with this humanity
To which I belong.[56]

Fourierism had died before its chief advocate. As a social science, it was doomed to oblivion by the empirical new social sciences that were to dominate the twentieth century; the limiting and fragmentary truths drawn from the observation of imperfect reality would replace the grand transcending truths that intuition had drawn from the cosmic order. As a practical effort at organic social regeneration, Associationism had shattered against the accumulating mass and momentum of modernizing society, convincing all but a faithful few that, whatever its theoretical virtues, it was not a practical solution to social problems.

Explanations for these failures vary with the ways that Fourierism was perceived. For conservatives, it was nothing more than a pretended social science, invalid in theory and impossible in practice—a scheme doomed by the imperfect character of man. For individualists like Emerson, in its addiction to contrivance it had considered everything except the spontaneous character of life itself. For religious radicals like Noyes, it had repeated the mistake of secular socialisms in ignoring the necessity of religious devotion as an animating and disciplining force. For Marxian Socialists, it was "utopian" and so doomed, because in its concern with the reconciliation of interests it failed to recognize that class conflict was the natural and irreversible force of social development. For the more sympathetic, the failure was a more limited and practical one, resulting from incidental imperfections in the associationist experiments: Insufficient capital, inadequate membership, poor leadership, bad location, and other reasons that had little to do with the intrinsic merits of the phalansterian system.

The most obvious explanation—on which virtually everyone can agree—is that the disciples simply failed to win much support from the American people. They received very little attention from those who most needed social redemption—workers and the poor—leading Greeley to complain that those who had nothing distrusted "any proposal to improve their condition." He might more accurately have said that those who were living on the edge had no time for schemes that did not address their immediate concerns. The great mass of farmers also had little interest in a movement essentially concerned with the needs of the new Urban Society.

Despite its professed concern for "the masses," though, Associationism was essentially designed for the broad middling class of ambitious small enterprisers and skilled craftsmen exposed to the ebbs and flows of a modernizing society. As such, it was particularly vulnerable to the mounting individualism of the times. The disciples rightly recognized that the prevailing social currents favored an atomizing individualism at the expense of community, but where they saw anarchy the great majority of ambitious people saw opportunity. Regardless of the promised benefits of phalansterian life, such people were inclined to agree with Emerson when he asked regarding Brook Farm "cannot I get the same advantages at home without pulling down my house."[57]

As for the gains supposedly to be derived from collective effort, the middle classes generally believed that they could benefit without tearing down the house of society. John Gray, one of the newest and least committed members of the North American Phalanx, spoke a fundamental truth when in 1851 he told a visitor "that society was progressing 'first rate' by means of Odd-Fellowship, Freemasonry, benevolent associations, railroads, steam boats, and especially all kinds of large manufactories without such little attempts as these of the North Americans to regenerate mankind." For the great majority, such familiar and partial associations as business corporations and fraternal societies provided enough cooperation without the distractions of a strange science and theology which few wanted to understand. On the basis of his own experience with social idealism, Thomas Low Nichols later wrote that "Fourierism has a religion and morality of its own, and Americans twenty years ago were not quite ready to abandon the religion and morals which they all professed."[58] The new movement was no match for Man's essential conservatism.

Conventional society was an obdurate reality that wore down the

wills even of dedicated Associationists. In 1853, Charles Sears summed up the essential frustration of many when he attempted to explain the troubles of the North American Phalanx: "If our organized society were the dominant order . . . so that our very social structure were not also an issue in every question of business, the efficient, the energetic, the enterprising would strike out as confidently as now and always in any established social order."[59] The inability of such Associations to overcome established social influences helped turn radical social reform away from communitarianism to the dream that some national regime would affect a total reorganization of the order and values of the entire society. While in Europe this manner of thinking led to the idea of some regenerative dictatorship of either the Right or the Left, its chief expression in the United States was the well-organized, bureaucratic national utopia of Edward Bellamy, whose *Looking Backward* was an appropriate successor to Fourier's works.

Later radicals, in support of their own forms of cooperative society, would sneer at Fourierism as an ineffectual and unrealistic joke to be ignored except for the negative lessons which it afforded. Whatever its deficiencies, however, it involved a vision of society which was to inspire generations to works of social improvement. Its chief aim was to expand and to elevate human freedom, to create a world in which every person would receive his just portion of the accumulating benefits of a modernizing society, and would be free from the privations, disruptions, wars, insecurities, and anxieties of the past. Although relatively few Americans accepted the Fourierist scheme and formula, many shared its dream of peace, plenty, and freedom. In pursuit of this dream, they invented other forms of social idealism that were further to enrich the search for a brotherly tomorrow.

IX

Preserving the American Eden

On its long passage to oblivion, Fourierism left a trail of broken social experiments unmatched in the history of utopia, a failure by pragmatic standards. Yet the extent of the failure was also a measure of its appeal to some basic human hopes. It offered what most people want: The advantages of complex urban life in the form of a small-scale community, prosperity and stability, order and liberty, social life and individual freedom—above all the great benefits of well-coordinated human energies and talents combined with opportunity for everyone to develop his or her unique personality. The phalanx embodied the dream of unlimited individuality and of unlimited human power.

Like other systems, however, Fourierism was founded on a restrictive conception of human life. The detailed catalogue of passions embraced in the system of passional attraction, while intended to allow for a full range of individualities, was at the same time limiting in the assumed completeness of its detail. This was especially evident in Brisbane's insistence that the phalanx was a "social mechanism" into which all human individualities would naturally fit. Conversely, the Fourierists believed that anyone's full individuality was attainable only as an integral element of a phalanx. "The members were made for the body," declared John S. Dwight, and only in that body could the individual find his natural self.[1]

This idea of total integration attracted a few men who hungered for mystical union with some great being—but only a few. In popular belief, America had made itself the Eden of the world by freeing individuals from the oppressive and limiting institutions of the past. In the land of freedom, what good were phalanxes and other social contrivances? Certainly, Americans agreed with Emerson's view that true individual depended on the freedom of the individual from any and all systems. As for cooperation, many also subscribed to his belief that the best form was the spontaneous cooperation of free-standing individuals, "the union of friends who live in different streets or towns."[2]

Emerson was generally content to preach his doctrines within the existing social order. This was not enough, however, for several social thinkers who believed that the American Eden required a different order to protect it against the depersonalizing tendencies of the Modern Age. Unlike the Fourierists, these thinkers attributed the troubles of society not to its individualism and to competition but to its failure to provide a basis for true personal independence. They dreamed of a society which would assure all men both individual freedom and the opportunity to freely cooperate when necessary. Where Fourierists saw the need for corporate association, these men hoped to establish conditions for the voluntary association of free-standing men.

One of the first to attempt to provide a social basis for spontaneous cooperation was the pioneer American anarchist, Josiah Warren, another Yankee social radical.[3] As a leading member of Owen's New Harmony community, Warren had acquired a permanent distaste for all systems and formal organizations. The failure of social experiments like New Harmony, he said later, was assured by the fact that human beings were "indestructible individualities" who would not conform to any preconceived social organization. Men like Owen had simply repeated the error of conventional society in ignoring this most basic fact of nature: "Our surrounding institutions, customs, and public opinion call for conformity; they require us to act in masses like herds of cattle; they do not recognize that we think and feel individually and ought to be at liberty to act individually." Warren came to oppose all forms of what he called "communism," i.e., any organization founded on joint ownership and responsibility; in this sense, communism included both the phalanx and the ordinary business corporation as well as Owen's Community of Equality. Collectivism of any sort served to smother individual responsibility and will, thereby weakening the personal effort that constituted the vital force in any society.[4] Only when every individual was assured complete liberty to act as he pleased would the good life be assured.

Warren envisioned a world where every man was "absolute despot or sovereign" over his life and property, but he also conceded the importance of some social arrangements. Although a Thoreau might attempt a life of self-reliance in the isolation of Walden Pond, Warren recognized that even self-sovereigns would need to cooperate in order to provide for their wellbeing, to build roads and schools, to buy and sell the products of their labors, and in other ways to extend their powers. In contrast to the Owenites and Fourierists, he believed that true cooperation depended not on social formulas, but on the spontaneous and free agreement of individuals, a "coincidence of interests and wills." Only when cooperation was founded on the free wills and self-directed interests of free individuals could it draw on the energies envisioned by the Fourierists and other organizers.[5]

In the three decades after New Harmony, Warren established three separate communities based on his principle of self-sovereignty: In the mid-1830s, the short-lived Equity community in Tuscarawas County, eastern Ohio; in the mid-1840s, the more successful hamlet of Utopia near the domain of the failed Clermont Phalanx outside of Cincinnati; in the early 1850s, the still more successful village of Modern Times located on Long Island some 40 miles from New York City.[6] Warren took particular pride in Modern Times as an example of what self-sovereignty could accomplish. Cooperative individualism had turned a wasteland into a small town of straight streets, homes, a railroad station, and a post office. Individual freedom had yielded a society without conflict and without crime: "They have no quarrels about what is called 'religion.' No demand for jails—No grog shops, no houses of prostitution. No fighting about politics—No man there has dashed his wife's brains with an axe."[7]

Personally, however, he did not like some of the people who settled in his village and in 1857 exercised his self-sovereignty by abandoning the experiment. This seems to have ended his active involvement in community-building, although after the Civil War he did dream of creating new equity villages in the Caribbean and in Central America.

Even before his death in 1874, Modern Times had rejected its anarchist past and, under the new name of Brentwood, was becoming a distant suburb of New York City.[8]

Warren belonged to a different and older part of the culture of dissent than the Fourierists. Unlike them, he was a freethinking rationalist who was suspicious of religion and churches in any form. While they dreamed of redirecting a changing America toward their Associationist future, he dreamed of preserving an older, essentially Jeffersonian America, an open land devoted to individual independence and opportunity. While they envisioned a world of phalanxes, he envisioned a world without institutions or formal organizations. While they drew a stark contrast between "anarchical" competition and well-organized cooperation, he pictured an open society where free individuals would engage in both friendly competition and useful cooperation. In a rare fit of millennial enthusiasm, he said that under his system competition "instead of being the fierce and terrible *ogre*—the Juggernaut of Civilization . . . becomes converted into a very comfortable carriage for the conveyance of passengers to the Holy Land"—if only the nation could be purged of all organizations which gave some men a suprapersonal power over others.[9]

Warren made some converts who carried his doctrines into the future, most notably Benjamin R. Tucker who fought a valiant but eventually losing battle for self-sovereignty in his journal, *Liberty,* between 1881 and 1908.[10] Very few Americans, however, were ready to sacrifice virtually the whole of organized society to the dream of individual independence. Warren insisted that true liberty had its price in that everyone was to exercise it as *his cost* and his alone regardless of how high that cost might be; no one had the right to expect assistance from any source beyond himself. Moreover, he gave little attention to the vital problem of assuring the possession of property, which seemed necessary for individual independence. Described by a contemporary as "an ingenious mechanic and artist," Warren was able to support himself by his innovations and inventions, particularly in the printing trade, but few people had either his talents or his self-confidence.[11] It was not surprising then, that most Americans should be content to live in Emersonian houses and dream Emersonian dreams of individualism among the social and economic organizations on which they came to depend.

The hopes for preserving an open land for individual independence and spontaneous brotherhood founded a safer and broader channel in

the National Land Reform movement, the chief secular rival to Fourierism in the world of social radicalism. The first National Reformer was
George Henry Evans, the older brother of Frederick Evans. Although
they were both English-born rationalists who shared an early interest in
Owenism, the Evans brothers pursued two very different paths in reactions to Owen's failure at New Harmony. While Frederick joined the
Shakers and eventually became the leading Shaker elder, George Evans
became an advocate for the rights of workingmen as the editor of several
labor newspapers in New York City. By the early 1840s, he believed
that he had found the reasons for the workers' apparently worsening
condition during this period. Like his fellow New Yorker Horace
Greeley, Evans concluded that there was a surplus of men competing
for jobs in the urban centers, a situation which forced down their wages
and left them defenseless against employers.[12] The logic of this analysis
led both journalists to conclude that it was necessary to stem the rush of
rural population to urban areas if industrial feudalism was to be avoided.

Greeley and his Fourierists friends promoted the phalanx as the way
to make rural life attractive enough to hold the rural population, but
Evans saw the problem and its solution differently. He believed that the
essential cause was land monopoly, especially the speculative withhold-
ing of land from the market, which denied many people the chance to
become landed proprietors. As a result, ambitious young Americans
were forced to migrate either to the wilderness beyond the reach of land
speculators or to the overcrowded cities, leaving depopulated rural areas
behind. If the cities were cursed with a surplus population, many rural
areas suffered socially and economically from underpopulation, which
reduced opportunities for needed cooperation, and the American dream
of freedom and plenty was denied to all but a few large propertyholders.[13]

Early in 1844, during the peak of the Fourierists boom, Evans met
with several other New Yorkers to form the National Reform movement. Although Evans had a farm in New Jersey, most of the National
Reformers were urban types (at least four were printers) who hoped to
create a rural world suited both to small farmers and to craftsmen like
themselves. The embodiment of their ideal, their version of the phalanx,
was the rural township, a six-mile square of land to be laid out in farms
of no more than 160 acres except for one square mile reserved for the
township center. This center would be laid out as a dispersed rural

village with mini-farm plots for craftsmen and others whose services were required by the farm population, and it would also include a park and sites for public buildings, the whole township being unified by roads from the center.[14]

The original population of the township would be approximately 1000 people. The expected increase in numbers over the years could be accommodated by subdividing the land into farms of as little as 20 acres each, allowing at least children and grandchildren to remain on their family homesteads. Except for a few necessary service cities, the future United States would become a nation of semi-autonomous townships, each with a population density sufficient to meet its economic and social needs. The majority of inhabitants would be independent land-owning farmers whose lives would be made easier by ready access to the benefits of the village center and by the use of steampowered machinery to eliminate the curse of manual labor; the craftsmen, printers, and others in the village would be protected from the competition of surplus workers and would also enjoy independence in their own houses on their own plots of land. "The whole system," promised Evans, "would tend to support the population on the smallest space consistent with health, comfort, and happiness, reversing exactly the crowded city and isolated country system now in vogue."[15] In this happy world of smiling fields and contented villages, individual Americans would engage in all the cooperation needed for prosperous, civilized life without the need for phalanxes and communistic associations.

This dream more closely matched traditional American ideals than most forms of social idealism, but the National Reformers were confronted with a major problem which most social radicals had avoided. In their various communitarian schemes, the Fourierists and others had chosen a nonpolitical way to the good society. The National Reformers, however, depended on government to prevent monopoly and to assure access to land for everyone who wanted it. They demanded a change in national land laws to provide, from the public domain, free homesteads for the landless and to prevent the engrossment of land by speculators; they wanted land grants limited to those who would actually reside on them. Beyond that, they advocated restrictions on the transfer and inheritance of land that involved virtually everyone. In 1847, for instance, land reformers in New York proposed that the legislature limit land subsequently acquired in the state to no more than 160 acres; those who inherited more than that amount would be required to sell the excess to others.[16] If the idea of free land was popular, such restrictions on property rights were not.

The future of homestead legislation might well have been predicted. The National Reformers were able to bring the idea before Congress, which debated several homestead bills before the Civil War. These bills, however, were not enacted—in part because of opposition from the slaveholding south but also because of wrangling over restrictions on the acquisition and transfer of the lands to be granted from the public domain. The removal of southern opposition during the Civil War finally opened the way for the enactment of a Homestead Act in 1862, but loopholes in the act led to the acquisition of much of the land by large-scale operators. Whatever the merits of the homestead dream, it was disappointed by the land legislation enacted under its name.[17]

The dream, however, survived. Although George Henry Evans died in 1856, his vision was kept alive by some of his associates. Lewis Masquerier, a convert from Owenism, revived it under the head of "The Paradise of Rural Cities" in his book, *Sociology: or, The Reconstruction of Society, Government and Property,* published in 1877: "Each of these homes, with the dwellings, barns, shops, and surrounding gardens, fields, and orchards, etc., will combine farm, village, and park into one, and make a rural city of the whole earth." Free from the dependencies, anxieties, and bad environment of the overcrowded city, every man could sit under his "own vine and fig tree" to eat the fruits of his own labor at peace with his brothers throughout the world; every woman, presumably, would be at her own stove in her own independent household.[18]

The Homestead vision in some form had broad appeal among cultural dissenters. As an ingredient in the boiling stew of antebellum radicalism, National Reform had connections with other radical efforts. At Modern Times, for instance, self-sovereignty was limited by a regulation that restricted individual purchases of land there to three acres. In part, this reflected Warren's hostility to land monopoly which in 1863 he denounced as a "civilized cannabalism" by which a few landowners waxed fat on the labor of the many. In part, it was also intended to prevent the wide diffusion of population that would reduce opportunities for spontaneous cooperation among individuals; the idea was to create a "town of diversified occupations" rather than a scattered farming community.[19] Similarly, National Reform and Fourierism had at least a limited influence on each other. The decision of the American Union of Associationists to the use the term "township" rather than phalanx in some of their statements seems to have been motivated by the hope of attracting Land Reformers, at least one of whom did respond by suggesting that the principles of the individual right to land and of limitations on landownership be added to the Associationist cause.[20]

In the late 1850s, this mixed influence appeared in the "Harmonial Township Association," formed in Worcester, Massachusetts, with the aim of assuring each of its members both a "home, sweet home" and the cooperative support of neighbors. The Association was a response to the depression following the Panic of 1857. Its aim was to raise enough money to buy and develop a "township" under a plan which would provide each member either with a farm or with a lot in a "well arranged Village Centre" under such rules as were needed to prevent "the trickery of monopoly and speculation." Outside the Village Centre, farm houses were to be grouped into sets of four or more; each set focused on a small park and constituted a neighborhood where "the material interest of each will be under his or her supervision and control, while the general welfare will be regarded mutually."[21] In this little world of independent propertyholders, inhabitants would have access to various kinds of cooperative organizations including a "Bank of Exchange" in which producers could "deposit" their products in exchange either for money or for articles deposited by other producers.[22]

The Harmonial Association was perhaps the most notable effort of the late 1850s to rally the dwindling forces of antebellum social radicalism and cultural dissent. It won the support of Adin Ballou, the Christian Socialist, who publicized it in his biweekly newspaper, *The Practical Christian,* and it also attracted some attention from the nation's many spiritualists. In September 1858, the Association held a convention at Worcester which drew delegates from New York and New Jersey as well as Massachusetts.[23]

A second meeting was held the next year which formed a "Harmonial and National Brotherhood" to organize "Branch Brotherhoods in every Town, City, State, and throughout all the nations of the World." The aims of the reorganized movement were to support the effort for a homestead act, lobby Congress into granting a township of public land for use by the Association, and to promote a national cooperative brotherhood of all producers. According to its leader, Daniel C. Gates of Worcester, the Brotherhood would "go to work in every town, city and state and set the wheels of organized industry rolling that have been blocked by speculators and the selfish capitalist."[24] If Gates's plan was great, however, his movement was little, and the Harmonial Brotherhood soon vanished under the deluge of national concerns that led to the Civil War.

After the War, the homestead vision was revived and partly realized by an enlightened Philadelphia land-developer, Charles K. Landis. In the early 1850s, Landis had laid out the town of Hammonton in southern New Jersey midway between Philadelphia and Atlantic City. A decade later he moved farther south in the state, purchasing 30,000 acres of what was then considered agriculturally worthless "Barrens" land.[25] Landis's scheme, which took advantage of a newly opened rail link with Philadelphia, was that of an unusually broad-minded developer. Recognizing, perhaps, that he needed some gimmick to attract people to the area, he sold his land at a fixed price of $25 per farm-acre and $150 per town lot, even after settlement had raised values much above those prices. Since he was prepared to sell on credit, he was later able to boast that he had given poor men a chance to acquire land for their families without having to migrate to the western frontier. Encouraged by Landis's policy, some "ten thousand intelligent and industrious people" had settled in this landowner's paradise by the mid-1870s.[26]

Vineland and its neighboring towns of Ancora and Hammonton became a special refuge for those who held what one observer called "an advanced position . . . on all questions of society and religion." They were freethinkers, Spiritualists, and a variety of other cultural dissenters, including at least a few "social architects" who in the mid-1870s attempted to launch at least five different experiments in cooperative living.[27] Many were attracted by another policy devised by Landis: Early in the history of his new community, he persuaded the settlers to prohibit the beer halls and saloons responsible for most cases of public drunkenness. In 1873, Landis estimated that this policy had saved Vineland the economic and social costs of 200 drinking places dispensing $300,000 in drink and disorder: "Here is a community where crime and pauperism are almost unknown, where taxes are nominal, where man's children are not contaminated by the evil language and influence of drunkards."[28]

Vineland also benefited from Landis's interest in developing an adequate road system for the area and from his requirements that land buyers within a year build a house on their properties and plant some shade trees and grass on their frontage. The small size of the farms, ranging from 10 to 60 acres, made for a compactly settled rural society where the settlers were able tⁿ associate for their mutual benefit. "They had," wrote one observer, 'what our American farmers have not in general, easy access to good schools for their children, to churches, and an intelligent society." By 1900, the year of Landis's death, central Vineland had developed into an industrial and commercial center for south New Jersey, with a diversified mix of manufacturing facilities, two banks, five newspapers, a public library, a high school, and other features of a practical paradise for a hardworking, law-abiding middle class.[29]

Vineland seemed to demonstrate that the imaginative could find more accessible and socially desirable frontiers than those of the distant west; one observer said that it indicated that Americans were awakening from their infatuation with the westward movement to an appreciation for lands closer to "their eastern homes and associates." In the 1870s, Thomas Low Nichols, a reformer and former member of Modern Times, concluded his memoir, *Forty Years of American Life,* by citing Vineland as an example of the existence of an eastern as well as western safety valve. His last words were a set of questions:

> What is there to prevent the formulation of a thousand just such colonies?
> Why may not a whole continent be covered over with Vinelands—with beautiful colonies, filled with industrious, intelligent, temperate, happy people?
> Why may it not be everywhere "On Earth AS IT IS IN HEAVEN?"
> *Why not?*[30]

There was only one Charles K. Landis, however, and Vineland remained a solitary social success in an isolated part of the Garden State. In any case, the times demanded a new and more comprehensive strategy to preserve the old America of open lands and open opportunities. By the early 1870s, the nation seemed to be moving rapidly toward the industrial feudalism and chaos which the Fourierists had earlier predicted would inevitably result from competitive individualism. The defects of the new order were given dramatic emphasis by the Panic of 1873, which created massive unemployment, and by a series of conflict between Labor and Capital that reached a climax in the violent railroad strikes of 1877.

Some social observers feared that America was fast giving way to a European-style world whose symbols were the bloated aristocrat of wealth and the rootless, jobless "tramp." Francis Wayland-Smith of the Oneida Community warned that some way had to be devised to protect the weak against the strong or risk the social turbulence of Europe, since the United States no longer could depend on its frontier to solve its social problems: "Most of our good land is taken up, there is an enormous stream of immigrants flowing in, both on the Atlantic and Pacific coasts, and the resident population is increasing rapidly by its own procreation."[31] Other social observers made the same point that the rapidly and chaotically growing industrial America would soon exhaust its natural advantages over Europe.

The sense of closing frontiers was a critical factor in making the 1870s a turning point for social radicalism in the United States, creating the need for a response to essential social evil more comprehensive than the communitarian solutions of the past. This need was first met in 1879 when Henry George published his *Progress and Poverty,* a book that had great effect in reviving hopes for preserving the American Eden. In it, he linked the essential character of the nation with its openness: "The general intelligence, the general comfort, the active invention, the power of adaptation and assimilation, the free, independent spirit, the energy and hopefulness that have marked our people are not causes, but results —they have sprung from unfenced land."[32] At a time when unfenced land was vanishing at an accelerating speed—in part as a result of the defective Homestead Act—George introduced a promising new way to protect and enrich the old society of individual independence and uncoerced cooperation.

Progress and Poverty owed much to varied sources of idealism, but its special character resulted from George's own personality and experiences. Physically a little man—he was less than five-and-a-half feet tall —his powerful intellect and imagination eventually yielded a social vision that would command the attention of millions of people in America and elsewhere. In the 1850s, the young man had attempted to escape from his lower middle class Philadelphia background to a life of individual freedom and adventure, first as a sailor on a merchant ship and then as a gold-seeker in California.[33] He soon discovered, however, that for him there was no escape, since in California the frontier was rapidly giving way to society. Finding himself poor and powerless in the booming city of San Francisco, he dreamed of escape to his own Eden: "How I long for the Gold-Age—for the Millennium, when each one will be free to follow his best and noblest impulses, unfettered by the restrictions and necessities which our present state of society imposes upon him."[34]

No millennium came for George; instead, he was to spend much of his life in a struggle to support himself, a wife, and a growing family as a laborer, printer, journalist, and sometimes editor. That life, however, was an effective tutor for one of America's most distinctive social thinkers. California's rapid growth from frontier to mature society convinced him that in a decade he had been able to view a compressed version of human social development whose lessons were applicable elsewhere. Where that development was headed he was soon to learn. In 1869, when on a visit to New York, he encountered the human misery of a great city, he had "a thought, a vision, a call—give it what name you please" that convinced him his experience was preparing him to answer the transcendent question of the Industrial Future: How was it that, in an age of such magnificent material progress, poverty and its degrading influences should have spread so rapidly over a once happy land? Why was it that "the 'tramp' comes with the locomotive?"[35]

He gave his answer in *Progress and Poverty,* which with an endearing lack of modesty he predicted would achieve greatness and would be read throughout the world. He was right; the book had an immense influence, especially in the United States and the British Isles. In England, it was a major inspiration for the development of Fabian Socialism.[36] What the reader got was a lengthy treatise on economics infused with millenarian enthusiasm. The "dismal science" became a science of hope, which promised to restore the frontier of freedom and opportunity in a form suited to the Industrial Age.

The book opens with the eloquent tribute to the progressive tendencies of a world where science and technology had brought "prodigious increase in wealth-producing power." That power promised to end age-old poverty and, by so doing, to bring "moral conditions realizing the golden age of which mankind always dreamed. Youth no longer stunted and starved; age no longer harried by avarice; the child at play with the tiger, the man with the muck-rake drinking in the glory of the stars!" Modernization had raised a powerful new set of hopes of mankind that could not be ignored: "They have sunk so deep into the popular mind as to radically change the currents of thought, to recast creeds and displace the most fundamental conceptions."[37]

The vision of unlimited plenty glimpsed by Robert Owen some 70 years before was within human grasp, but the hopes of the age were matched by its despair, since every increase in wealth seemingly caused new poverty and new misery, as if some wedge were being driven into society which further elevated the advantaged minority while crushing those below: "The association of poverty with progress is the great enigma of our times." Unless that enigma was soon solved, unless the widening social chasm was closed, the great progressing powers of modern civilization would serve only to destroy it: "The tower leans from its foundations, and every new story but hastens the final catastrophe." This frightening paradox, however, could be dispelled through a simple remedy based on a simple truth to which Americans had been kept blind by "a vast and dominating pecuniary interest."[38]

The truth was that society had allowed a privileged few to take for themselves the wealth which all Americans were producing for the benefit of all. The key to this exploitive system was the possession by the few of a near monopoly of mankinds' most basic and precious resource, land. So long as there had been an open west, this perhaps was tolerable; but civilization had reached the Pacific, and "the republic has entered upon a new era—an era in which monopoly of the land will tell with accelerating effect."[39] George believed that land monopoly afflicted all producers whether they were entrepreneurs or workers, city dwellers or farmers. Everywhere, large property owners were able to expropriate the increasing value of land created by the needs and work of an expanding population, and everywhere society suffered. In the country side, monopolists kept land from those farmers who needed it, causing rural poverty and driving many to the cities where they had difficulty finding jobs. In the cities, monopolists waxed rich on the excessive rents they charged, intensifying poverty and forcing the crowding of the poor into city slums. While rich parasites luxuriated on Fifth Avenue and at Newport, frustrated Americans fought over a system which might otherwise have assured wealth for all.[40]

This problem George promised to solve through the simple public remedy of taxation. In this, as well as in several other important particulars, he was anticipated some thirty years earlier by Dr. J. R. Buchanan of Cincinnati, a land reformer and an advocate of cooperative associations.[41] In a lengthy article, "The Land and the People," published by the *Herald of Truth* (Cincinnati) in 1847, Buchanan described a plan where, in lieu of outright nationalization of the soil, the people would levy "an ad valorem rent" on all land. Since rents would rise with the increase in land values produced by the growth of population, the revenue from this source would be so vast in itself as to eliminate the need for the other taxes while producing a surplus to fund a network of libraries, schools, and colleges and to construct local "free railroads."[42] These railroads would decrease the costs of necessities in the cities and reduce urban crowding by allowing city workers to settle in country residences.[43] The general result would be "the speedy abolition of ALL evil" and the transformation of the United States into a "MODEL REPUBLIC" where the people would be able to achieve their goals through cooperative associations.[44]

Similarly, George held that all land belonged to the people for their use. He believed that, while the value added to the land by its improvement belonged to individual owners, the "unearned increment" in value derived from the work of mankind belonged to the people and should be appropriate for social use through the mechanism of a "Single Tax," which was actually a form of rent. So great was the expected revenue derived from this one tax that George believed it could replace all other taxes. More significantly, the Single Tax would work a quiet revolution against privilege and for equality by forcing owners either to develop their lands or to sell them on the open market.[45] In either case, every man could acquire all of the space, rural or urban, which he could use.

George believed, as had Buchanan, that this one policy would enable modern America to re-create a Jeffersonian world of free and prosperous individuals without resorting to ineffectual homestead legislation. The opening of new lands for agriculture would give many Americans an independent life, and it would drain away that surplus of labor in urban and industrial centers which had led to mass poverty and the exploitation of workers: "The destruction of speculative land values would tend to diffuse population where it is too dense and to concentrate it where it is too sparse; to substitute for the tenement house, homes surrounded by gardens and fully to settle agricultural districts before people were driven far from neighbors to look for land."[46] In this way, the "Paradise of Rural Cities" envisioned by the National Reformers could be realized without their unpopular and ineffectual restrictions on property rights.

If Buchanan had anticipated most of these ideas, it was George who evoked a popular enthusiasm for them by combining a thoughtful study of economics with a distinctly millenial vision for modern society. *Progress and Poverty* is a great hymn to Liberty, written out of faith in the nearly infinite creative abilities of free men. Once freed from the tyranny of privilege and from the strangling grip of poverty, man would become an active and creative force; everyone, acting either individually or in voluntary association with his fellow men, would develop his natural capacities under the benevolent guardianship of a government dedicated to equal opportunity for all.[47] Human physical power would be freed from hunger, disease, and despair; mental power from greed, envy, and anxiety: "How infinitesimal are the forces that concure to the advance of civilization, as compared to the forces that lie latent?" If resources in land were ultimately limited, the greater resource of human creative power was not—and that power could be actualized in all of its glorious potency without resort to the passional contraptions of Fourier, whom George once took the trouble to dismiss as a "superficial thinker."[48]

Liberty, George believed, would enable mankind to control all creation for its benefit. To those who warned that contented men would lapse into idleness, he replied: "Man is the unsatisfied animal. He has but begun to explore, and the universe lies before him. Each step that he takes opens new vistas and kindles new desires. He builds, he improves, he invents, and puts together, and the greater the thing he does, the greater the thing he wants to do." To those haunted by Malthusian nightmares that a progressing mankind would exhaust the resources of Earth, he replied that the planet could sustain "a thousand billions of people," whose creative powers combined with their growing preference for spiritual over material things would assure continued human progress until the end of time.[49]

Little wonder that George was called, both in ridicule and reverence, the "Prophet of San Francisco." In writing *Progress and Poverty,* this self-tutored seer repaid America's debt to Owen and Fourier. By reformulating traditional American ideals, he laid new foundations for the hope that heaven indeed could be established on this earth without resort to a seemingly outmoded communitarianism. As he had predicted, the book was widely read. With the exception of the Bible, it was probably the most popular nonfiction book published in the English language before the twentieth century. The influence of his dream was wide and at least occasionally profound.[50] In 1890, the writer Hamlin Garland said of the Georgist movement that:

> It is at once intensely practical, and has all the allurement and intellectual exaltation of a radical humanitarian philosophy. When the word "single-tax" is spoken by single-tax men to each other, there is nothing prosaic in its sound. Vast dreams and gleaming vistas open in their minds. They see sun-lighted fields and shining cities towards which they are walking and expect to walk toilsomely (they have no wings), but their limbs are strong, their hearts invincible.[51]

George's vision, however, did not satisfy a great many Americans, especially when it became entangled in the murky world of politics. In the early 1880s, he attracted the interest of Americans who were disturbed by the deepening of social tensions and that verged on open war between Labor and Capital. At a time of violent railroad strikes and then of the Haymarket bombing, George offered the hope for a return to an older America where progress would be more orderly and sure. He won much support from both reformers and workers, particularly in New York City where in 1886 he ran for Mayor as the candidate of the Union Labor Party, coming in a strong second in a much publicized three-man race (the last was young Theodore Roosevelt).[52] For the first time, social idealism entered the political arena in a seemingly powerful form.

George's popularity, however, not only frightened conservatives but also drew him into the risky world of radical politics, which was then in the process of brewing modern socialism. Many Socialists initially supported Georgism as a promising movement for national regeneration superior at least to the ineffectual communitarianism of the past, but the social visions and programs of the two sides were essentially different. Although George had said "the idea of socialism is grand and noble," he had also warned that it could not be "manufactured" and had to grow naturally out of a free community, a warning especially directed toward those who were coming to see a strong, benevolent government as the savior of society.[53]

In 1887, George grew so convinced that association with the Socialists endangered his cause that he had them purged from the Union Labor Party in the vain hope of making it a national political organization. What followed was an open conflict in which each side accused the other of what George termed a "want of radicalism" for supposedly not getting to the root of the problem. For Socialists, the Single Tax was a weak nostrum for the disease of capitalism, and the Georgists themselves were "reformers" or even worse "utopians." For Georgists, the socialist scheme for an all-governing paternalistic state was a quack remedy that was worse than the disease.[54]

Outside of the radical world, the Georgists had to deal with a common tendency to lump them with the Socialists and other radicals. To establish their distinctive identity, they intensified their emphasis on the Single Tax, promoting it as the magical instrument to achieve all that the Socialists wanted while retaining the dynamism of competitive individualism. In the platform of their new Single-Tax League in 1890, the Georgists promised that their tax program would "solve the labor problem, do away with involuntary poverty, raise wages in all occupations to the full earnings of labor, make overproduction impossible until all human wants are satisfied, render labor-saving inventions a blessing to all, and cause such an enormous production and such an equitable distribution of wealth as would give to all comfort, leisure and participation in the advantages of an advancing civilization."[55]

In the same year, Hamlin Garland argued for the superiority of the Single Tax over any form of socialism. Contrary to the common belief of the times that society was naturally evolving toward increasingly organized forms of cooperation, said Garland, true progress meant the ever greater actualization of individual freedom. By breaking the hold of monopoly on land and other natural resources, the Tax would guarantee freedom by creating new employments for all people, to the special benefit of women, each of whom would have "the free opportunity to earn her own living independent of the man." Above all, the Single Tax would expand opportunities in the countryside and so increase rural population densities as to create better conditions for voluntary cooperation: "With the rise of towns and the concentration of rural population, swifter strides in civilization will come." Here, then, would be a world for "the fraternal, spontaneous, unconscious co-operation of individualism"—the unique American Eden preserved.[56]

This was an enthralling vision for Single-Taxers, but it had little appeal for most Americans, including those it was most designed to benefit. After he had briefly won some worker support as the head of the Union Labor Party, George lost most of it in large part because he had little to offer workingmen in their struggles with employers: he disliked strikes and feared labor violence, and his public acceptance of the execution of the alleged perpetrators of the Haymarket bombing excited accusations that he had betrayed the laboring classes. He had even less success with American farmers who, if they noticed him at all, tended to see in his attitudes toward land ownership a threat to their own land. For the dissatisfied agriculturalist, the Populist movement seemed to be a safer as well as more practical solution to his problems.

George received his most enthusiastic support from Irish immigrants with their bitter memories of landlordism in Ireland, but much of this support melted away when he became entangled in a lengthy dispute with the Roman Catholic hierarchy in New York.[57] He even encountered the enmity of two leading apostles of individualism and spontaneous cooperation: Benjamin Tucker, the anarchist, and Joshua K. Ingalls, the last survivor of the National Reform Movement; both condemned his program as emphasizing government action at the expense of individual freedom.[58]

Georgism continued to fade as a political movement during the 1890s, and with it went much of the enthusiasm first raised by *Progress and Poverty*. Although George tried to link his cause with that of Jesus, he could not revive his earlier fusion of millennialism and the American tradition. In 1897, he attempted to repeat his campaign for Mayor of New York City, but it was an uninspired effort by a wearied warrior, a dismal campaign further darkened by the bitter hostility of Benjamin Tucker; Tucker spent much energy and money to assure the maximum circulation of his pamphlet, *Henry George, Traitor,* in order to reduce the vote for his rival. It was not necessary. The campaign so exhausted George that he died shortly before the election at the age of 58; his son, Henry George Jr., won only four percent of the vote as his substitute.[59]

Death did not end George's influence. With the financial support of Joseph Fels, a wealthy soap manufacturer, his disciples continued to publish and promote his ideas for many years; if nothing else, they did educate Americans to the value of taxation as an instrument of social policy. A group of his disciples headed by Tom Johnson succeeded in making Cleveland a model of municipal reform.[60]

On another level, Georgism also became a new stimulus for traditional communitarianism: between 1895 and 1932, Americans formed at least ten single-tax colonies; the largest and most successful was Fairhope, Alabama, established in 1895 by an association of dissatisfied Iowans to free themselves from the tyranny of "the land speculator, the usurer, the monopolist of public service and all the other parasites who fatten upon industry."[61] The cumulative influence of Georgism was considerable, but it disappointed George's hopes for a national movement to revive the good old America of individual independence and voluntary cooperation.

This disappointment was as predictable as the disappearance of the geographic frontier. Both Georgism and National Reform had their greatest appeal during periods of especially disruptive economic and social change. During the stagnant and disorderly early 1840s and again in the 1880s, many Americans welcomed assurances that the traditional America still remained as a Gibraltar of American ideals and as a place of possible escape. *Progress and Poverty* especially seemed to confirm the hope that a period of national agony could be made the way to a national restoration of the old and pure republic that distinguished the real America from a corrupted Europe.[62]

It was a noble vision, but it became increasingly remote from the immediate hopes and fears of most people. Although both National Reformers and Georgists emphasized the importance of maintaining the traditional frontier safety valve for the good of urban labor, the working class itself generally ignored them. Having experienced the advantages of urban society, said Benjamin Tucker, the worker "will shiver in his garret and slowly waste away from inanimation ere he will exchange it for the semi-barbarous condition of the backwoodsman."[63]

Most Americans also wanted immediate answers to the accumulating problems of the promising but terrifying world of machines and big businesses that was gathering momentum around them. Georgism, with its emphasis on lands and hands, seemed to have little to say to the new age of steel and railroads and trusts and labor unions. After a promising start in politics, therefore, it was overwhelmed by more practical movements for more immediate objectives—by labor unions, farmer organizations, and middle-class reform.

Even in the realm of radical social idealism, the Georgian movement encountered the competition of rival visions that appealed to the same social concerns and the same constituency. Its birth in the early 1880s introduced three decades of social thought and practice that were to constitute a great new phase of radical idealism as Americans sought ways of controlling the new society that was growing up around them. Some ways were national and some were communitarian; some looked to the future and some to the past. Whatever their characters, however, their collective effect was to detract from George's effort to regenerate the old America of open frontiers and to initiate new movements seemingly more compatible with a modernizing urban-industrial society.

X

The Good Kings of Fouriana

Henry George was one spokesman for a variform idealism which envisioned a society to be created and sustained through the voluntary cooperation of freely acting men. This vision, however, was confounded by the general social inertia and passivity of men in reality. If anything, that social passivity had grown more pervasive as the new industrial and urban society gathered its momentum, overwhelming the feeble associations of the past. In the new age of giant business corporations and sprawling cities, it seemed less possible for men to work a significant change in their lives by their own efforts. Against mysterious and perhaps unmanageable new powers, how could human force be organized even to solve pressing social problems much less realize the good society?

Earlier, the Fourierists had tried to form a movement for change through their propaganda and had failed. George had resorted to prophetic inspiration and was to fail. What then? By the 1880s, another possible answer had appeared in the form of a new version of the old utopian hope that some Good King Utopus would work the social miracles that men in general could not achieve. In an industrial age, it was natural that some of these hopes should fall on the one human type who had seemingly mastered the mysteries of the times—the industrial entrepreneur.

In 1886, for instance, this was the main theme of Thomas Edwin Brown's *Studies in Modern Socialism,* a book intended to present a safe and practical alternative to social radicalism. Brown, a Baptist minister in Providence, Rhode Island, placed his hopes on the growing cadre of "Captains of Industry," those industrialists who, like the commanders of an army, were "the organizers, the leaders of our industrial forces." Brown's Captain of Industry was neither a capitalist nor a worker but a new entrepreneurial figure expert in managing the increasingly complex combinations of labor and capital required for modern industrial production. As a modern product elevated above the traditional concerns of both labor and capital, he was the most likely leader to end the industrial warfare which had broken out after 1870; as Brown would have him, he would pacify and elevate workers by assuring them adequate wages and decent working conditions as the wisest way to maintain both production and profits.[1]

Brown's thinking resembled traditional paternalism, but his distinction between managers and capitalists was a significant response to changing industrial conditions. Moreover, he added a new dimension to this industrial paternalism by proposing that his good kings create a system which directly involved workers in company affairs, at least in the form of a profit-sharing plan. As examples of industrial enlightenment, he mentioned some distinctly unconventional businessmen. One was Robert Owen, whose model community at New Lanark was a matter of history, but the other was a still living Frenchman, Jean Baptiste Godin, whose influence eventually involved nearly half a century and two distinct experiments in paternalism along Fourierist lines.[2]

Godin (1817–1888) was a Gallic Horatio Alger hero. Beginning as a blacksmith, he made a fortune as a manufacturer of iron stoves in Guise, northeast of Paris, but in the process he became deeply concerned over the social tensions generated by industrialization.[3] Sometime before the Revolution of 1848, Godin began to work out a system of industrial relationships with his employees, using Fourierism as his principal guide. To provide a home for himself and his phalanx of workers, he began in 1859 to build a version of the phalanstery, the "Social Palace." Consisting of three interlocking parallelograms, each with a glass-roofed center court, it contained apartments for workers along with a variety of cooperative stores and company facilities, the ensemble making the enclosed little world so favored by paternalistic employers.[4]

The Social Palace, however, was something more than a company town in phalansterian dress. Even before he began to build it, Godin instituted a system of profit-sharing based on the Fourierist formula for the division of profits among capital, talent, and labor. By 1870, he had also established funds to pay medical expenses and provide pensions for his workers and also to supplement the wages of his lowest-paid employees so as to guarantee them incomes sufficient to support their families. Along with the Social Palace and a school where worker children were educated along Fourierist lines, these funds constituted Godin's "Familistere," which he intended would eventually be managed and owned by the workers.[5]

Before he died in 1888, Godin attracted the attentions of many social observers, including a number of Americans. Felix Adler, the founder of the Ethical Culture Society, urged American employers to emulate Godin's accomplishments. Laurence Gronlund, the Socialist, doubted that the Social Palace would be welcomed in individualistic America, but in 1886 he did commend the Familistere as "the only instance in the world of a business enterprise, founded on Fourier's principles, meeting with a financial success . . . a splendid material prosperity."[6] Some observers were essentially hostile. Benjamin Tucker, an anarchist, described the Familistere as dominated by "an atmosphere of supervision and routine" and the Social Palace as needing only "a few bolts and bars to make it seem like a prison." And an old-line Fourierist complained that Godin was "but a routinist" who had developed "a narrow and superannuated system of discipline" which omitted the essential spirit of Fourierism.[7]

Despite such criticisms, the Social Palace enjoyed a generally positive image, thanks especially to the publicity given it by Edward and Marie Howland. The outlooks of both Howlands had been shaped by pre-Civil War radical reform. Edward, the Harvard-educated son of a southern cotton broker, moved to New York, where he became interested in a variety of "advanced" causes from free love to labor reform; he had some firsthand experience with Godin's experiment when he visited France in the early 1860s. Marie had had a much varied life as a Lowell factory girl, photographer, and teacher; before she married Howland, she had become involved with free-love, had been married and divorced, and had lived at Godin's Social Palace. Both had resided at Edward Underhill's Unity House, from which they may have visited the old North American Phalanx.[8] In 1868, the Howlands settled at Hammonton, New Jersey, where their home soon became part of the radical Hammonton-Vineland axis that had developed out of Charles K. Landis's land-development schemes; among their visitors were Albert Brisbane and some of the other social radicals of New York and Philadelphia.[9]

In 1872, Edward published a glowing account of the Social Palace in *Harper's Monthly,* presenting it as an example of how applied Fourierism could solve the problem of harmonizing labor and capital. Without displacing the individual family, Godin had created the conditions which led the members of his Familistere to act for the good of each other as one common family. Moreover, he had been able to make this model industrial community produce large profits for all concerned, thereby demonstrating the utility of the idea for profit-minded American capitalists. "In this country," said Howland in concluding his article, "there are most probably now in operation a thousand industrial enterprises employing capitals larger than that which produced the Familistere."[10] Although antebellum capitalists had failed to respond to the appeal of the phalanx, perhaps postwar Captains of Industry could be persuaded to adopt the model of the Familistere.

Marie Howland rather luridly embellished the Fourierist cause in 1874 by publishing her novel, *Papa's Own Girl,* based on her personal knowledge of life in the Social Palace. Twice republished, the book acquired some notoriety because of its advanced views of sexual relations; it was banned in Boston. It may also have had some influence on Edward Bellamy's *Looking Backward,* most of which was written shortly after *Papa's Own Girl's* republication in 1886.[11] Howland's novel reflects the influence of Fourierism in varied ways, including an expressed regret that Americans, instead of killing each other in the Civil War, had not "organized our vast army for the purpose of draining and reclaiming the Dismal Swamp," an industrial army that could have been inspired by "music and fancy-dress balls" to feats of heroic labor.[12]

The hero of *Papa's Own Girl,* is a European nobleman, Count Frauenstein, who brings Godin's gospel to the United states, where he is able to persuade a group of people to build a Social Palace for 2000 people, "a magnificent structure, besides which the palace of Versailles will seem the work of a 'prentice hand.' " Eventually, its inhabitants were to acquire ownership through the rents they paid for their apartments. In this Palace, everyone has access to material and social benefits not even available to the rich. "A man wants to have a home of his own," says Frauenstein; "leisure for studying social and political questions; he wants baths whereby to keep himself clean; good clothes for himself and his family; he wants his wife freed from the washtub and the cooking stove; he wants a guarantee of support for sickness and old age; and especially does he want to see his children educated and brought up to be noble men and women." The full range of the middle-class yearnings raised by modern progress is satisfied amid a highly civilized environment complete with schools, a theatre, a library, and an astronomical observatory plus a billiard-saloon and a large indoor swimming pool. The richman's mansion is opened to all.[13]

This fictional Familistere also realizes the old Fourierist promise of satisfying and efficient labor. The domestic drudgery of women is eliminated by the better organization of work and the use of machinery made possible by the collective household. Perhaps because she was less familiar with the working world of men, Marie has her Count speak rather vaguely of work scientifically organized on the basis of a scientific understanding of human nature: "We are just beginning to learn that man is not to be adapted to labor, but that labor, through machinery and scientific organization, is to be adapted to man." Properly organized, labor like life itself is a "pleasant exercise" that strengthens both body and mind, becoming so attractive that there is no question that all will work for the good of themselves and their community.[14]

Papa's Own Girl, being fiction, ends on a triumphant note. Under Count Frauenstein's leadership, the Social Palace is completed, its façade displaying in large letters the words "LIBERTY-EQUALITY-FRATERNITY," and it is opened in a great festive ceremony embellished with banners bearing Fourierist slogans like "the Series distributes the Harmonies." A new era has begun that will bring the perfection of the race in a harmonious society, totally refuting the obsolete notion preached by an obsolete theology that man was bad by nature. Cooperative society would soon spread over the earth, assisted by the railroad and the telegraph which were bringing mankind into a mutually dependent relationship: "This is our millennium, . . . the reign of peace, harmony, and love."[15]

All that was required was one Count Frauenstein, one visionary and prestigeous entrepreneur to bring the requisite people and capital together. Marie Howland's novel won some favorable notice, as had Edward's article two years before, but no captain of radical social reform came forth to follow up on the work of a Landis in New Jersey or a de Boissiere in Kansas.[16] The Howlands, however, did succeed in attracting the attention of an aspiring entrepreneur from nearby Pennsylvania. One day in 1874 Albert K. Owen visited them at their home in Hammonton, laying the basis for a partnership which eventually radically altered the course of all their lives.

Albert Kinsey Owen (1847–1916) was not related to Robert Owen, but there were notable similarities in their careers. The later Owen began as a civil engineer connected with the dominant industry of his day, railroads.[17] In the early 1870s, the young engineer left his Chester, Pennsylvania, home to work for the western railroad promoter General William J. Palmer. It was as part of a survey party sent by Palmer to Mexico that Owen first encountered his destiny when in 1872 he made his way to the Pacific Coast and found a harbor which he envisioned as the terminus of a great railroad. After naming the harbor Topolobampo (Hidden Water), he returned to the United States to begin a long series of efforts to raise support for the railroad, which he planned to build from the Rio Grande to the Pacific. His attempts to get congressional support failed, but in 1882 he did procure a concession from the Mexican government to build his Texas, Topolobampo, and Pacific Railway. By then, he had concluded that he needed a large town to serve as a terminus of and a source of labor for his railroad project, and so he turned his attentions to promoting the construction of a great new "Pacific City" at Topolobampo.[18]

The seemingly ever-energetic Owen was an exceptionally prolific author of pamphlets that promised great world benefits from his projects. In 1884, he began a new series of writings intended to raise popular interest in Pacific City and his own special formula for paradise, "Integral Cooperation," an idea which he apparently derived from the Knights of Labor of which he was a member. Some of the more radical Knights had previously argued that workers could escape from wage-slavery only through integral cooperation, i.e., through the formation of cooperative communities whose autonomy would be assured by the complete integration of both production and consumption. "Do not produce to sell," urged one proponent, "do not buy to consume. Be independent of capital, independent of markets and of the price of labor. Work for yourselves." Another advocate had published a book proposing that integral cooperation be applied in the form of a "self-supporting home colony" only shortly before Owen published his first work on the subject.[19]

Owen, however, was a eclectic thinker who concocted his own brand of integral cooperation from a variety of sources. At times, he sounded like Robert Owen (especially when he promised that "our machine will make good people out of bad persons") and at other times like Fourier; but the dominant voice was that of a post–Civil War engineer and railroad promoter who dreamed of adapting the model of an organized and disciplined army to his goals: "Just so must we lovers of peace, security, and beautiful homes organize our forces and marshall our columns for construction." The watchwords of the new movement were to be *"Duty, Interdependence and Equity,"* and the means were to be the organization of a great cooperative effort under the management of one company, which in 1886 he was able to incorporate in Colorado as the Credit Foncier Company of Sinaloa.[20]

Owen planned to raise the necessary capital for his project by mass merchandising the stock of the Credit Foncier Company, the principal attraction being the promise of a safe and secure home in a mild climate well away from the tensions and anxieties of industrial America. The company was authorized to issue 100,000 shares of capital stock at $10 each, purchases being limited to no more than 48 shares, presumably to protect against the influence of rich capitalists. For $20, the purchaser would get a share of stock and one "lot-interest" entitling him to occupy 400 square yards of the company lands at Pacific City.[21]

The company promised to erect separate dwellings, grouped in units of four, for families with lot-interests and to build "great palaces" for others, all as part of a well-planned metropolis covering 29 square miles. There would be centralized places for "cooking, washing, manufacturing and exchanging" to reduce drudgery, a network of "wires for heat, light, power and sound," and another network of underground pipes not only to provide water and steam but also to deliver packages and messages from place to place. It would be the world's first horseless city, since "in this age of electric motors, tricycles, and bicycles, horses can be excluded in largely settled cities." With its parks and green lawns,

Pacific City would provide an ideal combination of city and country life.[22]

The company itself would be a benevolent monopoly, managing all trade and production in the interests of efficiency and harmony. It would provide employment for everyone suited to his or her particular talents at equitable wages; women would receive the same pay as men for the same kind of work. Once Pacific City was established, everyone would attend school until the age of 20, work for the next 30 years, and then retire at 50 to a life of leisure. The company, the corporate embodiment of its stockholding inhabitants, would provide schools and cultural facilities, health care and pensions, and anything else that might be required for the happiness and well-being of its members.[23] It would be an all-governing, paternalistic protector of the people in capitalistic form. Harmony, security, health, and happiness could be purchased for only $20 a share.

Amid these happy promises, however, appeared the totalitarian tendencies of an efficiency engineer. The company was to make sure that the special talents of everyone were put to proper use for the good of the community: "The usefulness of every member in this way becomes absolutely interdependent and dovetailed with the interests of every other member." At Pacific City, there were to be no independent businesses, no churches or religious sects, no sexual relationship but monogamy, no political parties, and nothing else that might interfere with communal harmony. "Only when many think, work and rest together," said Owen in 1892, "under the rule of a certain measure of discipline is the divine spark in man able to redeem and enoble him."[24] Little wonder that Benjamin Tucker could warn that integral cooperation was "a very pretty name for absolute depotism" and a fellow anarchist, John W. Lloyd, could call the dream city a "one-horse heaven, where even Cupid has to submit to the 'directors' " of the company.[25]

Yet Tucker also noted that some anarchists and advocates of free love were attracted to Owen's scheme. In fact, the Topolobampo project seems to have become something of a rallying ground for the old-guard advocates of cooperative community, who were attracted to it by what became a national publicity campaign.[26] John W. Lovell, a New York bookseller, not only published Owen's *Integral Cooperation* but also contributed his own *A Co-Operative City* (1886) as well as money to the cause, which he hoped would prove to be "the happy medium" on which both radical socialists and anarchists could agree. Even greater support came from the Howlands who in 1885 began a one-couple propaganda blitz. Marie Howland, who called herself one of "the 'Old Guard' of reformers," published her translation of Godin's *Solutions Sociales* and republished her *Papa's Own Girl,* while Edward began to issue a bi-weekly newspaper, *The Credit Foncier of Sinaloa,* at Hammonton with the hopes of making it a new *Harbinger.*[27]

The Howlands' publicity efforts revealed a distinct intention of guiding the movement in the direction of Fourierism. Marie spoke of the "grand success" of the North American Phalanx owing to its "organization according to the series, as discovered by Charles Fourier." Edward went further by publishing Charles Sears' history of the Phalanx in order to provide a model for the organization of social life at Topolobampo. In his introduction, Howland expressed his enthusiasm for the Fourierist organization of labor and declared it "the only method of uniting harmonously by principles of democracy with all that is good in the one-man power." Since that organization provided for self-directing work groups, he probably hoped that it would serve as a check on Owens' one-man power at Pacific City; Owen had begun to refer to himself as "your leader" in his communications to the membership.[28]

The publicity efforts of the Howlands and others did attract attention to Topolobampo from as far away as England, where it was mocked by the *Saturday Review* as "Utopolobampo." Ebenezer Howard made reference to it in his *Garden Cities of Tomorrow,* although largely to indicate what his model city would not be, i.e., the exclusive employer of its citizens.[29] In America, the good news was spread across the Great Plains into Colorado and on to the Pacific, accompanied by predictions from the Howlands and others that integral cooperation was the highway to the Promised Land.[30] Owen himself described the Credit Foncier as "the Messiah which comes to lift us out of the present chaos of irresponsibility and crime" into a new era of harmony and order. His plan, he said at another time, was one "by which a colony of 500, or a nation of 600 million people might be united intelligently, forcibly, and amicably" as one well-integrated society.[31]

The effort resembled the propaganda blitz launched by Brisbane and other Fourierists in the early 1840s. The results were, if anything, even more disappointing. Although in 1887 one journal claimed that the project had the support of over 5000 members who had pledged more than half a million dollars to it, the pledges yielded only about $25,000 in cash.[32] As in the past, money was overstretched by enthusiasm, which led to a premature and doomed attempt to create Pacific City. By the end of 1886 more than 200 people had gathered at Topolobampo Bay, mostly from western states, to "eat mush and dream of utopia." Over the next seven years, some 1300 people tried life there for varying but generally short periods of time, arriving from 34 states and several foreign countries, the largest number coming from Kansas, Colorado, and California. Owen himself did not join the colony, concentrating his energies on an increasingly desperate search for money. In 1888, though, the Howlands settled there to claim their ten lot-shares in the hope that the warm Mexican sun would cure Edward's slow but steadily debilitating paralysis which had forced him into a wheelchair.[33]

Topolobampo was not a total disaster. Most of the people lived in tents or thatched huts, but they generally enjoyed the climate and the company, their lives enlivened by community dances, and an eleven-piece band. Although they fell short of the Howland's hopes for serial labor, they did apply some Fourierism to organize a community of work, paying themselves in the form of labor "credits" used for purchases within the community. Eventually, they were able to lay a basis for agricultural prosperity by digging a seven mile irrigation canal, a major achievement. They could boast that they had no rents to pay, no lawyers, no jails, and no crime. On the other hand, they had no electricity, no delivery tubes, no city, no railroad, and no viable economy. In 1890, one observer described life in the colony "as a long-drawn picnic where excesses have been avoided but where the ice-cream and cake have all been consumed." The colony was soon to be temporarily reinvigorated by new members and money, but the picnic was about to end.[34]

Instead of the harmony of integral cooperation, the colonists found ways of quarreling among themselves over personalities, over principles, and over water-rights in their irrigation ditch. Internal conflicts, isolation, deprivation, and disease led many to leave, shrinking the population from a peak of 300 to 240 by 1890. Although new arrivals increased the population to nearly 500 in 1892, the colony remained too small and poorly organized to support itself, much less build a city or a railroad. Pacific City might have been partly realized if Owen had succeeded in raising money for his railroad, but the utopian and "socialistic" reputation of the colony had further weakened the confidence of capitalists in his projects. Although he did succeed in persuading several other entrepreneurs to provide some money to keep the colony going, this soon led to quarrels with his new partners that disrupted the scheme at the top while quarrels among the colonists were weakening it at the bottom.[35]

These conflicts were virtually assured by Owen's booster tactics. In 1891, his Kansas-Sinaloa Investment Company, headquartered in the small southeastern Kansas town of Chetopa, advertised in Edward Bellamy's *New Nation* that its stock was a better investment than government bonds: "Friends of cooperation should avail themselves of the opportunity to aid the cause and at the time secure a safe and profitable investment." Soon after, he announced that he had enough money to construct the first 15 miles of his Mexican Central Railroad and that the colony could furnish the workers needed to construct and operate the line. In order to convince investors that he had found a way to reduce the costs of construction, he claimed that the colonists had agreed to provide their labor in exchange for stock in the railroad. Whatever the truth of this claim, it was a questionable way of fulfilling his promises, advertised elsewhere, that the worker would be assured "the full product of his labor."[36]

The suspicion that Owen was less interested in founding utopia than in finding a labor force for his "co-operative railroad" hardly inspired, confidence in his leadership, nor did much of his subsequent behavior. During the first five years of the Pacific colony, he had, like his earlier namesake, rarely been present in the community, his chief role being that of outside fund raiser and distant voice of hope; but in 1892 he did spend two months there, bringing a temporary revival of utopian enthusiasm among the colonists. This, however was soon followed by his promulgation of a new definition of governing principles intended to eliminate anything which was "not of an essentially business character," a policy at odds with hopes for a cooperative community. On net, the chief result of Owen's intrusion was to intensify opposition to his leadership and to further demoralize the colonists.[37]

One generally optimistic account of the colony in 1893 ended with the observation that "the lack of religious feeling, the endless grind for material things, the years of demand for hopefulness upon the spirit of each colonists, have been productive of discouragement for many." For a time, spirits were revived by rumors that "English capitalists with socialistic ideas" were preparing to invest in Owen's schemes, but that distant boon did not materialize. It became evident that no railroad would be built by any means in the foreseeable future (it was not completed until 1962), and even the most dedicated colonists began to leave. By 1898 Pacific City had withered away amid charges that Owen was an adventurer and swindler and Owen's own complaints that the colony had "been broken up by an organized set of speculators." In 1901, most of the land was sold to the Sinaloa Sugar Company, which developed it into a profitable agricultural operation; the last of the few remaining colonists at Topolobampo died in 1967 at the age of 94.[38]

This Mexican adventure left its principals poorer and perhaps a little wiser. Edward Howland died at Topolobampo in 1890, his dream of serial labor and attractive industry unfulfilled. Marie, who was rumored to have had an affair with Owen, eventually moved away from the colony in 1893, convinced that it had failed because of inexperienced management and a lack of money. Eventually, she joined the Georgist paradise at Fairhope, Alabama, where she used 1500 of her husband's books to found a public library. She died at Fairhope in 1921, three years after she published a third edition of her novel under a new title, *The Familistere*.[39]

Albert K. Owen formally abandoned the colony in 1898 and his railroad project a year later, but he did not give up his enthusiasms as a promoter and planner. In 1899, he spoke of plans to build a model city to aid in the development of the New South, and soon he was promoting a "Home Investment Company" to be financed from "some big money" that he expected to get from the sale of some land he owned in Texas. In his declining years, he tried to persuade Congress to fund a transcontinental "multi-highway" which had eleven lanes intended for everything from roller skates to "fast-moving automobiles." The incorrigible booster and visionary died in 1916.[40]

Owen tried to be a combined prophet and businessman, captain of radical reform as well as captain of industry. In doing so, he revived the old Fourierist hope for a beneficient combination of capitalism and cooperative community, only again to disappoint that hope not only by his failure to raise sufficient capital but also by his divided loyalties between cooperative dream and entrepreneurial ambition. Topolobampo was the final burial ground of the faith in a capitalistic form of organized cooperation, the dusty end of a fifty-year adventure in Fourierism. Even as Owen and the Howlands were attempting to revitalize the old faith in the late 1880s, they were already defeated even in the culture of dissent by the competition of a newer generation of social radicals who excluded capitalism from the old socialist camp in order to create what was intended to be a "modern" socialism.

XI

The Cooperative Commonwealth: Gronlund and Bellamy

The Topolobampo colony was still another failure of the Fourierist hope for some beneficent combination of capitalism and cooperative community. It was also one more defeat for a rapidly fading communitarianism as a way to radical social reform. By the 1880s, the concentration of industry and the consolidation of economic life had dampened the dream of regenerating the world through model communities and voluntary associations. The apparent lesson of these rapidly changing times was that a cooperative society could be established only by national means on national foundations. If the lesson seemed obvious, however, the way to implement it was not. How, especially, could the cause of radical reform find sufficient mass outside of the culture of dissent to overcome the social inertia of the general population? Georgism had attempted to find the answer, only to become entangled in politics and to fail.

How, then, could a truly cooperative society be established in the Industrial Age? The new times furnished a new answer. If the nationalization of life discouraged communitarian effort, it also raised hopes that the new society in itself contained forces for beneficial change—that the very momentum which had crushed communitarianism could take mankind to the promised land if only it were given the right direction. Although industrial monopoly and economic chaos threatened catastrophe for American society, the prospect of catastrophe raised the hope that Americans would be persuaded to take charge of their new destiny and to make the consolidating tendencies of their times a force for a national cooperative society beneficial for all.[1] This hope was first given form and a name by Laurence Gronlund in *The Cooperative Commonwealth,* a book which has an obscure but not insignificant history.

The Danish-born Gronlund had migrated to the United States soon after the Civil War, settling first in Milwaukee and then by the early 1880s in New York City, where his command of both German and English made him a mediator between the city's substantial Teutonic community and American Society. After abandoning a brief and unhappy try at the law, Gronlund determined to make himself the apostle among the Americans for what he called "German," i.e., Marxian, Socialism. He spent several years lecturing on that subject before he published, at his own expense, *The Cooperative Commonwealth* in 1884. By 1886, it was being sold for 25 cents as part of the "Standard Labor Literature" series issued by a Socialist publisher in New York.[2]

In New York, Gronlund seems to have become part of the radical subculture that had existed in that city at least since the days of Robert Owen. He was certainly exposed to the influence of Henry George, whose *Progress and Poverty* won his praise particularly for its service in demonstrating "the utter absurdity of the Malthusian philosophy." Rather than overpopulation causing misery, said Gronlund, "it is misery that causes overpopulation." The Dane, however, could not accept either George's individualism or his contention that land monopoly was the cause of contemporary problems.[3] Similarly, Gronlund dismissed communitarianism as belonging to an outmoded utopian phase of socialism. The "Modern Socialist," he claimed, did not pretend to have invented an ideal society as Marxists accused Owen and Fourier of doing. The Cooperative Commonwealth was not an invention, was not a human "edifice" dependent on the futile actions of individuals, but was a "historical product" in the process of being created by the natural evolution of society.[4]

Gronlund, however, was not content to present Socialism as Marx had developed it. In order to make it more palatable to Americans, he radically altered it along lines that suggest he was possibly influenced by Fourierism; the decade in which he had acculturated himself to American society had been the period of the Fourierist revival and of Noyes's efforts to promote the cause of American socialism. Anxious to strip Socialism of what he later called its "Continental prejudices," Gronlund in effect gutted Marxism by eliminating its emphasis on class conflict and the necessity of a revolutionary overthrow of the existing social order. He assured Americans that his new order of "social cooperation" would arrive by way of peaceful and harmonious evolution along American rather than European lines.[5]

Drawing on the new evolutionary doctrines of Charles Darwin, Gronlund held that society was an organic whole, a natural biological entity, which would evolve in its own special way into a completely integrated organism where "all important instruments of production" would be socialized. The great national monopolies being organized by the Captains of Industry were a natural and inevitable phase in the evolution of the Cooperative Commonwealth: "Is it utopian to expect that all enterprises will become more and more centralized, until in the fulness of time, they end in one monopoly of Society?" Once cooperation became the reigning principle of American society, all Americans would be freed from their present state of "social anarchy" and would merge peacefully into an organic system where they would find brotherhood and "the purest happiness, perfect blessedness."[6]

This heavenly condition would be attained when Americans could be persuaded to accept Gronlund's version of the paternalistic good-king, an all-embracing, organic national "State," 'which would take complete charge of the economy. His State, far from being simply a mediating government, constituted the whole of society. It did not merely resemble a biological organism; it "literally is an organism," which incorporated within itself all members of the nation. As an organic incorporation of all members of society, it would naturally provide for the welfare of all, its relationship to its citizens being "actually that of a tree to its cells." Having thus disposed of what he called "the pettiness and impotency of our individualism," Gronlund painted a glowing picture of the "New Order" which Americans would enjoy when they accepted the State as "man's greatest good."[7]

Gronlund's State would provide for every need. Incorporating as it would all citizens as "public functionaries," it would guarantee effective administration of all social affairs, mobilizing the whole of human competence for the social good. The State would eliminate depressions by equalizing supply and demand and assure an equitable distribution of the social product to the benefit of all. It would eliminate the need for lawyers and their obnoxious trade; it would free women from male tyranny and from "all drudgeries in housekeeping"; it would educate youth to their full potential, and in various other ways serve as the benevolent father of all people, even to the point of seeing to it "that there are no giddy girls running around on the streets." In the Cooperative Commonwealth, "perfect harmony will obtain between the interests of each citizen and those of the citizens at large, just as it now obtains between members of the well-ordered family."[8]

Having envisioned the social equivalent of a universal solvent which would dissolve all social problems, this self-avowed nonutopian faced the usual problems of realizing his ideal. By abandoning the Marxist faith in the proletariat as the instrument of social transformation, Gronlund left himself no recourse other than the hope of persuading society to swim with the tide of history. He did not anticipate a favorable reception from workers or from the general public, since he believed that the "majority are always ignorant, always indolent," but he did expect to persuade "a respectable minority" drawn from all levels of society to form a dynamic nucleus which would act as "the brains of the Revolution." In 1890, he said that six years earlier such a group had been formed in Chicago but had been forced to disband by the tumult caused by the Haymarket bombing. Writing in the anxious climate of the tumultuous 1880s in a nation not yet corrupted by European class prejudices, he hoped to persuade social idealists to unite in support of his all-controlling State. If only he had 10,000 dedicated men and twenty years, he could revolutionize America and establish a cooperative order that would eliminate forever the social anarchy of individualism.[9]

In this, he was to be personally disappointed. Not unexpectedly, anarchists denounced his deification of the State; Benjamin R. Tucker condemned him as "a conceited ignoramus and meddler" who served only to distract and divide workers. Henry George said that Gronlund's State was "an exotic born of European conditions that cannot take root or flourish on American soil."[10] Certainly, most Americans had little inclination to submerge themselves in the State, particularly when Gronlund insisted that the existing family would have no place in his Commonwealth, and neither would "the right of a person to dispose of himself in marriage as he pleases." In general, most American Socialists were embarrassed by Gronlund's enthusiasm for paternalistic government.[11]

The general idea of the cooperative commonwealth did receive a public hearing, but in ways that Gronlund had not anticipated. Having helped sow the seeds of a national utopia, it was his fate to see them sprout in unexpected forms, most notably the Americanized super-state of Edward Bellamy, whose novel *Looking Backward* almost totally obscured *The Cooperative Commonwealth* as the premier expression of national paternalism. The publication of Bellamy's book in 1888 proved to be a major event that marked the opening of a new but eventually troubling career for the cooperative ideal in America. The novel soon became *the* book of the decade and eventually the most popular utopian work ever written.[12] In his fictional paradise, Bellamy achieved a synthesis of ideals and techniques which satisfied a widespread need for assurance that the modern future could be made an age of prosperity and order.

It was Gronlund who best explained the character of both the novel and its author when in 1889 he said that *Looking Backward* was symptomatic of the thinking of the "intellectual classes," a mirror of the discontent of "a million Americans who are not workers" with the disorder and crassness of commercial society. Earlier these classes had turned to Fourierism in the hope of creating a society suited to themselves and, though that "mighty moment" had died, many of those most affected by the novel "undoubtedly are the sons of old Associationists."[13] Whatever the exact merits of Gronlund's genealogy, he was right in saying that Bellamy and many of his contemporaries, like Brisbane and his contemporaries, were driven by their discontents to dream of new societies suited to their personalities and talents. It was a measure of Bellamy's genius that, in fiction and then partly in fact, he succeeded in finding a suitable place for himself and for his generation.

Edward Bellamy (1850–1898) came from a New England family with roots in the millenarian tradition. His father and maternal grandfather were both ministers as was his great-great grandfather, Joseph Bellamy, who more than a century before *Looking Backward* had dreamed of his own millennial utopia where "peace and plenty, universal love and harmony range from town to town." The young Bellamy grew up comfortably in the peaceful factory town of Chicopee in western Massachusetts; the town was his home and his community, and there he was to die in 1898. For a young ambitious American attuned to the modern age, however, these roots were not enough. Rejecting the ministry as a career—to the disappointment of his deeply religious mother—he choose to venture out into the great world, first as an idealistic young traveler in Europe and then as a newspaperman in New York City in the early 1870s. In 1872, he returned to the Connecticut Valley as a writer and book reviewer for the *Springfield Union,* but he brought with him a deepening dissatisfaction both with the world and himself.[14]

In Europe and in New York, he had encountered what he later called "the inferno of poverty beneath our civilization," and the increasingly chaotic 1870s only intensified his feelings of disgust and anxiety over the times. His New England conscience and his ambitions demanded that he act in the interests of charity and order, but like many others he found himself impotent before the mysterious force of the new age. Sporadically weakened by poor health, he felt his powerlessness more than most other idealistic young men, and even more still when he could not find a support-group with which to identify. He had broken his ties with traditional religion and with his church. Although he might have identified with the reawakened Fourierism of the 1870s, he did not do so even though his brother, Frederick, had introduced him to Albert Brisbane in New York.[15] Instead, he retreated into himself, compounding his sense of frustration with the world and leaving him with a feeling that he was only "an atom or grain of sand on a boundless shore," as he said of individuals in general in 1874.[16]

By then, however, he was learning to find some salvation from his sense of personal insignificance, having worked out in an unpublished essay his own "Religion of Solidarity." While Brisbane and others had made Fourierism a link between themselves and the cosmos, Bellamy created his own escape from "the narrow grotto of the individual life" into a larger reinforcing spiritual reality. He concluded that every person lived a dual life, the narrow life of the individual self and the larger, liberating life of an "impersonal" self, a universal soul to which he and the rest of mankind belonged. By relating his personal self with the transcendent "soul of solidarity," he believed that he could attain "a stronger, intenser pulse of feeling than is allowable in the most vigorous assertion of the personality. Individuality, personality, partiality, is segregation, is partition, is confinement; is, in fine, a prison."[17]

The desire for some mystical merger with the universe was common to sensitive young men in perhaps every generation, but what was less common and certainly more noteworthy is Bellamy's comparison of the sense of solidarity to the feelings raised in a military parade, where under "the inspiration of martial music, combining with the instinct of nationalism . . . , the heart of the soldier melts into a happy rapture of self-devotion."[18] Having missed the Civil War, the noblest event of his young life, and also having been denied a much-desired appointment at West Point, it was not surprising that he should view the imagined solidarity of military life as a realized form of his self-invented religion, but it was to be more than a decade before he appreciated the full importance of the military metaphor to his personal search for a social place.

Bellamy left his essay on the Religion of Solidarity incomplete, but he did add a notation to the manuscript in 1887, the year in which he completed *Looking Backward,* that it represented "the germ of what has become my philosophy of life."[19] Although it provided a link with the spiritual realm, this "germ" did not in itself bring the meaningful connection with society he needed. Instead, he was left to pursue a modestly successful but solitary career as a journalist and writer; his work included two of the better novels of the period, *The Duke of Stockbridge* (1879) and *Dr. Heidenhoff's Process* (1881). While in the early 1880s he was drawn into the awakening public concern over social issues, he did not find the key to his problem until the fall of 1886 when he began to write the novel that became *Looking Backward.*[20]

Three years later, he recalled that he had set out to write "a mere literary fantasy, a fairy tale of social felicity . . . out of reach of the sordid and material world of the present," one which he intended to open in the year 3000 with a great parade of a world army. Somehow, early in the writing it occurred to him that this army could serve as "the vehicle of a definite scheme of industrial reorganization." He said that the idea was suggested to him by the military system adopted by European nations, but the timing raises the possibility that it came from Fourierism. In 1886, Marie Howland republished her *Papa's Own Girl,* a book with which Bellamy seems to have been familiar. Moreover, he seems to have been exposed to some of the propaganda churned out in support of Albert K. Owen's Topolobampo project.[21] Whatever the source of the inspiration, it provided the governing concept that transformed this "fairy tale" into a constructive social novel with a credible and original formula for dealing with the chaos of the Industrial Age.

When it was finished, no book better expressed the uneasy attitude of middle-class Americans toward the industrial world of rebellious workers and dominating capitalists. In its opening chapter, Bellamy's comparison of society to a nightmarish stagecoach graphically captured the fears and guilts of many advantaged idealists like himself. They ride on the coach in the sunny clear air, while a suffering many toil to pull its weight along the rocky road of contemporary life. Although the passengers are not without compassion for their human horses, self-interest compels them to concentrate on maintaining their own precarious positions on the swaying coach. In a world of labor strife and monopolistic power, there is no room for brotherly love and also no refuge from anxiety even for the advantaged. How can they be sure that the rebellious toilers, in their rage, will not tip the coach over or that the weaker passengers will not be elbowed off by the stronger?[22]

In *Looking Backward,* these Americans save themselves and the rest of humanity by making a fundamental change in direction which sets them all comfortably on a road to a future of harmony and prosperity set in the year 2000. The turn in the journey occurs when the less secure riders, especially small businessmen threatened by the merciless competition of Big Business, finally agree to change drivers in order to preserve themselves from the unfortunate toiler's lot. Having decided that the existing system of private property and competitive individualism was perilous to their future independence, Americans unite to change the system, not through revolution but through an accommodation with "industrial evolution." Rather than continuing their fruitless effort to destroy monopoly in the interest of petty enterprise, they determine to socialize the "prodigious" benefits associated with the concentration and organization of industry by merging all industry into one "Great Trust" owned by the nation and managed in the public interest.[23]

The most striking feature of the new industrial arrangement is its dependence on what might best be termed "human technology." Although machines evidently play a major role in Bellamy's industrial order, it is especially designed to mobilize human skills and talents for efficient production. In a significant footnote to his story, Bellamy said that "the failure of my age, in any systematic way to develop and utilize the natural aptitude of men for the industries and intellectual avocations was one of the great wastes, as well as one of the common causes of unhappiness of that time." In the year 2000, there is certainly no lack of system to develop and utilize human talents. Maximum efficiency is assured by the elimination of all social classes, which precludes disruptive class tensions while making it possible to deploy the whole population for productive labor on the basis of ability without concern for social standing. This, said Bellamy later, was "the only scientific plan for utilizing the energy of the people in wealth production." When combined with a national school system designed to realize the special aptitudes of every person, the industrial system produces such miracles of wealth as to make everyone rich.[24]

The linchpin of this system was an unqualified economic equality, Bellamy's most original idea. Without exception, healthy or handicapped, male or female, all citizens have equal shares of wealth and its advantages. The wage system has been eliminated in favor of the ruling principle that each person's humanity entitles him to his share of the social product regardless of his particular efforts or needs. Bellamy was particularly insistent on the importance of economic equality, which he called "the keystone of the arch." As an idealist, he believed that it furnished the only sound basis for human brotherhood. As a social architect, he thought that it made his system uniquely different from all other social systems, each of which made some provision for differential rewards based on either contributions or needs.[25]

Bellamy, like most social radicals, believed that money only served to feed man's selfishness. In place of the evil green, the society of the future provides every citizen with a credit card entitling him to an equal share of the national product. No one has any more credit than anyone else, but each person is free to spend his ample share as he pleases to satisfy himself and to embellish his private life. Some give priority to renting the best of the nationally owned housing; some to purchasing the finest of clothes and furnishings from centrally located national warehouses and others to the finest of dinners at public dining halls. Not only is consumption free from restraint but it is virtually required as a matter of policy; each person must use all of his yearly credit before the end of the year or have the unused portion revert to the nation. In a manner suited to the developing new age of mass consumption, the old virtue of thrift is denied, since savings threaten to produce both future concentrations of wealth and the fluctuations in consumer demand that hamper economic planning.[26]

This was the kind of paradise which the modern American could appreciate, especially when he faced the uncertainties of life in the Industrial Age. With public education guaranteed for all, there is no need to sacrifice for the education of children. With economic security assured and economic power socialized, there is no worry about unemployment or about a grinding, poverty-stricken old age. Jobs are made available for all, and there is a guaranteed retirement early enough to satisfy almost any civil servant. At age 21, all enter employment and, at age 45, all retire with a full credit to a life of carefree leisure. As good health care and security assured longevity, the citizens of the year 2000 have a long second life of uninhibited enjoyment: "At twenty-one we become men, but at forty-five we renew youth"—a scheme designed to assure that youth would not be wasted on the young.[27]

Bellamy responded to the realities of the new urban age by setting his paradise in the city of Boston, which in important respects is the Fourierist phalanstery writ large. People occupy private apartments where they enjoy a simple private life undisturbed by the distractions of household responsibilities or the annoyance of servants. Protected from inclement weather by covered walkways, they stroll to public restaurants where they dine in the splendor of their own dining halls on the cooking of professional chefs. All household work is done by "corps of domestic servants" from the Industrial Army, the equivalent of the domestic series of a phalanx: "Our washing is all done at public laundries at excessively cheap rates, and our cooking at public kitchens. The making and repairing of all we wear are done outside in public shops."[28] Bellamy's Boston was a world that advocates of the unitary household like Mrs. C. F. Peirce and Marie Howland could appreciate.

It was a world that promised special benefits to women—and without radical tampering with traditional sexual and family relationships. Within the framework of monogamy and private family life, women enjoy equal opportunities with men. Freed from household drudgery by public laundries and kitchens, they have the same access to education and to fulfilling careers. Although they labor in a separate work force in line with "the distinct individuality of the sexes," they occupy positions of comparable authority to men. As women receive equal credits, they enjoy economic independence, leaving them free to marry or not marry as they choose, and to marry for love and not for some degrading security as in the past. Since women can reject inferior men as the fathers of their children, "race purification" is assured by "sexual selection, with its tendency to preserve and transmit the better types of the race, and let the inferior types drop out."[29]

In the year 2000, harmony also prevails among all nations. Everyone is free to use his credit card to travel anywhere in the world, which has rid itself of national animosities. Unlike the utopias of Plato and More, both of which were geared for war, America makes no sacrifices on the altar of Mars, since it is a part of an international system of peaceful relations maintained by all of the modern nations, each of which has "remodelled" itself along American lines. This system is headed by an international council intended both to regulate relations among the civilized nations and to administer a "joint policy toward the more backward races, which are gradually being educated up to civilized institutions." Throughout the globe, humankind has freed itself from the twin curses of poverty and war.[30]

In these and other ways, the establishment of a nationally owned and managed economy results in a society without classes, human degradation, conflict, anxiety, crime, and unhappiness. In such a social environment, all but the most radically imperfect of men are good; human nature remains the same, but behavior has changed with the environment. No person is forced to steal or beg for his living; no personality and no body is twisted by poverty and care. Beyond that, all are free to realize their full creative potentials for the benefit of themselves and the human race. Inventions multiply, further reducing the need for labor; the arts, literature, and music flourish.[31] The society of the year 2000, near perfect though it is, stands on the threshold of an even greater perfection and at the gates of heaven itself: "The end is lost in light. For twofold is the return of man to God . . . the return of the individual by way of death, and the return of the race by the fulfillment of the evolution, when the divine secret hidden in the germ shall be perfectly unfolded. . . . Humanity has burst the chrysalis. The heavens are before it."[32] Pervading this happy scene is the benign influence of the Religion of Solidarity, which is realized on earth as it had been in Bellamy's youthful yearnings.

The mainspring of the coming Millennium, however, causes one to wonder whether Heaven had captured the Industrial Age or the reverse, since Bellamy's whole system depended on a decidedly mechanical organization of the labor force under rigorous management. In fact, his minutely systemized arrangement of labor strongly suggests that his version of the future was to be won chiefly by the Captains of Industry with an assist from the Prussian army. The main feature of *Looking Backward* is the "Industrial Army," basically a model national corporate bureaucracy equipped with both the trappings of a military force and the powers associated with universal compulsory military service. When they reach the age of 21, all citizens are drafted into the labor system, there to serve under the command of lieutenants, captains, and generals. Although they are ostensibly free to choose their line of work, the overriding reality is subjugation to the control and discipline of their superiors; the performance of each worker is carefully graded by his bureau chief, the reports being filed for later use in determining promotions or demotions from rank.[33]

In theory, the abuse of power by a superior is discouraged by the pervasive rule of economic equality—there would be no material profit in such an abuse, but Bellamy at the same time does provide incentives for effort in the form of psychological profits, especially promotions to higher levels of power and also various honors symbolized by white, blue, and red ribbons; an officer depends on his promotion to a higher rank on the reported efficiency of his men. In theory, too, little compulsion is needed to encourage men to work, since they are supposedly inspired to maximum exertion by a desire for public honors and, even more, by a civic patriotism equal to religious fervor. Yet in Bellamy's work force, officers are obligated to "hold their followers up to the highest standards of performance and permit no lagging," while anyone who persistently refused to give his best efforts runs the risk of "solitary imprisonment on bread and water until he consents."[34]

The chances of altering this system are few, since Bellamy, who was as contemptuous of politics as he was admiring of military efficiency, has abolished most of representative government. It is true that all major officers of the Industrial Army, including the President of the American nation, are elected, but voting is restricted to those who have already retired from the army. Although Bellamy mentions municipal governments (without reference to any mode of appointment), he has eliminated state governments, because they "would have interfered with the control and disciplines of the Industrial Army," while he also has reduced Congress to the status of a board of directors whose chief function is to approve or condemn the report of each retiring President.[35]

This was not a system that one would expect Bellamy himself to join, nor does he, since he exempts his kind from it. He has his *alter ego,* Julian West, conveniently enter the separate world of Dr. Leete and his daughter. What West learns of the Industrial Army is from Leete, who is not a part of it. The doctor belongs, instead, to a small meritocracy of professionals, scholars, scientists, and writers who escape service in the Army by passing a series of tests that qualify them for university training and for professional life. As they are not members of the industrial organization, they can hold no office in it, but this, if anything, is a blessing for those who like Bellamy were essentially apolitical. In this society, with well-regulated workers and without capitalists and politicians, where order is assured and production is automatic, there was no need for the Leetes and Bellamys to concern themselves with its affairs.

In general, this class is set apart from the mass and their sweaty world. Factories and farmers are beyond the horizon, and all goods are delivered impersonally by pneumatic tubes. The most notable bit of technology in the year 2000, the musical telephone or radio, keeps even culture and religion at a safe distance; a minister's sermon can be heard in the privacy of the Leete home.[36] The Brotherhood of Man has been established on earth, but these relationships were notably remote and impersonal. That was about as much solidarity as the frail and essentially private author could bear in his attempt to escape from the grotto of individual life.[37]

As the twentieth century was as yet unknown, it would unjust to accuse this friend of humanity of having consciously invented the modern totalitarian regime in order to make a secure place for his class. In fact, he offered his system as the best way to protect Americans from the tyranny of selfish and inefficient plutocrats, believing that modernization would inevitably bring the centralization of economic power. If so, then it was in the popular interest to place the economy under public control for public ends, free from both the power of monopolistic capitalists and the disharmonies of class conflict. He also convinced himself that, with the suppression of selfish individualism, the whole of national power would be directed by a religious dedication to the ideal of Brotherhood.[38]

Whatever his intentions, however, Bellamy's scheme did break rather ominously from the earlier spirit of social idealism. He insisted that his "Nationalism" was radically different both from earlier communitarianism and from Marxism, and he was right, although in a way he did not fully comprehend. In adapting the cooperative dream to a national society, he had altered its essential character as well as its scale. Not even Gronlund had founded his ideal society on a system so impersonally bureaucratic and so unrelenting in its corporate embrace. Despite Bellamy's clear distaste for industrial capitalism, *Looking Backward* does leave one to wonder whether society had absorbed the "Great Trust" or whether the Great Trust had absorbed society.[39]

Probably because it was so closely attuned to contemporary concerns and hopes, the book won a wider hearing than any other utopian work before or since. Although it was literarily inferior to some of Bellamy's earlier works, it was a superior utopian novel that attracted readers by its ingenious detail and by its gimmick whereby its hero, Julian West, is actually transported from contemporary to future Boston, the hub of the year 2000; undoubtedly many readers shared the pleased surprise of one reviewer when he discovered that what seemed to be a conventional fictional awakening from pleasing dreams to ugly realities in actuality is itself a nightmare from which West, new citizen of the future, recovers to claim his share of paradise.[40] With the support of this device, the novel appealed to those practical-minded readers who were less interested in social fantasy than they were in a credible prediction of a realizable future.

Groups as varied as Socialists, Populists, and the Women's Temperance Union praised the book as supporting their special hopes for the future. Mark Twain called *Looking Backward* "the latest and best of all Bibles," and said that Bellamy had "made the accepted heaven paltry by inventing a better one on earth." Those who shared Bellamy's hunger for a socializing religion saw the book as a herald of a new day when man's selfishly individualistic materialism would give way to a brotherhood of the spirit. Others were drawn to its promise of material plenty and comfort, one which William Dean Howells said appealed especially to small-town Americans: *"Looking Backward,* with its material delights, its communized facilities and luxuries, could not appeal to people on lonely farms who scarcely knew them, or to people in cities who were tired of them."[41]

Probably, however, the greatest attention came from America's fast growing professional and middle classes, enticed by Bellamy's dream of a stable, harmonious society in which middle class life would be secure from the threats posed by tyrannical capitalists, scruffy politicians, troublesome servants, and rebellious workers. William Morris, a rival English utopian, said that the governing ideal of men like Bellamy "is that of the industrious *professional* middle class of today, purified from the crime of complicity with the monopolistic class, and become independent instead of being, as they are now, parasitical."[42] Morris's observation could be applied to many of those who drifted toward some form of Socialism.

For these and other reasons, the book became a runaway best-seller. Within a decade, 400,000 copies had been distributed in the United States alone and many more elsewhere in the world; between 1890 and 1935, at least 235,000 copies were sold in England. *Looking Backward* was translated into Chinese and Japanese as well as every European language; some 50,000 copies were published in Russian before the Bolshevik Revolution.[43] One measure of the book's popularity was the readiness of some people to accuse Bellamy of plagiarizing from one source or another. Albert K. Owen claimed that the author got his ideas for economic organization from the published propaganda for the Topolobampo project: "Whole sentences are taken from our publications." Elder Frederick Evans charged that much of Bellamy's social scheme had been appropriated from the Shaker societies.[44] Among varied claims that *Looking Backward* was drawn from the literature of Socialism was the assertion of *Harper's Magazine* that Bellamy's all-powerful state "is constructed almost exactly upon the lines of Mr. Gronlund's *Co-operative Commonwealth*," a judgment which may have helped persuade Gronlund to temporarily withdraw his own book from circulation as an act of agreement with the more popular work.[45]

The extraordinary popularity of the novel attracted various social idealists who thought that it would help them attain their particular dreams. Gronlund hoped that it would rally "our well-off classes" behind his plan for a socialist elite to lead the masses, while Daniel DeLeon, the future leader of the Socialist Labor party, saw it as confirming his hopes for social revolution.[46] More broadly, the book served to mobilize a new generation of idealists who believed that the popular enthusiasm raised by it could be formed into force strong enough to transform society. By 1890, a movement had developed whose influence promised to be far greater than that of Associationism half a century before. Through the agency of Bellamy's social nationalism, the new decade might finally be made to yield the millennium which Samuel Hopkins had predicted a century earlier. To have practical effect, however, the nationalist movement was forced to move into the risky realm of national politics where, like the Georgist movement, it was soon to fail.

XII

The Nationalist Movement

Looking Backward was one of those rare books that had a significant impact on its own times. Even more than *Progress and Poverty*, it appealed to those many Americans who were anxious about their rapidly modernizing society. Many of the 200,000 people who bought the book in 1888 and 1889 belonged to the rapidly expanding new middle class of white-collar workers and salaried professionals, who wanted some way to protect themselves from the corruptions of partisan politics and the discontents of the lower classes as well as the despotism of concentrated capital. By providing for bureaucratic control over the consolidated economy, Bellamy promised to satisfy this need without the sacrifice of the benefits of industrial progress; his year 2000 was comfortably familiar territory to his readers, their own emerging modern future purged of its terrors.[1]

Bellamy's Nationalism had its most significant initial effect on the culture of dissent, which had grown larger and more complex with the progress of the century. A half century earlier, the combination of Fourierism and Swedenborgianism had established a respectable basis for dissent. Like them, Nationalism offered a form of cooperative brotherhood in which people of culture and sensibility would have an assured place without the distractions of power, the competition of money, or the presence of dissatisfied masses. For such people, Bellamy's plan for an equal sharing of economic abundance promised to end the ugly struggle over material things, and his Religion of Solidarity promised to be the new practical faith that would serve as the soul for the industrial age.

These cultural dissenters were only a small part of the total population, but their zeal and their talents made them able publicists for the new cause. Many of Bellamy's first allies were members of dissenting religions. The cult leader, Thomas Lake Harris (whose long career had taken him from a marginal involvement in the American Union of Associationists to the leadership of his own religious community at Fountaingrove, California) declared that the enthusiasm for Nationalism indicated that "paradise is in the air."[2] Especially important were the Theosophists, a comparatively new religious group whose beliefs mixed Christianity and Oriental religion. They saw in the Religion of Solidarity a way to realize their own ideals; in the words of the Boston Theosophist Sylvester Baxter, Nationalism would bring to "all men a realizing sense of the unity of all things, of the solidarity of the universe" and create the social form needed for true brotherhood.[3]

Theosophists like Baxter had a significant influence in persuading Bellamy to launch a movement to propagate his ideas. Before the end of 1888, Baxter and his fellow Theosophist Cyrus Field Willard had taken the lead in forming the first Boston Nationalist Club, whose 200 members were a fair cross-section of the early movement. Along with the Theosophists, there was a small company of retired army officers headed by Thomas Wentworth Higginson who were interested in Bellamy's plan for a well-organized solidarity; forty years earlier, Higginson had thought of surrendering himself to the impulse of a "new dawning Age of Faith" which he believed would eventually demand a new organization of society. At least 25 women joined the club, attracted by the cultural and moral character of Nationalism as well as by its emphasis on woman's rights; one of them was Frances E. Willard, a cousin of Cyrus Willard and the long-time president of the Woman's Christian Temperance Union. Other members were intellectuals, writers, and clerics. Solomon Schindler, a rabbi and radical reformer, proved to be an especially able publicist for Nationalism, his first contribution being the translation of *Looking Backward* into German.[4]

Many members accepted Bellamy's claim that the Religion of Solidarity was Christianity in its true social form. One early enthusiast, a "lady of culture and literary attainment," predicted that Nationalism would soon transform all of society, "for the message is so simple and plain, and the benefits so clearly discernible for the millions that when they hear the new truth and see how it can be realized, we will have practical Christianity for the first time realized in the state as well as in the heart of man." The writer William Dean Howells joined the Boston club in hope of finding what he later described as the "commonwealth of peace and goodwill" of the first Christians.[5] Nationalism had at least a temporary appeal for the many religious people who had been alienated from conventional Christianity by its apparent betrayal of the original ideal of brotherly love.

One of the most notable of these early Nationalists was Edward Everett Hale, the long-time minister of a Boston Unitarian church whose members included Cyrus Willard. Hale was a living link between Nationalism and the radical social idealism of the past. As a young minister in Worcester, he had been a leading figure in the formation of the New England Emigrant Aid Society, a cooperative effort to establish colonies of New Englanders in Kansas. After the Civil War, he published (1869) a long utopian story, "My Visit to Sybaris," describing an ideal society modeled on Charles K. Landis's experiment in land reform at Vineland, New Jersey. Soon, Hale began to dream of a "New Civilization" devoted to cooperative individualism under the ruling influence of the spirit of Christian brotherhood. In 1888, he gave this dream a corporate form in his *How They Lived at Hampton,* a novel featuring a model woolen-mill where skillful management and an employee profit-sharing plan maintain a productive cooperation between capital and labor.[6]

It is doubtful that Hale and some of the other well-bred Bostonians fully approved of Bellamy's scheme; Hale's own plan stressed voluntary cooperation on a communal basis. They did, however, see in *Looking Backward* the promise of a social order suited to the interests of their class. Bellamy was willing to encourage this view, as he indicated when he wrote in support of Willard's organization of the Boston Club that "I thoroughly approve what you say as to directing your efforts more particularly to the conversion of the cultured and cultivated class. That was precisely the special end for which *Looking Backward* was written."[7]

Like the Fourierists before him, he hoped to affect a union of Americans under the leadership of respectable people which could redeem society from the evils of competitive capitalism.

The formation of the Boston Nationalist Club led to the establishment in May 1889 of a monthly journal, the *Nationalist,* which was quickly followed by a burst of organized action.[8] By 1890, more than 150 Nationalist clubs had sprung up in many towns and cities outside the South. Generally, these clubs had weekly meetings for discussions of Bellamy's ideas and at least occasional public meetings to propagate the new faith. They appeared in most northern cities including New York (where the club included publisher John Lovell, a supporter of Albert K. Owen, and the Socialist Daniel DeLeon) and Chicago (where Clarence Darrow was a member), but they tended to cluster in two areas.[9] One was in eastern Massachusetts, an old center of cultural dissent. The other was on the opposite side of the continent in California, where the new enthusiasm, kindled by Theosophists and other dissenting religious groups, inspired the formation of some 60 clubs by the summer of 1890; one nationalist from San Diego even composed a hymn for the movement, "Tis the Rosy Dawn of Freedom." An observer said that these clubs were generally headed by people connected with literature and the professions, people who believed that Nationalism had, as one put it, "put a silk hat on socialism." by removing the socialist ideal from the grubby clutches of foreigners and radical workingmen.[10]

The most active of the California clubs was that in Los Angeles, one of the more than 30 clubs in the southern part of the state. It published a weekly Nationalist newspaper and held public meetings where lecturers such as H. Gaylord Wilshire—later the "Millionaire Socialist"—spoke to as many as a thousand people on the merits of nationalism. One notable lecturer was Charlotte Perkins Gilman, who was drawn to Bellamy's scheme by its combination of rational efficiency with "immense human love" as well as by its promise of independence for women. Another speaker was her uncle, Edward Everett Hale, who visited California in 1891 as an emissary of the Boston Club. Hale told his audience that they were the heirs of a distinctively American tradition of cooperation that had begun with the Pilgrims and that had found its best modern form in Nationalism.[11] California was the new New England that would, in union with the old, redeem the nation from its sins.

By the end of 1889, the Nationalists believed they had much to celebrate. Bellamy noted what he called a powerful "current which it is only needful to utilize in order to reach the desired haven" and then proceeded to describe the leading characteristics of the new movement. The first characteristic was also the most basic:

The sentiment of human brotherhood which is the animating principle is a religion in itself, and to understand it in its full significance implies a sense of consecration on the part of those who devote themselves to it. Nationalism is, indeed, based upon the soundest of economic laws; the principle of fraternal cooperation is as certainly the only true science of wealth-production, as it is the only moral basis for society.

The other characteristics flowed out of the first. As human brotherhood included even selfish capitalists, Nationalism was not a "class movement" which would stir up class hatreds but a "citizens' movement" designed to unite all Americans. It was inherently an expression of the highest form of American patriotism, and it was also the best form of American conservatism: "We are the true conservative party, because we are devoted to the maintenance of republican institutions against the revolution being effected by the money power." In this view, Nationalism was a logical and necessary step in the evolution of American democracy, adding economic equality to political equality and so eliminating forever the disparities of wealth and economic power that had disrupted the natural unity of the American people.[12]

Bellamy linked his cause to earlier movements for a cooperative society. Previously, Americans had formed "many movements for a nobler order of society which should embody and illustrate brotherly love, but they failed because the time was not right; that is to say because the material tendencies of the age did not work with the moral." The ideal of brotherly cooperation had had to wait until the trusts and industrial combinations had created the economic basis for a cooperative order. More explicitly, he traced the beginnings of Nationalism back to Associationism fifty years before. The Fourierists had begun a movement that had been interrupted by the conflict over slavery, but with the end of the Civil War "the progress of evolution toward economic Nationalism resumed its flow." With the assistance of such movements as Georgism, the ideal and spirit of brotherly cooperation had steadily developed its influence among Americans. Bellamy predicted that in the 1890s the moral and the economic trends toward national cooperation would naturally converge, creating the opportunity to dismiss the plutocratic money power and to advance American democracy to its completion—if only the people could be awakened to both the opportunity and the peril confronting them.[13]

In January 1891 Bellamy was persuaded to launch a new weekly paper, the *New Nation,* to spread the influence of Nationalist beyond the rather limited audience available to the *Nationalism* magazine, thereby repeating the shift from the *Phalanx* to the *Harbinger* that had marked the propaganda work of the earlier Associationists. This weekly was published in Boston with Bellamy as chief editor. In its prospectus, he pledged that it "will criticize the existing industrial system as radically wrong in morals and preposterous economically, and will advocate the substitution therefor, as rapidly as practicable of the plan of national industrial co-operation"; he also promised that, since "the Christian churches and other religious bodies" were beginning to recognize that Nationalism best embodied the principles of human brotherhood, he would make a significant place for religious news in the paper. Over the next three years, Bellamy and his managing editor, Mason Green, succeeded in making the *New Nation* one of the most respectable radical journals ever published in America, providing a broad though distinctly biased coverage of social, political, and economic developments in the hope of persuading "the thoughtful classes" that only Nationalism could eliminate "the modern never-ending industrial struggle" inherent to the competitive system.[14]

Bellamy and his associates tried to define their cause in a way that Americans could understand and appreciate. In large part, this involved indications of what Nationalism was not: It was not communism, because it was founded on the principle of equal reward rather than on the rule of to each according to need, nor was it socialistic, since socialism was a class movement and one that allowed for differential rewards. It was not anarchistic, because it retained faith in government as an instrument of cooperative order.[15] It was not paternalistic, since the people themselves would control the system (to say that Nationalism was paternalism was like saying "that a man can be his own father"). It was not a threat to individuality; rather it would "kill the trusts" that were threatening true individuality and initiate a new civilization in which every person would be free to develop his or her special self.[16] Nor would it provide a place for the lazy or the inefficient, since the Industrial Army would make "industry as scientific, as orderly, as efficient, as war"; and it would seize the lazy and vicious "by the scruff of the coat collar, and put them to work."[17]

Bellamy also defined Nationalism more directly: It was eminently democratic, a kind of New England town meeting shaped to the requirements of the Industrial Age: "Government action in a democracy is merely cooperative action. It is the people acting jointly instead of severally. Nationalism simply proposes to extend the scope of their cooperative action to business." It would compel all to work but this was simply the more systematic application of the popular belief that every able-bodied person had a social obligation to support himself. Nationalism would guarantee the right and enforce the duty to work; the new nation would not permit anyone either to starve or to loaf, "no man has a right to loaf." In response to the familiar charge that Nationalism would reduce everyone to parts of a great machine, Bellamy chose not to deny but to defend: "Well, aren't we parts of a great industrial machine now? The only difference is that the present machine is a bungling and misconstructed one, which grinds up the bodies and souls of those who work in it."[18]

In a more positive way, he explicitedly identified Nationalism with the millennial tradition: "Did you suppose that because it is called the millennium, it was never coming? . . . The world is on the verge of the realization of the vision of universal peace, love, and justice, which the seers and poets of all ages have more or less dimly foreseen." To become a Nationalist, he said, was "to be converted, and henceforth to see all things in a new light." Without the need for an apocalyptic Second Coming, the religion of Nationalism would convert everyone to a sense of human brotherhood that would make the cooperative commonwealth a living reality.[19]

This vision had particular appeal to the Theosophists and other religious dissenters who accepted Nationalism as a new version of the old hope for a regeneration of society outside of the corrupt and corrupting world of politics. By 1891, however, it was evident Bellamy had chosen a political as well as religious road to the millennium. In the prospectus of the *New Nation,* he outlined a program to begin the transformation of the nation. The first step would be a "radical form" of civil service involving the organization of all public employees on the basis of guaranteed employment and protection from political interference. He also called for the immediate nationalization of the telegraph, telephone, and railroad systems and of the coal mines and for a corresponding municipalization of gas, water and electric companies, mass transit lines, and other public services. Eventually, as he indicated elsewhere, all industry would be nationalized as would all land, permitting the reorganization of the entire labor force, agricultural as well as industrial, along the lines of the Industrial Army: "When this program is fulfilled there will be no private capitalists left and the proceeds of the National industries will be disposed of by the voice of the people, as the directors of the national corporation."[20]

Bellamy was notably less direct in his thoughts regarding the political means to affect these goals. When a group in Rhode Island formed a state Nationalist party, he applauded their effort and said that "the nationalist party is the legitimate heir to the principles and spirit of the patriots of 1776." He was not willing, though, to rest his hopes for a new American revolution on the immediate formation of a new party. Rather than involving Nationalism directly in politics, he aimed at developing a coalition of "the various reform bodies and industrial organizations, both of artisans and farmers" under the guidance and inspiration of his ideas. He expressed the confidence that "intelligent working-men" were already becoming aware that nationalism could "no longer be twitted as a 'kid-glove' movement" of the upper classes and could be trusted to protect their true interests. In the galaxy of cooperative organizations created by workers, farmers, and reformers over the previous decade, he saw an opportunity to forge one powerful force that could take control of American government on all levels, carrying out a peaceful revolution with a minimal involvement of nationalist leaders directly in the messy business of politics.[21]

Bellamy thought he saw the makings of such a force in the new People's Party which had begun to coalesce out of the Farmers Alliance, Knights of Labor, and other movements critical of the existing order. When these groups decided to meet at Cincinnati to form a political organization, he urged the various Nationalist clubs in the nation to send delegates to the conference. Although he was not satisfied with the preliminary platform of the new party, he did take heart from what he saw as a strong nationalist presence in the organization, particularly in the fact that eight of the 27 members of the party's national committee were Nationalists. The *New Nation* also found much hope in the formation of the Massachusetts Peoples Party, which adopted a platform more acceptably nationalist than that at Cincinnati. This state party did little to demonstrate the popularity of Nationalism, polling only slightly more than one percent of the vote, but Bellamy was already looking ahead to 1892, when he expected a grand coalescence of reform forces into "a political army" to occur.[22]

Much of this optimism depended on distant developments in Kansas, Nebraska, and other states of the Trans-Mississippi West—states which Bellamy had never seen. In March 1892, the *New Nation* declared that "the masses who are in sympathy with the people's party are today so largely leavened with nationalism that their entire and conscious acceptance of its program and ultimate aims is but a question of time."[23] Later in the year, Bellamy expressed satisfaction with the national platform of the new party, treating it as a sure sign of a drift in the West toward the ideas of "absolute economic equality and a nationalized system of industry." In order to foster this trend, the Nationalists organized a "national committee for propaganda" to spread their gospel both within and outside the Populist organization; eventually it claimed that it had members in 27 states.[24]

Bellamy took particular pleasure in the fact that farmers were setting "the pace for social reconstruction," citing it as a refutation of the claim made by Socialists that no radical reform could succeed unless it originated in the working class. Although he made occasional references to workers, he was far more comfortable with the agrarians than he was with the proletarians. He saw the People's Party as an American movement that was developing naturally as an American response to the transformation of the United States from a "peaceful agricultural state" to a mighty but conflict-ridden industrial power. Under the guidance of Nationalism, this party would restore to the true producers of the nation their rightful control over national affairs, and it would establish the permanent domination of the old values associated with the Protestant Ethic by giving them a new basis suited to the new age. In the process, it would eliminate the domineering plutocrats, demoralizing parasites, corrupting politicians and the rest of the poisonous crew who were spoiling the American Dream.[25]

The revivalist style of Populism appealed to the essentially apolitical

Bellamy, but his loyalty remained with the Nationalist cause. After the new party won more than a million votes in 1892, he wrote that "the political changes of the last election, by dislodging millions of voters from their former party affiliations, have created a wonderful opportunity for our missionary work."[26] The *New Nation* also found signs of progress at home as well as in the West. It hailed the publication of William Dean Howells "great nationalist story," *A Traveler from Altruria,* as a notable event in the history of the movement, and it gave special attention to signs in Massachusetts to an awakening of interest in the government ownership and operation of public services. Bellamy celebrated the opening of 1893 with the assertion that where before they had been ridiculed as being "fools enough to believe that God's Kingdom of fraternal equality ever could come to earth, the Nationalists today see their hope become the religion of hundreds of thousands," and he predicted that the practical program of Nationalism would prevail in the election of 1896.[27]

In April 1893, the editor made a small but significant change in the format of his newspaper by publishing on the front page of each issue a small box summarizing his doctrine of economic equality as the only way to create a true democracy for the Industrial Age: "Until economic equality shall give a basis to political equality, the latter is but a sham." His aim was to maintain the focus of the movement for radical reform on what he insisted was the central Nationalist ideal. The political significant of this tactic he made evident in September, when he proclaimed "economic inequality the root of the evil," condemned the drift of the Populist movement toward "the one-plank idea" of the free coinage of silver, and expressed the hope that the People's Party would complete its conversion to Nationalism by adopting economic equality as its primary campaign aim in 1896.[28]

The year strengthened Bellamy's hopes for the movement. The Panic of 1893 toppled the nation into a deep depression which threatened both individual opportunity and public order; the dangers of plutocratic rule had already been made manifest in the bloody Homestead Steel strike the previous year. The rapid rise of unemployment became a central social concern which Bellamy tried to turn to Nationalist advantage. In an article in the *Boston Traveller,* he urged government to take the initiative in creating a cooperative system which would enable the unemployed to support themselves. Under his plan, the state would provide the basic organization and the tools, land, and other facilities that the jobless needed to resume work. As this would be a comprehensive system, it would enable workers to apply their skills to produce various necessities which then could be exchanged among themselves; it would be a self-contained economy, with its own stores and currency, which Bellamy promised would not compete with employed workers. Eventually, he hoped, this system would prove so successful that it would not only "retain all who entered this cooperative service" but also furnish all workers with a permanent alternative to employment under capitalism. He was pleased that the Massachusetts Peoples Party had adopted this cooperative scheme as part of its platform for the gubernatorial election in 1893.[29]

Early in 1894, Bellamy summed up his ideas and expectations in a notable article for *Forum* magazine. He warned that in less than two generations an economic revolution resulting from the use of steampowered machinery had brought a rapid concentration and power in the hands of the few, making an economic system that resembled "a centralized government, or group of governments, administered by great capitalists."[30] Among other dangers of this new system, the increasingly hostile relationship between corporate management and labor threatened to intensify class conflict at the expense of social order. With the disappearance of the frontier, the only way to preserve both equality and order was to take control of this national economic organization away from capitalists and vest it in government:

> The industrial system that is to employ and maintain our dense population, under the present and future conditions of the country, must be a systematized, centralized, interlocking economic organization of the highest efficiency. It is a physical impossibility to restore to the people, as individuals, the government of their economic interests; but is feasible to bring it under their economic control, and that is the only possible alternative to economic oligarchy . . . We desire to see organized as public business all the industrial and commercial affairs of the people, so that they may be carried on henceforth, like all other public business, by responsible public agents, for the equal benefit of the citizens.[31]

Bellamy proposed a step-by-step process whereby government at all levels, local as well as national, would take over the economy, beginning with the nationalization of railroads and the "forestry business" followed by the expropriation of trusts and other consolidated business, all to be paid for on the basis of the current value of their physical facilities. Once begun, he promised, this process would proceed smoothly and with increasing speed, abetted by the popularity of the program among workers and the declining power of the oligarchs, until it would be possible to complete the program by "a process of systematization and equalizing of conditions under an already unified administration." Optimistically, he insisted that Nationalism had largely completed its educational phase and now was moving rapidly into political action. Nationalism was on the march.[32]

Even before 1894, however, it was evident that Nationalism was on the march toward oblivion, and that the political army that Bellamy hoped to guide to triumph in 1896 was melting away. As early as 1892, his attempt to involve Nationalism in Populist politics had alienated many of those whose enthusiasm had launched the movement in 1889. The Theosophists and other cultural dissenters, like previous generations of dissenters, were essentially hostile to politics; they hoped that Bellamy's Religion of Solidarity would be an effective nonpolitical influence for the national regeneration of society. Although the venture into politics did not antagonize all of them, it substantially weakened the zeal which had produced the remarkable proliferation of Nationalist clubs associated with the early movement. Many clubs continued to exist and some new ones were founded in 1891 and 1892, but a significant part of the energy was dissipated, especially in southern California where most of the clubs had vanished by 1892. It was the early activity of these clubs that had inspired Bellamy to predict that the Peoples Party would win California in the presidential election. Instead, the party ran a distant third in that state.[33]

The movement did little better in its other area of strength, eastern Massachusetts, where again the decline in enthusiasm for the Nationalist religion was not balanced by a notable increase in popular enthusiasm for the Nationalist political program, as the experience of the Peoples Party in Massachusetts made very clear. Conspicuously absent from the later movement were Cyrus F. Willard and some of the other Theosophists who had founded the First Boston Club; their places were taken by progressive social reformers like Frank Parsons and Benjamin O. Flower, who were interested chiefly in some of the practical aspects of Nationalism. In the state election of 1893, the Massachusetts party adopted a platform favoring the nationalization of all monopolies, state provisions for life and fire insurance at cost, the municipalization of public services, the establishment of civil service on all levels of government, and Bellamy's cooperative employment plan for the jobless. The *New Nation* did not expect to win the election, but it did hope that the Populist ticket would receive at least 10,000 votes. The ticket actually won little more than half that figure; the vote in Boston was notably weak despite the presence there of two Nationalist clubs.[34]

These ventures served only to demonstrate the political weakness of Nationalism even in areas of its greatest strength and so to diminish the ability of Nationalist leaders to influence the course of the national Peoples Party. That ability was further reduced when in February 1894 the *New Nation* abruptly suspended publication, noting that it had been run at "a pecuniary loss" from the beginning and that the hard times following the Panic of 1893 "have at last proved too much for us." Even before this loss, Bellamy's frail health had broken under the strain of his political activity, forcing him to retire to his old quiet world at Chicopee. It was no surprise that Populism should ignore his warning against "the one-plank idea," and that it should take its disastrous road toward "Free Silver" and eventual absorption by the Democratic party in 1896. Soon after the election of William McKinley, Bellamy washed his hands of party politics and dreamed of convening a convention of social radicals to issue a "manifesto" directly to what he thought were the now awakened people.[35]

The Nationalist entry into politics, however, had not only failed but also invited much criticism of Bellamy's ideas from social radicals as well as conservatives. When Laurence Gronlund published a revised edition of *The Cooperative Commonwealth* in 1890 he condemned Bellamy's insistence on economic equality ("decidedly unsocialistic") and on a disciplined labor force ("a dangerous militarism"); other Socialists were offended by Bellamy's open scorn of their proletarianism.[36] The advocates of the individualistic ideal also had their inning. Benjamin R. Tucker, an anarchist, warned that Nationalism was a form of "authoritarian reform" allied with "State Socialism." More significant opposition came from Henry George's followers, who denounced Bellamy's scheme as a threat to their dream of individuality and liberty. William Lloyd Garrison, the son of the great abolitionist, called Nationalism "the Mask of Tyranny," and Hamlin Garland said that reformers faced "the parting of two ways, one leading . . . to one great monopoly of all industry, controlled by the state, to be carried on by military regime; the other leading through the abolition of laws, through free trade, free production, free opportunity to free men." [37]

This conflict also found its way into fiction. In the 1890s, at least six explicitedly anti-Nationalist fictional works were published, four of them in 1890 alone. Each was set in a Bellamy-like future, generally with Bellamy's own characters, except that in these worlds Nationalist dreams have become nightmares. Arthur Vinton's *Looking Further Backward* describes a United States so weakened by its devotion to harmony and its addiction to routine that it is helpless before a Chinese invasion in 2020. J. W. Roberts, in his *Looking Within,* depicts a nation mired in indolence and intellectual sloth until Americans reject Nationalism in favor of a Single-Tax society. [38] Among these attacks, the most insightful was *Looking Further Forward* by Richard Michaelis, the editor of a German newspaper in Chicago and the advocate of a scheme of voluntary "mutual productive societies" for workers.

In Michaelis's Year 2000, the apparatus of the Industrial Army has been taken over by corrupt and greedy men who use it to maintain their power. Dissenters are confined in asylums for the insane on the pretext that only madmen would criticize the best society on earth. Those who wish to rise in the ranks of the army are forced to buy the friendship of their superiors, since they know that to do otherwise would turn their years of service into "hell on earth." The whole country is run by a bloated bureaucracy centered in Washington, D.C., which has become a center of prostitution owing to the presence there of many young women who are anxious to rise in the ranks. Although the government pretends otherwise, the economy is stagnating under the weight of a large unproductive class and of the absence of incentives to produce. And there is little hope that Americans will reverse this vicious descent, since they are helpless before the absolute power of the all-dominating state. [39] Michaelis's book foreshadowed the "dystopian" novels of the twentieth century; his Year 2000, thought it lacked literary merit, is not an unworthy ancestor of George Orwell's *1984.*

Probably the most incisive critique of Nationalism was made by the conservative William Graham Sumner in his "The Absurd Effort to Make the World Over," an essay published by the *Forum* in 1894 as a companion piece to Bellamy's own essay on the Nationalist program.

Sumner agreed with Bellamy that there was neither realism nor merit in the attempts to resist industrial consolidation and centralization: "The intensification of the social organization is what gives us greater social power. It is to it that we owe our increased comforts and abundance." He warned, however, that the Nationalists were naïve in assuming that it was possible to take over the industrial system without admitting the Captains of Industry to public power: "We may find that instead of democraticizing capitalism we have capitalized democracy . . . ,—that is, have the masterfulness, the overbearing disposition, the greed of gain, and the ruthlessness in methods, which are the faults of the master of industry at his worse."[40] Better, then, that political and economic authority be kept in separate places.

More basically, Sumner attacked the fundamental assumption that Bellamy shared with all radical social idealists, that it was possible to affect any significant change in society by human effort. Rather, "the turmoil of heterogeneous and antagonistic social whims and speculations in which we live is due to the failure to understand what the industrial organization is, and its all-prevading control over human life." The great gains derived from the increasing organization of society has been at the expense of creating an order which had become independent of human will. Whatever its defects, it was "a tough old world" that could be not changed except for some modifications of its tendencies: "Every one of us is the child of our age and cannot get out of it. . . . The men will be carried along with it and be made by it."[41] And so the conservative Sumner joined the radical Marx in dismissing as nothing more than ineffective utopian whim the hope of directing the tide of history toward Jerusalem.

Bellamy replied to both his critics and the course of events in a form most congenial to him, a second novel which, with significant emphasis, he called *Equality*. Apparently begun soon after he closed down the *New Nation* but not published until 1897, the new novel reflected the changes which had occurred both in the world and in his own experiences since the writing of *Looking Backward*. Although Bellamy presents it as an extension and elaboration of its his first work, it was a different book in significant ways. Most notably, it is inherently provincial and populist rather than urban and urbane. Part of it involved his efforts to incorporate his hopes for Populism into a story of triumph over Sumner's tough old world. Beginning in 1873, says Bellamy, a long period of economic distress incited an "irresistible conflict" between the people and plutocracy which brought into being the Populist movement which in turn gained control of "one of the great historic parties" for the Nationalist program.[42]

Not satisfied with politics alone, however, Bellamy makes this development the prelude for "the Great Revival" which transforms the spirit of the people by convincing them "that the ideal of a world of equal welfare, which has been represented to them by the clergy as a dangerous delusion, was no other than the very dream of Christ." Under the influence of the Religion of Solidarity, America goes through a great moral revolution in which the almighty good triumphs over the almighty dollar, converting even capitalists to the new order and completing the New Nation without conflict and disruption.[43] The Great Awakening, which had begun more than a century before with the millennial dreams of men like Joseph Bellamy and Samuel Hopkins and had reached one great triumph in the form of the abolition of slavery during Bellamy's early years, would complete itself in the form of the Nationalist millennium. In traditional American revivalism, Bellamy believed that he had found a moral tide far more powerful than the social tides of Sumner and Marx.

Bellamy, however, does not depend on human will alone. His great revival succeeds because "modern conditions" have evolved to the point where they provide a material basis for economic democracy. Where in Looking Backward he had emphasized the total organization of human power in the form of the Industrial Army, in Equality he depends on the new technology made available by electrical power. His future Americans have found ways of generating "practically exhaustless and costless" power whose most notable effect is to reinvigorate rural society. Work is now done with the aid of electric motors, including those used to drive great plows; run as easily by women as by men, these plows have revolutionized the once backbreaking labor of farmers. The telephone, already adapted to the transmission of music and of knowledge in Looking Backward, and the "electroscope" (television) have freed provincial people from their debilitating ignorance of the larger world.

"Navigation in the air" also has appeared in the year 2000, happily disassociated in an era of permanent international peace from the idea that its chief function would be "to drop dynamite bombs in the midst of crowded cities." There are no bombs and no crowded cities either, for the motor-carriage, benefiting from a network of roads constructed for it, has become a popular conveyance. The new technology permits a decentralization of population away from the congested cities; on New York's Manhattan Island, the population has been reduced to 250,000 people "living there among groves and fountains."[44]

Another notable addition in *Equality* is democracy. Where before politics was rejected as a danger to the discipline of the Industrial Army, now it runs from every pore. Not only are leaders selected by popular vote for fixed terms but they are subject to recall by the electorate at any time in their terms. Moreover, the telephone has been adapted to the principle of direct democracy, enabling people to vote in a wide variety of issues: "The people not only nominally but actually govern. . . . We vote a hundred times perhaps a year, on all manner of questions, from the temperature of the public baths . . . to the greatest questions of the world union." Government, far from being the unconstrained master of people's lives, is the universal servant of humanity.[45]

After gutting his year 2000 of its bureaucratic mainspring, Bellamy tried to find a substitute for it in his Religion of Solidarity. In economic affairs, noble impulses prevail, "the love of honor, the joy of beneficence, the delight of achievement, and the enthusiasm of humanity." The entire social order is permeated with the spirit of "modern religion . . . dominated by an impassioned sense of solidarity of humanity and of man with God: the religion of a race that knows itself divine and fears no evil." In such a social order, there is no need for compulsion—at least of white people; black Americans are admitted into paradise but in a way "perfectly consistent with any degree of race separation in industry which the most bigoted local prejudice might demand."[46]

Equality revealed, as had *Looking Backward,* that Bellamy was acutely sensitive to the trends and the thinking of his times. The difference between the two books reflects the changes which had taken place during the intervening decade: the criticisms leveled against Nationalism, the efforts to develop a politically effective Nationalist program, the emergence of Populism, the triumph of racial segregation, and especially the advent of a new technology associated with the internal combustion engine and with electricity. *Equality* thus heralded the end of the Age of Steam and of grimy industrialism in the name of a new phase of modernization.

In tuning his vision to the times, however, Bellamy sacrificed his earlier insight into one fundamental element of modern life. In *Looking Backward,* his emphasis on the efficient organization of human resources raised the specter of totalitarian rule, but it also forced the reader to consider the social interdependence and the bureaucratic tendencies in business and government which were to grow increasingly strong in the future. More than any other book of its time, it illuminated the special mixture of freedom and constraint encountered by the modern urban person: as a consumer, free to express one's individuality in the purchase of a distinctive style of life, but dependent on market situations beyond individual control; as a producer, ostensibly free to develop a special talent but often only within a larger system to which the individual has to conform.

For Bellamy, this modern situation was inevitable and good; the loss of individual autonomy was more than repaid by gains in opportunities for personal development as well as for physical well-being. If in *Looking Backward* he pushed his ideas to a disturbing extreme, he at least offered a powerful challenge to the traditional notion so strong among Americans that true freedom meant individual freedom from society. In *Equality,* he replaced the Prussian backbone of his dream with the mush of a provincial idealism. In significant respect, the second novel was a better book than the first, particularly in some of its predictions of twentieth-century reality, but it was weaker at the core. A decade after he had published one of the great books of his time, he unwittingly wrote that mere "fairy tale of social felicity" from which he had been saved in the 1880s.

Undoubtedly, he hoped to fulfill his scenario for the Great Revival, but it was a doomed hope. *Equality* did win the praise of some reviewers, including one who treated it as evidence that previous ages of muscle and brain were "about to yield to the age of heart." Another used his review of the book to argue that Bellamy's scheme was eminently practical and could be established with less trouble than that entailed by the establishment of the Constitution: "The people of the United States are now united in the homogeneous establishment of their interests, material and moral—they are susceptible of the highest civilization. The natural *espirit de corps* has never been so uniform and general in all sections of the country. . . . The Bellamy economy is . . . the legitimate conclusion of the argument of events." Overall, though, *Equality* raised little public interest.[47]

Rather than ignite the Great Revival, the book proved to be the last hurrah for both the movement and its author. Bellamy had completed it at the cost of his already enfeebled health, and in 1898 he died at the age of 47 from the combined causes of tuberculosis and bad medical treatment; Henry George had died in the previous year, and Laurence Gronlund was to die in 1899—three would-be remakers of society perishing with their century. In death, Bellamy received praise from, among others, the editor of the reform-oriented magazine, the *Arena,* who called him a prophet: "Had we the courage to . . . lay a new foundation, to bring in a new architecture that shall be consistent with itself and equal to the aspiration of the age, then we should all become apostles of Edward Bellamy."[48]

In the real world, though, the prophet had died without an organized following. As a movement, Nationalism had expired before Bellamy; its lifespan was shorter than that of Fourierism. By 1896, the attentions of Bellamy's largely middle-class audience had been distracted not only by reform politics but by a spate of rival utopian novels that served to dilute the vision that he had raised in *Looking Backward.*[49] The forces of radical social idealism which Bellamy had hoped to unite into one force became more dispersed than ever before. Few reformers gave even a thought to his most striking and original contribution, economic equality. Nationalism, however, had served to introduce thousands of Americans both to his ideas for a well-ordered economy and to his larger hopes for a cooperative commonwealth. From their ranks came a new generation of social idealists who continued the search for cooperative brotherhood into the first decades of the new century.

XIII

The Great Cooperative
National People's Trust

The 1890s, for many, was a time for anxious yet hopeful anticipation. By the end of the century, hundreds of utopian authors and social experts had joined Bellamy in the effort to envision the new times that seemed to be flooding over the old America. As early as 1893, a group of progressive thinkers in Boston had formed the Twentieth Century Club in order to prepare themselves for the new society. Henry Adams remembered that in "this last decade everyone talked, and seemed to feel *fin-de-siècle*," to sense an end and a beginning.[1] Amid a torrent of intellectual, technological, social, and industrial change in an era of great cities and business enterprises, Americans wondered where the momentum of "progress" was taking them. What would the new century bring?

Although there was no one answer to the question, many social observers saw a distinct tendency toward the integration of social and economic life into one national whole where the individualism of the past had little place. By the end of the 1890s, the return of prosperity was easing the social tensions and fears which had permeated the previous decades, but Americans continued to be concerned over the accelerating pace of economic concentration. Whatever their alleged virtues, the formation of Trusts and the general consolidation of business had raised a disturbing question: Was America to be ruled by a few privileged businessmen at the expense of the prosperity and the freedom of the people? In 1902, William T. Ghent predicted that by "a process of irresistible movement" the modern world was foiming itself into a "benevolent feudalism" where, in the interests of harmony and order, most people would be serfs bound to their jobs. Others doubted that the new order would be benevolent. "The Trust is virtually supreme in the United States," warned Henry Demarest Lloyd, "and when it has achieved the economic subjection of the old world it may consolidate the plutocratic system, against which the American people may be powerless."[2] The Industrial Feudalism that the Fourierists had predicted a half-century before seemed to be fast becoming a reality, as Lloyd tried to demonstrate in 1894 in his *Wealth Against Commonwealth*.

Social idealists, though, took comfort in the hope raised by thinkers like Gronlund and Bellamy that the evident advantages of the increasingly collectivized economy would be made available to all once the people were organized to take command of it away from its plutocratic masters. On Bellamy's death in 1898, the editor of the *Arena* magazine said that the novelist had seen "beyond the existing order arising in dim outline the COOPERATIVE COMMONWEALTH—a sort of socio-industrial, intellectual, and moral commune of associated interest, of mutual support, and counsel." Three years earlier, James G. Clark, in his article "The Coming Industrial Order," warned that it was either the Cooperative Commonwealth or growing economic chaos eventuating in "capitalistic oppression and, finally, military despotism in the name and mask of necessity." Clark and other social observers took comfort in the hope that industrial concentration and what they saw as a growing sense of human brotherhood were taking the world toward a cooperative life.[3]

This logic led, as Clark pointed out, to "Socialism as an idea," to some form of "cooperative interest and effort" involving a publicly managed economy.[4] Most American social idealists, however, resisted the Marxist emphasis on the necessity of class struggle and were little better disposed toward the "State Socialism" of either Gronlund or Bellamy. The title of Gronlund's book, *The Cooperative Commonwealth*, was an apt name for the yearning for national cooperative life, but his all-dominant organic State was not acceptable to the many idealists who had little faith in government or in any form of centralized power. These "socialists" looked for the Cooperative Commonwealth in what they saw as a growing tendency toward national cooperative life based on the American tradition of voluntary association.

The basis for this hope had been laid earlier in the century in part under the combined influence of Fourierism and Owenism. Association-ists like Horace Greeley had actively supported the formation of Work-ingmen's Protective Unions as a way of demonstrating to workers that cooperative associations would enable them to control their own eco-nomic destinies. By 1857, the American Protective Union claimed 327 local societies in ten states.[5] This effort, however, was soon overshad-owed by one imported from England where English workers, inspired by Owen's theories of cooperation, had begun the Rochdale Cooperative movement for the formation of consumer cooperatives. The success of the Rochdale stores intensified interest in voluntary cooperative organi-zations among Americans. In 1867, the National Labor Congress had urged workers to form all kinds of cooperative associations so that they could control their own economic lives:

> We confidently look forward to a period not remote when the cooperative principle will carry on the great works and improve-ments of the age. It will build our cities, dig our ores, fill the land with the noise of loom and spindle. The workingman as he is now in many instances his own purveyor through co-operative stores will become contractor, builder, manufacturer, reaping the rewards of his own industry, and profits of his own labor.[6]

By the 1880s, the cooperative idea had become familiar to many Americans, thanks especially to the influence of the Knights of Labor, whose leaders were inclined toward cooperation as an alternative to the violent strikes and industrial warfare of the period. The Knights started at least 185 producer cooperatives intended to give skilled workers control of the making and marketing of their products. In the early 1880s, they founded what they called "an absolutely independent com-munity" in southern Missouri where men could work for themselves "independent of markets and the price of labor." Despite the general failure of these schemes, the idea continued to appeal to artisans and other skilled workers as a way to maintain their independence from the new industrial order. In 1889, for instance, G.B. DeBarnardi of Sedalia in western Missouri initiated the Labor Exchange movement to furnish the means whereby workers could exchange goods and services among themselves. By 1896, after three years of depression, there were over 130 local exchanges with 6000 members in thirty-two states, and the movement had plans for factories, canneries, brickyards, and other enterprises to provide jobs for the unemployed.[7]

In the 1890s, Nationalism stimulated further interest in voluntary cooperatives, despite Bellamy's insistence that the only form of cooperation strong enough to survive in the modern world was "the co-operation of the people through and by their government." The *New Nation* itself occasionally reported examples of cooperative endeavor to illustrate the spreading influence of Nationalism. In Kansas, the "Bellamy Club" of Junction City established a cooperative kitchen to ease the work of the 44 women who belonged to the club. In San Francisco, a member of the local Nationalist Club attempted to establish a complex of cooperative boarding houses, restaurants, and stores which he called "the Commonwealth of Jesus." Bellamy hoped to incorporate the various forms of cooperation into the Nationalist movement, but Cooperationism constituted a movement in itself, and one which had strong appeal among the same classes attracted to Nationalism. In 1891, one proponent of the idea, Herbert Myrick, wrote "that the general success of cooperation must gradually precede much of the nationalistic and socialistic propositions of the day. Whether cooperators, having proved the utility and independence of self-help, could then desire to put it on a state or national basis, as advocated by the nationalist, time will reveal."[8]

Indeed, one of the apparent strengths of Cooperationism was that it did not depend on the risky world of politics. In theory, it offered the hope that cooperative society could be realized by the free action of the people without resort to any of the corrupted institutions of society. In this, it resembled communitarianism, but it did not depend on the old dream of creating miniature commonwealths apart from the existing society; rather, it seemed to be a way by which producers could carry out a piecemeal social reorganization suited to their interests. In 1884, for instance, the anarchist Benjamin Tucker proposed that workers organize themselves into a separate economy in cities where he believed that they had a better chance to succeed than in isolated communities; eventually, "a whole city would become a great hive of Anarchistic workers, prosperous and free individuals."[9]

Most workers, however, found little satisfaction in an idea that was best suited to the interests and ideals of a few independent-minded artisans and small businessmen. And the general failure of cooperationist ventures was a constant problem. They suffered from inadequate capital and inexperienced leadership that left them vulnerable to the competition of business enterprise. The situation seemed to demand that the various fragments of cooperation be consolidated into one movement capable of mobilizing the mass support and of mustering capital and organizational skills needed to establish an independent cooperationist world. In 1891, Herbert Myrick called for "a comprehensive union" to be launched by a Cooperative Congress which he hoped would be convened at the forthcoming Chicago World's Fair. Four years later, a group of reformers which included the old cooperationist and Nationalist, Edward Everett Hale, founded at Cambridge, Massachusetts, the Cooperative Union of America as an educational organization and a coordinating agency for local cooperatives. Although the Union published its *American Cooperative News* for three years, it had little influence either on the workers or on the general public.[10]

Cooperationism did have one notable success in the 1890s, but this did little to encourage hopes that workers would organize their own cooperative societies, since it was affected by a successful businessman. While Albert K. Owen was attempting to give life to his scheme for integral cooperation at Topolobampo, Nelson O. Nelson (1844–1922), a St. Louis manufacturer of plumbing supplies, was laying the basis for a model industrial community. Inspired by Godin's Familistere, Nelson decided to create a company town based on cooperationist principles. In 1890, he moved his plant and workers from St. Louis across the Mississippi to a new site near Edwardsville, Illinois. Like George Pullman, who had already built his big model company town outside of Chicago, he wanted to move his industrial operations away from the tumultuous and corrupting city to a more favorable environment with beauty and without saloons, but there the resemblance ends, since Nelson's new village of Leclaire (named after an early French pioneer in profit-sharing) was drawn to a smaller and far more democratic scale than the town of Pullman.[11]

By the end of the decade, Leclaire had become a suburban community of some 500 people, most of whom lived in their own houses on their own land, which Nelson sold to them on easy terms. Nelson's company paid regular union wages, operated a benefit fund to provide part-salary for sick workers, and maintained healthy and safe work conditions. It also provided the town with a kindergarten, a school, a library, and various recreation facilities, including a baseball field where Nelson himself played the game with his men. In its flower gardens, lawns, garden plots, and tree-lined streets, Leclaire provided a model physical environment.[12] It was a complete example of Welfare Capitalism, but it was also much more.

The essence of the Leclaire experiment was in its cooperative arrangements. Beginning with a cooperative store to reduce retail costs for the inhabitants, Nelson expanded the opportunity for active cooperation on the part of all who were involved in his business. Although entrepreneurs like himself were generally responsible for initiating businesses, he did not believe that this entitled them to permanent ownership and control. Therefore, he eventually arranged for a division of all profits among both employees and customers in the form of stock in the Nelson Company. He intended to transfer control of the business to them gradually. By 1914, both the company and the town had come under the joint ownership of his workers and customers, leading him to proclaim that he had found a proven way to create conditions, without the intrusion of government, in which business would be "conducted for the equal benefit of all, and with a greater efficiency because there is mutual interest."[13]

He was especially proud of his town, where he said everyone enjoyed the benefits of socialism without its constraints in a healthy society with "no policeman or [political] boss or the need of any, no migration of the young and a community where nearly all homes were owned by their occupants." In his enthusiasm for cooperation, he suggested that the approach could be applied to "making entire towns" on the model of Ebenezer Howard's Garden City. He expanded Howard's idea into a dream of towns where lands, public utilities, and businesses would all be cooperatively owned and managed, but where residents would have individual ownership of their homes. Although his dream of creating a cooperative community devoted to "Work, Education, Recreation, Beauty, Homes and Freedom" excited little general interest among either workers or capitalists, it did attract a number of admirers, one of whom proclaimed Leclaire "the Utopia where the capitalist and the workingman dwell in peace and perfect harmony."[14]

The depressed and troubled mid-1890s produced a varied crop of cooperative efforts, often with a strong booster flavor. In Maine, for instance, cooperationists founded the Industrial Brotherhood with the aim of mobilizing one million men and one hundred million dollars to establish a cooperative economy with its own factories, mines, and farms; this plan for "a marshalling of socialistic forces to capture the economic field" was one of several which promised to free workers and their producers from the control of capitalism so that they could enjoy the profits of their labor. In the West, hundreds of people invested money and energy in the Colorado Cooperative Company, a land-development scheme involving the construction of a fifteen mile long irrigation ditch intended to transform 40,000 acres of arid land into fertile fields. This effort resembled the earlier Union Colony at Greeley, Colorado, especially in its hopes that irrigation would foster the development of the cooperative spirit.[15]

The cooperative idea also appeared in the most bumptuous utopian novel of the 1890s, *The New Era* (1897), written and published by Charles Caryl, a Colorado businessman who billed himself as "One Who Dares to Plan." Caryl, president of the Gold Extraction Mining and Supply Company, was an experienced entrepreneur who also fitted readily into the culture of dissent, having a strong interest in Spiritualism and radical social idealism. Concerned over the widespread unemployment following the panic of 1893, he concocted what was certainly a daring plan for a network of worker-owned cooperatives to develop gold and coal mines, the profits which could be used to purchase "every other industry." This scheme was given a typical booster climax, the formation of "The New Era Model City. . . . The most stupendous and important enterprise ever accomplished on the planet by human beings." After the failure of both his book and his plan, Caryl became a member of the Brotherhood of Light, a cult that stressed Spiritualism, Vegetarianism, and communal living; in 1907, he led some of the brotherhood to California, where they formed a colony based on "the Caryl Cooperative Industrial system."[16]

Henry Demarest Lloyd gave the cooperative dream more significance in his *Labor Copartnership* (1898). Four years earlier, Lloyd had concluded his *Wealth Against Commonwealth* with some vague hopes for cooperation but no definite direction. His interest in Cooperationism took on a more definite form when in 1897 he and his friend N. O. Nelson attended the International Co-operative Congress at Delft, Holland, and then studied the cooperative movement in Great Britain. In Europe, he encountered what he called "a story of productive enterprises, including farms, started by workmen, owned by workmen, and managed by workingmen." He conceded that the idea had not yet won as much support among American workers, but he believed that a successful movement could be created if only "men of means, culture, and good will" would take the lead in organizing it. The problem, of course, was in finding such men with the right aims.[17]

The answer came in the form of another utopian novel, which precipitated what appeared to be a promising national movement for the creation of the Cooperative Commonwealth by popular nonpolitical means. This was *The World a Department Store* published in 1900 by its author, Bradford Peck, the owner of a successful department store in Lewiston, Maine. A businessman with a strong social conscience, Peck had reached the conclusion that only the reorganization of the nation along cooperative lines could save it from further social demoralization and industrial chaos.[18] In 1899, he had formed at Lewiston the Cooperative Association of America with the aim of uniting "producers and consumers through mill, farm, supply store, etc., into one combination, eliminating all waste and loss of energy, and for the benefit of all." He intended to use the profits from his book to help finance the Association, which in turn was to organize the mass popular enthusiasm which he expected the novel to inspire.[19]

Stylistically, *The World a Department Store* is burdened by the author's limited imagination and vocabulary; Peck's descriptions of his utopia depend heavily on such adjectives as "vast," "massive," "splendid," and especially "perfect." The novel, however, is enlivened by an enthusiasm for cooperation and efficient organization drawn from Peck's own experience as the department store king of northern New England. Its future is 1925, by which time the national economy has fallen under the control of the Cooperative Association, a "people's trust" owned cooperatively by everyone willing to invest $5.00 or more in the enterprise. The CAA has become the agency by which the people have availed themselves of all the advantages which the wealthy few had derived from the efficiencies of trusts like the Standard Oil Company. Rather than continuing their futile resistance to business consolidation, the people have taken command of the trend for themselves under the lead of "progressive, sagacious, and intelligent" captains of industry who have risen above the pettiness of individualism and the exclusiveness of capitalism to lend their talents to the creation of one "vast" super-efficient trust organization which has supplanted private business and reorganized the economy along the lines of a great department store.[20]

Under the control of the People's Trust, natural resources and human energies are so efficiently used as to produce a "truly heavenly existence on earth" more notable for its creature comforts than for its cultural and spiritual accomplishments. The Cooperative Association provides each of its adult members with a minimum yearly allowance sufficient to assure their economic well-being; above that level, there is a system of differential rewards which assures that everyone will be paid on the basis of his or her contribution to the general welfare. Under a board of engineers and architects, cities have been rebuilt into efficient, spacious places with splendid buildings and parks and without conniving politicians and corrupt bankers; rural areas have also been reorganized so that the farming population is concentrated in little towns, "thoroughly metropolitan in character," which are connected with each other by parkways. There is universal harmony and happiness thanks to an economic system that has achieved an almost perfect "conservation of energy." All of this has resulted from an understanding of God's will, which "was working by evolution in the development of those very octopuses called trusts and combinations which were the stepping stones that carried us up to the world's present great department stores."[21]

Peck's rehash of Fourierism and Nationalism could be easily forgotten if it were not for the means which he chose to attain his paradise. Peck intended the Cooperative Association to be a super-trust that would organize the many existing cooperatives in the United States into one integrated economic organization of workers and consumers. In theory at least, the People's Trust would be created and owned by the people themselves who would reap the benefits of the efficiencies of scale and the skills of enlightened businessmen; the only losers would be the wealthy owners of the old economic system who would either sink with the ship or join the People's Trust on its terms. Basically, business under the new system would involve a "copartnership" of workers and managers in which the people would have the upper hand, although Peck was notably vague on the distribution of power in this world.[22]

Peck hoped to begin what he called "a Social and Industrial Revolution" with the publication of his novel. In 1900, having gotten a state charter for the Cooperative Association of America, he constructed a two-story brick building in Lewiston to house both its offices and a cooperative grocery store, the first unit in the CAA's projected cooperative empire. After the grocery produced its first profits, Peck hailed it as the opening victory in the great "battle between the Trust for the People and the private monopolistic Trust whose designs are to absorb the wealth of the Nation." Determining to concentrate his energies on the CAA, he sold his department store to it in 1900 in exchange for its bonds; for ten years, the CAA operated the store on a profit-sharing arrangement with its employees. In less than two years, the new Association was able to claim that it did more than half-a-million dollars a year in business and had more than a thousand members, most of whom apparently joined it in order to get the promised dividends on their purchases in its stores.[23]

Peck's scheme soon attracted the attention of a few others who hoped to make the cooperative association a powerful weapon against the trusts. Most of them were essentially middle class radicals whose apparent purpose was, like Bellamy, to make a world suited to their interests and values. By activating and organizing the working class through cooperatives, they hoped to forge the lever that would move the corrupting world of the trusts off its foundations. Although they wanted to radically redirect the course of society, their revolution was to be a peaceful and conservative one, to be affected from the ground up by a coalition of workers, small businessmen, and idealists like themselves.

Aside from Henry Demarest Lloyd, they included Benjamin O. Flower, the editor of the Boston-based reform journal, the *Arena*. Flower literally was born into radical social idealism. The town of his birth, Albion, Illinois, had been founded by his grandfather, Richard Flower, who was the agent for the sale of nearby Harmonie, Indiana, to Robert Owen. In 1885, he moved to Boston where he founded the *Arena* with the intention of forming a cadre of young writers who would work for the cooperative cause, "a splendid minority in the struggle for human progress." Another supporter was a young minister, Ralph Albertson, who was rebounding from the collapse of his Christian Commonwealth Colony, an experiment in nonsectarian Christian communism in Georgia during the mid-1890s. Although the failure was a deeply painful experience, it did not deter Albertson from a lifelong search for cooperative brotherhood in some form.[24]

Even more active in the cooperative cause were Hiram G., Harry C., and Walter Vrooman, three reform-minded brothers, ministers, and founders of dozens of associations and societies for the radical improvement of society. Like Lloyd, the Vroomans dreamed of leading a fraternal alliance of workers against both the trusts and the various "social parasites" such as bankers and lawyers who feasted on the workingman's labor. As teenage spokesmen for the Socialist Labor Party in Kansas City, Walter and Harry had in 1887 attracted the notice of Karl Marx's daughter, Eleanor, but eventually they followed the non-Marxist lead of their older brother, Hiram, into Christian Socialism.[25]

In 1899, Hiram G. Vrooman, a minister in the Swedenborgian Church of the New Jerusalem in Baltimore, had founded the National Production Company, a cooperative association, which formed a small colony in Florida, mostly of refugees from Albertson's failed Commonwealth Colony. A year later, he was in Boston where he founded the Co-Workers Fraternity, intended to be a holding company for various cooperative enterprises, part of whose profits it would use to establish a university devoted to the interests of workers. Among the directors of this new organization were Flower, Albertson, and Lloyd. What followed the founding of the Co-Worker Fraternity was a spree of complicated cooperative trust building that might have bemused a John D. Rockefeller or a Samuel Insull.

The Fraternity first bought the stock of the National Production Company and then, having won the support of Peck, it purchased 90 percent of the stock in his Cooperative Association of America and its mini-empire of cooperatives.[26] In 1902, Hiram G. Vrooman further extended his efforts by getting a charter from the state of New Jersey for the Western Co-operative Association, whose president was Harry C. Vrooman. Soon after this, Walter V. Vrooman of Kansas City was able to incorporate another Western Co-operative Association in Missouri. In the same year (1902), Walter also incorporated the Multitude Unlimited, another intended holding company like the Co-Workers Fraternity, intended to take control of various regional cooperative association. Before long, the Multitude Unlimited made Ruskin College, founded by Walter in 1900, the first unit in its projected National University dedicated to disseminating the methods and virtues of cooperation. At its height, this holding company claimed control over the Florida colony established by the National Production Company, various agricultural enterprises, a cannery, a variety of retail stores, a chemical plant, and most of the business in the town of Trenton, Missouri, where it was headquartered.[27]

The great movement for a cooperative America seemed well underway, striking a blow not only against the trusts but also the hosts of parasitic middlemen whose exactions from producers and consumers alike would be eliminated by a well-organized cooperative system. Hiram Vrooman said that it would make workers co-partners with managers in all the advantages of machinery and large-scale organization. By joining this cooperative world, anyone could participate in the building of "a new and complete civilization" distinct from the corrupted society which it would replace. Once established, this new world would expand at an increasing rate as its advantages attracted workers and those managers who were ready to use their skills for the good of labor. As the managers of the new system were to be selected through "the highest form of civil-service examination," they would skillfully and honestly develop all the advantages of industrial cooperation, dramatically cutting the costs of production and distribution while also "doubling and then tripling" wages for workers.[28]

Universal prosperity would be accompanied by the emergence of a civilization unknown except in the imaginations of middle-class idealists, because the educational benefits of the Co-worker scheme "is sure to double and triple the intelligence of the average worker." A whole new society based on fraternal brotherhood could be created without class warfare and bloody revolution and without pain to anyone, since "it would not make the rich poor but it would make all the poor better off."[29] As cooperationism spread throughout the world, the movement would also fulfill Peck's prediction that by 1925 it would abolish "great ships of war" and wasteful armies in an atmosphere of international peace and good will.[30]

Fortified by their enthusiasms and by their early successes, the cooperationists issued a call for a great national convention to meet in June 1902 at Peck's hometown of Lewiston. Hiram Vrooman explained that the convention had been called to devise some way by which the many and varied cooperative societies in the United States "may all unite their forces and thereby give to the movement a momentum that will proceed with irresistible power in paving the way for the Cooperative Commonwealth." The convention itself was considerably less than the enthusiasm, attracting only some 50 delegates mostly from the Northeast, but it was heralded as another step forward in the battle against the Trusts. To publicize the cause, it created a new weekly newspaper, *The American Co-operator,* edited by Ralph Albertson. To provide for even greater national unity, it also merged the Co-Workers Fraternity and the Multitude Unlimited into one super "People's Trust of America" with a Boston department-store proprietor, George F. Washburn, as its general manager; a decade earlier, Washburn had been chairman of the Massachusetts Peoples Party.[31]

The new People's Trust began with the usual high expectations. Washburn, who noted that he had "twenty stores, two factories, a bank, and a trust company," hoped to organize all existing cooperatives into one national association that would provide the benefits of mass purchasing and mass merchandising to all its members. In an age of "combination and cooperation," he believed small proprietors could be persuaded to join the cooperative movement in order to protect themselves from the trusts. This would assure plenty of managerial and entrepreneurial skill for the expanding enterprise. Of the consequent savings in the costs of operation, half were to be apportioned among customers and the rest was to be divided between the management of the People's Trust and the Ruskin College of Social Science in Missouri; at the college, students paid for their education by working in cooperative enterprises. Aside from its merchandising and educational activities, the People's Trust was to expand its manufacturing and banking departments, making for itself a self-sufficient economy which soon would triumph over the less efficient and decidedly unpopular economy of the trusts.[32]

Having created the framework for what Hiram Vrooman called "a miniature civilization," the founders of the People's Trust hoped to attract droves of workers and small businessmen whose work in establishing cooperatives on the local level would give body to the organization. Workers, however, showed little disposition to join an organization which, at least in the form of the CAA, required them to enter into a contract binding them to submit to its authority and to accept their pay in the form of its notes rather than real money. Similarly, those who were inclined toward self-activity, notably small entrepreneurs and the leaders of worker cooperatives, were generally disinclined to accept any outside trust management whatever its ideals. In general, the talented and energetic believed they could find far more opportunities in the conventional world. Despite its booster pretensions, the People's Trust was little more than a small-town merchandising scheme which failed to break into the growing mass consumer markets of mainstream America.[33]

The new organization started to disintegrate soon after it was created, when its western branch, Walter Vrooman's Multitude Unlimited, encountered unexpected limits to its profits and broke down financially. In 1903, the Multitude Unlimited collapsed soon after Walter's wealthy wife divorced him (he had become involved with a young woman) and cut off his money supply; depressed by these events and exhausted by his efforts, he too collapsed and was put away in a New York hospital where he died in 1909 at the age of 40.[34]

Hiram Vrooman's eastern cooperative empire remained, but it consisted of little more than the Cooperative Association of America, which in turn was little more than Peck's still profitable businesses in Lewiston. In 1904, after a second feeble convention, the leadership decided to terminate the *American Co-operator,* and the People's Trust vanished. Although both Flower and Albertson continued to promote the cooperative ideal in the *Arena,* it was without reference to Vrooman's "miniature civilization." The CAA survived until 1912, when it was dissolved and its department store returned to Peck, whose family operated it at a profit for many years. Bradford Peck himself remained loyal to his dream of a cooperative society governed by brotherly love until his death at age 87 in 1935.[35]

Albertson rebounded from this disappointment to create his own little cooperative world. In 1909, he acquired a farm outside of Boston and established a small community open to those willing to commit themselves to the practice of brotherly love. Albertson's "the Farm" soon attracted some 30 or so residents who maintained a collective household. Like the Brook Farmers of 70 years before, the group had a satisfying, cultural and intellectual life, embellished by the visits of outside intellectuals; Walter Lippman (who married Albertson's daughter, Fay, in 1917) and Lincoln Steffens were frequent visitors. Albertson said that he enjoyed "the Fellowship that grows out of many people living together, the yeast of many ideas and opinions, the fair division of what there is to share." Like George Ripley, however, he did not enjoy the responsibilities of maintaining the Farm. Since it never achieved economic self-sufficiency, he was forced to work for the E. A. Filene Department store in Boston, spending only his weekends in the community. Too many bills and responsibilities eventually took their toll, and he deserted to other enterprises, leaving his wife to take care of the struggling Farm.[36]

Voluntary cooperative societies for specific purposes continued to be common, and the dream of one great national Cooperative Commonwealth remained alive. Throughout the previous half century, the succession of protective unions, consumer and producer cooperatives, labor exchanges, industrial brotherhoods, and various other kinds of associations raised hopes that cooperationism could be forged into a single force strong enough to resist the growing power of consolidated capital. A free people could, through their individual cooperative action, restore the old America of independent men in a modern form and without resort to the dubious sphere of politics and government. In 1909, Nelson O. Nelson expressed the confidence that "among the ten million or so members of co-operative business associations in the world there is a fast growing proportion of believers and workers for the voluntary co-operative commonwealth, a social state within a political state."[37]

The real future disappointed the dream. Successful cooperatives were far more likely to evolve into conventional businesses than to pave the way for cooperative society, while those launched with extravagant social objectives like the CAA expired for lack of popular support. In most cases, those who dreamed of cooperative independence were not likely to accept the direction of a national organization. Moreover, cooperation failed to mobilize the idealism of people in general and the advantaged in particular. Contrary to the hopes of men like Ely and the Vroomans, the cooperative was a poor instrument for the realization of the Kingdom of God on earth among a people who generally limited their religion to Sunday mornings.

The momentum which the founders of the People's Trust hoped to give to the cooperative commonwealth was a feeble counterforce to the momentum of business society. The Trust was the work of small-town businessmen and reformers in places like Lewiston, Maine, and Trenton, Missouri—an attempted rebellion of the provinces against the centers of economic power. If anything, it served chiefly to demonstrate the need for a very different way of achieving the Cooperative Commonwealth, political Socialism, which grew very rapidly during the first decade of the new century. Despite his distaste for class-oriented politics, Henry Demarest Lloyd had concluded before his death in 1903 that only the Socialist party was likely to reform American society and government.[38] The dream of voluntary cooperative community, however, remained alive in varied forms, some of which were to have a significant influence on the developing Socialist movement.

XIV

Socialism and "Utopia"

The rapid nationalization of American economic and social life in the late nineteenth century evoked a comparable nationalization of social idealism. By the 1890s, the combined influence of Henry George and Edward Bellamy had helped to shift attention away from communitarianism to politics and public policy. With the failure of both Georgism and Nationalism, this trend led to the emergency of modern socialism as the primary vehicle of radical social idealism. The new socialism, with its preference for Marxism in some form, seemed to be a distinctly new way to the Cooperative Commonwealth. As it grew, however, it had absorbed from earlier social idealism various social attitudes at odds with Marxist ideology. Throughout most of the century, the socialist idea had been defined so broadly as to include virtually every form of cooperative society, a tendency illustrated by John Humphrey Noyes, a religious communist, who spent most of his *History of American Socialisms* on a discussion of Fourierism, a species of cooperative capitalism.[1]

The diverse and, from a Marxian perspective, confused character of early socialism was exemplified by Albert Brisbane and his son, Arthur. The apostle of Fourierism had met Karl Marx in Cologne in 1848 and was impressed by the apostle of modern Communism. Later, he said that Marx, though he lacked the "genius" to conceive "any integral scientific organization of industry," was a modern Saint Paul who had inspired a powerful movement that was destined "to revolutionize the whole economy of our civilization." For Brisbane, though, this influence was not to result in Communism; rather, it would "introduce an entirely new order of society based on what we may call capitalistic equality."[2] Arthur Brisbane rejected his father's idealism and devoted himself to attaining wealth and power as a leading member of the Hearst newspaper organization. Eventually though, he orchestrated a sustained but notably unsuccessful campaign to promote William Randolph Hearst as a "socialist" candidate for various offices, including the presidency. Arthur Brisbane also was a leading investor in Milwaukee's Brisbane Hall (named after his father), the headquarters of Victor Berger's powerful Socialist organization, and a somewhat reluctant financial angel for Berger's newspaper, the *Leader*.[3]

Such connections were numerous enough to produce a major headache for those who wanted to purify and consolidate the modern movement. Orthodox Marxians, following the lead of Marx and Engels, tried to resolve the problem by insisting that Marxism was the only "scientific" and therefore the only possible way to the Cooperative Commonwealth. Other forms of socialism in this view were merely unrealistic and ineffectual forms of "utopianism," a judgment given an authoritative form by Engels in his influential book, *Socialism: Utopian and Scientific,* first published in 1880. Marxians treated "utopian" socialism as a premature effort to find a substitute for capitalistic society. Born out of the early stages of capitalism, it lacked the scientific understanding which Marx and Engels had drawn from their study of more mature stages: "To the crude conditions of capitalistic production and the crude class conditions," Engels wrote, "correspond crude theories. The solution of the social problems, which as yet lay hidden in undeveloped conditions, the Utopians attempted to evolve out of the human brain. . . . These new social systems were foredoomed as utopian; the more completely they were worked out in detail, the more they could not avoid drifting off into pure phantasy." Since it was not founded on fact, even the most logically developed social scheme was predestined to disintegrate under the force of the real world.[4]

The fundamental utopian mistake, Marxians said, was to ignore the existence of class interests and the necessity of class conflict as the driving force of social evolution. Instead of organizing the expanding working class for the overthrow of capitalism, men like Owen and Fourier dreamed of class harmony and designed schemes intended to appeal to all classes of society. They naïvely believed that even vested interests could be persuaded to forgo existing society in favor of a new and better world, an innocence that evoked a note of sarcasm in the *Communist Manifesto:* "For how can people, when once they understand their system, fail to see in it the best possible plan of the best possible society." Such confidence inspired the utopians to attempt to convert mankind through educational campaigns and experimental demonstrations. These efforts were innocent enough at the beginning, but the hostility of utopians to class conflict destined them to become increasingly reactionary as the modern class struggle developed.[5]

Orthodox Marxians were no more satisfied with the newer forms of American social idealism that appeared after 1880. Marx's daughter, Eleanor Aveling, and her husband, Edward, met Marie and Edward Howland and other supporters of Albert K. Owen's Topolobampo scheme when they visited the United States in the mid-1880s and concluded that the scheme was simply a somewhat larger version of the old ineffectual communitarianism: "The establishing of small islands of more or less incomplete communism in the midst of the present sea of capitalistic method of living, only ends in the overwhelming of the islands by the sea." Nor were they impressed by Bellamy's Nationalism, which they dismissed as a fantasy which served only "to reassure the bourgeois mind" that the impending revolution of society could be controlled by the middle class rather than by the proletariat.[6]

It is likely, though, that there would have been no significant socialist movement in the United States without that idealism, since socialism had to contend against both a general American hostility to the idea of class conflict and an unwillingness of most workers to view themselves as a distinct class. When in 1893 Engels attempted to explain why no strong socialist party had as yet appeared in America, he said that class feelings had been dampened among workers both by their ethnic and racial divisions and by their generally prosperous condition when compared to the European prroletariat.[7]

Many of those who did join the movement brought with them their own hopes for a peaceful transformation of society. They found support not only in the radical idealism of thinkers like George and Bellamy, but also in Darwinian evolution, a powerful but ambiguous influence on the social thought of the times. As they interpreted it, the new doctrine promised that society would naturally evolve into some form of the Cooperative Commonwealth, if only the people could be persuaded to work with rather than against social evolution.[8]

This hopeful attitude allowed some room for communitarianism, which continued to influence the thought and practice of many American idealists to the annoyance of orthodox Socialists and other advocates of a national approach. Ideological purists in the socialist movement took their signals from Marx and Engels, who had insisted that attempts to make "duodecimo editions of the New Jerusalem" were little more than reactionary utopianism disruptive of the class struggle.[9] Bellamy also rejected the approach. When asked to give his opinion regarding the founding of "Nationalist colonies" in 1893, he condemned the idea on the ground that such communities had little chance of success and, in the rare cases where they did succeed, benefited only a select few. He also rejected the old hope that one successful colony would begin the conversion of the world, noting that the many examples furnished by Christian saints had had little effect: "If you must lead men you must take them by the hand."[10] Few Americans, however, were willing to be led by the hand, and they continued to dream of creating little Jerusalems for themselves, particularly when they grew disillusioned with politics as a vehicle for progress.

The communitarian element appeared in many of the more than thirty utopian novels published in the 1890s, following the popularity of *Looking Backward*. The first was Alcander Longley's *What is Communism? A Narrative of the Relief Community*, a fictionalized tract on his own remedy for social ills. The veteran radical, who had begun his career before the Civil War, had long ago rejected Fourierism in favor of Robert Owen's vague communism, but he clung to the old communitarian dream. He advertised the book in Bellamy's *New Nation* as providing "a simple and practical plan by which communities may be established all over the country and consolidated so as to finally and speedily secure the adoption of common property and united labor by our government." Although he expected the book to raise at least some support for the Altruist community which he planned to establish outside of St. Louis, Longley's project was no more successful than the half dozen other schemes for social regeneration which he devised between 1850 and his death in 1918.[11]

Communitarianism was better publicized by the most popular Socialist novel of the decade, William Dean Howells' *A Traveler from Altruria,* written soon after the bloody Homestead Strike and published (1894) as a book in the year of the Pullman Strike. Like most idealists, Howells was disturbed by the apparent disappearance of any sense of community between American workers and their capitalistic employers. In the novel, he has a spokesman for employers say of striking workers: "They begin by boycotting and breaking the heads of the men who want to work. They destroy property and they interfere with business—the two most sacred things in the American religion. Then we call out the militia, and shoot a few of them, and their leaders declare the strike off. It is perfectly simple." [12]

Howells hoped that the nation would replace this regime with a Christian socialism notable for its democratic and communitarian tendencies. In the novel, he has a mythical visitor to America, a Mr. Homos, contrast life in the United States with that in his own distant Altruria, where community-building is a matter of national policy. Having grown tired of their own industrial warfare, the majority of Altrurians had simply voted capitalism out of existence in favor of Christian socialism. They had adopted national means to work a national change, but it is notable that the end result of their policies is essentially communitarian. Although Altruria has small regional capitals of administration and culture, the real life of the nation is in myriads of villages where the sense of community and the spirit of brotherhood reign supreme. [13]

Each community is a largely self-sufficient economy of farming and small-scale manufacturing done cooperatively "by companies of workers." These local communities are protected from outside competition by the national abolition of cities and factories, and they are secured against both greed and financial exploitation by the elimination of money. In such a society, no man works for another except in the form of voluntary cooperation, and "no man owns anything, but every man had the right to anything he could use." Gone was the old order of things where, as Howells put it with gentle sarcasm, upper class women sacrificed themselves by permitting others to do their work for them even at the risk of "suffering the nervous debility" so common to their class. The villages are too small to provide for much intellectual life, but the Altrurians have solved this problem by making it possible for everyone to travel to their cultural and administrative centers on publicly owned "electrical expresses" at 150 miles per hour. [14]

A Traveler from Altruria inspired at least two other communitarian novels, both published in 1895. John B. Walker's *A Brief History of Altruria* told the story of a cooperative experiment in Howells' utopia, while Titus K. Smith's *Altruria* was a more earthbound story of a successful cooperative town in Iowa. Smith carried the Altrurian tale back to its communitarian origins by presenting the familiar dream that such ventures would multiply until every township in America had become a miniature "industrial republic." In 1898, Zebina Forbush's mini-novel, *The Co-Opolitan,* describes a similar plan, whereby a cooperative community movement is able to take over the state of Idaho and, then, state-by-state, the entire nation.[15]

Such novels were part of a communitarian revival that began in the 1890s, in large part because the combined failures of Georgism, Nationalism, and Populism renewed the skepticism of some idealists regarding politics. If nothing else, communities could be justified as providing the experience in cooperation needed to prepare people for the eventual coming of the Cooperative Commonwealth. The new communitarian projects included the Single-Tax colony at Fairhope, an anarchist settlement at Home, Washington, and Ralph Albertson's experiment with Christian communism in Georgia. In 1894, a group in California established the short-lived colony of Altruria under the inspiration of Howells' novel. All told, more than thirty communities were attempted, twice as many as in the 1880s, when only the Topolobampo colony had much importance.[16] These efforts eventually came to dead ends, but at least two had great significance for socialism since they involved men who in the next decade were to do more than anyone else to make the Socialist movement a popular political cause.

The first was the Ruskin Colony, the brainchild of Julius A. Wayland (1854–1912). The Indiana-born Wayland had escaped from poverty by way of printing and land speculation in Missouri and then in Colorado, where he eventually became involved in Populism. In the early 1890s, under the influence of Populism and Nationalism, Wayland adopted what he believed was socialism, although most of it was derived from a reading of Bellamy's "wonderful book." Anticipating an economic collapse, he began in late 1892 to liquidate his assets and the next year moved to Greensburg, Indiana, where he established his newspaper, *The Coming Nation,* which he advertised as being "For a Government of, by, and for the People, as outlined in Bellamy's 'Looking Backward.' "[17]

The collapse which followed the Panic of 1893 convinced him that the time was ripe for socialist action. Beginning in the fall of 1893, he began to boost the circulation of his newspaper by promising to found a Socialist colony for his subscribers when he got 100,000 subscriptions. He figured that this number would provide him with enough money to buy 3000 or more acres of land. The land would then be developed by a joint-stock company that would provide homes and employment in a "cooperative village" for those who had purchased its stock.[18]

The nature of this scheme seems to owe less to either Bellamy or Marx than to Owen's Topolobampo project, which Wayland most probably had learned about during his Colorado days. It may have been that still existent project which led him to argue the practicality of his plan by citing the success of the captains of industry in using corporate association as the way to create the cooperation needed for a railroad or a great industry. Ordinary men could adapt the corporate form to their needs, protecting their interest from the wealthy by instituting the rule of one man one vote in corporate decisions regardless of the amount of stock owned by any particular individual. In association, they could pool their labor to create "for themselves good homes, scientifically constructed, supplied with every convenience that the rich enjoy, permanent employment at wages higher than ever dreamed of by laborers, with the advantages of good schools, free libraries, natatoriums, gymnasiums, lecture halls, parks, and playgrounds." Under the happy influence of the collective ownership and operation of economic and social institutions, members would work and live in "atmosphere of equality and brotherhood," protected from the poisons of competitive capitalism and the profit motive.[19]

Wayland fell far short of his goal of 100,000 subscribers, but he did tap into a broad vein of dissatisfaction raised by the Panic of 1893 and by the failures of Nationalism and other movements for radical change. Early in 1894, one subscriber from new Hampshire wrote to the *Coming Nation* that in America there were "no less than 100,000 socialist families," enough to form at least one great city of 50,000 or more people: Such a city "will be an object lesson that will convert the world. Our city of 'equal rights to all' will grow and expand and soon control the state. A socialist state will give us many miles of railroads, telegraphs and telephones, as well as all mines. Brothers, all that is required is intelligent work." It seemed easy for labor, the creator of wealth, to take charge of its own destiny, particularly when the movement was, as

Wayland enthused, "springing up in a hundred places" throughout the nation.[20]

This rising tide impelled Wayland to act on his promise, even though his subscriptions barely reached 60,000, and in 1894 he bought a thousand acres of land some 30 miles from Nashville, Tennessee. By the end of 1894, he and associated enthusiasts had begun to organize a colony open to all persons pledged to socialism, opposed to free love, and also able to afford a $500 membership fee in the Ruskin Cooperative Association, which was to own the property. Ruskin attracted a notable number of skilled workers and petty entrepreneurs from a wide area; by one count, members came from 16 states including New York and California. Before it began, Wayland boasted that "we have farmers, gardeners, brick masons, stone masons, carpenters, machinists, engineers, physicians, laborers, printers, and other needful vocations ready to locate in the colony and go to work." The members brought needed skills and some money, but they were hardly the naturally cooperative proletarians of the Marxist dream.[21]

The colony got off to a fast start with the aid of $18,000 raised from its first members. Eventually the colonists created a panoply of community facilities, including a library, school, art studio, theater, and town band; they tried to realize the dream of John Ruskin, after whom the colony was named, for a society where art would truly beautify the lives of the people. In the interests of socialism, they planned to establish a "college of the New Economy" with the intention of making Ruskin the intellectual Mecca of America; Henry Demarest Lloyd called it the "first Socialist College in the World" when he laid its cornerstone in 1897.

The colony operated a public steam laundry, communal kitchen (worked by men), and common dining hall to release women from domestic servitude so that they might share in opportunities for self-development. Supported by an array of machines beyond the dreams of most colonists, the Ruskinites worked a ten-hour day in the various departments to which they were assigned, generally on the basis of personal preference. In exchange, they received free meals, housing, medical assistance, shoe-repairing, laundry work, and education, along with a dollar each per week for incidentals.[22]

A new socialistic society was being born, raising the usual expectations for the regeneration of the world. One woman member, Lydia Kingsmill Commander, declared that the Ruskin ideal "is not simply to be a great business success, but to become the living embodiment of the ideal civilization, wherein skill in all industries shall be crowned by the highest mental and moral attainments, where the graces and joys of life shall be added to the sterner virtues." A sympathetic observer emphasized the ease with which the members had united in the active reshaping of their collective lives. Life at Ruskin, he said,

> becomes as natural as any other, and much more congenial and satisfactory to the mind and heart. Life loses its complex and bewildering aspect and becomes simple and comprehensive. The artificiality which is apt to nauseate us at times in the great gilded cities, gives place to a frank and open manner of life.
>
> The problems of overproduction and undercompensation no longer confuse the mind. . . . The snarled and twisted social problem becomes as straight as a telegraph wire. It is only how to work for others while others are working for you.[23]

For a time, the vigorous growth and vital life of Ruskin raised the familiar hope that some Americans had finally discovered a successful secular formula for a cooperative village life where the insecurities, class disharmonies, and degradations of urban-industrial society would be eliminated.

Ruskin, however, soon repeated the pattern of disaster first established at New Harmony. Like the two Owens before him, Wayland made the mistake of actually joining his colonists without having first worked out the details of his relationship with them. Less than half a year after he moved to Ruskin, he abandoned it when the majority made a logical Socialist claim to ownership of his newspaper, *The Coming Nation*. His angry departure in the summer of 1895 was followed by a series of conflicts among the members which belied the hope that brotherhood could be found in collective ownership.[24] Conflict not only undermined commitment and the willingness to work but also resulted in battles over the property that led some of the dissidents to force the colony into bankruptcy in 1899. When the receivers had finishing paying off Ruskin's debts, most of its estimated $94,000 in assets had been dispersed, as were the members, many of whom participated in the formation of a short-lived colony at Duke, Georgia; eventually, some of them found a safe refuge in the Single-Tax enclave at Fairhope.[25]

Julius Wayland fared much better than his colony. After leaving

Ruskin, he reestablished himself in Kansas as the publisher of the *Appeal to Reason,* which became the most popular American socialist newspapers of all time with a circulation of over 140,000 by 1900. Over the next decade, thousands of Americans were to learn their socialism from Wayland. His experience at Ruskin had left him with a permanent distaste for communitarianism. Yet there is some doubt as to how completely he broke with the past. Much of the boosterism that had led him to establish Ruskin remained alive in his outlook. Basically, he saw socialism as a new vehicle to carry on an old American fight of the true producers against parasitic capitalists, a vehicle that had ample room for entrepreneurs like himself. In his cooperative commonwealth, "men will have to do useful work to share in the benefits. Then the workers will be the capitalists." It was essentially a nationalized version of the joint-stock association attempted at Ruskin, although it is evident that in this new version he expected the *Appeal to Reason* to be made secure from the confiscation which had cost him the *Coming Nation*.[26]

The troubles at Ruskin had little effect on what began in 1897 as the most ambitious movement since the days of Fourierism to revolutionize society through communitarian means. The moving spirit behind this movement, and eventually behind American socialism generally, was Wayland's fellow Hoosier, Eugene V. Debs (1855–1926). Debs brought a new attitude to radical social idealism—one compounded out of hopes for the Cooperative Commonwealth and his own experiences as a worker and labor leader. By the early 1890s, the growing dominance of capital over labor had convinced him of the need for a union of workers strong enough to equal the consolidated force of big business; the dominating trend toward "consolidation, solidification, combination" required more consolidated labor organizations than the existing federations of railroad brotherhoods and craft unions. In 1893, he attempted to unite all railroad workers in one great industrial organization, the American Railway Union, with such success that, in the following year, the A.R.U. won an important strike against the Great Northern Railroad.[27]

Deb's concern with consolidating those whom he viewed as the productive class into an independent force was the dominant theme of his later career. In 1894, he believe that in the ARU he had found the way by which workers could protect their interests and achieve justice within the existing system. He hoped that the new union would enable labor to negotiate on a plane of equality with capital, thereby obviating strikes an other forms of discord that had disrupted industrial relations. Once workers had won the respect of employers, "the chasm between capital and labor" would be bridged, restoring the harmonious relations between the two great forces of productive society which Debs believed had existed during his days as young labor leader in his hometown of Terre Haute.[28]

This dream lasted for less than a year. In 1894, Debs was persuaded to swing his powerful union behind the strike initiated by the employees and residents of George Pullman's model factory town outside of Chicago. "You are," Debs told these workers, "striking to avert slavery and degradation." In the end, his intervention destroyed both his union and Pullman's capitalistic paradise. When the ARU refused to run trains which included Pullman's cars. the railroad companies resisted, creating a a near paralysis of the nation's railroad system. After the outbreak of violence, the Federal government intervened on the side of the railroad companies, and the strike was crushed. Debs himself was jailed for violating a federal injunction. It was while serving him time at Woodstock, Illinois, that he began to rethink his acceptance of the existing order, a process which soon led him to commit his talents to the Socialist cause.[29]

When he returned to his home in Terre Haute, however, he had yet to commit himself to anything beyond a general faith in cooperative society The influences on his thinking were as varied as the forms of social idealism that had appeared by the mid-1890s. He identified with the Cooperative Commonwealth of Laurence Gronlund, whom he described in 1896 as "one of the brainiest men of our times." He was also a friend and admirer of Henry Demarest Lloyd whose cooperationist ideals and analysis of society became ingredients in his own attitudes.[30] Likely, he was also influenced by the Ruskin Colony, whose newspaper, *The Coming Nation,* had won his attention by its support of the ARU during the Pullman strike.[31]

Debs took an even greater interest in Edward Bellamy. The Hoosier had been suspicious of the middle-class paternalism of the Nationalist movement, which he dismissed as "the Yankee Doodleism of the Boston savants," but he recommended *Looking Backward* to workers as an outline of what might be achieved even before the year 2000. He was also impressed by Bellamy's later writings, especially by *Equality,* which he saw as prophesying "the doom of our present competitive system."[32]

In early 1898, it was reported from Denver, Colorado (where Bellamy had gone for his health) that the Yankee and the Hoosier had joined together to resurrect the *New Nation;* whatever the exact truth of this, the *New Nation* was revived in Denver, with Bellamy as one of its directors, but before its first issue in June 1898 Bellamy had died.[33] In his obituary comments on Bellamy for a Terre Haute newspaper, Debs called him "a very warm friend of mine" and described him in a way that could also be applied to himself: "As a matter of course he was an idealist, but this only developed the practical side of the man and made it possible for him to present his theories so admirably and effectively as to captivate the mass of people in all civilized lands."[34]

After the Pullman strike, Debs had expressed his hopes of rebuilding the ARU in terms that Bellamy would have approved: "We shall take our time and have our machine in running order and our men trained and drilled and educated for action."[35] These hopes were disappointed, however, and he began to consider a political venture that resembled the Nationalist movement. In 1896, he supported the Free Silver campaign of William Jennings Bryan in the belief, as he said later, that it would become a rallying ground where the common people could be united against the power of concentrated capital "and once united could press forward in a solid phalanx in the crusade against social and industrial slavery . . . until the whole capitalistic system is abolished and the co-operative commonwealth has become an established fact." Like Bellamy, he found hope and inspiration in the great event of his boyhood, the Civil War, which he saw as the triumph of idealism over an earlier form of slavery.[36]

The Bryan campaign failed to dent the capitalistic system, but it did help prepare Debs for an ambitious effort to rally the forces of social idealism against competitive capitalism and for cooperative brotherhood. Soon after Bryan's defeat, Debs had requested Lloyd to advise with him about "a matter of importance." What that matter was first became apparent early in 1897 when, in an article addressed to members of the ARU and "other toilers," he proclaimed himself a Socialist who was prepared to find for all toilers "a highway of deliverance to new regions beyond the reach of Moloch maws and boodle beasts of prey." Under the system of competitive capitalism, "the producing many have been subjugated by degrees until millions work by permission and millions of others are tramping and starving to pauper graves. And all this amidst fabulous abundance."[37] The industrial feudalism which the Fourierists had predicted fifty years before had, for Debs, become a reality.

In May 1897, Debs announced that he had devised a new set of tactics founded on "common sense methods" to release workers from the domination of Capital. His plan was to unite workers "in a grand co-operative scheme in which they shall work together in harmony in every branch of industry, virtually being their own employers and receiving the whole product of their labor." He said that the new movement would be open to all classes of labor and to everyone regardless of nationality, sex, or color. As it would be necessary to educate the people to the virtues and requirements of cooperative society, he intended to start with a massive publishing and lecture campaign to bring the good news to all of the nation: "Some of the foremost men in the reform movement will head the crusade, and it is a foregone conclusion that it will grow more rapidly than any other organization that had preceded it, and being founded in the intelligence of the membership the growth will be healthy and substantial, and it will not be long until the movement will be one of the determining factors in shaping the policy and destiny of the republic."[38]

Debs hoped that his movement would succeed in organizing a massive campaign to "colonize" some western state with advocates of the Cooperative Commonwealth. The first objective of the colonists would be to create an independent worker-controlled economy that would provide employment for the masses of jobless workers to be directed to the state. In some respects, this resembled the various cooperationist schemes initiated at the time, especially the Brotherhood of the Cooperative Commonwealth conceived by the Maine cooperationist, Norman Wallace Lermond, to organize the scattered forces of American cooperationism into "one vast Fraternal organization." Earlier in 1897, Debs had in fact temporarily lent his organizing abilities to the BCC, which also had the support of the Ruskin's Colony's newspaper, *The Coming Nation*.[39]

Debs's new plan, however, marked a significant departure from such schemes, since it was cooperationism with a distinctly political soul. While most cooperationists had hoped to find an alternative to governmental action, Debs expected his Socialist pioneers to vote themselves into control of the state government and to legislate the Cooperative Commonwealth into full existence. He believed that the success of this model state commonwealth in creating a civilization superior to that of capitalism would soon convert the whole nation to socialism: "From one state the new life will rapidly overleap boundary lines," generating a great national enthusiasm which would enable "the great co-operative party" to take control of the United States by 1904.[40]

For a time, Debs's enthusiasm for the colonization scheme reached millenarian intensity. He dreamed of mobilizing a great army of workers who would march, "under perfect order and discipline," to the selected state. The march would be hard and demanding, but this would serve to "weed out all the lazy and worthless ones." By the time the survivors reached their target, "the conviction that they are the progenitors of a new humanity will burn and glow in their breasts with such intensity" that they would conquer every obstacle like some Puritan army. Since this movement would involve "a union of brain and brawn," it would soon succeed in creating a viable economy: "Factories will be built, mines opened, farm lands laid out, and cooperative industries of all kinds started."[41]

He expected to finance this invasion through membership fees collected from the 100,000 people who he believed were prepared to join the new organization. He also expected "many professional and business people" to provide assistance in some form. It was apparently this expectation which persuaded him in June 1897 to issue a public letter to John D. Rockefeller, the Standard Oil mogul, asking him for support. He informed Rockefeller that he aimed at substituting the Cooperative Commonwealth for the existing system, but he appealed to the great beneficiary of that system as "a Christian gentleman" to support the plan in the interests both of the unemployed and of the brotherhood of man: "In this movement there are no class distinctions. . . . There the strong will help the weak, the weak will love the strong, and Human brotherhood will transform the days to come into a virtual paradise."[42] No mogul's money came, but that did not dampen Debs's enthusiasm. To one audience, he presented a somewhat different vision of brotherhood when he predicted that the first state converted to worker control would be safe from the kind of federal intervention which had crushed the Pullman strike. If federal troops were sent, "they will find 300,000 at the state line ready to receive them."[43]

Debs's reputation and charismatic personality got the new movement off to a fast start. In June 1897 he was able to convene a meeting of both

ARU leaders and radical reformers at Chicago which created the Social Democracy of America, the successor to Nationalism and Populism. As he had proposed, the Social Democracy created a colonization commission. Both Gronlund and Lloyd disappointed Debs by declining to serve on the commission, but its membership did include at least one enthusiast, Cyrus F. Willard, the Theosophist who had helped launch the Nationalist club movement in 1889. In 1897, Willard and his colleagues tried to find a site for the first Social Democratic colony. The vagueness of their mission allowed them to consider first purchasing a tract of land in Tennessee and then investing $100,000 of the Social Democracy's money in a Colorado gold mine. After these ideas were rejected by the SDA, Willard finally succeeded in buying some land in the Puget Sound area of Washington State for what had by 1899 become a small colony called Burley in anticipation of a plan to make it a center of cigar-making.[44]

The Burley Colony had some success in creating a society modeled on a Nationalist version of socialism. By 1902, one of its members described it as "a village with no saloon, no sectarian church, no money, and no competitive stores, managed by the people themselves through a board of directors. Here is the beginning of a new civilization free from the evils of the old, which is to make actual the ideal proposed in Bellamy's 'Looking Backward.'" The members clung to the old dream that they were pioneers who would initiate a network of cooperative colonies that would replace the existing order. In fact, they were simply another group of dissenters who tried to escape from society to an isolated frontier, where they found something less than the brotherhood of man. Willard in particular grew convinced that some of the other colonists were out to make his life miserable, and he withdrew "entirely cured of socialism." He soon found a more comfortable refuge in the Point Loma colony which his fellow Theosophists had established outside of San Diego. Burley survived as a corporate entity until 1913, when it was dissolved into an ordinary agricultural and lumbering village.[45]

This was the first and also the last product of Debs's colonization scheme. Even before it was established, it was left high-and-dry by the rapid ebb of his enthusiasm for the idea. Undoubtedly, Debs expected the Social Democracy of America to serve his colonization plan, but many members of the new organization were critical of the plan from the beginning. One of the most influential of these critics was Victor Berger, the Milwaukee Socialist who wanted to convert the Hoosier leader to his German form of political socialism. In this, he was helped by Debs's experiences in the year following the founding of the SDA. On a tour of the Northeast in the fall of 1897, Debs encountered what he saw as a rapidly rising popular enthusiasm for the new movement.[46] Initially, he interpreted this as support for colonization, but eventually it led him to view the Social Democracy as a thing apart from his first plan. In March 1898, he described the objectives of the movement in a familiar way: "It sees cooperative workingmen in control of their own factories, their own machines and tools, regulating their own hours of labor and conditions of employment, working for themselves and their loved ones, owning their own homes, and knowing no master excepting the law, which as a 'rule of action' liberates instead of crushes and dwarfs their energies." Missing here, however, was any reference to colonization as a means to this end. Instead, he mentioned politics, and by May he had begun to refer to the SDA as "a Socialist party" opposed to any and all "capitalist" parties, including the remnant of Populism.[47]

Debs might have retained at least some of his enthusiasm for colonization if Willard and the other members of the Colonization Commission had been able to achieve anything. When in June the Social Democracy reconvened to debate its future, he made some effort to sustain his plan, but events soon indicated that he was disturbed both by failings of the Commission and by the tendency of Willard and other colonizers to disassociate the plan from political action. The debates came to a stormy climax when the advocates of political action accused the colonizers of trying to pack the convention with their supporters and withdrew from the meeting. To the shock of the colonizers, Debs sided with the bolters, adding his name to their bitter condemnation of the colonizers for betraying the political goals of the SDA. For Debs as for Berger, colonization had become an anathema to the Socialist cause.[48]

This split had immense importance for the future of socialism in America. In his last book, *The New Economy* (1898), Gronlund rejected "partisan socialism" in favor of colonization, but his nonpolitical approach had become a part of the vanishing past. Debs lent his influence and energies to the formation of a new politically oriented Socialist organization, the Social Democratic Party, abandoning his earlier hope of organizing a coalition of radical reformers: "The tendency is toward

Socialism and I think it better to make that fact clear and to unite those who grasp the true principles than to seek a union of elements who are at all the intermediary stages between Capitalism and Socialism." Henceforth, he would base the search for the Cooperative Commonwealth on a class-oriented party dedicated to waging political war against capitalism.[49]

In 1900, Debs accepted the presidential nomination of the Social Democratic Party, which he proclaimed "not a reform party, but a revolutionary party." His revolution, however, was to be a peaceful one to be completed by a people awakened to the true logic of their times: "The modern tendency is toward centralization and co-operation. It has given us the trust." Both capitalist parties, he predicted, would declare themselves enemies of the trusts, but this, he said, was as dishonest as it was ineffectual, since industrial consolidation was an "inevitable outgrowth of the competitive system." Eventually, under Socialist tutelage, Americans would recognize that consolidation pointed the way to the Cooperative Commonwealth and would peacefully establish the new Socialist society on a national basis by voting themselves into possession of the means of production and distribution.[50]

A new way to the old dream of cooperative society had been opened, and over the next decade Debs was able to win growing popular support for the cause. Contrary to Debs's pronouncements, however, the new movement was neither totally dedicated to the idea of class revolution nor wholly free from the older forms of "utopian" socialism. In fact, as it grew in size it became more like a new vehicle for various kinds of dissent than a proletarian party dedicated to social revolution along Marxian lines. In Debsian socialism, the dream of cooperative brotherhood which had been born in the culture of dissent nearly a century before would find its largest and, as time would eventually decree, its final home.

X V

Debsian Socialism

The formation in 1900 of the Social Democratic Party (soon to be renamed the Socialist Party of America) with Eugene V. Debs as its spokesman opened a distinctly new phase in the history of American radical social idealism. Over the next decade, the steady growth of modern socialism as a factor in political and social life inspired hopes that the concentration of industry and the national organization of economic life was revolutionizing the habits and perceptions of the people. Confronted by an all-embracing national economy, Americans would surely abandon their infantile preoccupation with voluntary associations, joint-stock enterprises, and miniature commonwealths in favor of one grand Cooperative Commonwealth to be managed by government for their benefit. By doing so, they would join Europeans in the grand march of international socialism toward the brotherhood of all mankind.[1]

This hope, however, did not square with the complex realities of American socialism. As various studies indicate, much of the party's success stemmed from its appeal to the local needs and concerns of Americans, including such matters as the demand for a sewer system in Jasonville, Indiana. It was more than practical politics, however, that gave socialism its "Golden Age" in America before World War I. In the process of its Americanization, the movement absorbed far more of the social radicalism of the past than its Marxist leaders either wanted or realized. Indeed, it was the continued influence of what Marxians had long denounced as "utopian" thinking that inspired much of the enthusiasm that enfused the Socialist cause. Without its connections with older dreams of cooperative association in particular, the cause would have made little headway among a people who traditionally were too individualistic and enterprising to accept a collectivism born from European circumstances.[2]

Some of the problems confronting socialism in America were illustrated by Daniel DeLeon, the dogmatic but perceptive leader of the Socialist Labor Party. DeLeon himself had come to Marxism by way of short but enthusiastic involvements in Georgism and Nationalism. Although *Looking Backward* had a permanent influence on his social ideals, DeLeon soon abandoned Nationalism for the hope of establishing the Cooperative Commonwealth through an organized movement of the working class. He had little success, however, in organizing workers, leading him to conclude that the western frontier, social diversity, and the general changefulness of American life had retarded the development of class consciousness. The United States was so large and so young, he wrote in 1908, that "primitive opportunities still occasionally crop up even in regions where capitalism is strongest." The result was a popular confidence in the existence of opportunity which discouraged class-consciousness even among immigrants, who generally accepted "the native's old illusions regarding material prospects." DeLeon's response to this situation was to attempt to make his Socialist Labor Party a sectarian organization, a disciplined party dedicated to preserving its purity from the corrupting influence of American illusions in preparation for the time when economic evolution would have prepared American workers to receive its message.[3]

DeLeon's strategy doomed his party to the status of a minuscule sect isolated from the mainstream. In contrast, Debs's Socialist Party of America made itself a rallying ground for radical social idealism, a place for those who were dissatisfied not only with conservative politics but also with the reforms proposed by the Progressive movement. In the process, however, it absorbed elements not in harmony with its official Marxian character, elements drawn from the Georgist, Nationalist, Co-

operationist, and communitarian past. Although officially Debsian socialism was a secular and "scientific" movement to place the economy
under government control, it had a strong millenarian and anti-government cast; although it was inherently hostile to communitarianism, it
attracted a significant number of people who viewed socialism as a new
basis on which they could actively organize their own social lives for
their own special benefit. For such people, a vote for socialism was not a
vote for the Socialist State but for an entirely new political order favorable to cooperative brotherhood.

This situation was embodied in the leader himself. In abandoning the
Social Democracy of America, Debs had rejected communitarianism in
favor of politics and Marxism, but the influences on his thought, including his experiences as an American, were too varied for him to fit readily
into any mold. He could identify with European socialism, noting in
1904 that it constituted the "only international political party in the
world," and yet his heart lay with the traditions of American freedom.
His greatest hero was not Karl Marx but the radical abolitionist John
Brown, and his model of revolutionary change was not the Paris Commune but the abolition of chattel slavery. In his "The American Movement" (1904), he emphasized the European origins of socialism but
gave unusual attention to the pioneering work of earlier American
communitarians, viewing Brook Farm as "something like a co-operative
commonwealth" and treating Greeley, Brisbane, and other Fourierists
with respect. Of Fourierism he wrote that "the dominant strain was
emotional and sympathetic but there was nevertheless a solid sub-stra-
tum of scientific soundness."[4]

Somewhat the same statement might have been made about Debs
himself. A scientific materialist, he was also a sentimentalist and romantic who quoted Victor Hugo more often than Marx. A fighter against
injustice and a bitter critic of capitalism, he showed an even greater
genius for love. A foe of orthodox religion and of churches, he could
sincerely identify his cause with that of Jesus, "the master proletarian
revolutionist," who offered a new hope for the world. Debs, said one of
his disciples, "was one of the few radicals who dared to mention the
name of God on a public platform, and one of the few who were not
ashamed to admit that he was an American." What might have been
hypocritical or contradictory or illogical in another man in Debs fused
into one inspiring vision of the future of mankind, a vision which with

the aid of his genius as an orator he was able to communicate with a sincerity even his enemies did not dispute.[5]

For him, brotherhood was not a concept but a necessity of his life. "We poor, petty individuals, as such, amount to little," he wrote in 1905, "but as we come in real touch with each other and draw upon each other for strength and size, and feel the essential unity of the race, we grow tall as gods, and our heads are among the stars." One tough-minded socialist said that he was sickened by sentimental gush over human brotherhood, but "the funny part of it is that when Debs says 'comrade' it's all right. He means it. That old man with the burning eyes actually believes that there can be such a thing as the brotherhood of man. And that's not the funniest part of it. As long as he is around I believe it myself."[6]

Socialism became not simply a movement but a cause when Debs began the first of his five campaigns for the presidency. Under Debs, the Socialist Party appealed to the hopes of many idealists for a party so radically new in spirit that it would be impervious to the temptations of conventional politics. As such, it promised to be a radical alternative to the reform-oriented progressivism as well as the conservatism of the times. Soon after Debs's first campaign, the veteran Socialist Charles Sotheran expressed the hope that the movement would bring a "splendid new era in Socialist politics, since the new party has come into the world armed with the lofty ideals of the utopian period, the scientific knowledge of the Marxian era and the spirit of the struggling, battling, fighting organization era." And so it seemed under Debs. A victim of capitalistic oppression during the Pullman strike, he spoke with bitterness against capitalism and made socialism into a fighting creed, declaring in 1905 that the "red flag . . . is the flag of revolt against robbery; the flag of the working class."[7] On the other hand, he offered the hope that the Socialist revolt would be accomplished by peaceful political means with harm to virtually no one.

His definition of the working class was so broad as to include nearly everyone, even those who managed the existing system: "Socialism counts among the world's workers all those who labor with hand or brain in the production of life's necessities and luxuries. The services of a general manager of a great railroad system, or the superintendent of a great department store, are quite as essential to modern civilization as are the section hand of the one or the delivery boy of the other, and the program of socialism appeals to the self-interest of every man and woman so employed." By that definition, the enemy consisted of a tiny band of powerful bankers and millionaires who, through their control over capital, owned the productive power of the nation. When the American majority was united against capitalism, the system could be voted out of existence with little turmoil or social damage; only the capitalists would lose their property through expropriation, and even they would be freed from their wealth to enjoy the greater benefits of the socialist order.[8]

This change would not significantly disrupt the economy, since the growing size and complexity of modern industry had ended the importance of the capitalist to the organization and management of production: "The process of industrial evolution," wrote Debs in 1908, "that has rendered the capitalist a useless functionary has at the same time evolved an organization, co-operative in character, whereby industry may be carried on without friction for the benefit of the whole people instead of for the profit of the individual capitalist. The conduct of industry will be entrusted to men who are technically familiar with its processes. . . . The whole industry will represent a great corporation in which all citizens are stockholders." Only a few years earlier, the People's Trust movement had raised a not dissimilar hope for an alliance of workers and managers, the two vital elements of the modern economy, which could eliminate a parasitic capitalism from the equation.[9]

In the new society, Debs predicted, "the class struggle must necessarily cease, for there will be no classes. Each individual will be his own economic master and all will be servants to the collectivity. Human brotherhood, as taught by Christ . . . will for the first time be realized." With the end of the class conflict would come peace at home and abroad, and mankind would finally be secure with itself.[10] Under socialism, he promised in 1908, "the mind and soul will be free to develop as they never were before. We shall have a literature and art such as the troubled heart and brain never before conceived. We shall have beautiful houses and happy homes such as want could never foster or drudgery secure." More than a century earlier, Samuel Hopkins had described the Millennium in similar terms.[11]

Debs rarely made such utopian predictions. He believed that his role was not to paint pictures of heaven but to agitate against the wrongs of capitalism; in the increasingly bitter times after 1912, his emphasis shifted from harmony to conflict. And yet no man of his generation was so successful in raising hopes for a cooperative order. In 1912, he offered Americans a choice: either to cling to an outmoded capitalism or to join the great Socialist march toward a new civilization, which would be "as far in advance of capitalism in its beneficence to mankind as capitalism is in advance of savagery." For the first time in history, the people through the power of their votes could emancipate themselves from the evils of the past without resort to "brute force."[12]

Debs was heartened by a steady and rapid increase of popular support for socialism since his first run for the presidency in 1900. Although the presidential election of 1912 brought no dramatic repudiation of capitalism, he did receive nearly 900,000 votes; he had won only 96,931 in 1900. Most of the support came from humble folk with personal grievances against the existing system, but the Socialist Party also attracted the support of a significant number of people with some influence in society. The number of dues-paying members of the party increased more than four-fold between 1906 and 1912 from 26,784 to 118,045; party membership, which had been mostly foreign-born in 1900, had become over 70 percent native-born by 1908, an indication of Debs's success in Americanizing the movement. Although members did tend to concentrate in the industrial northeast, they numbered a thousand or more in such states as California and Minnesota and Texas, providing some basis for the boast that there was at least one Socialist organization in every state.[13]

Political socialism, however, was less a class party than a coalition of varied groups with different visions of the cooperative future. The greatest influence within the party organization itself was exercised by a few dedicated men committed to European, especially German, socialism. Victor Berger, whom Sinclair Lewis called the Saint Paul of the movement, headed a distinctly Germanic local Socialist party in Milwaukee, and his New York associate, Morris Hillquit, also took German Social Democracy as his model. John Spargo, an English immigrant, was not happy with the Teutonic learnings of the party organization, but he used his considerable talents as a writer and a lecturer to support the official position. Berger, Hillquit, and Spargo constituted an informal guiding triumverate of "Constructivists," men who believed that the Cooperative Commonwealth could be gradually achieved through constructive political action. They hoped to recruit Americans to the cause by enacting social legislation which would demonstrate the benefits of socialism.[14]

This leadership gave coherence and direction to the party organization, and it won enough support from workers, especially those habituated to European socialism, to convince it that it headed an authentic proletarian movement. It did not, however, satisfy many social idealists. In part, its emphasis on legislative measures threatened to reduce socialism to a reform movement little different from the Progressivism that was influencing the programs of the two regular parties. Even more, its dependence on government and bureaucratic power seemed to betray the essential spirit of cooperative brotherhood. Those whose ideals had been shaped by the tradition of cooperative association, for example, found little satisfaction in Spargo's declaration that "the state must be superior to the employee and the employee subordinate to the state."[15] Certainly, the prospect of some future bureaucratic paradise to be attained under the lead of party bureaucrats did not please those many radicals who dreamed of creating by their own actions a cooperative world which they could manage for their benefit.

The Constructivist leaders, for their part, were not particularly pleased with the way that the movement had grown, particularly after 1905 when, as Hillquit later said, it "began to attract ever-growing numbers of men and women in literary and academic circles [and] Socialism became popular, almost a fad." These and other new recruits frequently brought attitudes that the leadership attempted to dismiss as "utopian." Spargo, for instance, denounced those who challenged his position as "empty-headed utopians, men with schemes for speedy salvation of mankind."[16] The leaders of the party, however, could not prevent units in the expanding Socialist army from pursuing their own roads to the brotherly tomorrow.

This was illustrated in a rather farcicial way by the novelist Upton Sinclair, one of the most influential of the new recruits. Sinclair had become a convert to socialism while he was writing *The Jungle,* whose muckracking of the meat-packing industry won wide acclaim when it was published in 1906. From this triumph, Sinclair went on to write *The Industrial Republic,* in which he predicted the coming of a Socialist millennium, of a world without conflict or crime, where material abundance was assured for all by the almost automatic workings of a well-organized cooperative society. Much of this enthusiasm stemmed from

Sinclair's confidence that he had not only seen the future but in small part was already participating in it. He closed *The Industrial Republic* with a lengthy description of a communitarian experiment which he had recently begun with the help of royalties from *The Jungle*.[17]

Sinclair's scheme would have pleased Albert Brisbane and other advocates of the Unitary Household, its aim being to form a "Home Colony," an organization for collective living to involve some 100 families. He argued that the cooperative household would eliminate the waste, inefficiency, and isolation of single-family life and would gain all the advantages of life among the rich. Of course, there would still be house work, but most of that work would be accomplished by labor-saving household machinery and by hired specialists, not servants but professionals who would have a status roughly equal to that of the members.[18]

Sinclair's plan evoked enough enthusiasm among like-circumstanced people for them to form the Home Colony Corporation, which proceeded to buy a former boy's school at Englewood, New Jersey, on the Palisades across the Hudson River from New York City. The author soon proclaimed that he had planted "the seed from which mighty forests are destined to grow . . . all the world will some day be following in our footsteps." He would later say that he had lived "in the future" and found it much to his liking. The future was short, however, since in less than a year this Socialist phalanstery was done in by that nemesis of many utopian communities, fire. Sinclair abandoned the burned wreckage of his dream for single-family living with the complaint that he had fallen from a truly modern civilization back into the dark ages.[19]

Another and more significant Socialist road was followed by Elizabeth Gurley Flynn who had joined the movement after having read Bellamy's *Looking Backward,* which she later recalled as providing a "convincing explanation of how peaceful, prosperous and happy America could be under a Socialist system of society." What began with Bellamy, however, soon took a radical turn when in 1906 Flynn joined the newly organized Industrial Workers of the World, the epitome of working-class socialism in America. The IWW was also the destination of young Ralph Chaplin, later the composer of some of its fighting songs, who came to it by way of a reading of Socialist literature and of Walt Whitman under the tutelage of Charles Kerr, publisher of utopian novels and of *The International Socialist Review*.[20]

The IWW was established in 1905 by Debs, Daniel DeLeon, and other radical-minded Socialists in an attempt to organize the entire working class rather than simply the "aristocracy" of skilled workers represented by the American Federation of Labor. It was intended to become one great industrial union that would serve as the economic complement to the Socialist political party, but it soon evolved into an alternative to Socialist politics for radicals disgusted with the political leadership. Rejecting the hopes of conservative Socialists for a peaceful and evolutionary transition to the new society by way of the ballot, the IWW leaned toward the idea of class struggle and a direct worker takeover of the economy. In the words of one of Ralph Chaplin's songs ("Paint 'Er Red") regarding the existing social system:

Our aim is not to patch it up, but build it anew,
And what we'll have for government,
when finally we're through,
is ONE BIG INDUSTRIAL UNION![21]

Hostile to rule by any class of managers and bureaucrats, socialistic as well as plutocratic, the "Wobblies" were driven by the dream of a world without formal government, where workers organize their own lives and work in voluntary brotherly cooperation. John Macy, proud that he was one of the few members of the middle class permitted to join the organization, said that its philosophy embodied "an idea vague enough to merit the complimentary reproach of 'utopianism,' yet definite enough to cause the arrest and imprisonment of those who preach it."[22] Its often violent confrontations with employers gave it great appeal for those who dreamed of a radical change in the course of society.

At least a few Socialists were intoxicated with the idea of revolution. The most notable was the novelist Jack London, whose revolutionary fantasies were something of an embarrassment to the cause. On the basis of some youthful experiences as a "tramp" and gold-seeker in Alaska, London convinced himself that he was an authentic spokesman for the American proletariat. In *The War of the Classes* (1905), he declared that socialism aimed "to pull down society to its foundations, and upon a new foundation to build a new society where shall reign order, equity and justice." By extrapolating the growth in the Socialist vote since 1888, he argued the inevitable coming of the great red tide which would sweep capitalism away, but he was not satisfied with the common

Socialist hope for a peaceful revolution through the ballot.[23] In *The Iron Heel* (1908), a rebuke to such conservatism, he presented a dystopian vision of a future under the heel of a despotic oligarchy which kept itself in power by force. The message was clear: Only by violent revolutionary war could the proletariat free itself from the iron power of capitalism.[24]

Socialist leaders ignored London whenever possible, although one of them, John Spargo, did denounce *The Iron Heel* as a "pathetic nightmare of melodrama and pessimism." Generally, London had no influence in the movement, but he did contribute to its development when in 1905 he helped found the Intercollegiate Socialist Society and became its first president. Originally the idea of Upton Sinclair, the society was founded to spread the Socialist message among college students.[25] Despite an aggressive lecture campaign initially headed by London, it made relatively few converts, but it did help add a significant new dimension to the movement and to its visions of the future.

Over the next decade the Intercollegiate Society became one of the links that developed between socialism and a new generation of young dissenters who brought with them their own distinctive vision of the good society. For them, joining the Socialist movement was an act of rebellion against what they believed was the oppressiveness of American society and its traditional ideals. They were essentially cultural rebels who sought a revolutionary new life style rather than soldiers in the army of social transformation; frequently, they were elitists who knew little and perhaps cared less about the real needs of the masses for whom the Socialists spoke. Basically, their Bohemia in Greenwich Village was an anarchist community devoted to their own personal liberation. And yet some could make a serious commitment to socialism as the most promising vehicle for their dreams and for their liberation.[26]

Max Eastman, for instance, became editor of the new Socialist journal, *The Masses,* in 1912 with the intention of making it "a Free Magazine ... A revolutionary and not a reform magazine" dedicated, as Eastman was to say later, to "freedom of mind and spirit, unqualified truth-telling, proletarian revolution, and state ownership of the means of production." Until it was suppressed during World War I, *The Masses* served as an open platform for socialism as well as for the cultural revolt.[27] Despite the title of his magazine, Eastman had little of Debs's sentimental faith in the masses. For him, the people were essentially irrational, governed by the need for faith in something greater than their own feeble selves. His Socialist world was to be governed by a cultural aristocracy who would be free to create, to manage, and to direct popular thought, a cultural priesthood that would satisfy the desire, as he said much later, "of God's orphans to believe in something beyond reality."[28]

If Eastman preferred to direct the Socialist parade from a distance, his friend and associate on *The Masses,* John Reed, dreamed of becoming its drum major. Reed, born to some affluence in Portland, Oregon, became one of the most radical of the cultural rebels.[29] The role of *The Masses,* he wrote, "is a social one: to everlastingly attack old systems, old morals, old prejudices—the whole weight of outworn thought that dead men saddled upon us—and to set up new ones in their places."[30] Not content simply with a war of words against the old order, Reed dreamed of a life of heroic action through militant class warfare against the capitalistic establishment, and in 1913 he became sufficiently involved in the IWW-led strike of Paterson, New Jersey textile workers to get himself thrown into jail with Elizabeth Gurley Flynn and other strike leaders. At Paterson, he had found the joy not only of direct action but also of comradeship with the real masses. Like other cultural radicals, he identified the largely immigrant strikers with a healthy and unrepressed life at war with the rottenness of traditional American society.[31]

At the opposite end of the Socialist spectrum was a far larger group who were more interested in the regeneration than the overthrow of the old society. They belonged to a world that constituted the heartland of Debsian Socialism, one far removed from the European-oriented radicalism of the Northeast. This heartland was not in Debs's own Indiana but was farther west and south in states like Illinois, Kansas, Oklahoma, and California where Populism, Nationalism, and other forms of the old radicalism lingered. In 1912, more than half of the votes for Debs came from the middle and Trans-Mississippi West.[32]

The most influential of the heartland Socialists was Debs's friend and fellow Hoosier, Julius Wayland. After his disastrous experience with the Ruskin Colony, Wayland had established the *Appeal to Reason* at Girard, Kansas, and soon built that weekly into the most popular socialist journal in American history. By 1908, the *Appeal* estimated it had more than 300,000 subscribers and claimed that a million and a half people were "animated by its spirit, and at least nominally enlisted to fulfill its mission." Although it had readers in nearly every state, nearly half of its circulation was in Oklahoma, California, Texas, Pennsylvania, Missouri, Ohio, Kansas, and Illinois. Earlier, Debs said that "wherever the *Appeal* is at work, and that seems everywhere, Socialism has at least a nucleus and the light is spreading."[33]

Wayland's experience with Ruskin had permanently embittered him against the colonization idea, and yet he retained much of his old hope for cooperative communities on the local level. His idea of socialism was "not one of force but of love—voluntary co-operation in its final stages." In reply to the view that socialism could not succeed without a fundamental change in human nature, he argued that the success of partnerships in business and elsewhere demonstrated that it was easy to transform men from rivals into cooperative brothers once they had a common stake in an endeavor; what had worked so well between two would also work among many. Essentially, his socialism was an extension of his earlier dream for voluntary association by which producers could achieve control over their own lives through "co-operated labor." Capitalism existed, he believed, only because workers and farmers had not tried to "co-operate themselves," permitting capitalists to do it for them at their cost.[34]

In 1908, Wayland warned that no producer was safe so long as society was controlled by the trusts: "Men worth millions last year are poor today; men with jobs last year today are jobless." Whatever independence small farmers still enjoyed would soon be destroyed by the organization of factory farms, whose efficient organization and use of machinery would do to them what industrial consolidation was doing to craftsmen and small businessmen. Once producers recognized that economic cooperation was their only defense, they would reject individualism and "social anarchy" in favor of socialism, which would eliminate capitalists and other parasites, putting all to work under the rule of "No Work, No Pay."[35]

Socialism, Wayland promised, would establish democratic control over industry, meaning "the control by all the workers, and not by a few so-called representatives or politicians." It would especially benefit small farmers by providing them with the advantages of machinery and of specialized labor on large cooperative farms. On such farms, they could maintain their own individual households and could use all the land they needed while also enjoying the benefits of urban life denied them by their present rural isolation, "The highest sanitary condition, heat, light, power, theatres, opera, library, museum, art galleries, parks, drives, and all the elevating influences their higher ideals can demand."[36]

Socialist influence over the heartland was strengthened by the *National Rip-Saw,* a rambunctious monthly with a circulation of 175,000 in 1912, whose motto was "Blind as a Bat to Everything But Right." Published in St. Louis, the *Rip-Saw* numbered among its editors and columnists several popular advocates of the Socialist cause, notably Debs (who eventually wrote many of its editorials), Oscar Ameringer, and the husband-and-wife team of Frank P. and Kate Richards O'Hare.[37]

Ameringer had been prepared for Socialism by *Progress and Poverty* and especially by *Looking Backward,* which he later called "the greatest, most prophetic book this country had ever produced." His conversion to socialism had been completed by his work with the tenant farmers of Oklahoma whose squalid poverty cured him of the notion that "all American farmers were capitalists and exploiters." Here were old-stock Americans who had tried to escape from industrial society by fleeing to one of the last frontiers only to fall into an existence as degrading as that of the city slums. The experience converted Ameringer to a full-time "world-saver."[38]

Another world-saver was Kate Richards O'Hare, whom Ameringer ranked "a close second to Debs as a riler-up of the people." She and her husband Frank gave their socialism the character of a revival movement. To extend the influence of the *Rip-Saw,* the O'Hares headed a corps of lecturers whose illustrated "stereopticon lectures and entertainments" could be obtained free by any group which had arranged to buy 1000 subscriptions to their magazine. Some of these lectures were the feature attractions of communal gatherings that resembled both revivalist camp meetings and small-town circuses. After the people were warmed up by the singing of radical songs, Kate O'Hare, Debs, and others would deliver their Socialist message of deliverance from the tyranny of the eastern money power. Undoubtedly more than a few in the *Rip-Saw* audience shared the view of one of its writers that "the Socialist party with its world-wide demand for Justice and Human Brotherhood, expresses more real religion to me than all the cant and creeds of all the churches in the world."[39]

The *Rip-Saw* and the *Appeal to Reason* had some of their greatest effect on small-town craftsmen, businessmen, and professionals. It was to these leaders in the various provincial centers that the *Rip-Saw* looked for the founders of the Socialist "locals"; in every town, there was such a leader: "Sometimes he is a carpenter, a drayman, a doctor or merchant, sometime he is a lawyer or preacher." In 1913, it noted the plight of the small-town merchant who was hedged in by "the mail order houses and the department store on one side and low wages of his patrons on the other."[40] Before socialism, Nationalism had found some of its greatest support among members of the small-town elites. Whatever their thoughts about the Cooperative Commonwealth, they had reason to take an interest in anything that promised protection from the new world of consolidated capitalism and big cities which was overwhelming the provinces. Such men added an element of oldtime American boosterism to socialism. Oscar Ameringer, who said that the Socialist local in one Oklahoma town was composed of the "banker, lumber-yard owner, druggist, and blacksmith," remembered that small-town business often welcomed Socialist camp meetings because they attracted patrons to town; in one town, "the show windows of the merchants displayed the red banners of international brotherhood."[41]

It was this boosterism that explained some rather anomalous projects that were launched with Socialist approval. In 1908, E. C. Howe, the business manager of the *Appeal to Reason,* gave his public endorsement to the American Farm Lands Association, a scheme to sell land in the Texas Panhandle on easy credit terms for settlement or speculation: "One of the last chances to clinch your share of America's virgin soil." Earlier, the *Appeal* had published an advertisement, addressed to "comrades," of a cooperative "Socialist Farm," which offered great profits to those who invested in it. A few years later, the *Rip-Saw* gave its approval to a cooperative land-development scheme in Florida.[42]

The booster element was only a small part of the larger movement that had formed behind Debs, but it calls attention to the fact that American socialism was far from being a proletarian movement. To the contrary, it was a loose coalition of intellectuals, workers, and dissenters of various shapes and sizes who had rejected progressivism and other reform movements out of the conviction that radical change was both necessary and possible. The common denominators were a hostility to monopoly capitalism and, on the positive side, a hope for the re-creation of society in some cooperative form. Although Debs generally kept his own utopian impulses in check, his inspiring influence had brought into being a political movement that was governed less by Marxian "science" than by millenarian hopes and resentments. This spirit was strongly expressed by Vachel Lindsay, a poet and crusader for the reinvigoration of provincial culture, when he urged Americans to follow him into socialism:

> Come, let us vote against our human
>   nature,
> Crying to God in all the polling
>   places
> To heal our everlasting sinfulness
> And makes us sages with transfigured
>   faces.[43]

Benjamin O. Flower, the old advocate of voluntary cooperation, called socialism "a philosophy of practical idealism . . . , a veritable evangel of gospel of men and women, filling them with an enthusiasm rarely matched since the days when Primitive Christianity swept irresistibly over the pagan world." In the heartland, where the movement found much support among dissenting members of rural evangelical churches, one Socialist declared that the movement was "the forerunner of the Second Coming of Jesus Christ," and another predicted that "the international socialist commonwealth—God's Kingdom—shall rise on the wreck and ruin of the world's present ruling powers." Margaret Sanger, the feminist and advocate of birth control, later said of this period that "a religion without a name was spreading over the country. The converts were liberals, anarchists, revolutionists of all shades. They were as fixed in their faith in the coming revolution as any Primitive Church in the immediate establishment of the Kingdom of Heaven."[44]

For enthusiasts, it was possible to believe that the new Socialist civilization lay ahead and to accept as prophecy Debs's statement in 1912 that humanity was seething with revolt throughout the earth: "It is the sure precursor of mighty changes, political, social and economic thruout the world." Although Debs in 1912 polled only 6 percent of the presidential vote, it did look as if his movement was riding a rising tide. The *Rip-Saw* boldly announced that "A MILLION VOTES MEANS THAT CAPITALISM is DOOMED in AMERICA." For the generations of social idealists exposed to the utopian writings of the 1880s and 1890s, the Cooperative Commonwealth seemed like an impending reality. One socialist later remembered that in 1912 "we all thought socialism was around the corner."[45]

Around the corner, however, waited disaster and the devastation of decades of accumulating hopes. The real future began to reveal itself even before the end of 1912. In November, Julius Wayland ended his long career as a spokesman for socialism by committing suicide. Depressed over the death of his wife from an auto accident (he was driving) the year before, the old warrior decided that "the struggle against the competitive system is not worth the effort."[46] The years that followed furnished little encouragement for the cause. Between 1912 and 1915, membership in the Socialist party declined by over 20 percent, and in 1914 there was a sharp drop in the Socialist vote. Even with Debs as its leader, the party of the working class failed to attract much support from the American workingman, nor was it able to overcome the general feeling that socialism was somehow "un-American."[47]

Moreover, the movement was weakened by differences among its members over its goals, and these differences tended to deepen after 1912. Much of this reflected a growing disillusionment with the gradualist politics favored by Constructivist leaders like John Spargo, Victor Berger, and Morris Hillquit, who believed that it was necessary to adapt to changing conditions in order to assure the eventual triumph of the party. Whatever the logic of this position, it raised suspicions that party leaders were sacrificing the spirit needed to lift society into the realm of brotherly cooperation. For those who dreamed of a cooperative society where workers would manage their own lives, there was little reason for joy in the distant prospect that Socialism would place the trusts under the management of government bureaucrats.[48]

The hostility to politics had its most militant form in the Industrial Workers of the World. Spokesmen for the IWW like William D. (Big Bill) Haywood and John Macy had a radical's scorn of compromising politicians and an anarchist's hostility to government. They dreamed of organizing all workers into a force so powerful that they could seize control of the industrial system, overthrowing both capitalism and conventional politics at the same time. "Under socialism we will have no congresses such as exist today," promised Haywood in 1912. "Our councils will not be filled with aspiring lawyers and ministers, but they will be conventions of the working class. We will then make machinery the slave of the working class." Direct action by the workers themselves against the industrial establishment would truly revolutionize society and create a cooperative commonwealth in which all would be workers.[49]

Political disillusionment also encouraged a resurgence of communitarianism. In 1913, for instance, Frank P. O'Hare of the *National Rip-Saw* began to take an interest in a cooperative community development scheme at Ruskin, Florida, which significantly was also the new home of the Ruskin College of Social Science founded a decade earlier at Trenton, Missouri, by Walter Vrooman. Ruskin advertised itself to "socialist homeseekers" as a new town where "a co-operative store, canning factory, and telephone company are in successful operation. Clauses in deeds protect against saloons, commercial competition and race antagonism. Only white people can acquire title." Its promoters saw nothing absurd in proclaiming it, in virtually the same breath, "strictly a white man's town" that was devoted to "a wholesome faith in humanity and the brotherhood of man." By 1917, Frank O'Hare had become president of the Ruskin Plaza development company and was offering land at Ruskin as prizes to those who got the most subscriptions for his journal.[50]

Early in 1916, the *Rip-Saw* took note of an even larger scheme for a Socialist community which it said involved at least one member of the National Committee of the Socialist party and "scores of other comrades who, for years, have been on the firing line." The chief inspiration behind this scheme was Job Harriman, who had been Debs's first running-mate in 1900; Harriman had first attracted notice in 1891 as an energetic organizer of Nationalist clubs in San Francisco and Cincinnati.[51] After 1912, Harriman abandoned politics for a scheme to build a model socialist city. He formed the Llano del Rio Corporation, capitalized at $2 million, which was to guarantee a house and employment to anyone who invested a thousand dollars in it. Harriman chose a dryland location about 45 miles north of Los Angeles and began to build a city for 10,000 people with the confidence that irrigation would make the desert around it "as green as the map of Ireland." Llano del Rio did attract some money and support, and by 1916 the place proclaimed itself "the World's Greatest Cooperative Community." In 1917, this socialist paradise had a population of over a thousand people and the beginnings of what was claimed to be a new civilization.[52]

The *Rip-Saw* initially endorsed the colony, as "a demonstration of the power of co-operation which may show the world the way to happiness through collective effort." A month later, however, it warned that anyone who bought stock in the Llano corporation was taking a gamble which he was likely to lose. In fact, Harriman's colony soon encountered shortages of both money and water and of the cooperative spirit as well, and it broke up after 1917 in conflict over the property.[53]

Brotherhood was not to be found in a colony, and neither was it to be found in a national party. Although Debs ignored the colonizing schemes and continued his political efforts, he became increasingly alienated from the party leadership: In 1918, he complained privately that "for years the National office under Berger, Spargo and Hillquit, the ruling trinity was decidedly opposed to me, that not a clerk who was friendly to me could stay in office and not an organizer who had a friendly word for me could stay on the road." Despite bouts of sickness which deepened his depression, he was able to retain some of his old fire and hopefulness, but he invested little of either in the party organization. In March 1914, he became the editor of the *Rip-Saw,* proclaiming it "a tremendous force in the American struggle to rid the world of capitalism and wage-slavery and make way for the industrial commonwealth and the Socialist Republic."[54] Over the next two years, he wrote many editorials for the monthly, few of which revealed any enthusiasm for party politics. Instead, he placed his greatest hopes in a plan to organize workers behind a two-pronged attack on wage-slavery and industrial despotism.

Debs's plan did provide some room for Socialist political action; he believed that a strong party was needed to promote worker interests and protect worker rights in existing society. He expressed little faith, however, in the party as the primary means of attaining the new order, and he warned that "the Socialist Republic cannot be created by a political majority alone"; to concentrate on politics would reduce the Socialist organization to "a mere political party whose advent to power will but signalize its impotency to carry out its own program." It was essential that workers be prepared to take charge of the worker's paradise when socialism won power and this, Debs believed, could be accomplished only by forming them into one great industrial union: "How can the workers be expected to take hold of the industries and operate them successfully, unless they have been trained and fitted by industrial co-operation as revolutionary unionists, and where but in the industrial union can they develop the economic power, capacity and self-discipline to assume the mastery and control of the nation's industry."[55] This was a new version of the hope for worker cooperation and control that had marked his first discouragement with politics in the 1890s.

In 1916, Debs declined to run for the presidency, but he did stand for Congress in order to speak on the issues. Although he gave much of his time to warning against America's involvement in World War I, he also urged every Socialist to work for the industrial organization of all workers without regard to nationality, sex, or, most significantly, race; there was to be no color line in Debs's Socialist Republic.[56] When the Socialist vote in 1916 declined by some 40 percent below 1912, he said that it was because the party "was controlled too largely by political considerations and paid too much attention to catching votes." He urged the party to concentrate on developing "the revolutionary spirit" among workers even at the sacrifice of its own political growth, warning that the party could not have "mushroom growth without at the same time being of mushroom softness and instability."[57]

Debs's position at this time suggests that he had drifted into a millenarian frame of mind. In the spring of 1917, the *Rip-Saw* changed its name to *Social Revolution* with the prediction that "the Social Revolution now pending is the greatest revolution in human history. It is the greatest thing on earth." In the midst of the Great War that was then convulsing the world, it was possible to dream apocalyptic dreams of collapse and rebirth which would reward those who had remained true to the faith. In an editorial for *Social Revolution* written at the beginning of its second year, Debs said that every day demonstrated that the long predicted collapse of capitalism was coming: "We must not waver. We must point the road to the co-operative commonwealth and pave the way to it by the industrial and political organization of the working class."[58]

The next years, however, brought the collapse not of capitalism but of hopes for the cooperative commonwealth as the Socialist movement was hammered by external persecution and torn apart by internal discord. Radical social idealism had reached the end of its golden age.

After Tomorrow

The years from 1916 through 1920 brought an unprecedented devastation of social idealism. Lewis Mumford, who had grown up with the optimism of socialism's golden age, later said that the period saw "the collapse of tomorrow."[1] The hope for a radically better society had encountered setbacks before, but nothing like the one which crippled it during the World War I era. Although Owenism, Fourierism, Georgism, Nationalism, and the other "isms" of the nineteenth century had failed, the cooperative ideal had survived and grown. The years surrounding the War, however, not only killed Debsian socialism but also broke the chain of hope that stretched back to the early years of the previous century.

The World War was surely the most serious challenge to the optimism which had flourished during the previous century. Since the days of Robert Owen, social idealists had dreamed of a world without war where the wastes of national conflicts would be replaced by the riches of international cooperation. The greatest conflict of that century, the American Civil War, did severely test social idealism, especially in its religious forms; the ideal of nonresistance which had inspired Adin Ballou's notable experiment in Christian socialism at Hopedale had been particularly devastated by the conflict.[2] For many idealists, though, the Civil War was a great regenerating victory of freedom over slavery and a model of constructive revolution. No such good could be found in the irrational conflict of armed nationalisms which had erupted in seemingly civilized Europe.

The conflict devastated the dream inspired by Bellamy and others of a peaceful international order managed by the civilized nations of the North Atlantic World. It had a particularly disruptive impact on international socialism. Before it began, there was widespread hope that socialism, with its commitment to international brotherhood and its growing power in Europe, would check the madness of nationalism and preserve the peace.[3] In fact, the Socialist movement had not only failed to prevent the outbreak of war but was itself deeply divided by national loyalties. North Atlantic socialism, said John Macy in 1916, was "in a state of confusion, obscured and torn, by the madness of the larger world that surrounds it." Macy and his fellow American Socialists themselves were being torn asunder by deep differences regarding the character of the European conflict. Was it, as John Reed and others insisted, simply a capitalistic war among the privileged classes which America should avoid, or was one side to be preferred as standing for right principle? By 1916, some members of the party like Spargo and Upton Sinclair had broken with its official position against the war in favor of moral support for England, from which they had derived much of their Socialism.[4]

When the United States entered the conflict in 1917, the majority of party representatives went on record against war and for the ideal of a new world of "peace, fraternity, and human brotherhood." That stand, however, brought socialism into direct confrontation with American nationalism. Previously, anti-state radicals like Macy had urged their brethren to make government obsolete and to prepare for the Cooperative Commonwealth by setting "to work to cleanse their own systems . . . of the superstition of nationalism," but nationalism proved difficult to purge and impossible to resist. Some Socialists chose nationalism, while the generally more idealistic anti-war faction was devastated by federal prosecutions and popular persecutions.[5]

The war was especially anguishing for Eugene V. Debs, whose faith in the coming of a better tomorrow was the strongest unifier of the Socialist coalition. Convinced that socialism was losing its essential brotherly soul, Debs became even more radical and more bitter in his hostility to capitalism. He condemned the war as a great act of "armed murder" where workers were the primary victims. When, in 1916, he accepted the Socialist nomination for Congress, he called on all his brothers to oppose American involvement in the madness and to continue the only war worth fighting, the class-war against industrial despotism and for industrial democracy: "The preparedness that the Socialist party stands for is the education and organization of the working class, for universal democracy, for mutual interest and good will among men, for the prosperity and peace of all—for a free people and a happy world." He soon privately warned Milwaukee's Socialist mayor, Daniel Hoan, that he would disown the party if it supported any preparation for war.[6]

The entry of the United States into the conflict in 1917 deepened his anger and drove him toward millenarian hopes for an apocalyptic destruction of capitalism. In the June issue of *Social Revolution* (the renamed *National Rip-Saw*), he declared that "capitalism lies disjointed and helpless in the midst of the wreck and ruin it has brought upon the world." The next year led him to renew his prediction that socialism would soon triumph—if the faithful remained true to their cause. He urged all Socialists to recognize that the war was a test of their faith and to renew their devotion to the cause of human brotherhood and the Workers Republic.[7] It was this confidence in the collapse of capitalism that led to a second renaming of the old *Rip-Saw*, which in May 1918 became *The Social Builder*. In explaining the change in title, Debs declared that the War had opened the way to "the cooperative commonwealth, based upon the collective ownership by all the people of the sources and means of wealth." It was necessary to prepare for the new time by organizing the awakening working class to take active control of industry; he was notably silent regarding the earlier Socialist hopes for progress through politics.[8]

Debs urged all Socialists to strengthen their dedication to the revolutionary spirit and to the ideal of social revolution so that they would be ready to confront what he called "the supreme crisis of the world." Weakened by ill health and overwork, which had left him in 1917 "literally fighting for my life," he drove himself on in the conviction that the convulsed and oppressive time was a great and redeeming trial for the Socialist spirit. By 1918, both official prosecution and private persecution were creating martyrs for the anti-war cause.[9] In order to inspire the revolutionary spirit, Debs apparently determined to add himself to their ranks: A month after he had introduced the new *Social Builder,* he made an anti-war speech at Canton, Ohio, that virtually invited prosecution under the war acts, and in September 1918 he was sentenced to a long term in Atlanta Penitentiary. The warm-hearted prophet of the new Socialist order became convict no. 9653, condemned by President Woodrow Wilson as a "traitor to his country."[10]

While awaiting his sentence, Debs had expressed his faith that a reunited socialism would eventually triumph: "In that day we shall have the universal commonwealth—the harmonious cooperation of every nation with every other nation on earth."[11] For a time in late 1918 and early 1919, there was some reason for optimism. The end of the "war to end all wars" revived hopes that the world would be reunited and with it the cause of international socialism.

The real future, however, arrived not in some winged chariot but on a steamroller. The war was officially ended at Versailles with a vengeful peace rather than in a spirit of world harmony. In the United States, the hopes for a resumption of prewar socialism were extinguished in 1919–20 by the often savage persecution of social radicals during the "Red Scare," which drew heavily on the nationalist feelings raised by the war. The hopeful radicalism of the past gave way to anxiety, resentment, and cynicism and the champions of cooperative brotherhood encountered a widespread tendency to treat them as if they were enemies of the best possible civilization in the world—the "American Way."

The fate of postwar radicalism was sealed by the Bolshevik Revolution in Russia. The overthrow of czarism in 1917 initially excited much enthusiasm among social radicals, since it was seemingly an omen of the long-hoped-for world revolution as well as a great victory over an oppressive and backward tyranny. By 1920, however, it had become an immensely divisive and disruptive influence on an already beleaguered American radicalism. Second thoughts began when the Revolution fell under control of Bolshevik Communists and then erupted into a bloody, vengeful civil war. They deepened when the Bolsheviks mounted a sustained effort to seize control of international socialism in order to promote their version of world revolution.[12]

Some American radicals supported Bolshevism, believing it to be the wave of the future. Max Eastman for a time attempted to convince himself that the Revolution had brought to power in Russia a scientific elite which would establish his version of socialist utopia. John Reed, true to his nature, threw himself actively into the cause in the belief that the Russians were "inventing a whole new form of civilization." In 1917, he had visited Russia and had been swept up in the excitement of the revolution, an excitement which he recorded in his classic book, *Ten Days that Shook the World.* Two years later, he returned to join the Bolshevik cause, only to die of typhus at the age of 33 in 1920. And so an American cultural dissenter was buried beside the Kremlin Wall, the hero of a foreign revolution.[13]

Many other Socialists, however, had none of Reed's youthful enthusiasm for the Bolsheviks. John Spargo, one of the leaders of the prewar party, at first dismissed Bolshevism as a "form of romanticism which cannot be of lasting influence" and then condemned it as a menace to civilization. In 1919, he attacked its American supporters as consisting largely of either the rootless and more violent element of the IWW or "hysterical" intellectuals. They were the ones, he said, who "embraced nearly every 'ism' as it arose . . . Anarchist-Communism, Marxian Socialism, Industrial Unionism, Syndicalism, Birth Control, Feminism, and many other movements and propagandas, each of which in its turn induced ecstatic visions of a new heaven and a new earth." Spargo belonged to the conservative wing of the Socialist movement; a few years later he urged the party to support the election of Calvin Coolidge.[14]

Debs, if only because his socialism was more radical, reacted to Bolshevism in a more complicated way. In the beginning, he had praised the Bolsheviks as the prophets of the world revolution which he expected from the war, and he declared himself to be a member of the new "Commonwealth of Comrades." However, their tactics in Russia and elsewhere would soon disturb and then outrage him. Lincoln Steffens, a sometime colleague of Reed, commented rather snidely after visiting the imprisoned leader in 1921 that, like other peaceful revolutionaries, "Debs the socialist could not abide the violence, bloodshed, tyranny. They all had their mental picture of the heaven on earth that was coming, and this was not what they had expected." Two years later, Debs privately called the new communism "the evil weed of an ungodly garden," expressing a hostility which previously he had reserved for the worst of capitalism.[15]

These years completed the breakdown of prewar socialism and of the hopes that had infused it. Out of this turmoil eventually came the new Communist party, a sectarian organization loyal to the Communist faith as it was defined in Moscow; its chief effect over the next decades was to seriously disrupt and embarrass the cause of social radicalism. The Socialist party survived but only in a much diminished and dispirited form; party membership plunged from 83,284 in 1916 to 13,484 in 1921.[16] It was hardly more than a shadow of its prewar self with little of the visionary radicalism that had enlivened it during its golden age.

Although Debs had polled close to a million votes in his presidential bid from prison in 1920, he had done so more as the gaunt victim of injustice than as the hopeful symbol of a radically better society. When he was finally released in 1922, it was into a depressingly different world than the one he had known before. For a time, he continued to hope for a reconciliation with the Communists and for a revival of the old radical movement. By 1925, however, he had broken openly with Communism and also had begun to doubt that Socialists had the zeal to carry on a meaningful movement. The great majority, he wrote privately in 1925, "are utterly lacking the spirit and fibre of revolutionary socialism and a party built of them is scheduled to go in the ditch."[17]

Debs attempted to carry on the old campaign, but the weakness of the party and his own failing health made it a wearisome cause, which ended in his death in 1926. Six years earlier he had summed up the new mood when he said bitterly: "The people can have anything they want. The trouble is they don't want anything. At least they vote that way on election day."[18]

Debs' complaint was an appropriate epitaph for the golden age of American socialism and for the whole century of hopes for cooperative brotherhood. Some elements of social radicalism survived the collapse, and at least a few radicals made a notable effort in the 1920s to resuscitate the cooperative movement. Although these efforts had some influence on the future, they proved to be more the survivals of a vanishing yesterday than the beginnings of a brotherly tomorrow. In significant ways, they served chiefly to provide a melancholy recapitulation of the previous century which brought that century back to its communitarian beginnings.

Among the more hopeful features of the 1920s was a continued interest in one form of voluntary association, the consumer cooperative, which involved thousands of Americans. Although most cooperatives were initiated by small groups to meet their immediate needs, they were also connected with a cooperative movement which took on some of the social radicalism of the past. The most prominent spokesman for the new cooperationism was James Peter Warbasse, the founder and long-term president of the Cooperative League of America. The League had been founded in New York City in 1916 to promote popular interest in the cooperative idea.[19] The early League had ties with socialism, but in the 1920s Warbasse presented his movement as providing a democratic and "non-governmental substitute" for the Socialistic State, which he insisted was inherently hostile to true cooperative life. In contrast to socialism, the cooperative movement would draw on the individual enterprise and ambition for property of Americans while also eliminating the selfish individualism that plagued American life. In Warbasse's plan, groups of consumers would form associations to provide themselves with what they needed and also to share in the profits that otherwise would have gone to capitalism.[20]

Warbasse made some appeal to the ordinary interests of people, but a significant part of his argument for cooperationism was couched in ambitiously radical terms reminiscent of Bradford Peck's National People's Trust before the war. In his *Co-operative Democracy* published in 1923, Warbasse described cooperationism as a peaceful and evolutionary "means for replacing the present system by something utterly and fundamentally different, whereby man is given a better attitude toward industry and toward his fellow man." By creating multitudes of cooperative societies, Americans could eventually replace government as well as capitalism with "a great Co-operating Society" that would be democratically managed by all the people. In the process of creating this new society, the actively cooperating people would evolve from their experiences the expertise needed to operate the new system and would also develop the cooperative habits, instincts, and sense of mutuality that would prepare them to "enter upon the era of brotherhood."[21]

In several ways, Warbasse drew on the basic elements of traditional communitarianism: The suspicions of government and politics, the hopes for expanding family feelings into a force for communal unity, and especially the emphasis on social forms that would encourage the maximum active participation of all members of the community—in sum, the dream of an activated people whose democratic cooperation would enable them to dispense with the whole existing order: "I hope for a world of nations made up of thousands of little communities; and each of these little communities I visualize as a self-governing society of neighbors." It would be a world free of the national madness that had caused the catastrophe of the Great War.[22]

Like most earlier advocates of seemingly new social formulas, Warbasse attempted to disassociate his plan from previous communitarian schemes. He contrasted his emphasis on the organization of a national movement of cooperative building with what he insisted was the past tendency to flee from capitalistic society by finding isolated colonies. Whether such colonies failed or succeeded in economic terms, they were doomed to fail as democratic communities since each was "a very small oasis in a very large desert. Profit-making business surrounds them"— and inevitably they were swallowed up by capitalism.[23]

Warbasse had some reason for confidence in his movement. During the early 1920s, the Cooperative League expanded rapidly until it embraced over 300 active societies engaged in various kinds of cooperative business; and it even won some praise from Debs, who in a letter to "comrade Warbasse" expressed his "appreciation of the splendid work the league is doing under your administration."[24] After 1925, however, many of the cooperative societies associated with the League failed, largely because of the changes brought by the boom years of the late twenties. It was a special misfortune for the cooperative ideal, therefore, that during its successful years the League should have opposed another experiment in cooperation.[25]

The other experiment was the New Llano colony, the last vestige of the communitarianism that had marked the growing disillusionment with Socialist politics after 1912. New Llano grew out of Job Harriman's experiences with both physical and human nature at Llano del Rio. In 1914, he had purchased a large tract of dryland in southern California, confident that it could be made productive by a system of irrigation to be constructed through the cooperative efforts of his Socialist followers. Like many Socialists, Harriman had believed that the consolidating trends of modern society were preparing the way for the Cooperative Commonwealth, especially by engendering a cooperative spirit among the members of the producing class. Impatient with political socialism, he had decided to establish his own little cooperative commonwealth to prove that in a Socialist world "the hearts and minds of men would be as sweet and gentle and loving as in babyhood."[26]

At Llano, however, he and his followers encountered a shortage of water that frustrated their hopes to create a rural city of 15,000 or more inhabitants. Even worse, they found little of the cooperative temper which they had expected from the new Socialist Man. Harriman, in particular, was upset by what he saw as sheer human nastiness, particularly in the form of an organized "brush gang" perversely hostile to his leadership. Especially disillusioning was the unexpected class behavior of many of the inhabitants. Where his economic determinism led him to expect a cooperative disposition among proletarians, his experience convinced him that "there was proportionately more selfishness among the poor" and an unexpectedly high degree of cooperativeness among the well-to-do.[27] His own middle-class background (he had begun his career life as a lawyer) may well have determined this experience, but he was confident that his experiment had demonstrated that conventional Marxist economic determinism was naïve.

Both the experience and the conclusion led Harriman to make a new experiment along more traditional communitarian lines. In 1918, he and a small band of followers made a trek from California to northwestern Louisiana, where they converted an abandoned mill village into the Llano Cooperative Colony. Having decided that a truly brotherly disposition would come only when the present generation had "undergone a long period of ethical or spiritual training," he placed his hopes in the educational and conditioning influence of communal living. Common work, common property, and the intimacy of communal life would gradually rework the psychology and behavior of individuals into cooperative dispositions with the assistance of Man's "fundamental gregarious urge."[28] The self-contained community would be the cradle of the new Socialist Man.

New Llano went through the equivalent of a frontier starving-time. In 1918, Harriman wrote to Debs requesting his assistance in finding Socialists wealthy enough to lend the $150,000 which he calculated would put the colony on a permanently profitable basis and enable it to demonstrate the feasibility of cooperative brotherhood: "It is up to us to develop a social spirit, a spirit of fellowship, and we are doing it in this colony and doing it magnificently."[29] Although Debs in his own disillusionment with politics may have been sympathetic, there is no evidence that he or anyone else came to Llano's aid. The failure to satisfy these financial ambitions, however, may have had some of the same saving influence on Llano that a similar experience had had on the North American Phalanx. Privation on the physical and social frontier was a great way to form a community of dedicated and cooperative people.

Hardships discouraged the sunshine soldiers of the cooperative army, but the grit and determination of a saving remnant of Llano's population pulled it though, and in the early 1920s it grew from a handful of dedicated families to over 150 inhabitants. The character of the population indicates that it had become something of a rallying-ground for the dispersed and depleted forces of the old idealism. There were anarchists, communists, socialists, pacificists, and radical feminists. One member had joined the original Llano venture after having read some of the works of Owen, Fourier, Bellamy, and George as well as Marx. One had begun his communitarian experience with Topolobampo and another with the colony of Equality in Washington. They were a diverse lot, but most of them had been attracted to the colony in the hope of finding what its newspaper called "the Religion of Cooperation."[30]

Reaching back to the Fourierist past, they adopted the joint-stock principle of property ownership. Llano was a corporation, chartered in Nevada, whose stock was available to anyone willing to put up a dollar per share. In 1923, it was estimated that it had close to 700 shareholders scattered all over America and embracing "all shades of economic heresy." Anyone could buy as many shares as he pleased, but to prevent the community from falling under the control of wealth no one could vote more than 2000 shares in corporate elections. Each head of a family was required to purchase 2000 shares, part of which were to be paid for in cash, in order to be admitted to membership. Every member was expected to contribute eight hours of work per day to the community in exchange for full access to everything available in the community.[31]

The members were able to cooperate sufficiently to attain what the *Llano Colonist* boasted in 1925 was "a miniature cooperative commonwealth, in which cooperation is the integral principal. . . . Instead of personal ambition and desires for personal gain, the colony is like a family in which the good of one is the good of all."[32] Along with this familiar ideal, New Llano also had the usual range of industries and institutions required for a miniature commonwealth: A printshop, bakery, steam laundry, hotel, machine shop, sawmill, and various other industries; a library, kindergarten, grammar school, and high school; a swimming pool, theater, dance hall, orchestra, evening classes, and discussion groups. It boasted that its children were educated in the practical experience and skills required for communal life and that its women had equal pay with men and an equal "right to work, live, love, and be happy."[33] At varying times, Llano's inhabitants proclaimed it the "Gateway to Freedom" (the title of a pamphlet advertising itself), a "fellowship of loving kindness," "a modern Garden of Eden," and the closest thing to "the Kingdom of Heaven on Earth"; one said that the members "approach very near the ideals and practices of the early Christians," although there was no church in this freethinking society.[34]

The inhabitants were satisfied with their isolation from the turmoils and uncertainties of the larger world, a world under the shadow of "Superdreadnaughts of the air," giant dirigibles "capable of destroying a city the size of New York in a few minutes by dropping powerful bombs." In contrast, New Llano was an island of peace through socialism. It was not, however, isolated from the larger world of hope. Its newspaper, the *Llano Colonist,* provided a clearing house for cooperative dreams and ideas in its column "Cooperation the World Over." It was able to attract some national attention, including some from Debs who at least considered visiting his "good comrades" in the colony. With some success came the usual hopes that a way had finally been found to the promised land. "They believe," one observer wrote of the colonists, "that that hard road to real cooperative life can best be blazed by small autonomous groups, and that the real nation or world-wide co-operative commonwealth will come by the ever-extending merger of these groups."[35]

Llano could claim at least one tie with a larger world of cooperative strivings. One of its former members reported his experiences with a communitarian experiment in the Kuzbas Basin of Soviet Siberia involving some 200 expatriated Americans headed by the old Wobbly, William D. Hayward; Hayward had fled from the United States after the war to avoid prosecution under the Sedition Act, an act that greatly disappointed some of his fellow members of the IWW. The Llano colonists took satisfaction from the belief that the Kuzbas Colony had been modeled on their own community, thereby refuting the belief of Moscow-leaning American Communists that nothing good had come from the United States. Although a world apart from the Siberian frontier, they could identify with those whom they imagined as possessing "the soul of the pioneer and vision of a co-operative commonwealth," a description which they undoubtedly also applied to themselves.[36]

This sense of importance was given a substantial boost in 1923 when Llano became the home of the *American Vanguard,* the direct descendant of the prewar organ of heartland socialism, the *National Rip-Saw.* The *Rip-Saw* had been suspended (under its third title, *The Social Builder*) by its managing editor, Phil Wagner, after its May 1918 issue, but the monthly was revived with its original title after the war by Frank P. and Kate Richards O'Hare, who renamed it *The American Vanguard* in 1922[37] It was inspired by the hope of retrieving the old dream of cooperative brotherhood from the ruins of socialism.

Kate Richards O'Hare said that, though the prewar Socialist party had educated Americans to the ideal of cooperation, it had been doomed by its emphasis on political action when "the World War proved that the real governing forces of the world are not political but industrial." It was time for the people to gain control of the industrial world by educating themselves to the techniques of cooperation, which she called "the only path out of the ruins of civilization that the war has wrought."[38] The *American Vanguard* did become a beacon for the old radicalism, but its circulation was far less than that of the prewar *Rip-Saw.* In order to save money and to enhance its image, the O'Hares decided to move their monthly from St. Louis to Llano, where they would have use of the colony's print shop.[39]

Llano's importance as the capital of the old radicalism was further enhanced later in 1923 when the O'Hares helped arrange for the establishment of Commonwealth College there. The College was directly descended from Ruskin College, which had originally been founded during the days of the National People's Trust; later it had been temporarily resurrected at Ruskin, Florida, in connection with a town development scheme with which Frank O'Hare was involved.[40] The new college was intended to provide higher education for the working classes and to begin a movement to overturn the existing university system which Kate O'Hare condemned as an instrument used by "the ruling classes to impose their ideals of culture." It would nurture and teach of a new culture, to "be born out of the mass mind and be the expression of the mass ideal."[41] On the basis of the new culture, workers would learn how to cooperate and to take control of their lives away from the ruling classes.

This new education experiment was more than vaguely reminiscent of the experiments attempted at Robert Owen's New Harmony and at Brook Farm. The emphasis was on blending education in the classroom with the education of real-life vocations; both instructors and students were to participate actively in the working life of the community. Although the College provided an extensive range of largely practical subjects, it gave special emphasis to the social sciences: "The development of social science," said Kate O'Hare, "holds out to workers the same hope for the mastery of the means of life that the development of physical science held out to the capitalist class a century ago. Physical science promised and kept that promise, to turn dirt into gold for the industrial masters, and social science promises to turn poverty, unrighteousness and war into social justice for the workers." When Commonwealth College opened in October 1923 with a faculty of eleven (which included both O'Hares in the Social Science Department), it promised to make Llano the new cradle of the old radicalism.[42]

The Llano of 1923 bore a close resemblance to the New Harmony of 1825; each was a frontier village which for a time could see itself as the starting point for the new world of cooperative brotherhood. "As our pioneer fathers and mothers went out into the wilderness to build a new civilization," wrote Kate O'Hare, "we go forth pioneers of a new culture."[43] Unfortunately for Llano, however, the similarity was too complete. In 1924, the new cooperative world experienced a crisis of authority that developed out of a struggle for control of the colony between Job Harriman and his chief lieutenant, George T. Pickett, an ex-insurance man whose business talents had kept the colony going.[44] When the majority of the colonists voted to support Pickett, Harriman left Llano, and with him went the whole faculty of Commonwealth College as well as some of his other supporters; among them were the O'Hares. Harriman died the next year from the tuberculosis which had burdened him as far back as his prewar career in Socialist politics, but the rest of the secessionists founded a small community in the Ozarks of western Arkansas and reestablished the College under the new name of Commonwealth University. Although the community soon failed, the University did survive into the 1930s; its most famous graduate was the later proletarian poet, Kenneth Patchen.[45]

Llano might have been killed by this loss, but it proved to be more durable than New Harmony, in part because of the practical business talents of George Pickett. Pickett had the same booster spirit that had characterized some of the more successful communities since the early days of Fourierism. In 1925, he advertised the sale of part of the colony's extensive holdings of second-rate land for sale at $15 per acre, "a wonderful opportunity as an investment or as a place to start that little home in the Western Highlands of Louisiana." The colony would serve as a cultural and marketing center for its new neighbors, who would not be bothered by any Socialist idealism: "There is nothing Utopian about Llano colony. It is a plain matter of fact proposition."[46] Such policies seemed to demonstrate the truth of Warbasse's warning that no cooperative oasis could long survive in a capitalistic desert, but Pickett's boosterism probably was critical to Llano's survival.

Certainly, the mixture of business and utopia that characterized the booster mentality was needed to sustain the colony through a decade of diminishing social idealism. Despite the efforts to publicize Llano as a workingman's paradise, it was generally ignored by both the Socialist party and organized labor—and with some reason, since it was far from demonstrating the virtues of cooperation. It boasted that it was a miniature commonwealth with a wide range of industries and skills, but these were generally the obsolete industries and skills being displaced by the economic progress of the larger society; the skills of the village shoemaker, sawyer, and mechanic did not add up to a viable much less prosperous local economy. Although this paradise of cooperation provided a better life than that of the average rural southern village, physically it was little more than a collection of rickety businesses and ramshackle buildings.[47]

Some of Pickett's growing number of critics charged that the colony was little more than a front for a scheme to attract donations and membership fees, that the Gateway to Freedom actually was "a mill through which twenty thousand idealists have been run only to come out stripped of their money." Whatever the truths of the charges, they reflected a persistent discontent among some of the members who believed that they put far more into the cooperative paradise than they received in return. For his part, Pickett complained of malingering and the theft of communal property. To make matters worse, he discovered that many of the young, despite their communal education, grew restless with the limited opportunities of the colony and abandoned it for the glamour and gold of the outside world.[48]

The determination of Pickett and the more idealistic members kept Llano going, although even that might not have succeeded without some $800,000 in outside wealth which by one estimate the colony had absorbed by 1928. Whatever its deficiencies, the community did attract and hold some good cooperationists. It was a miniaturized version of Gronlund's all benevolent state, providing for the health, welfare, and social life of its members from the cradle to the grave in exchange for an expected 48 hours of work for the common good. In the early 1930s, it temporarily acquired a new importance as its population more than doubled to nearly 500 people with the arrival of refugees from the Great Depression. Amid the ruins, it was a Socialist island of security and brotherhood, although one observer was so unkind as to say it had the "atmosphere of a Salvation Army refuge."[49]

This new role, however, intensified Llano's basic tensions. It accelerated the depletion of its capital at a time of dwindling outside support, and the newcomers soon overloaded the economy, adding new dissatisfactions to the old. On the one side, Pickett complained of the backbiting and shirking of some of the members. "Your fellow worker is your worst enemy," he told an outside observer. "They may be good enough co-operators in themselves, but they sure fight against the whole system of letting people try to live together in peace." On the other side, there was growing resentment over what was seen as Pickett's dictatorial leadership, and in 1935 he was voted out of his office when he stopped the playing of "modern" music at the colony's weekly dances.[50]

Pickett's overthrow was long overdue, said one critic, who charged that Llano had wound up with little more than a large debt and a low standard of living, "because he insisted on certain impractical utopian undertakings instead of putting all emphasis upon a realistic and working endeavor to build a successful cooperative colony."[51] It was, however, Pickett's booster enthusiasm which had carried Llano through its earlier crises. Deprived of that, the colony soon broke apart amid quarrels among its members. In 1939, after it failed to get financial support from the federal government, it went into receivership, its assets were sold off, and most of its inhabitants drifted away, leaving an aging few behind in the ruins of their utopia. Until he died in 1962, George Pickett lived a hermit-like existence on the outskirts of the decaying community.[52]

New Llano was the last stand of the cooperative commonwealth, the last remnant of an age which had died with the War. The great depression of the 1930s did revive some interest in cooperative colonies, but this was overshadowed by the policies of the National government which adopted "Socialistic" programs as part of a resolute effort to save the old order from the collapse which Socialists had long looked for. By the end of the 1930s, the New Deal had spent billions to maintain a capitalistic society and had not given a penny to Llano even though the colony was a refuge for some of the unemployed.[53] The great nineteenth century search for a brotherly tomorrow of harmony, happiness, and prosperity had become yesterday in the chaotically changing modern world.

EPILOGUE: YESTERDAY AND TOMORROW

The century between 1820 and 1920 brought a rising interest in the ideal of cooperative brotherhood. In varying forms, the ideal was a potential reality for generations of radical social idealists who saw in their fluid, changing times the opportunity to reconstruct society on an essentially new basis. Radical social idealism was above all a response to the modernization which first became significant in North Atlantic society after the end of the Napoleonic Wars. Modernization offered the hope that mankind, through the exercise of reason, could escape from the evils and miseries of the past. In physical science, Man could find the power to control the natural world; in social science, he could find the formula for the good society; in the cooperative use of the new powers, he could find the way, as one member of the Llano colony wrote in 1925, to "redeem the race and establish the Kingdom of Heaven on Earth."[1]

If modernization offered the possibility of a radically better society, however, it also threatened to create a system which would both deny modern reason its benefits and pervert it into a source of human misery. Whether called Industrial Feudalism or Plutocracy, the new system seemed to be a way by which the shrewd and ruthless few could reduce the many to some form of wage slavery. Although most Americans believed that their influence in politics and government would serve to protect them, social radicals saw no hope in a political order which itself was corrupted by the forces of evil. Instead, they expected that what they considered to be the essential oppressiveness of society would persuade the people of the need for a radically new tomorrow. Only when all things social, economic, and political were made new would humankind be saved from modern evil and be introduced into the modern heaven on earth.

Social radicalism was the province of a small minority whose personalities and experiences disposed them to be cultural dissenters, men and women at war not simply with the existing system but with the values and assumptions on which it was based. From the deterministic rationalism of Owen through the attractive industry of Brisbane and the sovereign individualism of Josiah Warren to the class-struggle doctrine of Debs, the underlying theme involved a rejection of existing conventions and dogmas in the belief that a fundamental transformation in human values and outlook was both possible and necessary. In the existing culture lay the roots of evil; in some new rationalist faith were the seeds of earthly salvation.

The hopes of social radicals involved some vision of cooperative community in either spontaneous or organized form. Whatever the form, it focused on the dream of a society in which all had an active part in the management of their own lives as willing members of a brotherly community large enough to meet each of their basic needs and small enough to allow every individual to participate in its collective life. In significant ways, the dream of cooperative community drew on nostalgic memories of idealized families and village communities. It also found much energy in boosterism with its hopeful belief that any group, by associating their efforts, could find profit for themselves in the open America of endless frontiers. One persistent feature of this dream was its promise that cooperation would assure all the people access to the social and especially the cultural riches enjoyed by the few. The boasts over the libraries, schools, theaters, musical groups, and other cultural facilities of cooperative communities expressed a deep hunger for such advantages.

At its core, the ideal cooperative community had a valuable vision of life as it might and could be in the modern world. In place of the debilitating and disruptive force of individual competition, it promised to mobilize the force of fraternal love to create not some static form of perfect harmony but a human and humane system in which all would work for the good of all. In place of an economy which often squandered the human talents it raised, it promised a union of talents and energies that would enable the people to satisfy all their needs. In place of a society where class differences were disproportionate to actual differences in character and contributions, it promised one where all would share in the benefits of human progress. Above all, it offered a social life in which all would feel at home and be free from the sense of alienation that afflicted modern times.

The manifold virtues of the ideal seemingly assured its success. Surely the contrast between what could be and what actually existed would mobilize the people to work a peaceful transformation of society on the basis of the Science of Circumstances, Attractive Industry, Individual Sovereignty, the Single Tax, the Religion of Solidarity, or the Industrial Republic of Workers: Owenism, Fourierism, Anarchism, Land Reform, Georgism, Nationalism, Cooperationism, and Socialism all involved the hope that the people would join the triumphant parade once they were made aware of the good news. Each new crisis in society evoked a new hope that the people could be awakened to the existence of the promised land that God, nature, and history had prepared for them.

In defiance of such faith, every movement eventually failed. Each could claim to have exercised an influence in teaching Americans some of the virtues of cooperation, but none affected the change in attitude and social organization which it sought. The model communities and colonies of the communitarians failed, largely because of internal defects; none of them was able to demonstrate that it was possible to create the necessary unity and commitment without the Millenarian religion of the Shakers and Harmonists, each oasis of the new life was eventually swallowed up by the desert. Such experiences seemed to indicate the need for some national effort to transform the whole society. The national movements, however, were no more successful. Land Reform, Georgism, and Nationalism all failed to create constituencies, and the seemingly more realistic Socialist effort to organize the working class had little effect. The challenge of finding a way to transfer the ideal of brotherly cooperation from its sectarian setting to the larger world had not been answered despite a century of effort.

These failures dashed all but the most stubbornly optimistic views of human nature. In 1923, one disillusioned Socialist gave this assessment of workers: "They find their greatest pleasures in the line of light amusement, religion, and carnal excitement. . . . They respond to the

Personality and not to the idea; hence they are forever led—easily and instinctively led—to build the very social structure by which they are enslaved."[2] The dream of cooperative community rested on the twin assumptions that people were naturally cooperative and naturally inclined to manage their own lives, but there was little to indicate that the masses of men had much interest in actively creating and operating their own economies, societies, and cultures. Only the spur of some booster enthusiasm or social necessity served to bring people out of their seemingly natural passivity.

Moreover, the easy confidence in the progress of humanity characteristic of nineteenth-century idealism was not only shaken by the Great War but eroded at its foundations by modernist thought. The old faith in the existence of a deductive social science lost its credibility in most intellectual circles, and the earlier influence of millennialism virtually disappeared from progressive social thought. In this new intellectual world, where evolutionism was the dominant concept of human development, the old hopes for the transformation of social forms seemed at best antiquated and naïve. The only realistic hope for a better world, then, lay in the progress of the existing social order, particularly in the accelerating development of science and technology and of the complex industrial machine that modern man was building.

By the 1920s the surest highway to heaven seemed to be the "second" industrial revolution associated with the new technology of internal combustion engines and electricity. The growing use of electrical power especially promised a peaceful revolution that would meet all material and social needs. In 1923, the *American Vanguard,* published the prediction of Charles Steinmetz, the "electrical wizard," that by the end of the next century, Americans would have four-hour work days and would have access to individual freedom and property in the new suburban life that was opening around the crowded cities. "We shall be more collectivistic in the operation of our essential productive life," said Steinmetz, "and individualistic in the pursuit of personal happiness and contentment."[3] Most people found this new industrial dream more appealing than that of cooperative brotherhood. With leisure and abundance, they could hope to find a utopia of love, harmony, and happiness in their own individual homes and, with the radio and the motion picture, they could satisfy at least some of the old cultural hungers without the sacrifice of private rights and private property.

The Great Depression dealt a severe shock to the new industrial economy, but it also evoked a great national effort to preserve it. Although some interest in cooperative brotherhood continued, there was little in the times of depression and then of war to support the old hope that mankind could be persuaded to practice brotherly love and to pool its energies and talents for the common good. Instead, the world seemed to demonstrate that conflict was more natural than cooperation and hatred more powerful than love. The most pronounced form of integral cooperation was a totalitarian dictatorship; the most compelling influences were fear and force.

Eventually, however, the "Youth Rebellion" of the 1960s did cause a rather spectacular eruption of communitarian activity as the young looked for ways to gain control of their own lives. In part because it lacked roots in the past, the communal movement proved to be an ephemeral one that crashed as quickly as it had taken flight, introducing a period which ranks as one of the least socially inspired in human history. And yet some elements of this movement have survived in the form of small communities that practice brotherly cooperation in various forms determined by their memberships. It is from the experiments of these "builders of the dawn," as the leaders of one community have described their brethren, that there may come a new and more successful phase in the search for a brotherly tomorrow.[4]

At its frequent best, the cooperative ideal embodied the noblest of human hopes for a community of self-acting individuals, whose members cared for each other out of a sense of humanity and where human virtue and talent could be realized for the good of all. From New Harmony to New Llano and beyond, these hopes have been disappointed, but a world without them is, regardless of the extent of its wealth, a poor and lonely place; a society without social inspiration is no society at all. Without such hopes and the imagination to give them meaningful form, tomorrow may well lack the social ideals it needs to guide modern power for human good. Indeed, in a world where calculation and force outrun social imagination, it is possible that, without some cooperative ideal, there may be no tomorrow at all.

NOTES

I: THE CHALLENGE OF THE CENTURY

1. The best general history of utopianism is Frank E. and Fritzie F. Manuel, *Utopian Thought in the Western World* (Cambridge, Mass., 1979). The best of several rather superficial and incomplete studies of American utopianism is Mark Holloway, *Heavens on Earth* (New York, 1966).

2. Samuel Hopkins, *A Treatise on the Millennium* (Repr.: New York, 1972), 45, 59–60, 84, 95, 117, 144. Also see Joseph A. Conforti, "Samuel Hopkins and the New Divinity," *William and Mary Quarterly,* 34 (1977), 585–87, and Joel Nydahl, "From Millennium to Utopia Americana" in Kenneth M. Roemer, *America as Utopia* (New York, 1981), 245–47.

3. Hopkins, *Treatise,* 65, 69–74.

4. See especially Edward D. Andrews, *The People Called Shakers* (New York, 1953), Henri Desroche, *The American Shakers,* translated and edited by John K. Savacool (Amherst, Mass., 1971), Flo Morse, *The Shakers and the World's People* (New York, 1980), and Robley Edward Whitson, *The Shakers: Two Centuries of Spiritual Reflection* (New York, 1983).

5. The best studies of the Harmonists remain Karl J. R. Arndt, *George Rapp's Harmony Society, 1785–1847* (Philadelphia, 1965) and, its sequel, *George Rapp's Successors and Material Heirs, 1847–1916* (Rutherford, N.J., 1971). Also, John Duse, *The Harmonists: A Personal History* (Repr.: Philadelphia, 1972) and Donald F. Pitzer and

Josephine Elliott, "New Harmony's First Utopians, 1804–1824," *Indiana Magazine of History*, 75 (1979).

6. Rosabeth Moss Kanter, *Commitment and Community: Communes and Utopias in Sociological Perspective* (Cambridge, Mass., 1972), 62–74. Andrews, *Shakers*, 152–75. Whitson, *Shakers*, 54–5, 118. Charles Nordhoff, *The Communistic Societies of the United States* (New York, 1965), 232–44. William M. Kephart, *Extraordinary Groups* (New York, 1976), 159–63.

7. Andrews, *Shakers*, 97, 178–81, 266–68. Kephart, *Extraordinary*, 175–76, 184. [Edward Everett], "The Shakers," *North American Review*, 16 (1823), 93–95. Arndt, *Harmony*, 17, 98, 235, 271, 358. Both groups believed that Adam had also been bisexual before he sinned.

8. Andrews, *Shakers*, 186–201. Arndt, *Harmony*, 210. Jeanette C. and Robert H. Lauer, "Sex Roles in Nineteenth Century American Communal Societies," *Communal Studies*, 3 (1981), 19–28. D'Ann Campbell, "Women's Life in Utopia: The Shaker Experience in Sexual Equality Reappraised—1810 to 1860," *New England Quarterly*, 51 (1978), 25–31.

9. Andrews, *Shakers*, 101, 185, 197–98. Duse, *Harmonists*, 418. Arndt, *Harmony*, 176, 202, 254.

10. Whitson, *Shakers*, 189–90, 194, 206, 300. Andrews, *Shakers*, 100–103. Nordhoff, *Communistic*, 147–48. Arndt, *Harmony*, 74ff.

11. Arndt, *Harmony*, 204–11. William E. Wilson, "Social Experiments on the Wabash," in Thomas C. Wheeler, ed., *A Vanishing America* (New York, 1964), 82–83. Paul H. Douglas, "Town Planning for the City of God," in Gairdner Moment and Otto F. Krausher, eds., *Utopias* (Metuchen, N.J., 1980), 103–25.

12. Andrews, *Shakers*, 116–25. Melcher, *Shaker Adventure*, 130–35. Rosemary D. Gooden, "A Preliminary Examination of the Shaker Attitude toward Work," *Communal Societies*, 3 (1983), 2–13.

13. Captain William N. Blane in Harlow Lindley, ed., *Indiana as Seen by Early Travelers* (Indianapolis, 1916), 290. Timothy Dwight, *Travels in New England and New York*, edited by Barbara Miller Solomon (Cambridge, Mass., 1969), III, 112.

14. *Ibid.*, 98–99, 101. Morse, *Shakers*, 85–88.

15. Robert Owen, *Life Written by Himself* (London, 1971), 242–43. The English traveler William Hebert wrote in 1823 that the Harmonists were "in an advanced state of improvement and accumulation," while William Cobbett saw them as "a wonderful example of skill, industry, and force combined." Lindley, *Indiana*, 329, 519.

16. Morse, *Shakers*, 91, and Whitson, *Shakers*, 23. Like most other outsiders, Engels dismissed the religion of both Shakers and Harmonists as no more than superstitious humbug.

17. Arndt, *Harmony*, 228–33, 244–51, 352.

18. Thomas Low Nichols, *Forty Years of American Life, 1821–1861* (New York, 1937, 238.

19. This paragraph is based on a consideration of the stated and implied intentions and hopes of participants in the varied communal experiments as well as on the judgments of various observers of the millenarian communities.

20. Thomas applies this term to the late nineteenth century in his *Alternative America* (Cambridge, Mass., 1983).

21. Frederick W. Evans, *Autobiography of a Shaker* (Mt. Lebanon, New York, 1869), 420–23.

22. Signe Toksvig, *Emmanuel Swedenborg: Scientist and Mystic* (New Haven, Conn., 1948), 12, 110–11, 278–79, 295. In 1745, Swedenborg wrote that he had been admitted into the spiritual world "by the Messiah himself" and had been able to converse "with those who are in heaven the same as my familiars here on earth." *Ibid.*, 153.

23. Marguerite Block, *The New Church in the New World* (New York, 1932), 79–173. The quotation is from the *New Jerusalem Missionary and Intellectual Repository* (New York), 1 (1823–24), 10. Robert Price, *Johnny Appleseed* (Glouster, Mass., 1967), 120–38.

24. Arthur Bestor, *Backwoods Utopias*, 2nd ed (Philadelphia, 1970), 97–99. Karl J. R. Arndt, ed. *A Documentary History of the Indiana Decade of the Harmony Society* (Indianapolis, 1975), II, 338, 388. Cornelius Blatchly, *An Essay on Common Wealths* (New York, 1822), 4. Blatchly's essay was published by the New York Society with its constitution and other material.

25. *Ibid.*, 3–4.

26. *Ibid.*, 9, 19.

27. *Ibid.*, 23–27, 32. Much of Blatchly's essay is reprinted in Albert Fried, ed. *Socialism in America* (Garden City, N.Y., 1970), see pages 85–88.

28. Blatchly, *Essay*, 33–36.

29. Arndt, *Documentary*, II, 338, 388–89.

30. *Ibid.*, 402–3.

31. *Ibid.*, 331n, 363–64, 513–15. Apparently Rapp did not reply to Blatchly's letter.

32. *Ibid.*, 515.

33. Blatchly, *Essay*, 30.

34. Paul Brown, *Twelve Months in New-Harmony* (Repr.: Philadelphia, 1972), 3–5.

35. Donald Macdonald, "Diaries . . . 1824–26," introduction by C. D. Snedeker, Indiana Historical Society, *Publications*, 14(2), 176. Arthur Bestor lists several plans for communities in the early 1820s, none of which came to life. *Backwoods*, 100–101.

36. Owen's tendency to view his company town as a model community was especially evident in such later writings as his "Address to New Lanark" (1816). In his autobiography, he said regarding New Lanark that "the superior condition of the schools, mills, establishments generally, was effected without religious interference, and solely by the dictates of common sense, applied to the study of humanity, of its natural wants, and of the easy natural means of supplying these wants." *Life*, 204.

37. Blatchly, *Essay*, 38. Fried, *Socialism*, 93. Brown, *Twelve*, 4–5.

38. Owen, *Life*, 243, 355–56. Arndt, *Documentary*, II, 90.

39. Arndt, *Harmony*, 288–89, and *Documentary*, II, 80, 865–66, 873. The Rapps apparently first offered to sell the town to Samuel Worcester, who declined on the grounds that his Boston friends had receded "from the principles necessary to form a fraternal commonwealth and are becoming more established in a different order of life." *Ibid.*, 833.

II: THE PROPHET OF NEW LANARK

1. Robert Owen, *Life Written by Himself* (Reprint of 1857 edition: New York, 1967), xliii.

II. The Prophet of New Lanark

2. *Ibid.*, 1–10, 65–71. In his not uncritical reminiscences of his father, Robert Dale Owen said that David Dale had already established both a successful mill operation and the beginnings of a benevolent policy toward his employees before Owen took charge of the partnerships. *Threading My Way* (Repr.: New York, 1967), 27–28, 34–39, 51–55. For a particularly negative view of Owen both at New Lanark and at New Harmony, see Anne Taylor, *Visions of Harmony: A Study in Nineteenth-Century Millenarianism* (Oxford England, 1987), especially pages 59–162.

3. Owen, *Life,* 60–4, 78–80, 135–36. G.D.H. Cole, *The Life of Robert Owen* (London, 1930), 90–115. J.F.C. Harrison, *Robert Owen and the Owenites in Britain and America* (London, 1969), 139–47, 153–57, 160–63. A.L. Morton, *The Life and Ideas of Robert Owen* (New York, 1969), 66–80. John Butt, ed. *Robert Owen* (New York, 1971), 15–16. Robert Owen, *A New View of Society and Other Writings,* introduction by G.D.H. Cole (New York, 1963), 20, 33.

4. Owen, *New View,* 157. Owen's estimates varied; somewhat later, he said that the advance of science and machinery had increased productive power between forty and a hundred times. *Ibid.,* 246.

5. *Ibid., 37,* 121–22. Owen, *Life,* 349–50. Robert Owen, *The Book of the New Moral World* (London, 1836, 1842–44; repr.: New York, 1970), vi, xxi. Morton, *Owen,* 75.

6. Owen, *New View,* 16–17, 110, 257, 271. In his autobiography, Owen used the term "science of the influence of surroundings." *Life,* xliii.

7. Owen, *New View,* 16–17, 33–7.

8. Owen, *Life,* 136–38.

9. *Ibid.,* 129–140. Karen C. Altfest, *Robert Owen as Educator* (Boston, 1977), 45–78.

10. Owen, *Life,* 340.

11. *Ibid.,* 347. Owen, *New View,* 21.

12. Owen, *Life,* 355–56.

13. Owen, *New View,* 158–59, 169, 238, 266, 271.

14. *Ibid.,* 165–69, 283–86.

15. *Ibid.,* 160–65, 265–68, 286.

16. *Ibid.,* 148, 286–87. Owen proposed that government in a village be placed in the hands of a committee of all inhabitants between ages 35 and 45 or 40 to 50.

17. Butt, *Owen,* 33. Andrews, *Shakers,* 131. Owen, *Life,* 242–45. In 1820, Owen denied that his villages in any way resembled "the associated communities in America," but this seems to have involved chiefly their sectarian character. Owen, *New View,* 266. Owen's rejection of rewards and punishments made him receptive to the general idea of communism without inducing any real thought regarding the matter. For other points of view, see Harrison, *Owen,* 75–6. Butt, *Owen,* 44–5. Bestor, *Backwoods,* 80–81.

18. Owen, *New View,* 212–215, 288–89.

19. *Ibid.,* 168, 289.

20. *Ibid.,* 248. Jeremy Bentham, *Works* (New York, 1962), X, 570.

21. Owen, *New View,* 122, 239, and *Life,* 154–63. Cole, *Owen,* 192–97, 208. Morton, *Owen,* 206–14.

22. Owen, *New View,* 239. Harrison, *Owen,* 95, 101, 135.

III. A New Harmony?

23. Owen did get a little support from a few influential Englishmen, who made an unsuccessful effort to raise some money for the purpose of establishing a model village. Although Owen remained a partner in the New Lanark concern until 1828, he broke his ties with his model company town in 1825. Cole, *Owen*, 212–14, 218–33. Harrison, *Owen*, 129.

24. *Ibid.*, 53, 72, 92. Macdonald, *Diaries*, 231, 263–65, 293.

25. *Ibid.*, 260, 294–95.

26. Thomas C. Pears, Jr., ed., *New Harmony, An Adventure in Happiness: Papers of Thomas and Sarah Pears*, Indiana Historical Society, *Publications*, 11(1), 92. William Pelham wrote in September 1826 that there was an "extensive brickyard" three miles south of New Harmony where "a number of men were busily employed in making bricks for the new village" to be located nearby. "Letters of William Pelham," in Lindley, *Indiana*, 396. The *New Harmony Gazette* (Oct. 13, 1825) estimated the acreage of the New Harmony estate at 30,000.

27. Oakley C. Johnson, ed., *Robert Owen in the United States* (New York, 1970), 23–37.

28. *Ibid.*, 46–53.

29. Alexis de Tocqueville, *Democracy in America*, ed. by Thomas Bender (New York, 1981), 152–53.

30. The New York *American Athenaeum* as reprinted in the Boston *Masonic Mirror*, May 28, 1825.

31. There has been no systematic study of these early inhabitants, but the comments of members and observers plus the nature of existing routes of travel to New Harmony seem to support these generalizations. William Pelham, for instance, wrote that "the more numerous sect, I believe, is that of persons who take delight in wandering with Baron Swedenborg in the regions of fancy." *Letters*, 379. Owen found many of his earliest recruits in the Cincinnati area, a center of Swedenborgianism. Part of this support, however, was soon diverted to the Yellow Springs (Ohio) community founded by Swendenborgians in 1825. Block, *New Church*, 118–19.

32. Pelham, *Letters*, 360, 371, 373, 386–87, 400, 423.

33. Macdonald, *Diaries*, 293–95. Bestor, *Backwoods*, 119–21. George B. Lockwood, *The New Harmony Movement* (New York, 1905), 83–91. *New Harmony Gazette*, 1 (1825–26), 2–3.

34. *Ibid.*, 1–3.

III: A NEW HARMONY?

1. Frederick Rapp added, however, that "in important matters the majority of votes always governs." Arndt, *Documentary*, II, 489, 513, 515n, and *Harmony*, 75, 217–29, 239–41.

2. Bestor, *Backwoods*, 230–31. Unfortunately, Bestor gives little attention to developing this concept.

3. Kanter, *Commitment*, 117–18.

III. A New Harmony?

4. Pears, *New Harmony*, 13. For various pictures relating to New Harmony, see especially Donald F. Carmony and Josephine Elliott, "New Harmony, Indiana: Robert Owen's Seedbed for Utopia," *Indiana Magazine of History*, 76 (1980), 161–261.

5. *New Harmony Gazette* (henceforth to be abbreviated as *NHG*), I, 1 (Oct. 1, 1825) and 14 (Oct. 8, 1825). The constitution of the Preliminary Society provided that "children will be located in the best possible manner in day-schools, and will board and sleep in their parents' houses." Lockwood, *New Harmony*, 89, 92–93.

6. Pears, *New Harmony*, 28. *NHG*, I, 103 (Dec. 21, 1825).

7. Pears, *New Harmony*, 15, 35. Owen, *New View*, 110. Bestor, *Backwoods*, 162–64. *NHG*, I, 30 (Oct. 28, 1825). Pelham, *Letters*, 383.

8. *Ibid.*, 376ff. *NHG*, I, 30 (Oct. 28, 1825). Carmony and Elliott, *New Harmony*, 202.

9. *NHG*, I, 102 (Dec. 21, 1825).

10. Pelham, *Letters*, 393. *NHG*, I, 1–2 (Oct. 1, 1825).

11. Pears, *New Harmony*, 24–26. *NHG*, I, 103 (Dec. 21, 1825).

12. Pelham, *Letters*, 392–93.

13. Harrison, *Owen*, 55. Macdonald, *Diaries*, 293–320. Bestor, 128–30. *NHG*, I, 118 (Jan. 4, 1826).

14. John Quincy Adams, *Memoirs*, edited by Charles Francis Adams (Philadelphia, 1874–77), VII, 68.

15. Macdonald, *Diaries*, 332. Robert Owen, "Retrospect of the Commencement and Progress of the New System of Society," in *NHG*, I, 262 (May 3, 1826). Bestor, *Backwoods*, 170–71. Much later, Robert Dale Owen wrote that his father's decision "took me by surprise," and yet in December 1825 a resident of Pittsburgh had written that it was his understanding that Owen planned to begin "a community" early in the spring. Robert Dale Owen, *Threading*, 285. Pelham, *Letters*, 405–6. Pears, *New Harmony*, 58.

16. Pelham, *Letters*, 406–8. Pelham reported the draft of the constitution prepared by the committee to the convention.

17. The constitution of the New Harmony of Equality was published in the *NHG*, I, 162–63 (Feb. 15, 1826). Also see Lockwood, *New Harmony*, 105–11, and Bestor, *Backwoods*, 172–74.

18. *NHG*, I, 161. During the discussions over the proposed constitution, Robert Dale Owen submitted a substitute plan which would have required six months probation for new members, but his father refused to support it. Richard W. Leopold, *Robert Dale Owen* (New York, 1969), 33.

19. Pears, *New Harmony*, 78. Bestor, *Backwoods*, 176–78. Lockwood, *New Harmony*, 113–16. In October 1826, Macluria broke up and its lands reverted to Owen's community. *Ibid.*, 151.

20. Bestor, *Backwoods*, 177, 202–16, 279. *NHG*, I, 363 (May 10, 1825); 276–79 (May 24, 1825). The best documented of these communities was founded by "The Friendly Association for Mutual Interest" at Kendall in northeastern Ohio. See Wendall P. Fox, "The Kendall Community," *Ohio Archaeological and Historical Quarterly*, 20(1911), 176–219.

21. *NHG*, I, 276. In the same issue were: 1)A notice signed by William Pelham to the "Friends of the Social System" that New Harmony was full and that no one should plan to join the community without prior acceptance, and 2) An announcement that the

III. A New Harmony?

federative arrangement was about to be applied to the internal affairs of the New Harmony community. *Ibid.*, 278–79 (May 24, 1826).

22. The principal members of the boatload of knowledge were William Maclure, naturalists Charles A. Lesuer and Thomas Say, educators Madame Marie Fretageot and William S. Phiquipal d'Arusemont, Robert Dale Owen, and Stedman Whitwell. Gerard Troost, naturalist, and Joseph Neef, educator, arrived separately. Bestor, *Backwoods*, 146–59. Lockwood, *New Harmony*, 73–78. Pears, *New Harmony*, 405.

23. Pelham, *Letters*, 410–11, 417. In April 1825, Owen had declared his intention "to have everything here of the best description in agriculture, manufacture . . . and whatever appertains to the improved state of society." *NHG*, I, 2 (Oct. 1, 1825). In April 1826, he spoke of introducing "steam-mills here in time from England" in response to the wearing-out of the Harmonist mill. Lindley, *Indiana*, 425. Owen, however, appears to have done virtually nothing along this line. Most of the tools and machinery either had been inherited from the Harmonists or introduced by the members themselves.

24. Lockwood, *New Harmony*, 233–54 *passim.* Pitzer, *Education in Utopia*, 91–93. Arthur E. Bestor, Jr. *Education and Reform at New Harmony: Correspondence of William Maclure and Marie Duclos Fratageot, 1820–1833,* Indiana Historical Society, *Publications* (Indianapolis, 1948), XV, 280–417. Gerard Lee Gutek, *Joseph Neef* (University, Ala., 1978).

25. Lockwood, *New Harmony*, 242–43. It is noteworthy that, under Maclure's plan, while the boys were taught industrial and agricultural skills, the girls were given practice either in the household arts or in the textile mills. Bestor, *Education*, 331.

26. Johnson, *Owen*, 68–75. *NHG*, I, 334–35 (July 12, 1826).

27. *NHG*, I, 335 (July 12) and 342 (July 19, 1826).

28. Bestor, *Backwoods*, 174. Lockwood, *New Harmony*, 113–14. The *Gazette* announced the decision obliquely by noting that "under the sole direction of Mr. Owen the most gratifying anticipations of the future" had been raised. It spoke of "considerable difficulty" in a "crowded population" and the problems of forming new communities. I, 190 (March 8, 1826). This step effectively abolished the Community of Equality without resolving any of the problems it had raised.

29. *NHG*, I, 207 (March 22, 1826). Bestor, *Backwoods*, 182. Later, Owen used the word "nucleus" as a synonym for community in his plan to establish "Home-colonies" in England. Owen, *New Moral World*, 58–59, 63, 76.

30. *NHG*, II, 255 (May 9, 1827). Leopold, *Robert Dale Owen*, 33. Pears, *New Harmony*, 58.

31. Robert Dale Owen, *Threading*, 281–84, and "My Experiences of Community Life," *Atlantic Monthly*, 32 (1873), 336–48. This Owen shared little of his father's idealism. Bestor, *Backwoods*, 179. Pears, *New Harmony*, 60, 68, 71.

32. *Ibid.*, 71–72. Lindley, *Indiana*, 425–33.

33. *NHG*, I, 3 (Oct. 1, 1825); 162–63 (Feb. 15, 1826). Later in life, Robert Dale Owen wrote: "I do not believe that any industrial experiment can succeed which proposes equal remuneration to all men" and said that such a scheme would soon eliminate the skilled and industrious, leaving "an ineffective and sluggish residue." *Threading*, 290.

34. *NHG*, I, 1–2 (Oct. 1, 1825); 162–63 (Feb. 15, 1826). Pears, *New Harmony*, 73. Bestor, *Education*, 332.

35. Bestor, *Backwoods*, 183. Pears, *New Harmony*, 73–74. Sarah Pears was also

unhappy with the decision to lodge her older children in the boarding school so that "instead of our own dear children each housekeeper is to receive two more families; each of which will have a child under two years." *Ibid.*, 72–73.

36. Jill Harsin, "Housework and Utopia: Women and the Owenite Communities," in Ruby Rohrich and Elaine H. Baruch, eds., *Women in Search of Utopia* (New York, 1984), 76–80.

37. *NHG*, I, 391 (Aug. 30, 1826). Pears, *New Harmony*, 81.

38. *NHG*, I, 163 (Feb. 15, 1826). Bestor, *Backwoods*, 174, 181.

39. Bestor, *Backwoods*, 180–81.

40. *Ibid.*, 181–82. Pears, *New Harmony*, 77. For an especially critical account of Owen's efforts to sell New Harmony, see Taylor, *Visions of Harmony*, 138–47.

41. *Ibid.*, 79, 83, 85, 94.

42. Bestor, *Education*, 312. This was six months after Maclure had visited New Lanark, where he had been impressed by Owen's educational system, although, with more truth than he intended, he compared it to "the moral experiment in the new jail of Philadelphia." *Ibid.*, 307.

43. *Ibid.*, 332. *NHG*, I, 276 (May 24, 1826). Bestor overstates the degree of separation involved in Maclure's plan. *Backwoods*, 193.

44. *Ibid.*, 184–86. Bestor, *Education*, 334. *NHG*, I, 279 (May 24, 1826).

45. Bestor, *Backwoods*, 186, 192, and *Education*, 354, 358, 361.

46. *NHG*, I, 390 (Aug. 30, 1826). The plan was approved "unanimously" by voice vote after Owen had assented vaguely to one member who asked "if this question is intended to test who are to remain here permanently and who are not." *Ibid.*

47. Bestor, *Education*, 337, 343–44, 357–58, 363, 365, 368, 378, and *Backwoods*, 197–98.

48. Printed in Indiana Historical Society, *Annual Report* (1978–79), 56.

49. Brown, *Twelve*, 14–17, 24, 33, 49, 54, 69, 87.

50. *Ibid.*, 107–8. Gutek, *Neef*, 58–61.

51. *NHG*, I, 342 (July 19), 351 (July 26), 365 (Aug. 9), and 391 (Aug. 30, 1826); II (May 9, 1827).

52. *Ibid.*, II, 15 (Oct. 11), 47 (Nov. 8), and 54 (Nov. 15, 1826). Lockwood, *New Harmony*, 125–26.

53. Bestor, *Backwoods*, 189–90, 194.

54. Pelham, *Letters*, 407, 409, 414–15.

55. Bestor, *Backwoods*, 194–95. *NHG*, II, 206 (March 28, 1827).

56. Bestor, *Backwoods*, 196–201. Lockwood, *New Harmony*, 172–76. Robert Dale Owen estimated that his father lost "upward of two hundred thousand dollars" in the experiment, about four-fifths of his estate, but it is unclear as to whether he considered as part of the loss the property which Owen transferred to his sons. Two of them each received a $50,000 share in the New Lanark mills and all four received a share in the New Harmony property, a source of considerable wealth for the family in the future. *Threading*, 293–95.

57. Brown, *Twelve*, 109.

58. Adams, *Memoirs*, XII, 117, 133. *Harbinger*, I (1845), 10–11.

59. The convention, which convened on October 1, 1845, elected Owen as its presi-

dent and supported his plan, announced the previous April, for a corporation "to form new and superior establishments for producing and distributing wealth," but this commitment was accomplished only after most of the delegates had withdrawn from the convention. John R. Commons, et. al., eds., *A Documentary History of American Industrial Society* (Repr.: New York, 1958), VII, 165, 182.

60. Robert Owen, *The Book of the New Moral World* (Repr.: New York, 1970), originally published in seven parts (London, 1842–44), xxi-xxvi; Part III, 78; Part V, 9–10, 19; Part VII, 4–5.

61. *Ibid.*, Part V, 11, 13, 17–19.

62. Post, *Popular Freethought,* 183. Bestor, *Backwoods,* 227–29.

IV: INDIVIDUALITY AND BROOK FARM

1. Among the periodicals publicizing the communitarian cause between 1840 and 1845 were the *Dial, Communitist, Practical Christian, Pathfinder, Present,* and *Phalanx.* Many newspapers at least occasionally took note of the movement. Arthur Bestor lists 77 communities of various sorts for the two decades after 1840. *Backwoods,* 280–84.

2. The most prominent members of this group were Stephen Pearl Andrews (1812–86), A. Bronson Alcott (1799–1888), Adin Ballou (1803–90), George W. Benson (1808–79), Albert Brisbane (1809–90), William Henry Channing (1810–84), John A. Collins (1810–79), Charles A. Dana (1819–97), Parke Godwin (1816–1904), Horace Greeley (1811–72), Thomas Low Nichols (1815–1901), John Humphrey Noyes (1811–86), George Ripley (1802–80), and Josiah Warren (1798–1874).

3. *Liberator,* 14 (1844), 3.

4. Quoted in Alice Felt Tyler, *Freedom's Ferment* (New York, 1962), 166. In 1846, William H. Fish, a founder of the Hopedale Community, said in an article on "the Community Enterprise" that "there was a simultaneous movement towards it, in various States, by men who had never had any intercourse or acquaintance with each other. The first public announcement of an intention to form a Community found a few in every direction who were prepared for the work—and several sprang up within the year." *Practical Christian* (Feb. 7, 1846).

5. The best sources for the Northamptom Association are Alice Eaton McBee, *From Utopia to Florence* (Northampton, Mass., 1947) and Charles A. Sheffeld, *The History of Florence* (Florence, Mass., 1895). For Hopedale, see Adin Ballou, *History of the Hopedale Community* (Repr.: Phila., 1972) and David M. Coffey, "The Hopedale Community," *The Historical Journal of Western Massachusetts,* 4 (1975), 16–26.

6. *Liberator,* 10 (1840), 208.

7. William Ellery Channing, *Works* IV, 78. Probably the best study of Transcendentalism remains Perry Miller's well-edited anthology, *The Transcendentalists* (Cambridge, Mass., 1971). Also see Emerson's essays, "Self-Reliance" and "New England Reformers," both commonly anthologized.

8. Tocqueville, *Democracy,* 395–97. Ralph Waldo Emerson, "The Character of the Present Age," *Early Lectures,* edited by Robert W. Spiller and Wallace E. Williams (Cambridge, Mass., 1972), III, 188–89.

9. Ralph Waldo Emerson, *Letters,* edited by Ralph L. Rusk (New York, 1939), II, 213.

10. Henry S. Canby, *Thoreau* (Boston, 1939), 205–15. Reginald Cook, *Passage to Walden* (New York, 1966). Henry David Thoreau, *Walden and Other Writings,* edited by Brooks Atkinson (New York, 1950), 5–9, 13–14, 17–18, 62, 65, 82, 156.

11. *Ibid.,* 123. Walter Harding, *The Days of Henry Thoreau* (New York, 1967), 125, 184, 336.

12. Emerson, "New England Reformers," in *The Complete Essays and Other Writings,* edited by Brooks Atkinson, (New York, 1950), 451.

13. *Ibid.,* 451–52. O. A. Brownson, "Brook Farm," *Democratic Review,* 11 (1842), 418–85. Miller, *Transcendentalists,* 187–88, 214–15, 258, 296–97, 432–33, 437–40.

14. Emerson, *Essays,* 452. John Weiss, *Life and Correspondence of Theodore Parker* (New York, 1864), II, 108. Theodore Parker, "Thoughts on Labor," *The Dial,* 1 (1840–41), 514–15.

15. Henry L. Golemba, *George Ripley* (Boston, 1977), 18–48. Also see Charles Crowe, *George Ripley: Transcendentalist and Utopian Socialist* (Athens, Ga., 1967).

16. Golemba, *Ripley,* 43, 48, 62. George Ripley, "Letter to the Church in Purchase Street" (1840), in Miller, *Transcendentalists,* 251–57.

17. Ripley, *Letter,* 254.

18. Ralph Waldo Emerson, *Letters,* edited by Ralph L. Rusk (New York, 1939), II, 347.

19. Golemba, *Ripley,* 62. In 1840, Ripley said that "the true followers are a band of brothers; they compose one family; they attach no importance whatever to the petty distinctions of birth, rank, wealth, and station." *Letter,* 253.

20. Henry W. Sams, *Autobiography of Brook Farm* (Englewood Cliffs, N.J., 1958), 6–7. John Humphrey Noyes, who called Brook Farm "an original Yankee attempt to embody Christianity," attributed the inspiration to the Unitarian leader William Ellery Channing. *American Socialisms,* 103–8, 117. In his 1841 introduction to his collected works, Channing did advance the idea of "a community, which shall open a great variety of spheres to its members, so that all might find free scope for their powers." *Works,* I, xxv. There is no question, however, that Ripley was the active originator of the experiment.

21. Sams, *Brook Farm,* 6–7.

22. *Ibid.,* 8. Golemba, *Ripley,* 70–72. Octavius B. Frothingham, *George Ripley* (Boston, 1888), 148. It was one of Ripley's principal strengths and weaknesses that he gave his attention to the actual work of the Farm rather than working up detailed plans or paper manifestoes, leaving most of the writing about his experiment to others. He had, however, a clear idea of his primary goals and of the general means to achieve them. See Sams, *Brook Farm,* 22.

23. *Ibid.,* 6.

24. Emerson, *Letters,* II, 369–72. Actually, Emerson had already decided against the experiment; in October, he had written in the privacy of his journal that to join such a community would be to "traverse all my long trumpeted theory . . . that one man is a counterpoise to a city. Even earlier, he had written that "perhaps it is folly this scheming to bring the good & like minded together into families, into a colony. Better that they

should disperse and so leaven the whole lump of society." *Journals,* edited by A. W. Plumstead and Harrison Hayford (Cambridge, Mass., 1969), VII, 401, 407–8.

25. Sams, *Brook Farm,* 26. Hawthorne made this assessment less than two months after his arrival and less than five months before he left in November. It is noteworthy that he was willing to subscribe to $1000 in Brook Farm stock even after he expressed doubts regarding the economic success of the Farm. *Ibid.,* 23. Also see James R. Mellow, *Nathaniel Hawthorne and His Times* (Boston, 1980), 178–92.

26. Sams, *Brook Farm,* 61. George P. Bradford, "Reminiscences of Brook Farm," *The Century,* 45 (1892–93), 143–44. James H. Wilson, *The Life of Charles A. Dana* (New York, 1907), 49, 526–27.

27. Sams, *Brook Farm,* 27, 47–8. Edith Roelker Curtis, *A Season in Utopia* (New York, 1961), 48–60.

28. Sams, *Brook Farm,* 61, 224. Golemba, *Ripley,* 79–80.

29. Sams, *Brook Farm,* 44–6.

30. *Ibid.,* 61–2. Wilson, *Dana,* 37. Lindsay Swift, *Brook Farm: Its Members, Scholars, and Visitors,* introduction by Joseph Schiffman (Repr.: Secaucus, N.J., 1973), 19–22. Emerson apparently did not reply to Ripley's request. In 1842, he was concerned about the failure of banks in which he owned stock to pay the expected returns on his investments. See *Letters,* III, 14, 88.

31. Arthur W. Brown, *William Ellery Channing* (Syracuse, 1956), 218–19.

32. Elizabeth Peabody, "A Glimpse of Christ's Idea of Society," *The Dial,* 2 (1841–42), 217–28, and "Plan for the West Roxbury Community," *Ibid.,* 361–72; also printed in Sams, *Brook Farm,* 62–72.

33. "The Social Evils and Their Remedy," *Boston Quarterly Review,* 4 (1841), 273–76, and "No Church, No Reform," *Brownson's Quarterly Review,* 1 (1844), 177–94.

34. Brownson, *Brook Farm,* 481–90. For Brownson's relationship with Brook Farm, see Arthur M. Schlesinger, Jr., *A Pilgrim's Progress: Orestes A. Brownson* (Boston, 1966), 150–55.

35. Brownson, *Brook Farm,* 488–90. Also see the anonymous letter dated August 1842 (probably written by Elizabeth Peabody) in the *Democratic Review,* 11 (1842), 696.

36. Golemba, *Ripley,* 80–82. Crowe, *Ripley,* 154–57. Sams, *Brook Farm,* 79.

37. Swift, *Brook Farm,* 69–94, 145–64. Both Dana and Dwight got their starts as journalists with the *Harbinger,* when it was published at Brook Farm. Wilson, *Dana,* 51–60. "John Sullivan Dwight," *Dictionary of American Biography,* V, 567. Also, George W. Cooke, ed. *Early Letters of George Wm. Curtis to John S. Dwight* (Repr.: New York, 1971), 41–64.

38. George William Curtis, *From the Easy Chair* (Repr.: New York, 1969), III, 15.

39. *Democratic Review,* 11 (1842), 492–94. Golemba, *Ripley,* 79. John V.D.Z. Sears, *My Friends at Brook Farm* (New York, 1912), 147.

40. Golemba, *Ripley,* 78, 84. John T. Codman, *Brook Farm: Historic and Personal Memories* (Boston, 1894), 217, 221.

41. Sams, *Brook Farm,* 79, 223.

42. Golemba, *Ripley,* 91. Frothingham, *Ripley,* 149. Curtis, *Brook Farm,* 144. Codman, *Brook Farm,* 29–30, 116. It seems likely that Ripley's own religious enthusiasms dwindled as he became preoccupied with day-by-day business. In July 1843, Sophia Eastman,

whose religious orthodoxy left her out of place at the Farm, wrote that many members had no apparent religious principles and added that "there are four ministers here who have . . . become Transcendentalists. They seldom attent Church on the Sabbath." Normally, there were no religious services at the Farm. Sams, *Brook Farm*, 81.

43. *Ibid.,* 84, 237. Curtis, *Brook Farm*, 142, 152, 159, 179.

44. "On Association and Attractive Industry," *Democratic Review*, 10 (1842), 30n.

45. *The Dial,* 3 (1842–43), 86.

46. *Ibid.,* 87–88, 90–95. Emerson, *Letters*, III, 51, 203; *Essays*, 458. In 1847, Emerson wrote that "Mr. Ripley & other members of the opposition came down the other night to hear Henry's Account of his housekeeping at Walden Pond." *Letters*, III, 377–78.

47. Golemba, *Ripley*, 89–91. Curtis, *Season*, 95–171. Wilson, *Dana*, 41–2, 529.

48. John S. Dwight, "Individuality in Association," the *Harbinger*, 1 (1845), 264–65. Also Sams, *Brook Farm*, 145. Curtis, *Season*, 171, 180.

49. Ripley in Miller, *Transcendentalists*, 469.

50. Sams, *Brook Farm*, 94–100.

51. Codman, *Brook Farm*, 31. Curtis, *Season*, 186. Elizabeth Peabody, "Fourierism," *The Dial*, 4 (1843–44), 481–83. Brownson, *Brook Farm*, 487. Mellow, *Hawthorne*, 248–49. In 1845, Hawthorne made things difficult for the Farm by suing it for the $560.62 still owed him on his original investment in it. Curtis, *Season*, 279–80. Mellow, *Hawthorne*, 263.

52. *Ibid.,* 172–207. Wilson, *Dana*, 531–32. Sams, *Brook Farm*, 118–32. Noyes, *American Socialisms*, 52–57.

V: FOURIERISM

1. Owen's judgment of Fourier was given privately to John Quincy Adams in 1844. Adams, *Memoirs*, XII, 117. Elsewhere, Owen claimed that Fourier had obtained his knowledge regarding the formation of ideal communities from Owen's "Report on New Lanark," only to make it part of "a confused medley of old and new notions, which can never be combined to work permanently together." Owen, *Life*, 234.

2. Nicholas V. Riasanovsky, *The Teaching of Charles Fourier* (Berkeley and Los Angeles, 1969), 2–23.

3. Jonathan Beecher and Richard Bienvenu, translators and editors, *The Utopian Vision of Charles Fourier: Selected Texts on Work, Love, and Passionate Attraction* (Boston, 1971), 1, 79, 82.

4. Manuel, *Utopian Thought*, 656–62. Charles Gide, ed., *Design for Utopia: Selected Writings of Charles Fourier*, with a new introduction by Frank Manuel (New York, 1971), 56–61. Albert Brisbane, *Treatise on the Functions of the Human Passions and An Outline of Fourier's System of Social Science* (Repr.: New York, 1972), 2–14.

5. Gide, *Design*, 55, 62–63.

6. *Ibid.,* 56–66, 83, 88. Manuel, *Utopian Thought*, 662–66.

7. Brisbane, *Treatise*, 31–34. Manuel, *Utopian Thought*, 659–60.

8. Gide, *Design*, 26, 60–61, 137, 139, 159, 164–66. Brisbane, *Treatise*, 144–55.

9. Gide, *Design*, 127–30, 159–60, 164, 180–89, 199–200. One-eighth of a phalanx was to "consist of capitalists, scholars, and artists." *Ibid.*, 142.

10. *Ibid.*, 165–70. Manuel, *Utopian Thought*, 642. Riasanovsky, *Fourier*, 50, 62–3.

11. Gide, *Design*, 109, 115, 179–80. Manuel, *Utopian Thought*, 667.

12. Gide, *Design*, 24, 137–48. Dolores Hayden, *Seven American Utopias: The Architecture of Communitarian Socialism, 1790–1975*. (Cambridge, Mass., 1976), 150–54.

13. Beecher and Bienvenu, *Fourier*, 55–61, 390ff. Manuel, *Utopian Thought*, 652, 655–56, 660–65.

14. Brisbane, *Treatise*, 4–10, 127, 133–36.

15. Riasanovsky, *Fourier*, 21–31, 144, 180. Gide said that there was some interest in Fourier's writings in France as late as the 1880s. *Design*, 40–42.

16. The best single source regarding Brisbane's life remains his autobiography published by his second wife after his death: Redelia Brisbane, *Albert Brisbane: A Mental Biography* (Boston, 1893).

17. *Ibid.*, 71, 114–15.

18. *Ibid.*, 171–79, 184–87.

19. Charles Fourier, *The Social Destiny of Man*, translated by Henry Clapp, Jr. with a preface by Albert Brisbane (Repr.: New York, 1972), x. Brisbane, *Treatise*, 49–50.

20. Codman, *Brook Farm*, 144. *The Dial*, 3 (1842–43), 95. George E. Mcdonald, *Fifty Years of Freethought* (Repr.: New York, 1972), I, 339.

21. Brisbane, *Brisbane*, 205. *The Dial*, 3 (1842–43), 90–94.

22. *Boston Quarterly Review*, 4 (1841), 128. *The Oxford Universal Dictionary* locates the origins of the word socialism in France in the 1830s. Horace Greeley referred to radical social reform as "this Socialism" in an article defending Fourierism. "The Idea of a Social Reform," *The Universalist Quarterly*, 2 (1845), 147.

23. Brisbane, *Brisbane*, 205. Horace Greeley, *Recollections of a Busy Life* (New York, 1868), 144–45. Edward K. Spann, *Ideals & Politics* (Albany, New York, 1972), 145–46.

24. Albert Brisbane, *Association; or A Concise Exposition of the Practical Part of Fourier's Social Science* (Repr.: New York, 1975), 8–9. *Phalanx*, Oct. 5, 1843. *Harbinger*, I (1845), 14, 19. Parke Godwin, *A Popular View of the Doctrines of Charles Fourier* (New York, 1844), 40, 59.

25. Greeley, *Recollections*, 144–50.

26. Godwin, *A Popular View*, 69. *The Pathfinder*, I (1843), 49, 97.

27. *The Pathfinder*, I (1843), 2, 44, 52. Brisbane, *Association*, 9–10, 29–30.

28. *Ibid.*, 10–13. Godwin, *Popular View*, 27–28, 57–69.

29. Brisbane, *Treatise*, 159.

30. *Ibid.*, 4, 9–10, 30–31 *passim*. Charles Sotheran, *Horace Greeley and Other Pioneers in American Socialism* (Repr.: New York, 1971), 122–25. *Phalanx*, April 1, 1844.

VI: THE MOVEMENT

1. [W.H. Fish], "The Community Enterprise," *Practical Christian* (Feb. 7, 21, 1846).

2. Ballou and Noyes each published a major work intended to educate Americans in his form of social organization: Adin Ballou, *Practical Christian Socialism* (Hopedale and New York, 1854) and John Humphrey Noyes, *The History of American Socialisms* (Philadelphia, 1870).

3. The best source regarding the radical periodicals of this period is Clarence L. F. Ghodes, *The Periodicals of American Transcendentalism* (Durham, N.C., 1931). Also, Sterling F. Delano, *The Harbinger and New England Transcendentalism* (Rutherford, N.J., 1983).

4. Michael Fellman, *The Unbounded Frame: Freedom and Community in Nineteenth Century Utopianism* (Westport, Conn., 1973), 5–15; Spann, *Ideals & Politics*, 145; Octavius Frothingham, *Memoir of William Henry Channing* (Boston and New York, 1886), 202–11.

5. See the Preamble and Resolutions adopted by the New York Convention of Associationists printed in John R. Commons, et al., eds., *A Documentary History of American Industrial Society* (Repr.: New York, 1958), VII, 193–96. Frothingham, *Channing*, 163–64 and *Present*, 1 (1843–44), 39–43. Spann, *Ideals & Politics*, 145–50.

6. Brisbane, "Means of Effecting A Final Reconciliation Between Religion and Science," *Dial*, 3 (1842–43), 90–95, and *Association*, 3.

7. Parke Godwin, *Out of the Past* (New York, 1870) and *Popular View of the Doctrines of Charles Fourier* (New York, 1844), 31.

8. *Harbinger*, 1 (1845), 187.

9. Brisbane, *Brisbane*, 208. *The Pathfinder*, 1 (1843), 49. Godwin, *Popular View*, 39–41.

10. The ablest discussion of this rebellion against conventional government is Lewis Perry, *Radical Abolitionism: Anarchy and the Government of God in Antislavery Thought* (Ithaca, New York, 1973).

11. Parke Godwin, *Democracy, Constructive and Pacific*, (New York, 1844), preface, 9–12, 22–5.

12. *Phalanx*, 1 (Oct. 5, 1843). Octavius Frothingham, *George Ripley* (Boston, 1882), 178–79. Dana said that the name "Harbinger" was chosen in order to avoid "the localism of New England periodicals. Our journal must touch the nerves of the whole country." Dana to Parke Godwin, Nov. 20, 1844 and Feb. 20, 1845, Bryant-Godwin Papers, New York Public Library. Also see Delano, *Harbinger*, for various details about this periodical.

13. *The Christian Examiner*, 37 (1844), 57–77. *Hunt's Merchants Magazine*, 11, (1844), 198. Kenneth Walter Cameron, *Research Keys to the American Renaissance* (Hartford, Conn., 1967).

14. Commons, *Documentary History*, VII, 190, 198. Horace Greeley, "The Idea of Social Reform," *The Universalist Quarterly*, 2 (1845), 147. Godwin, *Popular View*, 117. John S. Dwight, "Association the Body of Christianity," in Codman, *Brook Farm*, 309–12.

15. Brisbane, *Association*, 7–8, 25–7, 47–50, and "Association and Attractive Industry," *Democratic Review*, 10 (1842), 40. One-sixth of the wealth produced by a phalanx was to be allocated to talent. Dwight, *Association*, 312. *Harbinger*, II, 141. *Pathfinder*, I, 52.

16. Godwin, *Popular View*, 40, 69, 70, and *Democracy*, introduction and 9–12. *Pathfinder*, I, 97. *Harbinger*, VII, 60. Brisbane, *Association and Attractive Industry*, 38.

17. Brisbane, *Association*, 4, 9, 29.

18. Godwin, *Democracy*, 16–17.

19. Brisbane, *Association*, 9–10, 17–22, and *Association and Attractive Industry*, 569–73. *Harbinger*, I, 14, 222. Commons, *Documentary History*, VII, 193–94.

20. Brisbane, *Association*, 19–25.

21. *Ibid.*, 30–3, 38–40, and *Association and Attractive Industry*, 42–3. The motto regarding property is in the *Harbinger*, I, 304.

22. Brisbane, *Association*, 15–16, 19, 41, 51, 77.

23. *Ibid.*, 11–12, 16–18, 22–24, 73–75, 78, and *Association and Attractive Industry*, 31.

24. Emerson, *Letters*, III, 20. Sams, *Brook Farm*, 78.

25. Brisbane, *Brisbane*, 144ff. Commons, *Documentary History*, VII, 186. Greeley, *Recollections*, 145–49. Sotheran, *Greeley*, 124–25. Two early supporters of the movement in New York were the Swedenborgian ministers B. F. Barrett and Solyman Brown.

26. Brisbane, *Association*, 78ff.

27. *Phalanx*, Oct. 5, Nov. 4, Dec. 5, 1843; Jan. 5, 1844.

28. *Ibid.*, April 20, 1844. Commons, *Documentary History*, VII, 188–208.

29. *Ibid.*, 197–98. *Phalanx*, June 1, 1844.

30. The founding aims of the phalanxes ranged from the idealism of Brook Farm to the speculative aims of the Morehouse Union (New York), which was established by a large landowner to promote the sale of his surrounding acres. Generally, those who initiated these schemes intended to profit from the development of the phalanx property. For descriptions of the diverse phalanxes, see Noyes, *American Socialisms*, 200–536.

31. *Phalanx*, July 1, 1844.

32. Noyes, *American Socialisms*, 233–50. Horace Greeley was a leading member in the Sylvania Association. In July 1843, Henry Thoreau wrote after a visit with Greeley that the New Yorker "believes only or mainly, first in the Sylvania Association somewhere in Pennsylvania—and secondly and most of all, in a new association to go into operation soon in New Jersey [the North American Phalanx], with which he is connected." Thoreau, *Correspondence*, edited by Walter Harding and Carl Bode (New York, 1958), 128.

33. For the histories of these phalanxes, see Noyes, *American Socialisms*, 259–64.

34. *Ibid.*, 19, 224.

35. *Phalanx*, Oct. 5, 1843. Brisbane later claimed that the proliferation of such associations "under more or less imperfect circumstances" had caught him by surprise: "I had contemplated years of patient, careful propagation before the means of a single Asociation could be attained." Yet in May 1842, he expressed the hope in the *Tribune* that the first association "may be able to commence operations next spring." Brisbane, *Brisbane*, 212, 246. Commons, *Documentary History*, VII, 240.

36. *Phalanx*, April 20, 1844. Noyes, *American Socialisms*, 268–72. Commons, *Documentary History*, VII, 248–59.

37. *Harbinger*, V, 317–18. Noyes, *American Socialisms*, 278–302.

38. *Ibid.*, 440. *Phalanx*, Jan. 5, 1844. S. M. Pedrick, "The Wisconsin Phalanx at Ceresco," *Proceedings of the State Historical Society of Wisconsin* (1902), 199–200; this

article is based partly on the records of the Wisconsin Phalanx deposited with the Ripon Historical Society by the last president of the Phalanx before his death in 1901.

39. Warren Chase, *The Life Line of the Lone One*, 3rd ed. (Boston, 1861), 10–45 passim, 104–13.

40. *Ibid.*, 113–21.

41. *Ibid.*, 125. Noyes, *American Socialisms*, 416–40.

42. *Ibid.*, 443–44. Chase, *Life-Line*, 126–27.

43. Commons, *Documentary History*, VII, 267–70.

44. Noyes, *American Socialisms*, 431, 443. Chase, *Life-Line*, 122–23.

45. Warren Chase, *Forty Years on the Spiritual Rostrum* (Boston, 1888), 12, 70. Commons, *Documentary History*, VII, 272–84. Noyes, *American Socialisms*, 446–48. Pedrick, *Wisconsin Phalanx*, 222–25. Chase said that the members at Ceresco were temporarily successful in resisting the name and influence of Ripon, "but the speculative Ripon at last outgrew and conquered its rival." *Life-Line*, 144.

46. Sams, *Brook Farm*, 93–97.

47. *Ibid.*, 137–40. The three Brook Farmers contributed nearly 200 major articles to the *Phalanx* and the *Harbinger*. Noyes, *American Socialisms*, 212.

48. Sams, *Brook Farm*, 128, 207. Golemba, *Ripley*, 79. Curtis, *Seasons*, 179. Crowe, *Ripley*, 172–81.

49. Marianne Dwight Orvis, *Letters from Brook Farm*, edited by Amy L. Reed (Repr.: Philadelphia, 1972), 33, 94&n, 102, 120.

50. Orvis, *Letters*, 69. Sams, *Brook Farm*, 128. Curtis, 194–95 *passim*. Marianne Dwight wrote in December 1844 that, with the collapse of some of the other phalanxes, "friends of Association in New York and elsewhere are beginning to see the need of concentrating their efforts in some one undertaking, and it is to Brook Farm that they look." Orvis, *Letters*, 52, 82.

51. *Ibid.*, 89–90, 92. Sams, *Brook Farm*, 134–36.

52. Orvis, *Letters*, 126–37. Sams, *Brook Farm*, 170–74.

53. *Ibid.*, 170–74.

54. *Ibid.*, 201–2. Curtis, *Season*, 279–80 *passim*. Wilson, *Dana*, 533. Swift, *Brook Farm*, 25–6. *Harbinger*, I, 222. See Emerson's fine praise for the community, which he did little to support, in Sams, *Brook Farm*, 225.

55. Ripley, by one estimate, wrote 315 articles for both the *Phalanx* and the *Harbinger*, second only to John S. Dwight's 324.

56. Curtis, *Season*, 299. Codman, *Brook Farm*, 214–15. Noyes, *American Socialisms*, 557. Orvis, *Letters*, 167–72.

57. *Ibid.*, III, 14–15.

58. *Ibid.*, 14–16, 410–11. Frothingham, *Channing*, 214–37. *Practical Christian* (Jan. 23, 1847).

59. *Harbinger*, III, 16, 47, 80, 302, 410; IV, 386–87. Sams, *Brook Farm*, 190. Commons, *Documentary History*, VII, 203–6.

60. *Harbinger*, VI, 12, 203. For Kriege also see David Herreshof, *American Disciples of Marx* (Detroit, 1967), 48–52.

61. Commons, *Documentary History* VII, 229–33.

62. Godwin, *Popular Views*, 57–8. Taylor Stoehr, *Free Love in America: A Documen-*

tary History (New York, 1979), 406–8. Brisbane, "American Associationists," *Democratic Review,* 18 (1846), 147. Brisbane concluded his later *Treatise on the Functions of the Human Passions* (Repr.: New York, 1972) with a section on "The Marriage Question," in which he denied that Fourier advocated "a system of promiscuity, license, and sensuality." But he then gave much attention to describing an ideal world where there would be "the full, free, natural, and harmonious development of Love in all its shades and varieties." Pages 161–70.

In 1848, one reader of the *Harbinger* wrote to Godwin to inform him that he had kept a recent issue of that journal out of the hands of friends because of Godwin's "discussion of matrimonial and sexual relations." He went on to say that "if the Mastadon . . . possessed the peculiar endowment of the Skunk" he would sooner attack it than "to assail the popular sentiments on the subject of love with the weapons of mere reason." Joseph R. Buchanan to Parke Godwin. Bryant-Godwin Papers, New York Public Library.

63. Commons, *Documentary History,* VII, 209–16.

64. *Harbinger,* VII, 12–13.

65. Hugh Doherty (an English Fourierist leader) to Parke Godwin, March 5 and Aug. 17, 1847, Bryant-Godwin Papers. Commons, *Documentary History,* VII, 237. *Harbinger,* VII, 13; VIII, 116. Brisbane, *Brisbane,* 292–300.

66. From a notice of *The Spirit of the Age* published in the *Practical Christian,* July 21, 1849.

67. Frothingham, *Channing,* 294–95.

VII: THE PHALANX IN DREAM AND REALITY

1. Ralph Waldo Emerson, *Complete Works* (Boston and New York), 1903–1904, X, 349. Godwin, *Democracy,* Introduction. Codman, *Brook Farm,* 144.

2. Brisbane, *Brisbane,* 313–18.

3. Albert Brisbane, *Treatise on the Functions of the Human Passions and An Outline of Fourier's System of Social Sciences* (Repr.: New York, 1972), 12, 131–34. Brisbane said that the "Soul" was a unity of passions. He described the passions as "spontaneously active and self-determining forces; they are the thinking, feeling, creating principles in Man. . . . They are the agents of supreme wisdom, the motors implanted in him by that Wisdom to impel him to fulfill his Destiny on Earth. *Ibid.,* 2.

4. *Ibid.,* 93, 132–33, 138–40. Brisbane emphasized that only in a social "mechanism" or organization which conformed to the passions would the passions work as God had intended them to function. *Ibid.,* 2.

5. Brisbane, *American Associationists,* 145.

6. Brisbane, *Association,* 43–49. In the fully organized phalanx, groups would be divided into subgroups which would be friendly rivals in the same work.

7. *Ibid.,* 51–52, 56, 62–64.

8. *Ibid.,* 17, 52–53. Brisbane gave little special attention to women, and he identified them with traditional woman's work, but his system did allow women greater freedom of choice than they had in conventional society. More explicitly, Godwin promised that

Association would enhance the status and eliminate the burdens of housework and motherhood. *Popular View*, 58–59.

9. Brisbane, *Association*, 53–54.

10. *Ibid.*, 9. Among the many Americans interested in this problem was Horace Greeley, who gave particular emphasis to Association as a way of shoring up rural life against urban temptation. Greeley. *Recollections*, 147–50.

11. Brisbane, *Association*, 53–54.

12. *Ibid.*, 33–38, 62. Also, see Godwin's *Popular View*, 65–68, where he defines profit to mean "benefits and gains of all kind, whatever recompenses the services rendered, whether honors, ranks, decorations, influences, or power, as well as money."

13. Brisbane, *Association*, 58–62. Key elements of this scheme reappear in Bellamy's *Looking Backward*.

14. Brisbane, *Association*, 71–72.

15. Brisbane, *Treatise*, 138–39.

16. *Ibid.*, 141, and *Association*, 15, 17–23.

17. *Ibid.*, 19–26.

18. Brisbane, *Treatise*, 133–34, 143, and *American Associationists*, 147.

19. *Ibid.*, 147, and Brisbane, *Treatise*, 142. Dolores Hayden, *The Grand Domestic Revolution* (Cambridge, Mass., 1981), 36–37.

20. Brisbane, *Association*, 64.

21. Godwin wrote that "in Association, which denies none and accepts all, liberty of the individual is conciliated with the order of the state, distinctions or rank harmonized with the guaranteed rights of the masses. There is *absolute* unity of purpose . . . , the guaranteed minimum and freedom of all classes, and the utmost *individuality* allowed to every person." *Popular View*, 72.

22. *Ibid.*, 117. *Harbinger*, IV, 12 (Greeley), 94 (Ripley). Brisbane, *Association*, 15.

23. The best study of these early years is Herman J. Belz, "The North American Phalanx: Experiment in Socialism," *Proceedings of New Jersey Historical Society*, 81 (1963), 219–25. Also, Charles Sears, *The North American, An Historical and Descriptive Sketch* (Prescott, Wisc., 1886). Sears' short pamphlet is reprinted, without pagination and with some pages out of order, in a compilation entitled *Exposé of the conditions and the Progress of the North American Phalanx* (Philadelphia, 1971).

24. North American Phalanx, *Exposé* reprinted in *Ibid.* (pages 1–28), 16. Norman Lippinscott Swan, "The North American Phalanx," in the compilation noted above, 50–55. Also, "A History of the First Nine Years of the North American Phalanx," written by Charles Sears in 1852 and published in Noyes, *American Socialisms* (pages 450–67), 461–62.

25. Belz, *North American*, 227–29. Noyes, *American Socialisms*, 477–78. Also see the three tables regarding production and earnings in North American Phalanx, *Exposé*, 25–28. Sears described the members as being mostly "mechanics, merchants and professional men and their families, with a fair proportion of single people of both sexes. Most of the heads of families had a knowledge of farming." Sears, *The North American*, 4. According to George Kirchmann, the Phalanx later rejected applicants for membership who did not have agricultural experience. "Why Did They Stay? Communal Life of the North American Phalanx," in P. A. Stellhorn, ed. *Planned and Utopian Experiments* (Trenton, N.J., 1908), 16–17.

26. Belz, *North American*, 228–29.

27. Sears, *The North American*, 13. Noyes, *American Socialisms*, 467.

28. *Ibid.*, 454, 456. Sears, *The North American*, 9–10. Belz, *North American*, 225.

29. *Ibid.*, 225–26. Sears, *The North American*, 5–7.

30. *Ibid.*, 7. North American Phalanx, *Exposé*, 13–14. Noyes, *American Socialisms*, 482.

31. Sears, *The North American*, 7–8, 10–11. In 1852, the North Americans said that "all our labor is paid for in domestic currency. In other words, when value is produced, a representation of the value is issued to the producer." One member said he got "cash every two weeks," out of which he paid a weekly rate for board. Noyes, *American Socialisms*, 465, 476, 478–79, 481–82.

32. North American Phalanx, *Exposé*, 10–11, 21. Noyes, *American Socialisms*, 463, 471, 484.

33. North American Phalanx, *Exposé*, 10–11. In the early 1850s, one member said that he received 90 cents per day and that he paid $1.50 per week for board plus $12 a year rent for "a snug little room." Prices in the Phalanx "restaurant" ranged from 1½ to 3½ cents for breakfast to 4½ to 8 cents for supper. Noyes, *American Socialisms*, 478–79, 482.

34. North American Phalanx, *Exposé*, 12, 15–16. Sears, *The North American*, 1–2, 4, 8–9.

35. After noting Fourier's prediction that "Civilization" would eventually give way to a new age of "Guaranteeism," Godwin defined "guaranteeism" as "a general system of mutual insurance . . . in which the separate interests of different classes might be combined, so that each would be directly interested in the general welfare of of every other." He went on to say, however, that "being of secondary importance, Guaranteeism may be safely left out of the account of the societary Reformer who should labor for the direct introduction of what is strictly Association." *Popular View*, 40–41.

36. Noyes, *American Socialisms*, 455, 459. North American Phalanx, *Exposé*, 10–16.

37. *Ibid.*, 9, 12, 20. Noyes, *American Socialisms*, 459–60. Frederick Law Olmsted, "Association: The Phalanstery and the Phalansterians," reprinted from the New York *Tribune* (1852) in Robert H. Walker, ed., *The Reform Spirit in America* (New York, 1976), 520. Thomas Dublin, ed. *Farm to Factory: Women's Letters, 1830–1860* (New York, 1981), 112–14, 117–19.

38. Noyes, *American Socialisms*, 460, 467.

39. *Ibid.*, 477. Sears, *The North American*, 8–9. North American Phalanx, *Exposé*, 20.

40. Noyes, *American Socialisms*, 456–57. Sears, *The North American*, 15. Frederick Law Olmsted in 1852 said that the chief weakness of the Phalanx was its failure to pay adequate attention to intellectual matters and claimed that children there were growing up without proper discipline of mind, and yet he also noted that older ones were maturing into "young *ladies* and young *gentlemen* naturally." He concluded that if he had a sixteen year old son who had been adequately exposed to formal education, "I would . . . prefer that he spend his next few years of life as a working member of the North American Phalanx than at Yale or Harvard." *Association*, 524.

41. *Ibid.*, 523. Noyes, *American Socialisms*, 461–63.

42. Swan, *North American*, 62–3. North American Phalanx, *Exposé*, 27. Two of the largest stockholders were Sears (203 shares) and Greeley (197).

43. Brisbane, *Brisbane*, 213. Rather than swinging their influence behind either the North American or Brook Farm, Brisbane and some of the other leaders dreamed of raising money for a full-fledged new phalanx. In December 1845, Marianne Dwight of Brook Farm wrote that Brisbane "and other friends to the cause in New York, instead of trying to concentrate all efforts upon Brook Farm as promised, have . . . taken up a vast plan of getting $100,000 and starting anew." Orvis, *Letters*, 137. The Brook Farmers, apparently, were led by Brisbane to the erroneous belief that the North Americans were receiving support at their expense. Crowe, *Ripley*, 185, 187.

44. *Harbinger*, IV, 222–23. Noyes, *American Socialisms*, 458.

45. *Harbinger*, IV, 390–391. Belz, *North American*, 233–36. Noyes, *American Socialisms*, 461. It is not clear as to how the money from the fund was actually channeled to the Phalanx except that it was made in the form of loans to individual stockholders. Perhaps this translated into new purchases of Phalanx stock since after 1848 there was a 70 percent increase in dividends paid to stockholders (from $1335 to $2242) between 1848 and 1850, at a time when the Phalanx continued to run a deficit. North American Phalanx, *Expose*, 27–8.

46. Noyes, *American Socialisms*, 476. Olmsted, *Association*, 519. Swan, *North American*, 55–6. Dolores Hayden, *Seven American Utopias: The Architecture of Communitarian Socialism* (Cambridge, Mass., 1976), 161–74.

47. *Ibid.*, 52. North American Phalanx, *Expose*, 16.

48. Noyes, *American Socialisms*, 477–84.

49. Joshua K. Ingalls, *Reminiscences* (Elmira, N.Y., 1897), 54.

50. North American Phalanx, *Exposé*, 12–14. Noyes, *American Socialisms*, 509. Belz, *North American*, 242–43.

51. *Ibid.*, 236–37. George Kirchmann, "Unsettled Utopians: The North American Phalanx and the Raritan Bay Union," *New Jersey History*, 97 (1979), 29–32. Frothingham, *Channing*, 210–16.

52. Belz, *North American*, 236–37. Sears, *The North American*, 12–13. Olmsted, *Association*, 522.

53. Kirchmann, *Unsettled*, 32–34. Sears, *The North American*, 12.

54. Jayme A. Sokolow, "Culture and Utopia: The Raritan Bay Union," *New Jersey History*, 94 (1976), 89–100. Belz, *North American*, 239–45. Benjamin Thomas, *Theodore Weld* (New Brunswick, N.J., 1950), 125–32.

55. Sokolow, *Culture*, 97–100. Frothingham, *Channing*, 242. Canby, *Thoreau*, 408–11. Thoreau, *Works*, VI, 286–87.

56. Reprinted from the *Republic Arbeiter* in the *Practical Christian*, XIV (1853–54), 80. North American Phalanx, *Expose*, 5–6.

57. *Ibid.*, 17.

58. *Ibid.*, 13.

59. Dublin, *Farm to Factory*, 118–20.

60. Kirshmann, *Unsettled*, 35–6. Belz, *North American*, 244. Noyes, *American Socialisms*, 495–96. Sears, *The North American*, 16, 18. Dublin, *Farm to Factory*, 120.

61. Sears, *The North American*, 17–18. Belz, *North American*, 244–45. Noyes, *American Socialisms*, 499. By 1855, the Texas project was drawing attention from the reform press; see *Oneida Circular*, IV, 158.

62. Sears, *The North American,* 16, 18. The Phalanx had already (by 1852) paid more than $13,000 in dividends to its stockholders. North American Phalanx, *Exposé,* 27–28. Horace Greeley, one of its stockholders, estimated that each stockholder got back "about 65 per cent of his investment with interest." He also estimated that about $100,000 (including loans) had been invested in the North American. *Recollections,* 153.

63. *American Socialist,* 1 (1876), 293.

64. Federal Writers Project, *New Jersey* (New York, 1939), 589. Kirchmann, *Why Did They Stay?,* 14.

VIII: A TWILIGHT LONG GLEAMING

1. Dublin, *Farm to Factory,* 121–26.

2. Noyes, *American Socialisms,* 366–76.

3. *Harbinger,* III, 191; IV, 112. Enthusiasm for Fourierism in Cincinnati had been temporarily increased by the missionary activity of John Allen, the agent of the A.U.A. in 1848. In April of that year there were enough Fourierists in the city to hold "a delightful party" in honor of Fourier's birthday. *Herald of Truth,* III (1848), 399. *Practical Christian,* 18 (1857–58), 34. This last periodical is a good source for radical idealism, since it reprinted various articles from obscure reform journals, some of which are unobtainable.

4. *Ibid.,* 34, 74, 87.

5. *Ibid.,* 19 (1858–59), 2, 55.

6. Noyes, *American Socialisms,* 660. Brisbane, *Brisbane,* 213–18. George E. Macdonald, *Fifty Years of Freethought* (Repr.: New York, 1972), I, 339. It should be noted that, when Brisbane was allowed to publish a series of essays in John Humphrey Noyes's *American Socialist,* he treated Fourier in what Noyes called a "patronizing" way, and Noyes suspended the series because he believed that Brisbane was interested chiefly in presenting "an interminable train of his own lucubrations." *American Socialist,* II, 26, 188.

7. Nichols, *Forty Years,* 242.

8. Delano, *Harbinger,* 91–95. For Brisbane and other associationists, the combination of Fourier and Swedenborg seem to provide the basis for a harmony between religion and both social and physical science. Brisbane said in 1843 that "the illustrious Swedenborg had discovered some portion of those laws of Universal Harmony" on which Fourierism was based. *American Associationists,* 143. John S. Dwight, under the influence of Swedenborgianism, promised that "Association would spiritualize matter, make the senses minister to the soul." *Harbinger,* II, 141.

9. John Humphrey Noyes, who was attracted to spiritualism as well as Fourierism, emphasized—indeed overemphasized—this connection in his *History of American Socialisms,* 539–50. Also, *American Socialist,* 1 (1876), 256. Chase, *Forty Years,* especially 15, 23–26, 44–47.

10. For Thomas Lake Harris, see Herbert W. Schneider and George Lawson, *A Prophet and A Pilgrim* (New York, 1942). Also, Noyes's chapter on the Brocton Community in *American Socialisms,* 577–94. *Harbinger,* IV, 385.

11. Hale, *Greeley*, 103–4. Hal D. Sears, *The Sex Radicals* (Lawrence, Kansas, 1977), 6–9.

12. Henry Edgar to Auguste Comte in Hawkins, *Positivism*, 134.

13. Sears, *Sex Radicals*, 9–10. Brisbane, *Treatise*, 161–99.

14. Godwin, *Popular View*, 78–79. *The Harbinger*, VII, 116.

15. Brisbane, *Treatise*, 158–59. *Practical Christian*, 19 (1858–59), 8.

16. *Harbinger*, IV, 254, 409. Edward K. Spann, *The New Metropolis: New York City, 1840–57* (New York, 1981), 151–53. Commons, *Documentary History*, VII, 236–37.

17. *Ibid.*, 232–35. *Practical Christian*, 19 (1858–59), 69.

18. *Harbinger*, IV, 254, 409.

19. *New York Times*, Sept. 26, 1860. Hayden, *Grand Domestic*, 95–6.

20. Laura Stedman and George M. Gould, *Life and Letters of Edmund Clarence Stedman* (New York, 1910), I, 156–60, 179.

21. *New York Times*, Sept. 21, 1860. Also see *Oneida Circular*, 7 (1858–59), 90, where Underhill denied the charge directed against the Home but did say that personally he believed "the institution of civilized marriage to be at variance with the interests of human nature."

22. *American Socialist*, 2 (1877), 389; 3 (1878), 1–2, 258, 282.

23. Mrs. C. F. Peirce, "Co-operative Housekeeping," *Atlantic Monthly*, 22 (1868), 514–21, 523, 683–95. Hayden, *Grand Domestic*, 66–72.

24. Peirce, "Co-operative Housekeeping," *Atlantic Monthly*, 23 (1868), 286–99.

25. Hayden, *Grand Domestic*, 80–9.

26. *American Socialist*, II (1877), 45.

27. The prospectus of the colony as it was presented in the *Oneida Circular*, 4 (1854–55), 158. Also, the *Practical Christian*, Sept. 8, Oct. 6, Dec. 29, 1855.

28. Godwin in the 1840s had been hostile to Abolitionism, because it diverted attention away from Associationism, but in the 1850s he became a leading spokesman for the Republic party. Spann, *Ideals & Politics*, 174–76. For Dana's part in the Civil War see Wilson, *Dana*, 194–369.

29. Noyes, "Deductive and Inductive Socialisms," *American Socialisms*, 658–72. *American Socialist*, 2 (1877), 28.

30. Oneida Community, *Bible Communism* (Oneida, 1853), 7–8. Noyes, *American Socialisms*, 1–9. The Macdonald manuscripts are now at Yale University. It is noteworthy that Noyes's book was issued by a commercial publisher, J. B. Lippincott of Philadelphia.

31. *Ibid.*, 9, 13, 22–9. In response to the charge that his book was mostly Macdonald's, Noyes said that only 168 of the book's 672 pages had been derived from Macdonald. *Oneida Circular*, n.s. 5 (1869–70), 413.

32. *American Socialist*, 1 (1876), 1; 2 (1877), 28.

33. *Ibid.*, 1 (1876), 1; 2 (1877), 28. In introducing the writings of the American Fourierists, Noyes declared that "their work was the noblest which men ever undertook." *Ibid.*, 1 (1876). For the collapse of the Oneida Community, see especially Constance Noyes Robertson, *Oneida Community: The Breakup, 1876–1881* (Syracuse, New York, 1972).

34. *American Socialist*, 3 (1878), 141. Wilson, *Dana*, 529–30, 534.

35. In 1877, Brisbane denied that Greeley had been a Fourierist or that the journalist

had any real understanding of Fourierism. *American Socialist*, 2 (1877), 45. Greeley, writing a decade earlier, said that he saw "much error" in Fourier's doctrines, but he also believed that Fourier was the "most suggestive and practical" of the would-be reformers of society. *Recollections*, 147–48.

36. *Ibid.*, 158.

37. For the Trumbull Phalanx, see Noyes, *American Socialisms*, 328–53; for Meeker, see especially 337–39, 344–45. In 1877, Meeker wrote that he and his wife agreed "that if the ague had not prevailed the company [the Trumbull Phalanx] might have prospered to this day." *American Socialist*, 2 (1877), 669.

38. *Ibid.*, 3. Noyes, *American Socialisms*, 348–49, 501.

39. *Harbinger*, IV, 27. *Practical Christian*, 19 (1858–59), 11, 86.

40. William E. Smythe, "Real Utopias of the Arid West," *Atlantic Monthly*, 79 (1897), 599–601. James F. Willard, ed. *The Union Colony of Greeley, Colorado, 1869–71* (Boulder, Col., 1918) documents the first two years of the colony. Hayden, *Seven American Utopias*, has an excellent chapter on the Union Colony.

41. Smythe, *Real Utopias*, 600, 603. Although Associationism was not explicitedly committed to temperance, it did recruit heavily from those who were. The members of the Wisconsin Phalanx were described as being "all temperance men and women," while at the North American Phalanx "good cold water was the only beverage." Noyes, *American Socialisms*, 444, 469.

42. Glynden G. Van Deusen, *Horace Greeley* (Philadelphia, 1953), 378–79, 397n. Hale, *Greeley*, 309–10. Willard, *Union Colony*, 6, 171–73.

43. Hale, *Greeley*, 351–52.

44. Smythe, *Real Utopias*, 601–4. Richard T. Ely, "A Study of a 'Decreed' Town," *Harpers Magazine*, 106 (1903), 390–401. *American Socialist*, 2 (1877), 402.

45. Ely, *Decreed*, 401. Hayden, *Seven American Utopias*, 284–85. *American Socialist*, 4 (1879), 324.

46. Sears, *North American*, 17. Sears first made this assessment in a long letter published in the *American Socialist*, 4 (1879), 163.

47. *Ibid.*, 1 (1876), 69.

48. *Ibid.*, 69. In the introduction to his history of the North American Phalanx, Sears wrote that in the 1870s "the great movement has revived," but he also noted that "it is narrower in scope, being limited mostly to co-operative production and co-operative distribution." *The North American*, 3.

49. Garrett R. Carpenter, "Silkville: A Kansas Attempt in the History of Fourierist Utopia, 1869–1892," *The Emporia State Research Studies*, 3 (1954), no. 2, 5–22. *Oneida Circular*, n.s. 6 (1869), 136.

50. Nordhoff, *Communistic Societies*, 376.

51. *Ibid.*, 377–80.

52. *Ibid.*, 378. Carpenter, *Silkville*, 22–29. *American Socialist*, 3 (1878), 172. Alexander Kent, "Cooperative Communities in the United States," *Bulletin of the Department of Labor*, 6 (1901), 641.

53. Wilson, *Dana*, 455, 533. Godwin, for instance, served as the last editor of the *Harbinger* and then went on to become the political editor of *Putnam's Monthly*, where in 1854 he helped mobilize support for the creation of the modern Republican party. Spann, *Ideals*, 175–77.

54. Orvis, *Letters*, 93. Brisbane, *Brisbane*, 9, 11.
55. *Ibid.*, 213–15. Noyes, *American Socialisms*, 658–63.
56. Brisbane, *Brisbane*, 13, 27–40.
57. Sams, *Brook Farm*, 9–10.
58. Noyes, *American Socialisms*, 480. Nichols, *Forty Years*, 197.
59. North American Phalanx, *Exposé*, 22.

IX: PRESERVING THE AMERICAN EDEN

1. Sams, *Brook Farm*, 154. *Harbinger*, 1 (1845), 264.
2. Emerson, *New England Reformers*, 458.
3. For Warren, see William Bailie, *Josiah Warren: The First American Anarchist* (Repr.: Brooklyn, New York) and Frederick D. Buchstein, "Josiah Warren: The Peaceful Revolutionist," *The Cincinnati Historical Society Bulletin*, 32 (1974), 61–71.
4. Bailie, *Warren*, 5. Selections from Warren's *Equitable Commerce* in Adin Ballou, *Practical Christian Socialism* (Repr.: New York, 1974), 607, and in M. S. Shatz, ed. *The Essential Works of Anarchism* (New York, 1971), 433, 442. Also, Bowman H. Hall, "The Economic Ideas of Josiah Warren," *History of Political Economy*, 6 (1974), 102–3. Fellman, *Unbounded*, 3, 11. The most thorough discussion of Warren's philosophy can be found in Eunice M. Schuster, *Native American Anarchism* (Repr.: New York, 1970), 92–105.
5. Josiah Warren, *True Civilization* (Repr.: New York, 1967), 13, 113–48, 154–60, 164–68, 182–83. Shatz, *Anarchism*, 428–40.
6. Buchstein, *Warren*, 65–66. Bailie, *Warren*, 29–38, 47–55, 63–7. John C. Spurlock, "Anarchy & Community at Modern Times, 1851–1863," *Communal Societies*, 3 (1983), 29–38. Madeleine B. Stern, *The Pantarch: A Biography of Stephen Pearl Andrews* (Austin, Texas, 1968), 76–79.
7. Shatz, *Anarchism*, 447–49. Henry Edger, *Modern Times, The Labor Question, and the Family* (New York, 1855), 2–5. Richard L. Hawkins, *Positivism in the United States (1853–1861)* (Cambridge, Mass., 1938), 116; Hawkins prints several of Edger's letters regarding Modern Times.
8. Spurlock, *Anarchy*, 42–47. Buchstein, *Warren*, 68–69. Bailie, *Warren*, 77. Hawkins, *Positivism*, 120–23 *passim*.
9. Warren, *True Civilization*, 112.
10. For Tucker's life and influence, see Schuster, *Native American Anarchism*, 138–43 *passim*, and Charles A. Madison, "Benjamin Tucker: Individualist and Anarchist," *New England Quarterly*, 16 (1943), 444–67.
11. Schuster, *Native American Anarchism*, 154–60. Buchstein, *Warren*, 61–63. Bailie, *Warren*, 34–47.
12. Lewis Masquerier, *Sociology; or the Reconstruction of Society, Government and Property* (New York, 1877), 94–95. Greeley, *Recollections*, 147–50. *The Radical*, 1 (1841), 6–8, 21.
13. *Ibid.*, 21. *Working Man's Advocate*, April 6, 1844. Commons, *Documentary History*, IV, 300–304.

14. *The Radical,* I (1841), 21. *Working Man's Advocate,* March 16, 1844.

15. *Ibid.,* March 16, April 6, 1844. Commons, *Documentary History,* V, 319; VIII, 36. Masquerier, *Sociology,* 13–19.

16. Helen Sara Zahler, *Eastern Workingmen and National Land Policy, 1829–1862* (New York, 1941), 34. Commons, *Documentary History,* VIII, 313–17. New York State Assembly, *Documents* (1847), 6–7.

17. Zahler, *Eastern Workingmen,* 127–201. Roy M. Robbins, *Our Landed Heritage* (New York, 1950), 217–54.

18. Masquerier, *Sociology,* 13, 19. Also Thomas A. Devyr, *The Odd Book of the Nineteenth Century* . . . (Greenpoint, New York, 1882), ix. The National Land Reform Association was headquartered on the east side of New York City, with Joshua K. Ingalls as its long-term secretary. Ingalls, *Reminiscences,* 60–61, 81.

19. Spurlock, *Anarchy,* 37–38. Warren, *True Civilization,* 76–79.

20. *Harbinger,* III, 155, 319–20. The use of the word "township" may have originated with Horace Greeley, who published a plan for "An Associative Township in the West" in *Ibid.,* IV, 27.

21. *Practical Christian,* 19 (1858–59), 4, 27, 46, 59–60, 72.

22. *Ibid.,* 4, 27, 85.

23. *Ibid.,* 27, 46. Adin Ballou, who was intensely interested in Spiritualism, drafted the "constitutional compact" of the Association. In one appeal for support, the Association issued a call: "Come *Mediums,* and let *Spirits* and *Angels* speak their approval." *Ibid.,* 56.

24. *Ibid.,* 20 (1859–60), 47, 67.

25. Nordhoff, *Communistic Societies,* 366–67. William McMahon, *South Jersey Towns* (New Brunswick, N.J., 1973), 181–83, 224.

26. Nordhoff, *Communistic Societies,* 367–69. *Oneida Circular,* n.s. 12 (1874–75), 227.

27. *American Socialist,* I (1876), 240, 286, 303.

28. Nordhoff, *Communistic Societies,* 373–75.

29. *Ibid.,* 367–69. *Johnson's Universal Cyclopaedia* (New York, 1896), VIII, 526–27.

30. Nichols, *Forty Years,* 414–15.

31. *American Socialist,* 2 (1877), 233, 236.

32. Henry George, *Progress and Poverty* (New York, 1937), 390.

33. Charles A. Barker, *Henry George* (New York, 1955), 3–48. Among other biographies of George are two by his children: Anne George de Mille, *Henry George: Citizen of the World,* edited by Don C. Shoemaker (Chapel Hill, N.C., 1958) and Henry George, Jr., *The Life of Henry George* (Garden City, New York). Also, George R. Geiger, *The Philosophy of Henry George* (New York, 1933) and John L. Thomas, *Alternative America: Henry George, Edward Bellamy, Henry Demerest Lloyd and the Adversary Tradition* (Cambridge, Mass., 1983).

34. Barker, *George,* 55. George, *Henry George,* 117.

35. Daniel Aaron, *Men of Good Hope* (New York, 1951), 63–4. George, *Progress and Poverty,* 3–8.

36. Aaron, *Men,* 65, 78. Robert V. Andelson, ed. *Critics of Henry George* (Rutherford, N.J., 1979). In 1887, John Rae wrote that among Englishmen *Progress and Poverty* "was

enthusiastically circulated like the testament of a new dispensation." *Contemporary Social-ism* (New York, 1887), 380. H. G. Wells recalled that it was under the influence of George that "I became a Socialist in the Resentful Phase." *Experiment in Autobiography* (New York, 1934), 142.

37. George, *Progress and Poverty*, 3–5.

38. *Ibid.*, 9–13.

39. *Ibid.*, 391.

40. *Ibid.*, 164–72, 272–73, 354. Barker, *George*, 211, 239.

41. *Herald of Truth*, 2 (1847), 135–40; 3 (1848), 467ff.

42. J. R. Buchanan, "The Land and the People," *Herald of Truth*, 2 (1847), 168–81 and 249–64. Reprinted in *Arena*, 3 (1890–91), 401n, 586–600.

43. *Herald of Truth*, 2 (1847), 252–59.

44. *Ibid.*, 258, 261–64.

45. George, *Progress and Poverty*, 328–30, 504–7.

46. *Ibid.*, 433–39, 451.

47. *Ibid.*, 456. Barker, *George*, 426–27.

48. George, *Progress and Poverty*, 465–67, 469, 545. Edward T. Rose, *Henry George* (New York, 1968), 115.

49. *Ibid.*, 133–39, 466n, 545, 552. George believed that population increase would slow "as the higher development of the individual became possible and the perpetuity of the race is assured." *Ibid.*, 132.

50. Louis F. Post, *The Prophet of San Francisco* (New York, 1930), 3–19. Hillquit, *History*, 251–52.

51. *Arena*, 3 (1890–91), 159.

52. Barker, *George*, 455–81. George won the political endorsement of Shaker Elder Daniel Frazier, the only known case of Shaker involvement in politics. Desroche, *Shakers*, 276–79.

53. George, *Progress and Poverty*, 320–21.

54. Henry George, "Open Letter to Pope Leo XIII" (1891), in *The Land Question* (New York, 1941), 58. Barker, *George*, 482–507.

55. Arthur N. Young, *The Single Tax Movement in the United States* (Princeton, N.J., 1916), 323.

56. Hamlin Garland, "A New Declaration of Rights," *Arena*, 3 (1890–91), 168–84.

57. Barker, *George*, 504–7, 514, 555–77. Benjamin R. Tucker denounced George as a "traitor" to the cause of human rights because of his refusal to support clemency for the Haymarket anarchists. *Liberty*, No. 356 (Oct. 1897), 1.

58. Both George's son, Henry Jr., and his chief disciple, Louis Post, were Sweden-borgians. Block, *New Church*, 345. The Spiritualist and former leader of the Wisconsin Phalanx, Warren Chase, favored George. Chase, *Forty Years*, 77. Ingalls, *Reminiscences*, 67–70, 103–5. Bowman N. Hall, "Joshua K. Ingalls, American Individualist," *American Journal of Economics and Sociology*, 39 (1980), 390–94. *Liberty*, no. 23 (June 24, 1882), 2; no. 267 (April 1893), 2; no. 287 (May 19, 1894), 1.

59. Thomas, *Alternative America*, 198–202, 325–26. Rose, *George*, 145–46. Barker, *George*, 610–19. *Liberty*, no. 356 (Oct. 1897), 1.

60. Barker, *George*, 620–35. Rose, *George*, 157. Tom L. Johnson, *My Story* (Repr.:

X: The Good Kings of Fouriana

Seattle, Wa., 1970), 48–58, 107, 112, 307–10. Frederick Howe, *Confessions of a Reformer* (Repr.: Chicago, 1967), 95–97, 125–43, 225–30.
61. Young, *Single Tax*, 250–56. Paul E. and Blanche E. Alyea, *Fairhope, 1894–1954: The Story of a Single-Tax Colony* (Tuscaloosa, Ala., 1956), 1–21. Ernest Gaston, "Fairhope, the Home of the Single Tax and the Referendum," *Independent*, 55 (1903), 1670–73; Gaston was the principal founder of the Fairhope Industrial Association. Also, R. F. Powell, "A Single Tax Colony," *Review of Reviews*, 76 (1921), 187–90. C. Montoliu, "Fairhope—A Town Planning Scheme for the Development of an Organic City," *American City*, 24 (1921), 355–56. *Llano Colonist*, 5 (1926), 6.
62. For a recent and notably able development of this view see Thomas, *Alternative America*, especially 1–17, 50–55, and 332–66.
63. *Liberty*, No. 108 (Sept. 24, 1887), 4.

X: THE GOOD KINGS OF FOURIANA

1. T. Edwin Brown, *Studies in Modern Socialism and Labor Problems* (New York, 1886), 142–52.
2. *Ibid.*, 149–54.
3. Robert F. Fogarty, introduction to Marie Howland, *The Familistere* (Philadelphia, 1975), ii–iii. Edward Howland, "The Social Palace at Guise," *Harper's Magazine*, 44 (1871–72), 701–2.
4. *Ibid.*, 914–18. Edward Howland, "The Familistere at Guise, France," *Harper's Magazine*, 71 (1885), 912–13.
5. *Ibid.*, 914–18. Howland, *Social Palace*, 712–16. Laurence Gronlund, "Godin's 'Social Palace'," *Arena*, 1 (1889–90), 691–95.
6. Felix Adler in Albert K. Owen, *Integral Cooperation*, introduction by R. S. Fogarty (Repr.: Philadelphia, 1975), 67. Gronlund, *Social Palace*, 691.
7. Tucker, *Instead*, 485–86. *Liberty*, no. 83 (July 3, 1886), 7.
8. Ray Reynolds, *Cat'spaw Utopia* (El Cajon, Calif., 1972), 37–38. Fogarty, introduction to *The Familistere*, i. Hayden, *Grand Domestic*, 95–96.
9. Fogarty, *Familistere*, ii. Reynolds, *Cat'spaw*, 39.
10. Howland, *Social Palace*, 702, 716.
11. The following is based on the third edition of *Papa's Own Girl* published in 1918 as *The Familistere* (see note 3). Reynolds, *Cat'spaw*, 37–38, 86. The specific influence allegedly was on Bellamy's views of women. Arthur E. Morgan, *Edward Bellamy* (New York, 1944), 221.
12. Marie Howland, *The Familistere*, 158, 160.
13. *Ibid.*, 372, 412–13, 422–23, 441, 461, 474–75, 510, 524.
14. *Ibid.*, 423, 507, 515, 532, 534–35.
15. *Ibid.*, 265, 507–9, 539, 541, 545.
16. The editor of *Harper's Magazine* wrote that "no novel has yet appeared so comprehensive in its range, bearing upon the great social questions of the day." 49 (1874), 443. The novel, however, was not widely noticed.
17. The two best sources on Owen's life are Reynolds, *Cat'spaw*, 1–12 *passim*, and

David M. Pletcher, *Rails, Mines, and Progress: Seven American Promoters in Mexico, 1867–1911* (Ithaca, New York, 1948), chapter 4. For Owen's relationship to sociological thought, see the chapter on "The Albert Kinsey Owen Group" in L. L. and Jessie Bernard, *Origins of American Sociology* (New York: 1943), 359–71.

18. Pletcher, *Rails*, 107–21. Reynolds, *Cat'spaw*, 5–23. For a short history of the Topolobampo Colony see Fogarty, *American Communes*, 155–57.

19. Herbert B. Adams, *History of Cooperation in the United States* (Baltimore, 1888), 398–400. Reynolds, *Cat'spaw*, 30.

20. Albert K. Owen, *Integral Cooperation*, introduction by R. S. Fogarty (Repr.: Philadelphia, 1975), 8, 151. Reynolds, *Cat'spaw*, 32–36.

21. *Ibid.*, documents regarding the Credit Foncier Company following page 36. Owen, *Integral Cooperation*, 21–24. The constitution of the company is reprinted in Leopold Katscher, "Owen's Topolobampo Colony, Mexico," *American Journal of Sociology*, 12 (1906), 148–51.

22. *Ibid.*, 165–66. Owen, *Integral Cooperation*, 42, 116–19, 197. Reynolds, *Cat'spaw*, 26–9. J. Leon Williams, an Englishman who claimed to have seen Owen's detailed plans, said that "nothing had been overlooked—except a few of the most fundamental qualities of human nature." Williams, "An Experiment in Socialism," *Fortnightly Review*, 89 (1900), 363.

23. Reynolds, *Cat'spaw*, 25–26 and the "principles" of the Credit Foncier Company following page 36. Katscher, *Topolobampo Colony*, 148–51.

24. *Ibid.*, 145–52. Owen's obsession with efficient organization is also evident in his pamphlet, *A Dream of An Ideal City*, where he said that "if we must put our trust in Trusts, let us make a Trust big enough to include every citizen in the city" and where he described his ideal as a city "laid out, built up, and managed with order, system and authority from the start to the finish." Revised edition (London, 1897), 5, 7.

25. *Liberty*, no. 83 (July 3, 1886), 1; no. 101 (June 18, 1887), 7.

26. *Ibid.*, no. 83 (July 3, 1886), 1; no. 89 (Nov. 30, 1886). One veteran association-ist, Stephen Young, died at Topolobampo, the last of various communities he had joined beginning with the Sylvania and the North American phalanxes. Bestor, *Backwoods*, 57 and n. Reynolds, *Cat'spaw*, 41. At least 36 of those who came to Topolobampo were from Greeley, Colorado, founded as the Union Colony less than two decades earlier. *Ibid.*, 151–52.

27. *Ibid.*, 39–40. Bernard, *Origins of Sociology*, 364–65. Owen, *Integral Cooperation*, iii. Lovell, a publisher of inexpensive books and a socialist, played a major role in forming the Credit Foncier Company as well as in the publicity effort. See Madeleine B. Stern, *Imprints on History* (Bloomington, Ind., 1956), chapter 16.

28. Bernard, *Origins of Sociology*, 360–61, 365. Owen, *Integral Cooperation*, iii. Edward Howland's introduction to Sears, *North American Phalanx*, i–ii.

29. "Topolobampo," *Saturday Review*, 63 (1887), 360–61. Ebenezer Howard, *Garden Cities of Tomorrow* (Cambridge, Mass., 1965), 115–16. In 1897, Murdoch & Company of London published the revised edition of Owen's *A Dream of An Ideal City* as part of a series which included works on the Shakers and on Brook Farm. The publisher explained that he was publishing the Owen pamphlet to "encourage and stimulate those who, on this side of the Atlantic, are looking forward to the establishment of a new order of society, and the building up of the Kingdom of Heaven on earth."

30. Bernard, *Origins of Sociology*, 367, 374n.

31. Fogarty, *American Communes*, 156. Reynolds, *Cat'spaw*, third page of the document following page 36.

32. Bernard, *Origins of Sociology*, 366. Pletcher, *Rails*, 129, 138.

33. *Ibid.*, 106. Reynolds, *Cat'spaw*, 39, 72, 77–78. Reynolds estimates the number of colonists for each year on page 149 and lists the colonists by state of origin on pages 150–60.

34. *Ibid.*, 59–80 (see especially the photographs following page 68), 92–9ff. Pletcher, *Rails*, 138–42. "The Topolobampo Colony," reprinted from the St. Louis *Globe-Democrat* in *The American Architect and Building News*, 30 (1890), 26–27.

35. Reynolds, *Cat'spaw*, 59–68, 90–95, 111. Pletcher, *Rails*, 129–42.

36. *New Nation*, 1 (1891), 132, 635.

37. Pletcher, *Rails*, 141–42. Reynolds, *Cat'spaw*, 100–109. "A Latter-Day Utopia: The Socialist Colony of Topolobampo," *Review of Reviews*, 8 (1893), 572–73.

38. *Ibid.*, 573. Reynolds, *Cat'spaw*, 110–30. Pletcher, *Rails*, 141–47. Katscher, *Topolobampo Colony*, 173.

39. Marie Howland, *The Familistere*, ii. *Llano Colonist*, 5 (1926), 6.

40. Reynolds, *Cat'spaw*, 130–32. Katscher, *Topolobampo Colony*, 175.

XI: THE COOPERATIVE COMMONWEALTH: GRONLUND AND BELLAMY

1. For the cataclysmic elements in American thought during this period, see Frederic C. Jaher, *Doubters and Dissenters* (New York, 1964), especially pages 19–32. For the positive side of this thinking, see Kenneth M. Roemer, *The Obsolete Necessity: America in Utopian Writings, 1888–1900* (Kent, Ohio, 1976), especially pages 1–7 and 171–80.

2. Stowe Persons, introduction to Laurence Gronlund, *The Cooperative Commonwealth* (Cambridge, Mass., 1965), xx–xxv. *Liberty*, no. 79 (April 17, 1886), 5.

3. Gronlund, *Cooperative Commonwealth*, 32, 76, 81, 116.

4. *Ibid.*, 89–90. Hillquit, *History*, 18–19.

5. Gronlund, *Cooperative Commonwealth*, 5–7, 65.

6. *Ibid.*, 7–9, 70–77, 90, 235, 247–48. *Arena*, 18 (1897), 355. Richard Hofstadter, *Social Darwinism in American Thought* (Boston, 1955), 115.

7. Gronlund, *Cooperative Commonwealth*, 67–73, 83–84. *Arena*, 18 (1897), 354–55.

8. Gronlund, *Cooperative Commonwealth*, 65, 93–95, 113, 128, 160, 190–91, 226.

9. *Ibid.*, 237–38.

10. *Liberty*, no. 145 (May 18, 1889), 1; no. 167 (Sept. 13, 1890), 1. Barker, *George*, 497–98. *The Cooperative Commonwealth* seems to have received popular notice only after the publication of Bellamy's *Looking Backward*, when it was treated as precursor to that novel. See, for instance, the *Atlantic Monthly*, 61 (1888), 845, and *Harper's Magazine*, 77 (1888), 154.

11. Gronlund, *Cooperative Commonwealth*, 74, 199–200.

12. During its first half-century, some 530,000 copies of *Looking Backward* were sold in the United States alone and another 235,000 copies in Great Britain. Sylvia E.

XI: Cooperative Commonwealth

Bowman, *The Year 2000: A Critical Biography of Edward Bellamy* (New York, 1958), 121.

13. Laurence Gronlund, "Nationalism," *Arena,* 1 (1889–90), 153–55.

14. Arthur E. Morgan, *Edward Bellamy* (New York, 1944), 1–58, 116–21, 172–82, 215–216. Bowman, *Year 2000,* 14–36. Also, see the chapter on Bellamy in Steven Kesselman, *The Modernization of American Reform* (New York, 1979), 122–40.

15. Morgan, *Bellamy,* 135, 225, 369. R. Jackson Wilson, "Experience and Utopia: The Making of Edward Bellamy's *Looking Backwards," Journal of American Studies,* 11 (1977), 51–60.

16. *Ibid.,* 54–55. Thomas A. Sancton, "Looking Inward: Edward Bellamy's Spiritual Crisis," *American Quarterly,* 25 (1973), 538–48. Edward Bellamy, *Selected Writings on Religion and Society,* edited by Joseph Schiffman (New York, 1955), 6–7.

17. *Ibid.,* 8–18.

18. *Ibid.,* 21. George M. Frederickson, *The Inner Civil War: Northern Intellectuals and the Crisis of the Union* (New York, 1965), 14–36.

19. Bellamy, *Selected Writings,* 26.

20. Morgan, *Bellamy,* 55–65, 123–31, 183–99. Thomas, *Alternative America,* 152–67.

21. Edward Bellamy, "Why I Wrote Looking Backward" (1890), in *Edward Bellamy Speaks Again* (Kansas City, 1937), 199–203. He emphasized a different point in "How I Wrote 'Looking Backward' " (1894), one better suited to his political interests at that time. *Ibid.,* 217–27. Arthur E. Morgan notes similarities of expression regarding women between the Howland and Bellamy novels. *Bellamy,* 221. As for Topolobampo, Bellamy, inviting Albert K. Owen to meet with him in 1888, said that someone had, at an unspecified time, sent him "Topolobampo papers" which he had read. Reynolds, *Cat'spaw,* 85.

22. Edward Bellamy, *Looking Backward,* edited by John L. Thomas (Cambridge, Mass., 1967), 96–102. For a detailed critique of the novel as an example of utopian thinking, see Elizabeth Hansot, *Perfection and Progress* (Cambridge, Mass., 1974), 116–44.

23. *Looking Backward,* 124–28.

24. *Ibid.,* 171–76, 181–82n, 242–54. Morgan, *Bellamy,* 227. Bellamy, *Speaks Again,* 60.

25. *Ibid.,* 60, 71, 90, 237–39. Bellamy, *Looking Backward,* 77–8, 151–54.

26. *Ibid.,* 147–50, 157–62, 178, 203, 225, 248–49.

27. *Ibid.,* 132–34, 178, 217, 222–23, 236–41. In a rather curious break with his emphasis on equality, Bellamy also provided for retirement at age 33 on half-credit. *Ibid.,* 204.

28. *Ibid.,* 168–69, 192–96.

29. *Ibid.,* 168–69, 263–71. For Howland, see note 21, above.

30. Bellamy, *Looking Backward,* 184–88.

31. *Ibid.,* 198–203, 221–22, 225–27, 238–41. Bellamy attempted to work out safeguards against government censorship. *Ibid.,* 199–200. Joseph Schiffman, "Edward Bellamy's Altruistic Man," *American Quarterly,* 6 (1954), 205–6, and "Edward Bellamy's Thought," *PMLA,* 68 (1953), 728–30.

32. Bellamy, *Looking Backward*, 285.

33. *Ibid.*, 131–37, 171–77, 215–16, 253.

34. *Ibid.*, 133–37, 171–77.

35. *Ibid.*, 218–20, 229–31. In a hostile review of *Looking Backward*, Francis A. Walker called the provision for election by retirees the most original element in the book, but he said that, contrary to Bellamy's assurances, these electors would be a meddlesome and disruptive influence on the Industrial Army. *Atlantic Monthly*, 65 (1890), 254–55.

36. Bellamy, *Looking Backward*, 137–38, 170, 219–20. Like Albert Brisbane, Bellamy's chief interest seemed to be to organize the working classes to suit the needs of the middle class intellectuals. In this connection, see Arthur Lipow, *Authoritarian Socialism: Edward Bellamy & the Nationalist Movement* (Berkeley and Los Angeles, 1982).

37. John L. Thomas notes the impersonality of Bellamy's ideal world in his *Alternative America*, 253–58.

38. Bellamy, *Looking Backward*, 246–54, 275–85, 314, and *Speaks Again*, 22–23, 43–44, 104, 174. In 1889, Bellamy said that "patriotism, though so often misdirected, is the grandest and most potent form under which the enthusiasm of humanity has yet shown itself capable of moving great masses." *Ibid.*, 177.

39. For the authoritarian side of Bellamy's "barracks Socialism," see Lipow, *Authoritarian Socialism*, especially pages 72–118, 201–21. David DeLeon judges Bellamy more sympathetically, but even he concludes that "Bellamy's reliance on institutional power . . . compels one to the unavoidable conclusion that he is essentially outside the company of American libertarians." *The American as Anarchist* (Baltimore, 1978), 91–93.

40. Bellamy, *Looking Backward*, 105–6, 295–311. *Atlantic Monthly*, 61 (1888), 846.

41. Bowman, *Year 2000*, 119. Morgan, *Bellamy*, 262–63, 393–94. Frederick Anderson, et al., eds., *Selected Mark Twain–Howells Letters* (Cambridge, Mass., 1967), 291n. William Dean Howells, "Edward Bellamy," *Atlantic Monthly*, 61 (1898), 255.

42. Quoted in Hansot, *Perfection*, 122. Lipow, *Authoritarian Socialism*, 16–56, 96–221.

43. Bowman, *Year 2000*, 121. Sylvia E. Powers, et al., *Edward Bellamy Abroad* (New York, 1962), 70–74, 97–107, 277, 329.

44. Reynolds, *Cat'spaw*, 85. Desroche, *Shakers*, 275.

45. *Harper's Magazine*, 77 (1888), 154. Morgan, *Bellamy*, 235–45, 389.

46. Gronlund, *Nationalism*, 155–58. Carl Reeve, *The Life and Times of Daniel De-Leon* (New York, 1972), 5, 18–18, 28–9. The Socialist Charles Sotheran wrote that the spirit of Bellamy's Nationalism was almost identical to that of the Socialist Labor Party. Sotheran, *Greeley*, 24. John Chamberlain later said that DeLeon was initially influenced by Bellamy and went on, in turn, to influence Lenin: "The American Daniel DeLeon first formulated the idea of a Soviet Government which grew up on his idea . . . The germ of DeLeon's system may be found in Bellamy's novel." *Farewell to Reform* (New York, 1932), 84.

XII: THE NATIONALIST MOVEMENT

1. Elizabeth Sadler, "One Book's Influence. Edward Bellamy's 'Looking Backward,' " *New England Quarterly*, 17 (1944), 530–37. Bowman, *Year 2000*, 155–22. Lipow,

Authoritarian Socialism, especially the chapter "Organization for the Unorganizable: *Looking Backward* and the Crisis of the Middle Class."

2. The *New Nation,* 1 (1891), 123. Having created his own cult, the Brotherhood of the New Life, Harris had founded a "New Eden of the West" in the form of his Fountaingrove Community near Santa Rosa. For his life, see Herbert W. Schneider and George Lawson, *A Prophet and A Pilgrim* (New York, 1942). The freethinker George E. Macdonald called Nationalism "razzle-dazzle Socialism" and said regarding it that "the Eddyite said it was Christian Science; Theosophists recognized it as Theosophy; it was generally accepted as harmonizing with the Spiritualist philosophy." *Fifty Years of Freethought* (Repr.: New York, 1972), I, 478, 511.

3. Morgan, *Bellamy,* 260–68. *New Nation,* 2 (1892), 738. Thomas Wentworth Higginson, *Letters and Journals,* edited by Mary T. Higginson (Repr.: New York, 1969), 15.

4. Morgan, *Bellamy,* 65, 247–52. Bowman, *Year 2000,* 124–26.

5. B. O. Flower, *Progressive Men, Women and Movements of the Past Twenty-Five Years* (Boston, 1914), 82–83. William Dean Howells, *A Traveler from Altruria,* introduction by Howard Mumford Jones (New York, 1958), 171.

6. Jean Holloway, *Edward Everett Hale* (Austin, Texas, 1956), 105, 168–72, 208, 225. Edward Everett Hale, *How They Lived at Hampton* (Boston, 1888), especially 10, 12, 27, 262–64, 269–72.

7. Morgan, *Bellamy,* 249.

8. *Ibid.,* 249–50, 263, 267. Some of Bellamy's own writings for the *Nationalist* are reprinted in *Edward Bellamy Speaks Again* (Kansas City, Mo., 1937).

9. Morgan, *Bellamy,* 252–275. Bowman, *Year 2000,* 127–28. In 1891, the *New Nation* reported regularly on the activities of various clubs.

10. Morgan, *Bellamy,* 266–67. F. I. Vassault, "Nationalism in California," *Overland Monthly,* ser. 2, 15 (1890), 660. *New Nation,* 1 (1891), 147, 179.

11. *Ibid.,* I (1891), 147, 307. Mary A. Hill, *Charlotte Perkins Gilman: The Making of a Radical Feminist, 1860–1896* (Phila., 1980), 171–79.

12. Morgan, *Bellamy,* 254–58. Bellamy, *Bellamy Speaks,* 171–77.

13. *Ibid.,* 43–44, 133–36.

14. *New Nation,* 1 (1891), 7, 11.

15. *Ibid.,* 2 (1892), 196. Bellamy, *Bellamy Speaks,* 27, 29, 90.

16. *New Nation,* 1 (1891), 127, 264, 328.

17. *Ibid.,* 1 (1891), 189; 2 (1892), 8.

18. *Ibid.,* 1 (1891), 127, 264–65.

19. *Ibid.,* 144.

20. *Ibid.,* 13, 118, 124, 193, 303; 2 (1892), 567.

21. *Ibid.,* 1 (1891), 118, 124, 209.

22. *Ibid.,* 284, 286, 485–86, 496, 662, 668.

23. *Ibid.,* 284; 2 (1892), 98, 146. Also, Christine McHugh, "Midwestern Populist Leadership and Edward Bellamy," *American Studies,* 19 (1978), 57–74.

24. *New Nation,* 2 (1892), 48, 146, 152, 440, 530, 548, 697–98; 3 (1893), 267, 428.

25. *Ibid.,* 2 (1892), 529–30; 3 (1893), 237–38. Thomas, *Alternative America,* 312–15.

26. *New Nation*, 2 (1892), 98, 146, 582, 666, 698; 3 (1893), 2.

27. *Ibid.*, II (1892), 113, 577–78, 607; III (1893), 2, 458.

28. *Ibid.*, 177, 215–16, 426–27, 475, 524.

29. *Ibid.*, 44–45, 535, 544; 4 (1894), 25–27, 45. Morgan, *Bellamy*, 284–85.

30. Edward Bellamy, "The Programme of the Nationalists," *Forum*, 17 (1894), 83.

31. *Ibid.*, 84–85.

32. *Ibid.*, 86–90.

33. See especially Morgan, *Bellamy*, 268–75. *New Nation*, 2 (1892), 520, 546, 548.

34. *Ibid.*, 3 (1893), 442, 489, 517. For Parsons and Flower, see Arthur Mann, *Yankee Reformers in the Urban Age* (New York, 1954), especially 131–41, 167–70. An able discussion of Nationalism in Massachusetts is provided in Henry F. Bedford, *Socialism and the Workers in Massachusetts, 1886–1912* (Amberst, Mass., 1966), 11–21.

35. Thomas, *Alternative America*, 316–17. Morgan, *Bellamy*, 286. *New Nation*, 4 (1894), 49–50.

36. Morgan, *Bellamy*, 288–89, 291, 375, 389–90.

37. *Liberty*, no. 144 (March 16, 1889), 1; no. 146 (June 8, 1889), 1; No. 158 (May 24, 1890), 1. *Arena*, 2 (1889–90), 3, 533–59; 3 (1890–91), 184; 4 (1891), 311–21. Barker, *George*, 540.

38. Vernon L. Parrington, Jr., *American Dreams: A Study of Utopias*, 2nd ed. (New York, 1964), 80–82. Frances T. Russell, *Touring Utopia* (New York, 1932), 207–9, 220–21. Also see the annotated bibliography in Roemer, *Obsolete Necessity*, 188–206.

39. Richard Michaelis, *Looking Further Forward* (Repr.: New York, 1971), iii–vii, 22, 26, 32, 41–3, 46–47, 53–56, 86–87, 91. At the end of the book, Dr. Leete is brutally killed by a mob of communistic rebels.

40. William Graham Sumner, "The Absurd Effort to Make the World Over," *Forum*, 17 (1894), 94–101.

41. *Ibid.*, 93–94, 101–2.

42. Edward Bellamy, *Equality* (Repr.: New York, 1974), vii, 69. Bowman, *Year 2000*, 138–46. Thomas, *Alternative America*, 340–41. Some critics mistakenly treat *Equality* simply as an extension of *Looking Backward;* for instance, see Hansot, *Perfection*, 114ff.

43. Bellamy *Equality*, 301–45.

44. *Ibid.*, 157, 205, 247, 254–57, 272–73, 298–300, 378–80.

45. *Ibid.*, 274–75, 344–45, 408–9. Bellamy does briefly reintroduce the Industrial Army, but this is largely to answer what he called "the lack of incentive objection" (390).

46. *Ibid.*, 344–45, 365, 381. In 1889, Bellamy said that Nationalism "will be an ideal system for developing, guiding and elevating the recently emancipated colored race." *Bellamy Speaks*, 69.

47. *Arena*, 18 (1897), 518–19. Alfred C. Coursen, "Is Bellamy's Idea Feasible?", *Arena*, 21 (1899), 602–9.

48. "Is the Prophet Dead," *Area*, 20 (1898), 284–88.

49. Roemer, *Obsolete Necessity*, lists more than one hundred utopian works published between 1888 and 1897.

XIII: THE GREAT NATIONAL
COOPERATIVE PEOPLE'S TRUST

1. Mann, *Yankee Reformers*, 172. Arthur M. Schlesinger, *The Rise of the City, 1878–1898* (New York, 1933), 421–36.

2. William J. Ghent, *Our Benevolent Feudalism* (New York, 1902), 2–10, 181–98. Thomas, *Alternative America*, 344.

3. *Arena*, 11 (1894–95), 238–43; 20 (1898), 287.

4. *Ibid.*, 11 (1894–95), 238–39.

5. Commons, *Documentary History*, VII, 236–37; VIII, 285–96, 303–9.

6. "The Address of the National Labor Congress," Commons, *Documentary History*, IX, 142–52.

7. David Thelen, *Paths of Resistance: Tradition and Dignity in Industrializing Missouri* (New York, 1986), 161–62. Florence E. Parker, *The First Hundred Years: A History of Distributive and Service Cooperation in the United States* (Superior, Wisc., 1956), 17–23.

8. *New Nation*, 2 (1891), 113, 198; 2 (1892), 106. Herbert Myrick, *How to Cooperate*, 2nd ed. (New York, 1912), 252–53.

9. Tucker, *Instead*, 108–14. 423–24.

10. Parker, *First 125 Years*, 23–24, 31. Myrick, *Cooperate*, 219–27.

11. See especially George W. Eads, "N. O. Nelson, Practical Cooperator," *Arena*, 36 (1906), 463–80, and N. O. Nelson, "Leclaire—An Existing City of the Future," *Independent*, 77 (1914), 100. Also, John S. Garner, "Leclaire, Illinois: A Model Company Town, 1890–1934," *Journal of the Society of Architectural Historians*, 30 (1971), 219–27.

12. Eads, *Nelson*, 467–75.

13. Aside from Nelson's article, "Leclaire," see his articles on profit-sharing and cooperation in the *Independent*, 58 (1905), 1179–82; 66 (1909), 1136–37; 71 (1911), 643–45 and 858–60.

14. Nelson, *Leclaire*, 100, and "Experiments in Cooperation," *Independent*, 66 (1909), 1136–37. *Arena*, 36 (1906), 467, 474; 38 (1907), 334–35.

15. Kent, *Cooperative Communities*, 622–25.

16. Charles W. Caryl, *New Era* (Denver [1897?]), 6–10, 15, 44–7. H. Roger Grant, "'One Who Dares to Plan': Charles W. Caryl and the New Era Union," *The Colorado Magazine*, 51 (1974), 13–25.

17. Chester M. Destler, *Henry Demarest Lloyd and the Empire of Reform* (Philadelphia, 1963), 274, 281, 380–83, 389, 395–98. Thomas, *Alternative America*, 289–308, 327–31. Henry Demarest Lloyd, *Labor Copartnership* (New York, 1898), 1–8.

18. For Peck and his career, see Francine C. Cary, "The World A Department Store: Bardford Peck and the Utopian Endeavor," *American Quarterly*, 29 (1977), 370–84, and Wallace E. Davies, "A Collectivist Experiment Down East: Bradford Peck and the Cooperative Association of America," *New England Quarterly*, 20 (1947), 471–91.

19. Bradford Peck, *The World A Department Store* (Lewiston, Maine; repr.: New York, 1971), vii-viii. Davies, *Collectivist*, 478–80.

20. Peck, *World*, 20–23, 33–34, 73, 85–86, 154, 181, 242, 293, 299–301.

21. *Ibid.*, 35–39, 70–72, 194–201, 230–33, 240, 258, 293, 298–99.

22. *Ibid.*, 186, 258, 302–3, 306, 311.

23. Davies, *Collectivist*, 479–83. Cary, *World*, 379–84.

24. Mann, *Yankee Reformers*, 163–71. John O. Fish, "The Christian Commonwealth Colony: A Georgia Experiment, 1896–1900," *Georgia Historical Quarterly*, 57 (1973), 213–26. For Albertson, see Francis Davis, *A Fearful Innocence* (Kent, Ohio, 1981), 6–20 *passim*.

25. Ross E. Paulson, *Radicalism & Reform: The Vrooman Family and American Social Thought, 1837–1937* (Lexington, Ky., 1968), 59–125. Edward B. and Eleanor Marx Aveling, *The Working-Class Movement in America*, 2nd ed. (London, 1891), 210–12.

26. Paulson, *Radicalism*, 160–63, 170. Davies, *Collectivist*, 483–85.

27. Paulson, *Radicalism*, 170, 174–78. Earl A. Collins, "The Multitude Unlimited," *Missouri Historical Review*, 27 (1932–33), 303–6. Thelen, *Paths of Resistance*, 163.

28. Hiram G. Vrooman, "The Co-Operative Association of America," *Arena*, 26 (1901), 578–87.

29. *Ibid.*, 585–87. Davis, *Collectivist*, 485. Peck, *World*, 268–69.

30. Cooperationists like Nelson and Lloyd were in close touch with the cooperative movement in England and northern Europe. Destler, *Lloyd*, 383–91.

31. Davies, *Collectivist*, 486–87. Paulson, *Radicalism*, 178–79. *Arena*, 27 (1902), 611–14; 28 (1902), 321–22. *New Nation*, 2 (1892), 542, 559.

32. *Arena*, 28 (1902), 406–15, 434–35.

33. Kent, *Cooperative Communities*, 630–31. *Arena*, 28 (1902), 604–5. Washburn's proudest boast was that the People's Trust controlled "almost the entire business of Trenton, Missouri through the Western Cooperative Association." *Ibid.*, 409. Trenton, a town in northern Missouri, had somewhat less than 6000 people.

34. Paulson, *Radicalism*, 181–83. Collins, *Multitude*, 306.

35. Paulson, *Radicalism*, 183–85. Cary, *World*, 383–84. Davies, *Collectivist*, 488–90.

36. Davis, *Fearful Innocence*, 24–76.

37. N. O. Nelson, "The Co-Operative Movement in the United States," *Outlook*, 89 (1908), 529. After the termination of *The Cooperator*, Ralph Albertson continued to promote the cooperative ideal in the *Arena* as editor of its cooperative news column and as Secretary of the Coopertive Association, but he also devoted much of his time to municipal ownership and other progressive reforms. See, for instance, the *Arena*, 37 and 38 (1907).

38. Thomas, *Alternative America*, 349. As early as 1901, Lloyd had concluded that the cooperative movement would be defeated by business consolidation and by the mechanization of agriculture. Destler, *Lloyd*, 399, 510.

XIV: Socialism and "Utopia"

1. It is worth noting that Noyes believed that all forms of American Socialism shared a common ideal, "the enlargement of home—the extension of family union beyond the little man-and-wife circle to large corporations," a definition well suited to his own experiment in communism at Oneida. *American Socialisms*, 23.

2. Brisbane, *Brisbane*, 273–75.

3. Oliver Carlson, *Brisbane* (New York, 1937), 79, 113, 142–213, 247. Edward J.

Myzik, *Victor Berger, A Biography*. Ph.D. dissertation, Northwestern University (1960), 244–48.

4. Friedrich Engels, *Socialism: Utopian and Scientific*, translated by Edward Aveling (Chicago, 1914), 58, 74–75.

5. *Ibid.*, 58, 74–75, 91–93. Karl Marx and Friedrich Engels, *Basic Writings on Politics and Philosophy*, edited by Lewis S. Feuer (New York, 1959).

6. Aveling, *Working-Class*, 191–93, 237–38.

7. Marx and Engels, *Basic Writings*, 456, 458, 489–97.

8. Richard Hofstadter, *Social Darwinism in American Thought* (Boston, 1955), especially chapters 4 and 6.

9. Marx and Engels, *Basic Writings*, 39.

10. *New Nation*, 1 (1891), 222; 2 (1892), 36.

11. Alcander Longley, *What Is Communism?* (Repr.: New York 1976). *New Nation*, 2 (1892), 189. H. Roger Grant, "Missouri's Utopian Communities," *Missouri Historical Review*, 66 (Oct. 1971), 38–44.

12. William Dean Howells, *A Traveler from Altruia* (New York, 1957), 147–49, 179–80. By the time he published *A Traveler from Altruria*, Howells had finished a sequel, which owing to the reluctance of his publisher was not published until 1907 as *Through the Eye of the Needle*. William Dean Howells, *A Life in Letters*, edited by Mildred Howell (New York, 1968), II, 25–26, 36. Edwin D. Cady, *The Realist at War: The Mature Years, 1885–1920* (Syracuse, N.Y., 1950), 146, 154–55. 197–98. Howells' two novels are analyzed by Elizabeth Hansot, *Perfection*, 170–92.

13. Howells, *Traveler*, 180–84.

14. *Ibid.*, 137–38, 186–91, 202.

15. Titus K. Smith, *Altruria* (Repr.: New York, 1971), 31, 42, 84–5. Parrington, *American Dreams*, 120.

16. Robert S. Fogarty has found 37 colonies in the 1890s and 22 more in the period, 1900–1919. *American Communes*, 157–62. Also, Bushee, *Communistic Societies*, 661–64. For the Home Colony, see Charles Pierce LeWarne, *Utopias on Puget Sound, 1885–1915* (Seattle, 1975), chapter 6. Morris I. Swift, "Altruria in California," *Overland Monthly*, 29 (1897), 643–45.

17. Howard Quint, "Julius Wayland, Pioneer Socialist Propagandist," *Mississippi Valley Historical Review*, 35 (1948–49), 585–606. Francela Butler, "The Ruskin Commonwealth," *Tennessee Historical Quarterly*, 23 (1964), 333–42. *New Nation*, 3 (1893), 432.

18. *The Coming Nation*, Dec. 3, 1893.

19. *Ibid.*, Dec. 2, 16, 23, 30, 1893.

20. *Ibid.*, Jan. 6, Feb. 3, 1894.

21. *Ibid.*, Dec. 23, 1893; March 16, April 16, June 8, Aug. 3, 195. Bushee, *Communistic Societies*, 632. J. W. Braam, "The Ruskin Co-operative Colony," *American Journal of Sociology*, 8 (1902–3), 667–68. Herbert N. Casson, "The Ruskin Co-operative Colony," *Independent*, 51 (1899), 192–93.

22. *Ibid.*, 193–95. Bushee, *Communistic Societies*, 632. Braam, *Ruskin*, 673–76. Butler, *Ruskin*, 331.

23. Casson, *Ruskin*, 194–95.

24. Braam, *Ruskin*, 668–71. Bushee, *Communistic Societies, 632–33*. In March 1895, the first issue of *The Coming Nation* was published from "Tennessee City"; in July came the announcement that Wayland "has severed his connection with the *Coming Nation* and the Ruskin Co-operative Association." (July 27, 1895).

25. Isaac Broome, *The Last Days of the Ruskin Co-operative Association* (Chicago, 1902), 52. In this highly biased account, Broome attributed the failure not to the cooperative idea but to the membership, "a medley of untrained people whose most prominent characteristic is ignorance," a people who had fallen into the habit of "begging" from the outside rather than working for themselves. *Ibid.*, 15–18, 30–1. For another personal account of life and conflict at Ruskin, see Charles H. Kegel, ed. "Earl Miller's 'Recollections of the Ruskin Cooperative Association'," *Tennessee Historical Quarterly*, 17 (1958), 45–69.

26. Quint, *Wayland*, 595–99. Ernest S. Wooster, *Communities of the Past and Present* (Repr.: New York, 1974), 45. For Wayland's later attitudes, see the compilation of his editorials for the *Appeal to Reason*, J. A. Wayland, *Leaves of Life* (Girard, Kansas, 1912), especially 77, 82–3, 118, 229–30.

27. Nick Salvatore, *Eugene V. Debs: Citizen and Socialist* (Urbana, Ill., 1982), 109–23. Eugene V. Debs, "Consolidation" (Jan. 15, 1896) in Eugene V. Debs, *Papers*, microfilm edition, edited by J. Robert Constantine, et al. (Terre Haute, 1984), Reel 6.

28. Salvatore, *Debs*, 17–55, 124.

29. *Ibid.*, 127–39. Ginger, *Debs*, 129ff.

30. Debs to Frank X. Holl (March 24, 1896) and Debs to Henry Demerest Lloyd (Aug. 15, Dec. 10, 1894; Feb. 1, Dec. 12, 1896), *Papers*, Reel 1. Salvatore, *Debs*, 151.

31. Debs to the *Coming Nation* (Sept. 2, 1899), *Papers*, Reel 6.

32. *Ibid.*, 101. Ginger, *Debs*, 86. "Mr. Debs on Bellamy" (May 29, 1898), *Papers*, Reel 6.

33. Clipping, "Debs and Bellamy Start the New Nation" attached to a letter (May 29, 1898), *Papers*, Reel 1. Bowman, *Year 2000*, 151–52.

34. "Mr. Debs on Bellamy" (May 29, 1898), *Papers*, Reel 6.

35. Debs to Frank X. Holl (May 15, 1895), *Papers*, Reel 1.

36. Debs, "Present Condition and Future Duties" (Jan. 1, 1897), *Papers*, Reel 6.

37. *Ibid.*, Debs to Henry Demerest Lloyd (Dec. 12, 1896), *Papers*, Reel 1. For Lloyd on this matter, see Destler, *Lloyd*, 380–382.

38. Debs, "It is Coming" (May 1, 1897), *Papers*, Reel 6.

39. Quint, *Forging*, 282–85.

40. Debs, "It is Coming" (May 1, 1897) and "Coming Republic" (June 1, 1897), *Papers*, Reel 6. Debs to Frank X. Holl (May 31, 1897), *Papers*, Reel 1. Eugene V. Debs, "The Social Democracy," *The New Times* (Aug. 1897), 78–9.

41. Debs, "Coming Republic," (June 1, 1897), *Papers*, Reel 6.

42. *Ibid.*, "Letter to John D. Rockefeller" (June 19, 1897) and "Now for Action" (Sept. 23, 1897), *Papers*, Reel 6. Debs, *Social Democracy*, 78–9. Also Bernard J. Brommel, "Debs Co-operative Commonwealth for Workers," *Labor History*, 12 (1971), 560–69.

43. Bernard J. Brommel, *Eugene V. Debs: Spokesman for Labor and Socialism* (Chicago, 1978), 46–49, and *Cooperative Commonwealth*, 540.

44. LeWarne, *Utopias on Puget Sound,* 130–34. Quint, *Forging* 305–6.

45. *Ibid.,* 142–67. W. E. Copeland, "The Cooperative Brotherhood," *Arena,* 28 (1902), 403–5, and "The Cooperative Brotherhood and Its Colony," *Independent,* 55 (1903), 317–23.

46. Salvatore, *Debs,* 163–65. In his August 1897 article, "Social Democracy," Debs noted that most of the criticism of the SDA was directed against colonization, only to defend the idea by arguing that its aim was not "to organize isolated colonies" but to attain control of a state. For his optimistic assessment of the future of the SDA, see "Debs Gives a Brief Account of Progress in the East" (Nov. 4, 1897) and his letter to *The Coming Nation* (Oct. 27, 1897), *Papers,* Reel 6.

47. Debs, "Social Democracy" (Oct. 27, 1898) and his rejection of a proposal to fuse with the Populist party (May 14, 1898), *Papers,* Reel 6.

48. Salvatore, *Debs,* 165–67. LeWarne, *Utopias on Puget Sound,* 134–36. Debs, et al., "The Address of the Social Democratic Party of America" (June 16, 1898), *Papers,* Reel 6.

49. Lipow, *Authoritarian Socialism,* 277. Debs to Ignatius Donnelly (Aug. 17, 1898) and to Samuel M. Jones (March 6 and July 24, 1899), *Papers,* Reel 1.

50. Salvatore, *Debs,* 170–77. Debs, "The Social Democratic Convention" (March 24, 1900), *Papers,* Reel 6.

XV: DEBSIAN SOCIALISM

1. For examples of this reasoning, see Morris Hillquit, *Socialism in Theory and Practice* (New York, 1909), especially pages 111–33, and Jesse W. Hughan, *American Socialism* (New York, 1912), 112.

2. The practical and local side of Socialism is especially well discussed in two collections of essays: Bruce Stave, ed. *Socialism and the Cities* (Port Washington, New York, 1975) and Donald T. Critchlow, ed., *Socialism in the Heartland* (Notre Dame, Ind. 1986). The plight of Socialism in America is thoroughly debated in John H. M. Laslett and Seymour Martin Lipset, *Failure of a Dream? Essays in the History of American Socialism* (Berkeley and Los Angeles, 1984), 333–482. There is little here to refute the much earlier claim of Nicholas Paine Gilman that a Socialism which made "no room for voluntary cooperation" would have little appeal to Americans. Nathan Paine Gilman, *Socialism and the American Spirit* (Boston and New York, 1896), v–viii, 57–83, 181–89, 334.

3. L. Glen Seretan, *Daniel DeLeon: The Odyssey of an American Marxist* (Cambridge, Mass., 1979), 24–44, 126–35.

4. Eugene V. Debs, "How I Became a Socialist," in Ronald Radosh, ed. *Debs* (Englewood Cliffs, N.J., 1971), 18–19. Eugene V. Debs, "The Social Democratic Party's Appeal," *Independent,* 57 (1904), 837, and "The American Movement," in *Writings and Speeches,* edited by Arthur Schlesinger, Jr. (New York, 1948), 77–79, 81–82, 88–89, 94.

5. Lincoln Steffens, "Eugene V. Debs," *Everybody's,* 19 (1908), 457–59, 469. Ginger, *Debs,* 285, 305. Ralph Chaplin, *Wobbly* (Chicago, 1948), 342–43.

6. Debs to Joseph A. Labadie, Dec. 12, 1905, Debs *Papers,* Reel 1. Emma Gold-man, *Living My Life* (New York, 1934), 220. Milton Cantor, *Max Eastman* (New York, 1970), 78.

7. Sotheran, *Greeley,* xxxvii. Debs, *Writings and Speeches,* 119, 125, 137–38, 166. For an early expression of the hope for a new kind of party, see Benjamin Fay Mills, "The New Party," *Arena,* 22 (1899), 1–14.

8. Debs, "The Socialist Party's Appeal," *Independent,* 73 (1912), 950–52. H. Wayne Morgan, "The Utopia of Eugene V. Debs," *American Quarterly,* 11 (1959), 121–30. Steffens, *Debs,* 467–69.

9. Debs, "Socialist Party's Appeal," *Independent,* 65 (1908), 878–80. Steffens, *Debs,* 467.

10. Debs, *Appeal* (1908), 878–80, and *Writings and Speeches,* 125, 310, 320.

11. Eugene V. Debs, "Socialist Ideals," *Arena,* 40 (1908), 433–34. Also H. Wayne Morgan, *Eugene V. Debs: Socialist for President* (Westport, Conn., 1973), 23–24, and *Utopia,* 120–35; David Karsner, *Debs: His Authorized Life and Letters* (New York, 1919), 204.

12. Robert M. Hyfler, *American Socialist Thought: From Debs to Harrington.* Ph.D. dissertation, University of Massachusetts (1980), 180, 184, 190, 213–14. Debs, *Appeal* (1912), 450–52.

13. Harry W. Laidler, *The History of Socialism* (New York, 1968), 588–93. Morris Hillquit, *Loose Leaves From a Busy Life* (New York, 1943), 55, 70, 74. Morgan, *Debs,* 90–91. Membership figures, *Appeal to Reason* (March 14, 1908), 3.

14. Hughan, *American Socialism,* 236–37. Robert M. Hyfler discusses the outlook of Berger, Hillquit, and Spargo in a chapter aptly titled, "The Conservative Uses of Marxism," *Prophets of the Left* (Westport, Conn., 1984), 15–46. Hillquit, *Loose Leaves,* 41–43, 51–52, and *Socialism,* 110–12. Muzik, *Berger,* 196–207. The best overall study of Socialism as a political movement is Ira Kipnis, *The American Socialist Movement, 1897–1912* (New York, 1952).

15. Hyfler, *Socialist Thought,* 58–59, 87. John Spargo, *Socialism,* revised edition (New York, 1912), 18–25, 294, 299, 308. Kipnis, *American Socialist Movement,* 294–311.

16. Hillquit, *Loose Leaves,* 55. Hughan, *American Socialism,* 227. Probably some middle-class adherents looked to socialism as a defense against industrial concentration under capitalism, to which H. G. Wells referred when he wrote that "for a century or more the grinding of the middle class has been going on . . . Which is the better master— the democratic State or a 'combine' of millionaires?" Wells, "The Middle Class Between the Millstones," *Independent,* 62 (1907), 1085–86. Socialism also attracted the wealthy and influential J. C. Phelps Stokes, who declared that the working class exploited by capitalism consisted "of the manual and mental worker together from the executive officers of the corporation to the coal-heavers." Stokes, "Reasons for Supporting Debs," *Outlook,* 90 (1908), 380.

17. Leon Harris, *Upton Sinclair: An American Rebel* (New York, 1975), 58–75.

18. Upton Sinclair, *The Industrial Republic* (New York, 1907), 216, 260–84, and "A Home Colony," *Independent,* 60 (1906), 1401–8. Lawrence Kaplan, "A Utopian During

the Progressive Era: The Helicon Home Colony, 1906–1907," *American Studies,* 25 (1980), 59–73.

19. Sinclair, *Industrial Republic,* 284. Upton Sinclair, *Autobiography* (New York, 1962), 127–36, 162–64.

20. Elizabeth Gurley Flynn, *I Speak My Own Piece* (New York, 1955), 37, 41, 68. Chaplin, *Wobbly,* 71, 98, 104.

21. Paul F. Brissenden, *The I.W.W.: A Study of American Syndicalism* (New York, 1957), 67–82, 91–110, 241–42, appendices I and III. John Spargo, *The Psychology of Bolshevism* (New York, 1919), 66. Salvadore, *Debs,* 205–12. Melvin Dubofsky, "Socialism and Syndicalism" in Laslett and Lipset, *Failure of a Dream?,* 170–203.

22. Brissenden, *I.W.W.,* 136–54, 163–64, 213 *passim,* 376. John Macy, *Socialism in America* (Garden City, New York, 1916), 45–7, 157–63, 177, 194, 223. Macy, a Harvard graduate and the husband of Anne M. Sullivan (the teacher of Helen Keller), formally became a Socialist in 1909.

23. Two very different views of London and his background are presented in Philip S. Foner, *Jack London: An American Rebel* (New York, 1964), 8–45, 403–6, 453, and John Perry, *Jack London: An American Myth* (Chicago, 1981), 6–67. Also, Jack London, "How I Became a Socialist," in Foner, *London,* 362–65, and *War of the Classes* (New York, 1905), xiii–x, xiii.

24. Gordon Beauchamp, "Jack London's Utopian Dystopia and Dystopian Utopia," in Roemer, *America as Utopia,* 91–107. Foner, *London,* 85–95. Perry, *London,* 118–20.

25. Harris, *Sinclair,* 75–76. Foner, *London,* 69–77. Hillquit, *History,* 355, and *Loose Leaves,* 60–61.

26. Three especially good books on the subject are Henry F. May, *The End of American Innocence* (Chicago, 1964), especially 219–52, Robert E. Humphrey, *Children of Fantasy: The First Rebels of Greenwich Village* (New York, 1978), especially 3–8, 236–53, and Leslie Fishbein, *Rebels in Bohemia: The Radicals of the Masses, 1911–1917* (Chapel Hill, N.C., 1982).

27. William L. O'Neill, *Echoes of Revolt: The Masses, 1911–1917* (Chicago, 1966), 28–9 *passim.* Cantor, *Max Eastman,* 58–70.

28. O'Neill, *Echo,* 289–92, 303. Humphrey, *Children of Fantasy,* 179–82.

29. Granville Hicks, *John Reed: The Making of a Revolutionary* (New York, 1936), 1–78.

30. *Ibid.,* 73, 78, 94.

31. *Ibid.,* 94–138. Richard O'Conner and Dale L. Walker, *The Last Revolutionary: A Biography of John Reed* (New York, 1967), 75–84.

32. See James R. Green, *Grass-Roots Socialism: Radical Movements in the Southwest, 1895–1943* (Baton Rouge, La., 1978).

33. Quint, *Wayland,* 594–606. *Appeal to Reason* (Jan. 18, 1908), 3, 6. Wayland, *Leaves,* 38, 339. Salvatore, *Debs,* 191, 234.

34. Wayland, *Leaves,* 76, 80–83, 219.

35. *Ibid.,* 56, 90–95, 114, 182–84, 189, 211, 217. *Appeal to Reason* (Feb. 15, 1908), 6.

36. Quint, *Wayland,* 599–605. Wayland, *Leaves,* 82–83, 134, 218–19. *Appeal to Reason* (May 9, 1908), 2, 4.

37. For a brief history of the *National Rip-Saw,* see Phil Wagner, "The Story of the Rip-Saw" (March 1914), 13.

38. Oscar Ameringer, *If You Don't Weaken: The Autobiography of Oscar Ameringer,* introduction by James R. Green (Norman, Okla., 1983), 181–82, 233–34.

39. Neil Basen, "Kate Richards O'Hare: The 'First Lady' of American Socialism, 1901–1917," *Labor History,* 21 (1980), 165–99. Ameringer, *Don't Weaken,* 263–69. *Rip-Saw* (Nov. 1912), 24; (Dec. 1912), 20; (Jan. 1913), 17, 25. Henry M. Tichenor, "The Religion of One Socialist," *Ibid.* (Feb. 1913), 27.

40. *Ibid.,* (Jan. 1913), 31; (April 1913), 4. See, however, Garin Burbank, *When Farmers Voted Red* (Westport, Conn., 1976). For an analysis of the class backgrounds of a select but significant group of heartland Socialists, see James R. Green, "The 'Salesmen-Soldiers' of the *Appeal* Army" in Stave, *Socialism and the Cities,* 13–40.

41. Ameringer, *Don't Weaken,* 263–64.

42. *Appeal to Reason* (Feb. 1, 1908); (Feb. 15, 1908), 8; (May 16, 1908), 3. *Rip-Saw* (May 1913), 2, 22.

43. V. Lindsay, "Why I Voted the Socialist Ticket," *Independent,* 68 (1910), 1086.

44. *Arena,* 41 (1909), 92. Green, *Grass-Roots,* 164–65, 174. Harris, *Sinclair,* 129.

45. Debs *Appeal* (1912), 952. *Rip-Saw* (Dec. 1912), 6. John R. Chamberlain later wrote that in 1912 it looked like "a fairly intelligent, fairly good natured and fairly easy transition . . . to the millennium." *Farewell to Reform* (New York, 1932), 278. Kipnis, *American Socialist Movement,* 335–69.

46. Salvatore, *Debs,* 272. H. G. Creel, "A Memoir of Wayland," *Rip-Saw* (Dec. 1912), 22.

47. Salvatore, *Debs,* 265–71. Laidler, *Socialism,* 591.

48. *Ibid.,* 260–61. In 1912, Jessie W. Hughan, a perceptive student of Socialism, said that "the extreme democratic ideal in the American movement is doubtless responsible for the lapses into Utopianism which run through the ultimate program." Hughan, *American Socialism,* 120–22, 144–45.

49. Fried, *Socialism,* 497–503. Macy, *Socialism,* 161, 163, 177, 194. The most thorough discussion of the conflicts within the party is provided by Kipnis, *American Socialist Movement,* especially pages 370–420 and 423–28.

50. *Rip-Saw* (May 1913), 2, 22; (May 1914), 20. Another Socialist colony at Fallon, Nevada, attracted the interests of Phil Wagner, the managing editor of the *Rip-saw,* and of Fred Warren, Wayland's successor as editor of the *Appeal to Reason. Social Revolution* (March 1917), 13; (June 1917), 13; (Sept. 1917), 11.

51. *Rip-Saw* (Feb. 1916), 8, 22–23. *New Nation,* I (1891), 450.

52. Paul Conkin, *Two Paths to Utopia: The Hutterites and the Llano Colony* (Lincoln, Neb., 1964), 108–11. Hayden, *Seven American Utopias,* 289–309. Aldous Huxley, "Llano Del Rio," *California Historical Quarterly,* 51 (1971), 119–30, and Paul Kagan, "Llano Del Rio," *Ibid.,* 131–54.

53. *Rip-Saw* (Feb. 1916), 23; (March 1916), 18.

54. Debs to Frank P. O'Hare, Jan. 2, 1918, Debs *Papers,* Reel 2. *Rip-Saw* (Feb. 1914), 1.

55. *Ibid.,* (March 1914), 30: (Dec. 1914), 18–19; (June 1916), 15; (Nov. 1916), 4.

56. *Ibid.,* (May 1916), 19; (June 1916), 15; (Nov. 1916), 4.

57. *Ibid.,* (Jan. 1917), 30.
58. *Social Revolution* (March 1917), 1; (April 1918), 5.

XVI: AFTER TOMORROW

1. Lewis Mumford, *Findings and Keepings* (New York, 1975), 61.

2. The best book on antebellum Nonresistance is Lewis Perry, *Radical Abolitionism: Anarchy and the Government of God in Anti-Slavery Thought* (Ithaca, New York, 1973).

3. John Spargo and George L. Arner, *Elements of Socialism* (New York, 1917); this book was first published in 1912. Hillquit, *Loose Leaves,* 145.

4. Macy, *Socialism,* 18. Hillquit, *Loose Leaves,* 145–46. Hicks, *Reed,* 177. Harris, *Sinclair,* 158. Salvatore, *Debs,* 75–76, 280–85.

5. Fried, *Socialism,* 521–26. Macy, *Socialism,* 194, 222. Ginger, *Debs,* 394–95, 407–8. Salvatore, *Debs,* 291–302.

6. Debs to Upton Sinclair, Jan. 12, 1916, and to Daniel Hoan, Aug. 17, 1916, *Papers,* Reel 2. *Rip-Saw* (May 1916), 19.

7. *Social Revolution* (June 1917), 3; (Sept. 1917), 15; (April 1918), 5.

8. *Social Builder* (May 1918), 5; this was its only issue.

9. Debs to George D. Herron, Jan. 23, 1917, and to Frank P. O'Hare, Jan. 2, 1918, *Papers,* Reel 2. Basen, *O'Hare,* 198.

10. Salvatore, *Debs,* 291–302; Ginger, *Debs,* 394–95, 407–8.

11. Radosh, *Debs,* 82–3. Salvatore, *Debs,* 298–99.

12. For the favorable response to the Bolsheviks, see Philip Foner, *The Bolshevik Revolution: Its Impact on American Radicals, Liberals, and Labor* (New York, 1967). Salvatore, *Debs,* 290–92. Hillquit, *Loose Leaves,* 277–99. John Spargo, *Social Democracy Explained* (New York and London, 1918), preface.

13. Cantor, *Eastman,* 83. Humphrey, *Children of Fantasy,* 146–47, 196. Hicks, *Reed,* 299–354.

14. Spargo, *Social Democracy Explained,* preface, and *The Psychology of Bolshevism* (New York, 1919), 31–2, 149–50.

15. Ginger, *Debs,* 401. Foner, *Bolshevik,* 90, 125–26, 154. Lincoln Steffens, *Autobiography* (New York, 1931), 844. Chaplin, *Wobbly,* 342.

16. Morgan, *Debs,* 161–66. Laidler, *Socialism,* 591–93. Hillquit, *Loose Leaves,* 300–23.

17. See especially Theodore Debs to David Karsner, March 11, 1925, and Debs to Bertha Hale White, June 11, 1925, *Papers,* Reel 4.

18. Morgan, *Debs,* 189. Salvatore, *Debs,* 325–41.

19. Ellis Cowling, *Co-operation in America* (New York, 1938), 107–9. Jerry Voorhis, *American Cooperatives* (New York, 1961), 187–88.

20. James Peter Warbasse, *Co-operative Democracy* (New York, 1923), 113, 116, 122, 130, 143, 189.

21. *Ibid.,* viii–ix, 42, 49, 56–7, 84, 97, 103.

22. *Ibid.,* 10–11, 45, 101–3, 197.

23. *Ibid.,* 341–46.

24. Cowling, *Co-operation*, 110. Debs to Warbasse, Oct. 27, 1922, *Papers*, Reel 4.

25. Warbasse ignored the Llano Colony in his book, but, according to Paul Conkin, *Co-operation*, the official publication of the League, "endlessly condemned" Llano, Conkin, *Two Paths*, 122, and 123n. Also see Frank O'Hare's review of Warbasse's book in the *American Vanguard* (Oct. 1923), 8.

26. The story of Llano colony is best told by Conkin, *Two Paths*, 103–85; for the California phase of the colony, see pages 103–13. Ernest S. Wooster, *Communities of the Past and Present* (New Llano, La., 1924; repr.: New York, 1974), 121. Kagan, *Llano del Rio*, 145.

27. *Ibid.*, 147–54. Wooster, *Communities*, v–vi.

28. *Ibid.*, vi–x. Conkin, *Two Paths*, 113–18.

29. Job Harriman to Debs, July 24, 1918, Debs *Papers*, Reel 2.

30. Conkin, *Two Paths* 115–17. *Llano Colonist* (Jan. 9, 1925), 12: (July 3, 1926), 6; (Aug. 28, 1926), 6. Bob Brown, *Can We Co-operate?* (Staten Island, New York, 1940), 41, 46–8, 128, 161.

31. Conkin, *Two Paths*, 111, 119. *American Vanguard* (April 1923), 5. Between February 1923 and June 1924, Kate Richards O'Hare published a series of articles on Llano in the *American Vanguard* under the title, "Kuzbasing in Dixie."

32. *Llano Colonist*, June 5, 1925, p. 15.

33. Wooster, *Communities*, 132–33. Charles Gide, *Communist and Cooperative Communities*, translated by E. F. Rowe (New York, 1930), 205–6. *Llano Colonist*, Aug. 15, 1925, p. 8.

34. *Ibid.*, May 8, p. 14; June 5, p. 15; July 6, p. 7; Aug. 15, 1925, p. 8.

35. Wooster, *Communities*, 131. *Llano Colonist*, June 13, 1925, p. 8. Theodore Debs to Frank P. O'Hare, July 9 and Dec. 22, 1923, Debs *Papers*, Reel 4. *American Vanguard* (Feb. 1923), 13–14. Among the cooperative news published in the *Colonist* was an announcement of a convention to be held at Columbus, Ohio, "for inaugurating the foundation of communists [sic] co-operative colonies" to restore to workers the "self-support and independence, taken from many by modern methods, inventions, progress, and so called civilization; to awaken to action our unused labor or man power." July 24, 1926, p. 2.

36. Wooster, *Communities*, 138–40. *American Vanguard* (Feb. 1923), 13.

37. Phil Wagner told Debs that he had to suspend the monthly, because "I found it impossible to continue under the heavy burden." May 17, 1918, Debs *Papers*, Reel 2. The *Rip-Saw* was revived in late 1920 with Kate Richards O'Hare as editor and Frank P. O'Hare as manager; in 1921, it claimed 50,000 "actual paid-in-subscribers." (June 1921), 4.

38. *American Vanguard* (Nov. 1923), 1.

39. *Ibid.*, (Feb. 1923), 4; (March 1923), 6; (April 1923), 4.

40. Frank P. O'Hare refers to the history of the college in *Ibid.* (April 1923), 8.

41. *Ibid.*, (May 1923), 11: (Oct. 1923), 6.

42. *Ibid.*, (Sept. 1923), 9; (Oct. 1923), 3, 6ff.

43. *Ibid.*, (Oct. 1923), 7.

44. Conkin, *Two Paths*, 116–20.

45. *Ibid.*, 117–18. *American Vanguard* (Sept. 24), 10–11. *Llano Colonist* (Aug. 5, 1925), 1.

46. *Ibid.*, (June 6, 1925), 11; (July 4, 1925), 12.

47. Brown, *Can We Co-operate?*, 17ff, 208. Gide, *Communist*, 204–7. Conkin, *Two Paths*, 125, 154. Later, one member recalled that "our greatest opposition during the whole life of Llano Colony came not from the capitalists," but from union labor and the Socialist party, because the colonists did not support the strategies of either. Yaacon Oved, "Communes & the Outside World," *Communal Societies*, 3 (1983), 91.

48. Brown, *Can We Co-operate?*, 176–79, 191–92, 217. Conkin, *Two Paths*, 172.

49. Gide, *Communist*, 203–7. Conkin, *Two Paths*, 119–23. "Llano Cooperative Colony," *Monthly Labor Review*, 32 (1931), 1133–39. Brown, *Can We Co-operate?*, 17, 33–35.

50. *Ibid.*, 38–9, 207. Conkin, *Two Paths*, 142–44.

51. *Christian Century*, 53 (1936), 608.

52. Conkin, *Two Paths*, 172–83. Henrik F. Infield, *Cooperative Communities* (New York, 1945), 49–52.

53. Conkin, *Two Paths*, 173–74.

EPILOGUE: YESTERDAY AND TOMORROW
I. *Llano Colonist* (June 6, 1925), 7.

1. *Llano Colonist* (June 6, 1925), 7.

2. L. G. Atkins, who claimed "twenty-six years of Socialist activity," to the *American Vanguard* (Oct. 1923), 13.

3. *American Vanguard* (Nov. 1923), 12.

4. Corinne McLaughlin and Gordon Davidson, *Builders of the Dawn* (Walpole, N.H., 1985).

BIBLIOGRAPHY

SPECIAL PERIODICALS
(Used consistently for the years indicated)

American Socialist (1876–1979).
American Vanguard (1923–24).
Appeal to Reason (1908).
Coming Nation (1893–1897).
Dial (1840–1844).
Harbinger (1845–1849).
Herald of Truth [Cincinnati] (1847–1848).
Liberty (1881–1900).
Llano Colonist (1925–1926).
National Rip-Saw (1914–1918).
New Harmony Gazette (1825–1827).
New Nation, (1891–1894).
Oneida Circular (1853–56; 1875–76).
Phalanx (1843–1844).
Practical Christian (1843–1859).

3 2 7

ARTICLES

Albertson, Ralph. "A Survey of Mutualistic Communities in America." *Iowa Journal of History and Politics,* 34 (1936), 375–444.

Arndt, Karl J. R. and Patrick Brostowin, "Pragmatists and Prophets: George Rapp and J. A. Roebling *versus* J. A. Etzler and Count Leon," *The Western Pennsylvania Historical Magazine,* 52 (1969), 1–27, 171–98.

Baker, Ray S. "The Debs Cooperative Commonwealth." *Outlook,* 56 (1897), 538–40.

Basen, Neil K. "Kate Richards O'Hare: The 'First Lady' of American Socialism." *Labor History,* 21 (1980), 165–99.

Baxter, Sylvester. "How the Bills of Socialism Will Be Paid." *Forum,* 17 (1894), 699–709.

Bellamy, Edward. "The Programme of the Nationalists." *Forum,* 17 (1894), 81–91.

—— "The Religion of Solidarity," *Selected Writings on Religion and Society,* Joseph Schiffman, ed. New York: Liberal Arts Press, 1955.

Bellamy, Francis. "The Tyranny of All the People." *Arena,* 4 (1891), 180–91.

Blez, Herman J. "The North American Phalanx: Experiment in Socialism." *Proceedings of the New Jersey Historical Society,* 81 (1963), 215–47.

Bestor, Arthur, Jr. "Albert Brisbane: Propagandist for Socialism in the 1840's." *New York History,* 28 (1947), 128–58.

Braam, J. W. "The Ruskin Colony." *American Journal of Sociology,* 8 (1902–1903), 667–80.

Bradford, George P. "Reminiscences of Brook Farm." *The Century,* 45 (1892–1893), 141–48.

Bridge, John R. "Nationalistic Socialism." *Arena,* 1 (1889–1890), 184–95.

Brisbane, Albert. "The American Associationists." *United States and Democratic Review,* 18 (1846), 142–47.

—— "Association and Attractive Industry." *Ibid.,* 10 (1842), 30–44.

Brommel, Bernard J. "Debs's Cooperative Commonwealth Plan for Workers." *Labor History,* 12 (1971), 560–69.

Buchanan, J. R. "The Land and the People." *Herald of Truth,* 2 (1847), 169–81 and 249–64.

Buchstein, Frederick. "Josiah Warren: The Peaceful Revolutionist." *The Cincinnati Historical Society Bulletin,* 32 (1974), 61–71.

Bushee, Frederick A. "Communistic Societies in the United States." *Political Science Quarterly,* 20 (1905), 625–64.

Butler, Francelia. "The Ruskin Commonwealth." *Tennessee Historical Quarterly,* 23 (1964), 333–42.

Campbell, D'Ann. "Women's Life in Utopia: The Shaker Experiment in Sexual Equality Reappraised—1810–1860." *New England Quarterly,* 51 (1978), 23–38.

Carpenter, Frederic, ed. "A Letter from Tolstoy." *Ibid.,* 4 (1931), 777–82.

Carpenter, Garrett R. "Silkville: A Kansas Attempt in the History of Fourierist Utopia, 1869–1892." *The Emporia State Research Studies,* 3(2) (1954).

Cary, Francine C. "The World A Department Store: Bradford Peck and the Utopian Endeavor." *American Quarterly,* 29 (1977), 370–84.

Bibliography: Articles

Carmony, Donald F. and Joseph M. Elliott. "New Harmony, Indiana: Robert Owen's Seedbed for Utopia." *Indiana Magazine of History,* 76 (1980), 161–161.

Casson, Herbert N. "The Ruskin Co-operative Colony." *Independent,* 51 (1899), 192–95.

Collins, Earl A. "The Multitude Incorporated." *Missouri Historical Review,* 27 (1932–33), 303–6.

Conforti, Joseph A. "Samuel Hopkins and the New Divinity." *William & Mary Quarterly,* 34 (1977), 572–89.

Copeland, W. E. "The Co-operative Brotherhood." *Arena,* 28 (1902), 403–5.

——— "The Cooperative Brotherhood and Its Colony." *Independent,* 55 (1903), 317–23.

Coursen, Alfred C. "Is Bellamy's Idea Feasible?" *Arena,* 21 (1899), 602–9.

Cox, J. Sullivan. "Imaginary Commonwealths." *The United States and Democratic Review,* 19 (1846), 175–85.

Curtis, George William. "Hawthorne and Brook Farm." *From the Easy Chair* (Repr.: New York: Greenwood, 1969), 3, 1–19.

Davies, Wallace Evan. "A Collectivist Experiment Down East: Bradford Peck and the Cooperative Association of America." *New England Quarterly,* 20 (1947), 471–91.

Debs, Eugene V. "The Social Democracy." *The New Times* (Aug. 1897), 78–79.

——— "The Socialist Party's Appeal." *Independent,* 57 (1904), 835–40; 65 (1908), 875–80; 73 (1912), 950–52.

Dubofsky, Melvyn. "Socialism and Syndicalism." In John H. M. Laslett and Seymour Lipset, eds. *Failure of a Dream? Essays in the History of American Socialism.* Garden City, N.Y.: Doubleday, 1974, 252–81.

Eads, George W. "N. O. Nelson, Practical Cooperator and the Great Work He is Accomplishing for Human Uplift." *Arena,* 36 (1906), 463–80.

Ely, Richard T. "Pullman: A Social Study." *Harper's Magazine,* 70 (1885), 452–61.

——— "A Study of a 'Decreed' Town [Greeley]." *Harpers Monthly,* 106 (1903), 390–401.

Evans, Frederick W. "Autobiography of a Shaker." *Atlantic Monthly,* 23 (1869), 415–25.

[Everett, Edward]. "The Shakers." *North American Review,* 16 (1823), 76–102.

Fish, John O. "The Christian Commonwealth Colony: A Georgia Experiment, 1896–1900." *Georgia Historical Quarterly,* 57 (1973), 213–26.

Flower, Benjamin O. "Is Socialism Desirable?" *Arena,* 3 (1890–91), 753–64.

Fogarty, Robert S. "American Communes, 1865–1914." *Journal of American Studies,* 9 (1975), 145–62.

——— "Oneida: A Utopian Search for Religious Security." *Labor History,* 14 (1973), 202–27.

Fox, Wendall P. "The Kendall Community." *Ohio Archaelogical and Historical Quarterly,* 29 (1911), 176–219.

Gooden, Rosemary. "A Preliminary Examination of the Shaker Attitude Toward Work." *Communal Societies,* 3 (1983), 1–15.

Garland, Hamlin. "A New Declaration of Rights." *Arena,* 3 (1890–91), 157–84.

Garrison, William Lloyd. "The Mask of Tyranny." *Ibid.,* 1 (1889–90), 553–59.

Gaskins, J. W. "The Anarchists at Home, Washington." *Independent,* 68 (1910), 914–22.

Gaston, Ernest B. "Fairhope, the Home of the Single Tax and the Referendum." *Ibid.,* 55 (1903), 1670–77.

Bibliography: Articles

Grant, H. Roger. "Henry Olerich and the Utopian Ideal." *Nebraska History,* 56 (1975), 248–58.

—— "Missouri's Utopian Communities." *Missouri Historical Review,* 66 (1971), 20–48.

—— " 'One Who Dares to Plan': Charles W. Caryl and the New Era Union." *The Colorado Magazine,* 51 (1974), 13–25.

Green, James R. "The 'Salesmen-Soldiers' of the *Appeal* Army." In Bruch Stave, ed. *Socialism and the Cities.* Port Washington, N.Y.: Kennikat Press, 1975, 13–40.

Hall, Bowman N. "The Economic Ideas of Josiah Warren, First American Anarchist." *History of Political Economy,* 6 (1974), 95–108.

—— "Joshua K. Ingalls, American Individualist." *American Journal of Economics and Sociology,* 39 (1980), 383–96.

Harsin, Jill. "Housework and Utopia: Women and the Owenite Socialist Communities." In Ruby Rohrlich and Elain Baruch, eds. *Women in Search of Utopia.* New York: Schocken Books, 1984.

Hebert, William. "A Visit to the Colony of Harmony." *Indiana As Seen By Early Travelers.* Indianapolis: Indiana Historical Commission, 1916.

Howells, William Dean. "A Shaker Village." *Atlantic Monthly,* 37 (1876), 699–710.

Howland, Edward. "The Familistere at Guise, France." *Harper's Magazine,* 71 (1885), 912–18.

—— "The Social Palace at Guise." *Ibid.,* 44 (1871–72), 701–16.

Huxley, Aldous. "Llano Del Rio: Oxymondius, the Utopia that Failed." *California Historical Quarterly,* 51 (1971), 119–30.

Kagan, Paul. "Llano Del Rio: Portrait of a California Utopia." *Ibid.,* 131–54.

Kaplan, Lawrence. "A Utopia During the Progressive Era: The Helicon Home Colony, 1906–1907. *American Studies,* 25 (1980), 59–73.

Katscher, Leopold. "Owen's Topolobampo Colony, Mexico." *American Journal of Sociology,* 12 (1906), 145–75.

Kegel, Charles H., ed. "Earl Miller's Recollections of the Ruskin Cooperative Association." *Tennessee Historical Quarterly,* 17 (1958), 45–69.

Kent, Alexander. "Cooperative Communities in the United States." *Bulletin of the Department of Labor,* 6 (1901), 563–646.

Kirchmann, George. "Why Did They Stay? Communal Life at the North American Phalanx." *Planned and Utopian Experiments: Four New Jersey Towns,* Paul A. Stellhorn, ed. Trenton: New Jersey Historical Commission, 1980.

—— "Unsettled Utopias: The North American Phalanx and the Raritan Bay Union." *New Jersey History,* 97 (1979), 25–36.

Lauer, Jeanette C. and Robert H. Lauer, "Sex Roles in Nineteenth-Century American Communal Societies." *Communal Societies,* 3 (1983), 16–28.

"Llano Cooperative Colony." *Monthly Labor Review,* 32 (1931), 1133–41.

McHugh, Christine. "Midwestern Populist Leadership and Edward Bellamy." *American Studies,* 19 (Fall 1978), 57–74.

McMullin, Thomas A. "Lost Alternative: The Urban Industrial Utopia of William D. Howland." *New England Quarterly,* 55 (1982), 25–38.

Madison, Charles A. "Benjamin Tucker: Individualist and Anarchist." *New England Quarterly,* 16 (1943), 444–67.

Bibliography: Articles

Mills, Benjamin Fay. "The New Party." *Arena,* 21 (1899), 1–14.

Montoliu, C. "Fairhope—A Town-Planning Scheme for Its Development into an Organic City." *American City,* 24 (1921), 355–59.

Moorhead, James H. "The Erosion of Postmillennialism in American Religious Thought, 1865–1925." *Church History,* 53 (1984), 61–77.

Morgan, H. Wayne. "The Utopia of Eugene V. Debs." *American Quarterly,* 11 (1959), 120–35.

Nelson, N. O. "Co-operation." *Independent,* 71 (1911), 643–45.

—— "Leclaire—An Existing City of the Future." *Ibid.,* 77 (1914), 100.

—— "Profit Sharing." *Ibid.,* 71 (1911), 858–60.

—— "Profit-Sharing with the Customer." *Ibid.,* 58 (1905), 1179–82.

Olin, Spencer C., Jr. "The Oneida Community and the Instability of Charismatic Leadership." *Journal of American History,* 67 (1980), 285–300.

Oved, Yaacov. "Communes & the Outside World." *Communal Societies,* 3 (1983), 83–92.

Owen, Robert Dale. "The Social Experiment at New Harmony: A Chapter of Autobiography." *Atlantic Monthly,* 32 (1873), 224–36.

—— "My Experiences of Community Life." *Ibid.,* 336–48.

Pedrick, S. M. "The Wisconsin Phalanx at Ceresco." *Proceedings of the State Historical Society of Wisconsin* (1902), 190–226.

Peirce, Mrs. C. F. "Co-operative Housekeeping." *Atlantic Monthly,* 22 (1868), 513–24, 682–97; 23 (1868), 29–39, 161–71, 186–99.

Perella, Frank. "Henry George, the Classical Model and Technological Change." *American Journal of Economics and Sociology,* 40 (1981), 191–206.

Pitzer, Donald E. "Education in Utopia: The New Harmony Experience," Indiana Historical Society, *Lectures, 1976–1977.* Indianapolis, 1978, 74–101.

Powell, R. F. "A Single-Tax Colony: An Economic Experiment at Fairhope, Alabama." *Review of Reviews,* 76 (1927), 187–92.

Quint, Howard H. "Julius Wayland, Pioneer Socialist Propagandist." *Mississippi Valley Historical Review,* 35(1948–49), 585–606.

Robertson, Constance Noyes. "The Oneida Community." *New York History,* 30 (1949), 131–50.

Rollins, Richard M. "Adin Ballou and the Perfectionist Dilemma." *Journal of Church and State,* 17 (1975), 459–76.

Sadler, Elizabeth. "One Book's Influence. Edward Bellamy's 'Looking Backward.' " *New England Quarterly,* 17 (1944), 530–37.

Schiffman, Joseph. "Edward Bellamy's Altruistic Man." *American Quarterly,* 6 (1954), 195–209.

—— "Edward Bellamy's Religious Thought." PMLA, 68 (1963), 716–32.

Shoemaker, Joel. "A Co-operative Commonwealth." *Arena,* 27 (1902), 164–73.

—— "The New Eden." *Overland,* 61 (1913), 291–94.

Sinclair, Upton. "A Home Colony." *Independent,* 60 (1906), 1401–8.

Slosson, E. E. "An Experiment in Anarchy." *Ibid.,* 55 (1903), 779–85.

Smythe, William E. "Real Utopias in the Arid West." *Atlantic Monthly,* 78 (1897), 599–609.

Bibliography: Articles

Sokolow, Jayme A. "Culture and Utopia: The Raritan Bay Union." *New Jersey History*, 94 (1976), 89–100.

Spurlock, John Calvin. "Anarchy & Community at Modern Times, 1851–1863." *Communal Societies*, 3 (1983), 29–47.

Steffens, Lincoln. "Eugene V. Debs." *Everybody's*, 19 (1908), 455–69.

Stokes, J. G. Phelps. "Reasons for Supporting Debs." *Outlook*, 90 (1908), 378–81.

Sumner, W. G. "The Absurd Effort to Make the World Over." *Forum*, 19 (1894), 92–102.

Swift, Morris I. "Altruria in California." *Overland Monthly*, ser. 2, 29 (1897), 643–45.

Vassault, F. I. "Nationalism in California." *Overland Monthly*, ser. 2, 15 (1890), 659–61.

Vrooman, Hiram. "The Co-operative Association of America." *Arena*, 28 (1902), 602–9.

—— "A National Co-operative Conference." *Ibid.*, 27 (1902), 611–14.

[Washburn, George F.] "A Conversation with George F. Washburn. . . . How to Meet the Trust Problem through Co-operation." *Ibid.*, 28 (1902), 406–15.

Wilson, Lewis G. "Hopedale and Its Founder." *New England Magazine*, n.s. 4 (1891), 197–212.

Wilson, R. Jackson. "Experience and Utopia: The Making of Edward Bellamy's *Looking Backward*." *Journal of American Studies*, 11 (1977), 45–60.

Wilson, William E. "The Boatload of Knowledge: The Journey of Robert Owen's Disciples by Keelboat." *South Atlantic Quarterly*, 74 (1975), 104–17.

—— "Social Experiments on the Wabash: New Harmony, Indiana." *A Vanishing America*, Thomas C. Wheeler, ed. New York: Holt, Rhinehart and Winston, 1964.

Winter, Donald E. "The Utopianism of Survival: Bellamy's *Looking Backward* and Twain's *A Connecticut Yankee*." *American Studies*, 21 (Fall 1980), 23–38.

Wisbey, Herbert A., Jr. "Research Note: Rufus Rockwell Wilson's Tour of Five Utopian Communities in 1888." *Communal Societies*, 3 (1983), 140–46.

BOOKS

Aaron, Daniel. *Men of Good Hope*. New York: Oxford University Press, 1951.

Adams, Herbert, et. al. *History of Cooperation in the United States*. Baltimore, 1888.

Adams, John Quincy. *Memoirs*, Charles Francis Adams, ed. 12 vols. Philadelphia, 1874–77.

Albertson, Ralph. *A Survey of Mutualistic Communities in America*. Repr.: New York: AMS Press, 1973.

Altfest, Karen Caplan. *Robert Owen as Educator*. Boston: Twayne, 1977.

Alyea, Paul E. and Blanche R. *Fairhope, 1894–1954*. Tuscaloosa: University of Alabama Press, 1956.

Ameringer, Oscar. *If You Don't Weaken*, introduction by James R. Green. Norman: University of Oklahoma Press, 1983.

Andelson, Robert V., ed. *Critics of Henry George*. Rutherford, N.J.: Fairleigh Dickinson University Press, 1979.

Anderson, Frederick, et. al., eds. *Selected Mark Twain-Howells Letters, 1872–1910*. Cambridge: Harvard University Press, 1967.

Bibliography: Books

Andrews, Edward D. *The People Called Shakers*. New York: Oxford University Press, 1953.

Arndt, Karl J. R. *George Rapp's Harmony Society, 1785–1847*. Philadelphia: University of Pennsylvania Press, 1965.

—— *George Rapp's Successors and Material Heirs, 1847–1916*. Rutherford: N.J.: Fairleigh Dickinson University Press, 1971.

Arndt, Karl J. R., ed. *A Documentary History of the Indiana Decade of the Harmony Society*. 2 vols. Indianapolis: Indiana Historical Society, 1975.

Aveling, Edward B. and Eleanor Marx. *The Working-Class Movement in America*. London, 1981.

Bailie, William. *Josiah Warren: The First American Anarchist*. Repr.: Brooklyn, N.Y.: Herbert C. Roseman, 1971.

Ballou, Adin. *History of Hopedale Community*. Repr.: Philadelphia: Porcupine Press, 1972.

—— *Practical Christian Socialism*. Repr.: N.Y.: AMS Press, 1974.

Barker, Charles A. *Henry George*. New York: Oxford University Press, 1955.

Bedford, Henry F. *Socialism and the Workers in Massachusetts, 1886–1912*. Amherst: University of Massachusetts Press, 1966.

Bauman, Zygmunt. *Socialism: The Active Utopia*. New York: Holmes & Meier, 1976.

Bellamy, Edward. *Edward Bellamy Speaks Again*. Kansas City: The Peerage Press, 1937.

—— *Equality*. Repr.: New York: AMS Press, 1970.

—— *Looking Backward*, John L. Thomas, ed. Cambridge, Mass.: Harvard University Press, 1967.

—— *Selected Writings on Religion and Society*, Joseph Schiffman, ed. New York: Liberal Arts Press, 1955.

Bender, Thomas. *Community and Social Change in America*. New Brunswick, N.J.: Rutgers University Press, 1978.

Bernard, L. L. and Jessie. *Origins of American Sociology*. New York: Thomas Y. Crowell, 1943.

Bestor, Arthur E., Jr. *Backwoods Utopias: The Sectarian and Owenite Phases of Communitarian Socialism in America, 1663–1829*. Philadelphia: University of Pennsylvania Press, 1950.

Bestor, Arthur E., Jr., ed. *Education and Reform at New Harmony: Correspondence of William Maclure and Marie Duclos Fretageot, 1820–1833*. Indianapolis: Indiana Historical Society, 1949.

Blatchly, Cornelius. *An Essay on Commonwealths*. New York, 1823.

Block, Marguerite B. *The New Church in the New World: A Study of Swedenborgianism in America*. New York: Henry Holt, 1932.

Bowman, Sylvia E., et al. *Edward Bellamy Abroad: An American Prophet's Influence*. New York: Twayne, 1962.

—— *The Year 2000: A Critical Biography of Edward Bellamy*. New York: Bookman Associates, 1958.

Brisbane, Albert. *Association; or A Concise Exposition of the Practical Part of Fourier's Social Science*. Repr.: New York: AMS Press, 1975.

—— *Social Destiny of Man, or Association and Reorganization of Industry*. Repr.: August M. Kelley, 1969.

Bibliography: Books

—— *Treatise on the Functions of the Human Passions and An Outline of Fourier's System of Social Science*. Repr.: Gordon Press, 1972.

Brisbane, Redelia. *Albert Brisbane: A Mental Biography*. Boston, 1893.

Brissenden, Paul F. *The I.W.W.: A Study of American Syndicalism*. New York: Russell & Russell, 1957.

Brommel, Bernard J. *Eugene V. Debs: Spokesman for Labor and Socialism*. Chicago: Charles H. Kerr, 1978.

Broome, Isaac. *The Last Days of the Ruskin Co-operative Association*. Chicago: Charles H. Kerr, 1902.

Brown, Bob. *Can We Co-operate?* Staten Island, N.Y.: Roving Eye Press, 1940.

Brown, Paul. *Twelve Months in New-Harmony*. Repr.: Philadelphia: Porcupine Press, 1972.

Brown, T. Edwin. *Studies in Modern Socialism and Labor Problems*. New York, 1886.

Bruce, Robert V. *1877: Year of Violence*. Indianapolis: Bobbs-Merrill, 1959.

Buder, Stanley. *Pullman: An Experiment in Industrial Order and Community Planning, 1880–1930*. New York: Oxford University Press, 1967.

Buhle, Paul M. *Marxism in the United States, 1900–1940*. Ph.D. dissertation: University of Wisconsin. 1975 (University Microfilms).

Burbank, Garin. *When Farmers Voted Red: The Gospel of Socialism in the Oklahoma Countryside, 1910–1924*. Westport, Conn.: Greenwood, 1976.

Butt, John, ed. *Robert Owen: Aspects of His Life and Work—A Symposium*. New York: Humanities Press, 1971.

Cady, Edwin H. *William Dean Howells . . . 1885–1920*. Syracuse: Syracuse University Press, 1958.

Canby, Henry S. *Thoreau*. Boston: Beacon Press, 1939.

Cantor, Milton. *Max Eastman*. New York: Twayne, 1970.

Carden, Maren L. *Oneida: Utopian Community to Modern Corporation*. New York: Harper & Row, 1971.

Carlson, Oliver. *Brisbane: A Candid Biography*. New York: Stackpole, 1937.

Carter, Paul A. *The Spiritual Crisis of the Gilded Age*. DeKalb, Ill.: Northern Illinois University Press, 1971.

Chamberlain, John. *Farewell to Reform*. New York: Liveright, 1932.

Chaplin, Ralph. *Wobbly*. Chicago: University of Chicago Press, 1948.

Chase, Warren. *Forty Years on the Spiritual Rostrum*. Boston, 1888.

—— *The Life-Line of the Lone One*. 3rd ed. Boston, 1861.

Codman, John T. *Brook Farm: Historic and Personal Memoir*. Boston, 1894.

Cole, G. D. H. *The Life of Robert Owen*. London: Macmillan, 1930.

Commons, John R., et al. *A Documentary History of American Industrial Society*. 10 vols. Repr.: New York: Russell & Russell, 1958.

Conkin, Paul K. *Two Paths to Utopia: The Hutterites and the Llano Colony*. Lincoln: University of Nebraska Press, 1964.

Conway, Moncure D. *Autobiography*. 2 vols. Boston and N.Y.: Houghton and Mifflin, 1904.

Cook, Reginald L. *Passage to Walden*. New York: Russell & Russell, 1966.

Cowling, Ellis. *Co-operation in America*. New York: Coward-McCann, 1938.

Bibliography: Books

Critchlow, Donald T. *Socialism in the Heartland: The Midwestern Experience, 1900–1925.* Notre Dame, Ind.: University of Notre Dame Press, 1986.

Cross, Whitney R. *The Burned-Over District: The Social and Intellectual History of Enthusiastic Religion in Western New York, 1800–1850.* New York: Harper & Row, 1950.

Crowe, Charles. *George Ripley: Transcendentalist and Utopian Socialist.* Athens: University of Georgia Press, 1967.

Curtis, Edith Roelker. *A Season in Utopia: The Story of Brook Farm.* New York, 1961.

Davis, Frances. *A Fearful Innocence.* Kent, Ohio: Kent State University, Press, 1981.

Debs, Eugene V. *Papers,* microfilm edition, edited by J. Robert Constantine, et. al. Terre Haute: Indiana State University, 1984.

—— *Writings and Speeches,* Arthur M. Schlesinger, Jr., ed. New York: Hermitage Press, 1948.

Delano, Sterling F. *The Harbinger and New England Transcendentalism.* Rutherford, N.J.: Fairleigh Dickinson University Press, 1983.

DeLeon, David. *The American as Anarchist: Reflections on Indigenous Radicalism.* Baltimore: The Johns Hopkins University Press, 1978.

De Mille, Anna George. *Henry George: Citizen of the World,* Don C. Shoemaker, ed. Chapel Hill: University of North Carolina Press, 1950.

Desroche, Henri. *The American Shakers: From Neo-Christianity to Presocialism,* John K. Savacool, trans. and ed. Amherst: University of Massachusetts Press, 1971.

Destler, Chester M. *Henry Demarest Lloyd and the Empire of Reform.* Philadelphia: University of Pennsylvania Press, 1963.

Dombrowski, James. *The Early Days of Christian Socialism in America.* New York: Columbia University Press, 1936.

Dublin, Thomas, ed. *Farm to Factory: Women's Letters, 1830–1860.* New York: Columbia University Press, 1981.

Duss, John S. *The Harmonists: A Personal History.* Philadelphia: Porcupine Press, 1972.

Dwight, Timothy. *Travels in New England and New York,* Barbara Solomon, ed. 4 vols. Cambridge, Mass.: Harvard University Press, 1967.

Edger, Henry. *Modern Times, The Labor Question, and the Family.* New York, 1855.

Edson, Milan C. *Solaris Farm.* Repr.: New York: Arno, 1971.

Ellis, John B. *Free Love and Its Votaries: American Socialism Unmasked.* Repr.: New York: AMS, 1971.

Emerson, Ralph Waldo. *The Complete Essays,* Brooks Atkinson, ed. New York: Modern Library, 1950.

—— *Letters,* Ralph L. Rusk, ed. 6 vols. New York: Columbia University Press, 1939.

Engels, Friedrich. *Socialism: Utopian and Scientific,* Edward Aveling, trans. Chicago: Charles H. Kerr, 1914.

Etzler, John Adophus. *The Collected Works,* Joel Nydahl, ed. Delmar, N.Y.: Scholars' Facsimiles & Reprints, 1977.

—— *The Paradise Within the Reach of Man, Without Labor, By Powers of Nature and Machinery.* Pittsburgh, 1833.

Evans, Frederick William. *Autobiography of a Shaker.* Mt. Lebanon, N.Y., 1869.

Federal Writers Project. *Alabama.* New York: Richard B. Smith, 1941.

—— *California.* New York: Hastings House, 1941.

—— *Florida*. New York: Oxford University Press, 1939.

—— *New Jersey*. New York: Viking, 1939.

—— *Wisconsin*. Duell, Sloan and Pearce, 1941.

Fellman, Michael. *The Unbounded Frame: Freedom and Community in Nineteenth Century American Utopianism*. Westport, Conn., 1973.

Feuer, Lewis S., ed. *Marx & Engels: Basic Writings on Politics & Philosophy*. New York: Doubleday, 1959.

Fishbein, Leslie. *Rebels in Bohemia: The Radicals of the Masses, 1911–1917*. Chapel Hill: University of North Carolina Press, 1982.

Flower, Benjamin O. *Progressive Men, Women, and Movements of the Past Twenty-Five Years*. Boston: New Arena, 1914.

Flynn, Elizabeth Gurley. *I Speak My Own Piece*. New York: Masses & Mainstream, 1955.

Foner, Philip S. *The Bolshevik Revolution: Its Impact on American Radicals, Liberals, and Labor*. New York: International, 1967.

—— *Jack London: American Rebel*. New York: Citadel, 1964.

Foster, Lawrence. *Religion and Sexuality: Three American Communal Experiments of the Nineteenth Century*. New York: Oxford University Press, 1981.

Fourier, Charles. *Design for Utopia: Selected Writings*, edited by Charles Gide and with a new introduction by Frank Manuel. New York: Schocken Books, 1971.

—— *The Social Destiny of Man*, translated by Henry Clapp, Jr. Repr.: New York: Gordon Press, 1972.

—— *The Utopian Vision of Charles Fourier: Selected Texts on Work, Love, and Passionate Attraction*, translated and edited by Jonathan Beecher and Richard Bienvenu. Boston, 1971.

Fredrickson, George M. *The Inner Civil War: Northern Intellectuals and the Crisis of Union*. New York: Harper & Row, 1965.

Fried, Albert, ed. *Socialism in America. From the Shakers to the Third International: A Documentary History*. Garden City, New York: Doubleday, 1970.

Frothingham, Octavius Brooks. *George Ripley*. Boston, 1888.

—— *Memoir of William Henry Channing*. Boston, 1886.

Gausted, Edwin S., ed. *The Rise of Adventism*. New York: Harper & Row, 1974.

Geiger, George R. *The Philosophy of Henry George*. New York: Macmillan, 1933.

Geissler, L. A. *Looking Beyond, a Sequel to "Looking Backward" and An Answer to "Looking Further Forward."* London, 1891.

George, Henry. *The Land Question*. New York: Robert Schalkenbach Foundation, 1941.

—— *Our Land and Land Policy*. New York: Doubleday and McClure, 1902.

—— *Progress and Poverty: An Inquiry into the Cause of Industrial Depressions and of Increase of Want with Increase of Wealth*. New York: Robert Schalkenbach Foundation, 1937.

George, Henry, Jr. *The Life of Henry George*. Garden City, N.Y.: Doubleday, Doran, 1930.

Ghent, William J. *Our Benevolent Feudalism*. New York: Macmillan, 1902.

Gide, Charles. *Communist and Co-operative Colonies*, E. F. Rowe, trans. New York: Crowell, 1930.

Gilman, Charlotte Perkins. *The Living of Charlotte Perkins Gilman*. New York: D. Appleton-Century, 1935.

—— *Herland,* with an introduction by Ann J. Lane. New York: Pantheon, 1979.
Gilman, Nicholas Paine. *Socialism and the American Spirit.* Boston and N.Y., 1893.
Ginger, Ray. *Eugene V. Debs.* New York: Macmillan, 1962.
Godwin, Parke. *Democracy, Constructive and Pacific.* New York, 1844.
—— *A Popular View of the Doctrines of Charles Fourier.* Repr.: Philadelphia: Porcupine Press, 1972.
Goldman, Emma. *Living My Life.* New York: Knopf, 1934.
Golemba, Henry L. *George Ripley.* Boston: Twayne, 1977.
Gooch, G. P. *English Democratic Ideas in the 17th Century.* New York: Harper & Brothers, 1959.
Greeley, Horace. *Recollections of a Busy Life.* New York, 1868.
Green, James R. *Grass-Roots Socialism: Radical Movements in the Southwest, 1895–1943.* Baton Rouge: Louisiana State University Press, 1978.
Greenwalt, Emmett A. *California Utopia: Point Loma, 1897–1942.* San Diego: Point Loma, 1978.
Gronlund, Laurence. *The Cooperative Commonwealth,* Stowe Persons, ed. Cambridge, Mass.: Harvard University Press, 1965.
Gutek, Gerald Lee. *Joseph Neef: The Americanization of Pestalozzianism.* Tuscaloosa: University of Alabama Press, 1978.
Hale, Edward Everett. *How They Lived in Hampton.* Boston, 1888.
Hale, William H. *Horace Greeley: Voice of the People.* New York: Harper & Brothers, 1950.
Handlin, Oscar and Mary F. *Facing Life: Youth and the Family in American History.* Boston: Atlantic Monthly, 1971.
Hansot, Elizabeth. *Perfection and Progress: Two Modes of Utopian Thought.* Cambridge, Mass: MIT Press, 1974.
Harding, Walter. *The Days of Henry Thoreau.* New York: Knopf, 1967.
Harmony Society. *A Documentary History of the Indiana Decade of the Harmony Society,* Karl J. R. Arndt, ed. 2 vols. Indianapolis: Indiana Historical Society, 1975.
Harris, Leon. *Upton Sinclair: American Rebel.* New York: Crowell, 1975.
Harrison, J. F. C. *Robert Owen and the Owenites in Britain and America.* London, 1969.
—— *The Second Coming: Popular Millenarianism, 1780–1850.* New Brunswick, N.J.: Rutgers University Press, 1979.
Hawkins, Richard L. *Positivism in the United States (1853–1861).* Cambridge: Harvard University Press, 1938.
Hayden, Dolores. *The Grand Domestic Revolution: A History of Feminist Designs for American Homes, Neighborhoods, and Cities.* Cambridge: MIT Press, 1981.
—— *Seven American Utopias: The Architecture of Communitarian Socialism, 1790–1975.* Cambridge: MIT Press, 1976.
Hecht, David. *Russian Radicals Look to America, 1825–1894.* Cambridge: Harvard University Press, 1947.
Herreshoff, David. *American Disciples of Marx: From the Age of Jackson to the Progressive Era.* Detroit: Wayne State University Press, 1967.
Hertzler, Joyce O. *The History of Utopian Thought.* New York: Macmillan, 1923.
Hicks, Granville. *John Reed: The Making of a Revolutionary.* New York: Macmillan, 1936.

Bibliography: Books

Higginson, Thomas Wentworth. *Letters and Journals,* edited by Mary T. Higginson. Repr.: New York: Negro Universities Press, 1969.
Hill, Mary A. *Charlotte Perkins Gilman: The Making of a Radical Feminist, 1860–1896.* Philadelphia: Temple University Press, 1980.
Hillquit, Morris. *History of Socialism in the United States,* fifth revision. New York: Funk & Wagnalls, 1910.
—— *Loose Leaves from a Busy Life.* New York: Macmillan, 1934.
—— *Socialism in Theory and Practice.* N.Y.: Macmillan, 1907.
Hinds, William A. *American Communities.* Oneida, N.Y., 1878.
Hine, Robert V. *California's Utopian Colonies.* San Marino, Calif.: Huntington Library, 1953.
Hobston, J. A. *John Ruskin: Social Reformer.* Boston, 1898.
Hofstadter, Richard. *Social Darwinism in American Thought.* Boston: Beacon Press, 1955.
Holloway, Jean. *Edward Everett Hale.* Austin: University of Texas Press, 1956.
Holloway, Mark. *Heavens on Earth: Utopian Communities in America, 1680–1880.* New York: Dover, 1966.
Hopkins, Samuel. *A Treatise on the Millennium.* Repr.: New York: Arno, 1972.
Horgan, Edward R. *The Shaker Holy Land: A Community Portrait.* Harvard, Mass: Harvard Common Press, 1982.
Howells, William Dean. *Life in Letters,* Mildred Howells, ed. 2 vols. New York: Russell & Russell, 1968.
—— *A Traveler from Altruria,* introduction by Howard Mumford Jones. New York: Sagamore Press, 1957.
Howland, Marie. *The Familistere,* introduction by Robert S. Fogarty. Repr.: Philadelphia: Porcupine Press, 1975.
Hughan, Jessie W. *American Socialism of the Present Day.* New York: John Lane, 1912.
Humphrey, Robert E. *Children of Fantasy: The First Rebels of Greenwich Village.* New York: Wiley, 1978.
Hyfler, Robert M. *American Socialist Thought: From Debs to Harrington.* Ph.D. dissertation: University of Massachusetts, 1980 (University Microfilms).
—— *Prophets of the Left: American Socialist Thought in the Twentieth Century.* Westport, Conn.: Greenwood, 1984.
Infield, Henrik F. *Cooperative Communities at Work.* New York: The Dryden Press, 1945.
—— *Utopia and Experiment: Essays in the Sociology of Cooperation.* New York: Paeger, 1955.
Ingalls, Joshua King. *Reminiscences of an Octogenarian.* Elmira, N.Y., 1897.
Jackson, Holbrook. *Dreamers of Dreams: The Rise and Fall of 19th Century Idealism.* London: Faber and Faber, 1948.
Jaher, Frederic Cople. *Doubters and Dissenters: Cataclysmic Thought in America, 1885–1918.* N.Y.: Free Press of Glencoe, 1964.
Johnson, Oakley C., ed. *Robert Owen in the United States.* New York: Humanities Press, 1970.
Johnson, Paul E. *A Shopkeeper's Millennium: Society and Revivals in Rochester, New York, 1815–1837.* New York: Hill & Wang, 1978.

Kanter, Rosabeth Moss. *Commitment and Community: Communes and Utopias in Sociological Perspective.* Cambridge: Harvard University Press, 1972.

Kaplan, Justin. *Lincoln Steffens.* New York: Simon & Schuster, 1974.

Karsner, David. *Debs: His Authorized Life and Letters.* New York: Boni and Liveright, 1919.

Kelly, Edmond. *Twentieth Century Socialism.* New York: Longmans, Greene, 1913.

Kephart, William M. *Extraordinary Groups: The Sociology of Unconventional Life-Styles.* New York: St. Martin's, 1976.

Kern, Louis J. *An Ordered Love: Sex Roles and Sexuality in Victorian Utopias.* Chapel Hill: University of North Carolina Press, 1981.

Kesselman, Steven. *The Modernization of American Reform.* New York: Garland, 1979.

Kipnis, Ira. *The American Socialist Movement, 1897–1912.* New York: Columbia University Press, 1952.

Kring, Hilda A. *The Harmonists: A Folk-Cultural Approach.* Metuchen, N.J.: Scarecrow Press, 1973.

Kuklick, Bruce. *Josiah Royce: An Intellectual Biography.* Indianapolis: Bobbs-Merrill, 1972.

Laidler, Harry W. *The History of Socialism.* New York: Crowell, 1968.

Laslett, John H. M. and Seymour Martin Lipset, eds., *Failure of a Dream? Essays in the History of American Socialism.* Berkeley and Los Angeles: University of California Press, 1984.

Leavitt, Fred and Nancy Miller. *Pullman: Portrait of a Landmark Community.* Chicago: Historic Pullman Foundation, 1981.

Leopold, Richard W. *Robert Dale Owen.* Repr.: New York: Octagon, 1969.

LeWarne, Charles P. *Utopias on Puget Sound, 1885–1915.* Seattle: University of Washington Press, 1975.

Lewis, Arthur M. *Ten Blind Leaders of the Blind.* Chicago: Charles Kerr, 1919.

Lindley, Harlow, ed. *Indiana As Seen By Early Travelers.* Indianapolis: Indiana Historical Commission, 1916.

Lindsay, Nicholas Vachel. *Adventures, Rhymes & Designs,* with an essay by Robert F. Sayre. New York: The Eakins Press, 1968.

—— *The Golden Book of Springfield.* New York: Macmillan, 1920.

—— *Letters,* Marc Chenetier, ed. New York: Burt Franklin, 1979.

Lindsey, Almont. *The Pullman Strike.* Chicago: University of Chicago Press, 1942.

Lipow, Arthur. *Authoritarian Socialism in America: Edward Bellamy & the Nationalist Movement.* Berkeley and Los Angeles: University of California Press, 1982.

Lockwood, George B. *The New Harmony Movement.* New York: D. Appleton, 1905.

Lloyd, J. William. *The Natural Man: A Romance of the Golden Age.* Newark, N.J.: Benedict Prieth, 1902.

London, Jack. *War of the Classes.* New York: Macmillan, 1905.

Longley, Alcander. *What is Communism? A Narrative of the Relief Community.* Repr.: New York: AMS, 1976.

Macdonald, Donald. *Diaries . . . 1824–1826,* Caroline Dean Snedeker, ed. Indiana Historical Society, *Publications,* vol. 14, no. 2.

Macdonald, George E. *Fifty Years of Freethought.* 2 vols. Repr.: New York: Arno, 1972.

McLaughlin, Corinne and Gordon Davidson. *Builders of the Dawn*. Walpole, N.H.: Stillpoint Publishing, 1985.

MaMahon, William. *South Jersey Towns: History and Legend*. New Brunswick, N.J.: Rutgers University Press, 1973.

Macy, John. *Socialism in America*. Garden City, N.Y.: Doubleday, Page, 1916.

Malin, James C. *A Concern About Humanity. Notes on Reform, 1872–1912, At the National and Kansas Levels of Thought*. Lawrence, Kansas: James C. Malin, 1964.

Mannheim, Karl. *Ideology and Utopia*. New York: International Library, 1936.

Mann, Arthur. *Yankee Reformers in the Urban Age*. New York: Harper & Row, 1966.

Manuel, Frank E. *The Prophets of Paris*. Cambridge: Harvard University Press, 1962.

Manuel, Frank E. and Fritzie. *Utopian Thought in the Western World*. Cambridge: Harvard University Press, 1979.

Martin, Rose L. *Fabian Freeway: High Road to Socialism in the U.S.A., 1884–1966*. Chicago: Heritage Foundation, 1966.

Marsh, Margaret S. *Anarchist Women, 1870–1920*. Philadelphia: Temple University Press, 1981.

May, Henry F. *The End of American Innocence*. Chicago: Quadrangle, 1964.

Melcher, Marguerite Fellows. *The Shaker Adventure*. Princeton, N.J.: Princeton University Press, 1941.

Mellow, James R. *Nathaniel Hawthorne and His Times*. Boston: Houghton Mifflin, 1980.

Meyers, Mary Ann. *A New World Jerusalem: The Swedenborgian Experience in Community Construction*. Westport, Conn.: Greenwood, 1983.

Michaelis, Richard. *Looking Further Forward*. Repr.: New York: Arno, 1971.

Miers, Earl Schenck. *Down in New Jersey*. New Brunswick, N.J.: Rutgers University Press, 1973.

Miller, Perry. *The Transcendentalists: An Anthology*. Cambridge: Harvard University Press, 1950.

Moment, Gairdner and Otto F. Krauschaar, eds. *Utopias: The American Experience*. Metuchen, N.J.: Scarecrow Press, 1980.

Morgan, Arthur E. *Edward Bellamy*. New York: Columbia University Press, 1944.

Morgan, H. Wayne. *Eugene V. Debs: Socialist for President*. Westport, Conn.: Greenwood, 1973.

Morse, Flo. *The Shakers and the World's People*. New York: Dodd, Mead, 1980.

Morton, A. L. *The Life and Ideas of Robert Owen*. New York: International, 1969.

Mumford, Lewis. *Findings and Keepings: Analects for an Autobiography*. New York: Harcourt Brace Jovanovich, 1975.

—— *My Works and Days*. New York: Harcourt Brace Jovanovich, 1979.

—— *The Story of Utopias*. New York: Viking, 1962.

Muncy, Raymond L. *Sex and Marriage in Utopian Communities: 19th Century America*. Bloomington: Indiana University Press, 1973.

Myrick, Herbert. *How To Cooperate*. New York: Orange Judd Co., 1912.

Muzik, Edward J. *Victor Berger: A Biography*. Ph.D. dissertation: Northwestern University, 1980 (University Microfilms).

Nearing, Scott. *The Making of a Radical*. New York: Harper & Row, 1972.

Nichols, Thomas Low. *Forty Years of American Life, 1821–1861*. New York: Stackpole Sons, 1937.

Nordhoff, Charles. *The Communistic Societies of the United States*. New York: Schocken, 1965.

[North American Phalanx]. *Exposé of the Conditions and Progress of the North American Phalanx*, with an introduction by N. L. Swan and appendices by Fredrika Bremer and Charles Sears. Philadelphia: Porcupine Press, 1975.

Noyes, John Humphrey. *History of American Socialisms*. Repr.: New York, Dover, 1966.

—— *Home-Talks,* Alfred Barron and George Noyes Miller, eds. Repr.: AMS, 1975.

Olerich, Henry. *A Cityless and Countryless World: An Outline of Practical Co-operative Individualism*. Holstein, Iowa, 1893.

Oneida Community. *Bible Communism*. Repr.: Philadelphia: Porcupine Press, 1972.

O'Neill, William L. *Echoes of Revolt: The Masses, 1911–1917*. Chicago: Quadrangle, 1966.

Orvis, Marianne (Dwight). *Letters from Brook Farm, 1844–1847,* Amy L. Reed, ed. Repr.: Philadelphia: Porcupine Press, 1972.

Owen, Albert K. *Integral Co-operation: Its Practical Operation,* with an introduction by Robert S. Fogarty. Repr.: Philadelphia: Porcupine Press, 1975.

Owen, Robert. *The Life of Robert Owen*. Repr.: New York: August M. Kelly, 1971.

—— *The Life of Robert Owen,* with an introduction by John Butt. London: Charles Knight, 1971.

—— *A New View of Society and Other Writings,* introduction by G. D. H. Cole. New York: Dutton, 1963.

—— *The Book of the New Moral World*. 7 parts. Repr.: New York: August M. Kelly, 1970.

Owen, Robert Dale. *Threading My Way: Twenty-seven Years of Autobiography*. Repr.: New York: August M. Kelly, 1967.

Owen, William. *Diary . . . November 10, 1824 to April 20, 1825,* Joel W. Hiatt, ed. Indiana Historical Society, *Publications,* 4 (1906), no. 1.

Parker, Florence E. *The First Hundred Years: A History of Distributive and Service Cooperation in the United States*. Superior, Wisc., 1956.

Parker, Robert Allerton. *A Yankee Saint: John Humphrey Noyes and the Oneida Community*. New York: Putnam, 1935.

Parrington, Vernon L., Jr. *American Dreams: A Study of American Utopias*. New York: Russell & Russell, 1947.

Paulson, Ross E. *Radicalism & Reform: The Vrooman Family and American Social Thought, 1837–1937*. Lexington: University of Kentucky Press, 1968.

Pears, Thomas Clinton, Jr., ed. *New Harmony, An Adventure in Happiness: Papers of Thomas and Sarah Pears*. Indiana Historical Society. *Publications,* 11 (1937), no. 1.

Peck, Bradford. *The World A Department Store*. Repr.: New York: Arno, 1971.

Pelham, William. *Letters . . . 1825 and 1826* in Harlow Lindley, ed. *Indiana As Seen By Early Travelers*. Indianapolis: Indiana Historical Commission, 1916.

Perry, John. *Jack London: An American Myth*. Chicago: Nelson-Hall, 1981.

Persons, Stowe. *Free Religion*. New Haven: Yale University Press, 1947.

Pierson, George W. *Tocqueville in America,* abridged by D. C. Lunt. Garden City, N.Y.: Doubleday, 1959.

Pletcher, David M. *Rails, Mines, and Progress: Seven American Promoters in Mexico, 1867–1911*. Ithaca, N.Y.: Cornell University Press, 1958.

Podmore, Frank. *Modern Spiritualism.* 2 vols. London and New York: Methuen, 1902.

Post, Louis F. *The Prophet of San Francisco: Personal Memories and Interpretations of Henry George.* New York: Vanguard, 1930.

Price, Robert. *Johnny Appleseed, Man and Myth.* Repr.: Glouster, Mass.: Peter Smith, 1967.

Quint, Howard H. *The Forging of American Socialism.* Columbia: University of South Carolina Press, 1953.

Radosh, Ronald, ed. *Debs.* Englewood Cliffs, N.J.: Prentice-Hall, 1971.

Rae, John. *Contemporary Socialism.* New York, 1887.

Rauschenbusch, Walter. *A Theory for the Social Gospel.* New York and Nashville: Abingdon, 1945.

Reichert, William O. *Partisans of Freedom: A Study of American Anarchism.* Bowling Green, Ohio: Bowling Green Popular Press, 1976.

Reeve, Carl. *The Life and Times of Daniel DeLeon.* New York: Humanities Press, 1972.

Reps, John W. *The Making of Urban America: A History of City Planning in the United States.* Princeton, N.J.: Princeton University Press, 1965.

Reynolds, Ray. *Cat'spaw Utopia.* El Cajon, Calif.: The author, 1972.

Riasanovsky, Nicholas V. *The Teaching of Charles Fourier.* Berkeley and Los Angeles: University of California Press, 1969.

Robertson, Constance Noyes. *Oneida Community: The Breakup, 1876–1881.* Syracuse: Syracuse University Press, 1972.

Roemer, Kenneth M., ed. *America as Utopia.* New York: Burt Franklin, 1981.

—— *The Obsolete Necessity: America in Utopian Writings, 1888–1900.* Kent, Ohio: Kent State University Press, 1976.

Rose, Edward J. *Henry George.* New York: Twayne, 1968.

Rugoff, Milton. *Prudery and Passion.* New York: Putnam, 1971.

Salvatore, Nick. *Eugene V. Debs: Citizen and Socialist.* Urbana: University of Illinois Press, 1982.

Sams, Henry W., ed. *Autobiography of Brook Farm.* Englewood Cliffs, N.J.: Prentice-Hall, 1958.

Schuster, Eunice Minette. *Native American Anarchism: A Study of Left-Wing American Individualism.* Northampton, Mass.: Smith College Studies, 1932.

Sears, Charles. *The North American Phalanx: An Historical and Descriptive Sketch,* introduction by Edward Howland. Prescott, Wisc., 1886.

Sears, Clara Endicott. *Gleanings from Old Shaker Journals.* Boston and New York: Houghton Mifflin, 1916.

Sears, Hal D. *The Sex Radicals: Free Love in High Victorian America.* Lawrence: The Regents Press of Kansas, 1977.

Seretan, L. Glen. *Daniel DeLeon: The Odyssey of an American Marxist.* Cambridge: Harvard University Press, 1979.

Shatz, M. S., ed. *The Essential Works of Anarchism.* New York: 1971.

Sinclair, Upton. *Autobiography.* New York: Harcourt, Brace & World, 1962.

—— *The Industrial Republic.* New York: Doubleday, Page, 1907.

Smith, Titus. *Altruria.* Repr.: New York: Arno, 1971.

Sotheran, Charles. *Horace Greeley and Other Pioneers of American Socialism.* Repr.: New York: Haskell House, 1971.

Spargo, John. *The Psychology of Bolshevism*. New York: Harper & Brothers, 1919.
—— *Social Democracy Explained*. New York: Harper & Brothers, 1918.
—— *Socialism*. New York: Macmillan, 1912.
—— *The Substance of Socialism*. New York: Macmillan, 1909.
Spargo, John and George Louis Arner. *Elements of Socialism*. N.Y.: Macmillan, 1917.
Stalley, Marshall, ed. *Patrick Geddes: Spokesman for Man and the Environment*. New Brunswick, N.J.: Rutgers University Press, 1972.
Stedman, Laura and George M. Gould. *Life and Letters of Edmund Clarence Stedman*. 2 vols. New York: Moffit, Yard, 1910.
Steffens, Lincoln. *Autobiography*. New York: Harcourt, Brace, 1931.
Stern, Madeleine B. *Imprints on History: Book Publishers and American Frontiers*. Bloomington: Indiana University Press, 1956.
—— *The Pantarch: A Biography of Stephen Pearl Andrews*. Austin: University of Texas Press, 1968.
Stevens, Errol Wayne. *Heartland Socialism: The Socialist Party of America in Four Midwestern Communities, 1898–1920*. Ph.D. dissertation: Indiana University, 1978.
Stoehr, Taylor. *Free Love in America: A Documentary History*. New York: AMS, 1979.
Swift, Lindsay. *Brook Farm: Its Members, Scholars, and Visitors,* introduction by Joseph Schiffman. Repr. Secaucus, N.J.: The Citadel Press, 1973.
Symes, Lillian and Travers Clement. *Rebel America: The Story of Social Revolt in the United States*. Boston: Beacon Press, 1972.
Taylor, Anne. *Visions of Harmony: A Study in Nineteenth-Century Millenarianism*. Oxford, England: Clarendon Press, 1987.
Thelen, David. *Paths of Resistance: Tradition and Dignity in Industrializing Missouri*. New York: Oxford University Press, 1986.
Thomas, Benjamin. *Theodore Weld: Crusader for Freedom*. New Brunswick, N.J.: Rutgers University Press, 1950.
Thomas, John L. *Alternative America: Henry George, Edward Bellamy, Henry Demarest Lloyd, and the Adversary Tradition*. Cambridge, Mass.: Harvard University Press, 1983.
Thoreau, Henry David. *Correspondence,* Walter Harding and Carl Bode, eds. New York: New York University Press, 1958.
—— *Reform Papers,* Wendell Glick, ed. Princeton: N.J.: Princeton University Press, 1973.
—— *Walden and Other Writings,* Brooks Atkinson, ed. New York: Modern Library, 1950.
—— *Writings* (Walden Edition). 20 vols. Repr.: New York: AMS, 1968.
Toksvig, Signe. *Emmanuel Swedenborg: Scientist and Mystic*. New Haven: Yale University Press, 1948.
Tucker, Benjamin R. *Instead of a Book*. Repr.: New York: Gordon Press, 1972.
Tyler, Alice Felt. *Freedom's Ferment*. New York: Harper & Brothers, 1962.
Ubbelohde, Carl. *A Colorado History*. Boulder, Col.: Pruett Publishing, 1976.
Van Deusen, Glyndon G. *Horace Greeley: Nineteenth-Century Crusader*. Philadelphia: University of Pennsylvania Press, 1953.
Veysey, Laurence. *The Communal Experience: Anarchist and Mystical Counter-Cultures in America*. New York, 1973.
Voorhis, Jerry. *American Cooperatives*. New York: Harper & Brothers, 1961.

Bibliography: Books

Walling, William English. *The Larger Aspect of Socialism*. New York: Macmillan, 1913.

Warbasse, James Peter. *Co-operative Democracy*. N.Y.: Macmillan, 1923.

Warren, Josiah. *True Civilization: An Immediate Necessity and the Last Ground of Hope for Mankind*. Repr.: New York: Burt Franklin, 1967.

Wayland, Julius A. *Leaves of Life*. Girard, Kansas: Appeal to Reason, 1912.

Weinberg, Arthur and Lila, eds. *Passport to Utopia*. Chicago: Quadrangle, 1968.

Whitson, Robley Edward. *The Shakers: Two Centuries of Spiritual Reflection*. New York, Ramsey, Toronto: Paulist Press, 1983.

Whitworth, John M. *God's Blueprints: A Sociological Study of Three Utopian Sects*. London and Boston: Routledge & Kegan Paul, 1975.

White, Ronald C., Jr. and C. Howard Hopkins. *The Social Gospel: Religion and Reform in Changing America*. Philadelphia: Temple University Press, 1976.

Wiebe, Robert H. *The Segmented Society*. New York: Oxford University Press, 1975.

Willard, James F., ed. *The Union Colony at Greeley, Colorado, 1869–1871*. Boulder, Col., 1918.

Williams, Aaron. *The Harmony Society at Economy, Penn'a*. Repr.: AMS, 1971.

Wilson, James H. *The Life of Charles A. Dana*. New York: Harper & Brothers, 1907.

Wilson, R. Jackson. *In Quest of Community: Social Philosophy in the United States*. New York, 1968.

Wooster, Ernest S. *Communities of the Past and Present*. Repr.: New York: AMS, 1974.

Yarmolinsky, Abraham. *A Russian American Dream: A Memoir on William Frey*. Lawrence: University of Kansas Press, 1965.

Yorburg, Betty. *Utopia and Reality*. New York: Columbia University Press, 1969.

Young, Arthur N. *The Single Tax Movement in the United States*. Princeton, N.J.: Princeton University Press, 1916.

Zahler, Helene S. *Eastern Workingmen and National Land Policy, 1829–1862*. New York: Columbia University Press, 1941.

INDEX

Index

Index

Index

349

Index

Index